THE DEATH OF INNOCENCE

THE DEATH OF INNOCENCE:

A Socio-Historical Study
of Middle Jewish/Christological Communities
in the Diaspora of Second Temple Judaism
out of which Emerged
the Eschatological/Apocalyptic Gatherings
that became the Christian Church

by
Lindley Ross Johns

Amanda

Your life and presence has made my life worthwhile.
You are my greatest joy and blessing.

CONTENTS

PART ONE

Foundational Era: *Preparation* 200 B.C.E. to 29 B.C.E.
The nascent christological communities are established.

PART TWO

Transitional Era: *Revelation* 30 B.C.E. to 59 C.E.
The primitive christological fellowships expand in the Diaspora.

PART THREE

Formative Era: *Demonstration* 60 C.E. to 115 C.E.
The christological groups reformulate a historicized kerygma.

PART FOUR

Canonical Era: *Confirmation* 116 C.E. to 325 C.E.
The Orthodox Christian Church affirms its official Christology.

PREFACE

Theory like mist on eyeglasses, obscure facts.
Charlie Chan

Myth, as part of the ancient world mind-set was just one of many socio-religious constructs that helped to identify a sense of historical understandings of those great social, religious, economic, and political forces in the Hellenistic world. It not only shaped the world of their social reality; but, it added to a sense of historical continuity with past generations of those who were or had been part of an ongoing historical community. Myth is understood as a narrative story that explains or describes natural phenomena by the use of images, metaphors, symbols, and other mental constructs to demonstrate the intervention of deities into the affairs of humanity, usually as mystic and ritualized communal experiences. Thus, history according to its literary record never develops as a planned course of action that eventually comes into existence fulfilling all the expectations of a past generation's hopes. Those desires became the social matrix and an understanding of their own participation in the overall historic process.

This study is basically a historical, social, and religious analysis. It uses a symbolic hermeneutic (a particularized theological interpretation) to disclose the non-existent and so-called historical Jesus. This process analyzes, as a literary creation, the theological framework of Paul's religion via his letters, which incorporated Platonic categories, midrashic themes, and the early Christian mythothemes that became reflected through the later fabricated 'life of Jesus' narrative in the Gospel of Mark. The Christian Faith, which had emerged out of this socio-religious mythology, had developed piecemeal, in tension with traditional understandings. Thus, it was a confrontational faith, within an existing socio-religious world structure, even as it struggled to gain a hearing among the current voices of ancient world religiosities. This historic process gave birth to the latter Orthodox Christian Church and was only accomplished after several hundred years of cultural adaptation, absorption, social acculturation, and amelioration with other esoteric, mystery religions, philosophies, and cultural mythologies of the Greco-Roman world.

After more than half a century of scholarly analysis of the biblical tradition, there seems to be no substantive finality that would bring about a meaningful conclusion to the 'historical Jesus' debates by modern scholarship. Many biblical scholars still have a concern over some basic religious misapprehensions, which were created by the historical Jesus studies that relate to the historical, philosophical, and sociological dilemmas, even within the biblical text itself. There are several new theological questions that still relate to the Pauline corpus and its mystical content that tend to cause some difficulty in selecting a viable methodology for a relevant theological understanding of the biblical tradition's historicity. Most of the current studies have not adequately provided substantial theological, socio-religious, cultural, and historical answers to those questions that have been raised by contemporary biblical scholarship within the context of the historical Jesus debate.

Therefore, a radical theological shift used for a historical analysis is proposed concerning the socio-historical context within the Hellenistic world. Certain issues will be identified as they relate to the actual development of theological concepts within the diaspora faith of the early Jewish christological gatherings. A different methodology for a new socio-historical trajectory will be proposed to explain the rise and development of the Platonic mythothemes embedded within the emerging biblical text of the New Testament. These christological developments are seen as the socio-religious structures of the new faith communities (the body of the Christ), the Jewish christological gatherings. Their communal existence and an emerging religiosity still reflect an original symbolic and mystical understanding. It was represented in literary form by their missionary, the Apostle Paul. This new methodological posture will necessitate that a symbolic understanding be used to explain mystical religiosity within a Jewish historical context. This should provide a greater hermeneutical degree of socio-historical understanding and an appreciation of the various christological developments within the Second Temple Judaisms and the pre-Christian gatherings. Some theological issues, concerning a non-historical Jesus, are reconsidered; and hopefully, this current study of Middle Judaisms will provide some legitimate historical and sociological answers.

For instance, how and why did some Hellenistic Jews during the time of the 'historical Jesus' (identified as *Yeshua*) of the Gospel literature come to accept an incarnational presence of the divine in which the persona of the deity took on human flesh? Especially since this persona (within the biblical kerygmatic drama of the Second Temple period in Mark's narrative) was portrayed mythologically in the narrative text of the expanded covenantal literature of the early Christian faith. It is especially questionable since, according to the traditional Jewish faith, Jewish authorities abhorred any thought of physical objectification of their God, YHWH. Furthermore, the earliest letters of Paul and the other apostolic literature of the canonical text, prior to the Gospel narratives, provide no reference to or historical evidence of any actual person called Jesus. He was not known to anyone outside of the canonical texts 'until' Mark's Gospel written toward the end of the first century as a historical person.

Another issue is: To what extent and when did the early Jewish christological gatherings maintain historic Messianic expectations that included the many-faceted political and cultural trappings of the original Hebraic, covenantal biblical tradition? The earliest Christian literature, the letters of the Apostle Paul, maintains a mystical heavenly Christ, God's son, as the anointed one, that formulated the basis for his proclamation. And, the symbolic understanding of the earliest Gentile, christological communities' mystical union was perceived as an anointing by YHWH. How and when did this theological posture, which embraced Platonic, mystical, and linguistically mythical categories in Paul's understanding, emerge and crystallize into a religious literalism, within the later literary context of the Christian, fabricated Gospel narratives with Jesus as the Messiah? Besides, the traditional Messianic expectation did not seem to be a theological aspect of Paul's creative mystical experience and proclamation of his heavenly Christ. It was suggestive of a divine revelatory anointing of an Essence-like community whose mystical faith experience identified YHWH's divine presence among them. This became the religious impetus out of which the Apostle Paul voiced his mystical understanding through his own "gospel" proclamations.

Why did the socio-political, religious category of Jewish thought find such a distinctive historical place in a literary form, where the anointing appears as a spiritualized, quasi-historical, and Hellenized formulation for the conceptualization of Jewish Messianism? Mark's Gospel was written sometime around or after the devastation of the Jewish/Roman war of 66-73 CE. Furthermore, those biblical passages in the Gospels of the Christian tradition that reflect a semblance of historicity in the accounts of Jesus' life and ministry, by the end of the Second Century, were becoming accepted and interpreted as historically, factual narrative accounts. Most of these literary constructs are indicative of an extensive kerygmatic and intentional fabrication by the evangelist, Mark. Therefore, to what extent, if any, can the biblical textual tradition reflect any authentic history, let alone provide a historical representation of an actual person, namely, the biblical Jesus who has emerged, theologically, symbolically, and metaphorically, as the biblical Christ figure within the Romanized Christian Faith of orthodoxy?

Another area of hermeneutical concern that has always been problematic is how to identify and provide a name for these earliest groups of Second Temple Hellenistic Jews, who diverged in their traditionalist thinking (the conservatives) and embraced the new Jewish christological mythothemes (the progressives). It was within the diaspora that a segment of christological Judaism remained theologically faithful to the religious sentiments of biblical Judaism, in all its diversity. Nevertheless, some the various Judaisms' creative spirit can be seen in its several historical forms: Essenism, Ebionites, Enochic Judaism, Samaritanism, Zadokite Judaism, Nazoraeans, the Zealots, the Sicarii, Pharisaism, Saduceeism, the Qumran community, early Christianity, and the roots of Rabbinic Judaism. These are just a few of the various

Jewish socio-religious expressions, historically based, of which we currently have literary and archaeological documentation. There were several Jewish Diaspora fellowships out of which some of the christological Jewish members expanded their new mystical, religious, and communal categories of theological and Hellenistic philosophical understanding. They had not yet become 'Christianized.' By the Fourth century, these gatherings together with their mystical, religious life style, became reflected in the literary collection, the expanded covenantal literature (the New Testament) and later became known under the power and authority of Rome, as the 'Christian Church.'

Therefore, what should we call these early eschatological, mystical, and religious gatherings that were within the parameters and socio-historical context of the Hellenistic world, whose earlier hermeneutical posture maintained a symbolic understanding? The term Jewish-Christian remains problematic, both from a sociological and a historical perspective. Some have suggested the term proto-Christian or pre-Christian; yet, this omits a vital aspect of the new emerging theological pattern of thought along Jewish eschatological and apocalyptic lines. A more historical nomenclature, which captures the basic cultural Jewishness and directs our attention to the christological significance and the eschatological dimensions in the lives of these diaspora, Jewish faithful, is offered. These groups made socio-political concessions and accommodations, which affected their apocalyptic and eschatological engagement within the Hellenistic world. It is suggested that we refer to these fellowships simply as 'Jewish christological gatherings,' 'Jewish christological fellowships,' or the 'christological communities within several divergent Judaisms,' etc. The key mystical and mythological term, that is used to identify them, is their 'christological' self-identification, as the community's divine 'anointing' by the Spirit of YHWH's presence. These categories of identification are essential historically when identifying the sociological, religious, and historic context of Paul's letters. These will be the designations used to identify the earliest of those faithful Hellenistic, Jewish believers within the Middle, Second Temple Judaisms, especially in the diaspora. It was due to an understanding of this self-identification that they were transformed by religious and theological categories and mythothemes. These had a tendency to be of a gnostic quality in their religious and metaphorical formulations. They maintained a definitely mystical understanding in their perceived religious experience as a 'communal' union with their Lord. They established their communal self-identity along with an apocalyptic understanding and lived out their eschatological perceptions with a philosophic basis according to newly established Hellenistic patterns. These were similarly used by Paul, which also had communal and christological significance.

An additional aspect of this Jewish, christological development needs to be clarified. A significant theological emphasis within the mindset of the Jewish, christological community's leaders was their apocalyptic understanding of the eschatological 'anointing' as the 'spiritual presence and power' of YHWH. It was the dawning of the end times. Thus, it was perceived as the christological act of God within the new faith gatherings' relationship and systemic union with their Heavenly Father. This idea is also found in gnostic and mystery religious thought. An understanding of the 'gospel of God' (the forgiveness of sins through a mystical union with God) was proclaimed by Paul as a resurrection from death to life in the communal body of the Christ (1 Corinthians 15). Paul and other apostles of the Essene-like communities proclaimed the 'revelatory' gospel of God's presence as a mystical union in Platonic fashion as the body of the Christ. Paul proclaimed his symbolic imagery (the *Christos* event), purely in mythical terms and not as some Messianic and theological expectation involving a historical Jesus.

The last issue that concerns our historical and sociological approach finds expression in the Ezekielian apocalyptic and eschatological theme, the 'son of man.' This also relates to the christological communities' self-identity. It was this theological understanding that established the apocalyptic parameters of their religious and social existence. The Son of Man, as an apocalyptic mythotheme, continued to influence them. It later became the dominant expression that entered the literary arena in Mark's gospel narrative. The literary expression (the Son of Man) that is found in Mark's Gospel coming from the lips of Jesus is embedded in Apocalypticism, and its meaning must be extrapolated from the kerygmatic, biblical tradition through textual analysis by tearing apart the very fabric of the theological socio-religious matrix. In this way, we can separate the religious myth from the historical reality. No historical evidence 'outside of the biblical tradition' has been found that would validate any words either spoken or associated with a real historical person, as Jesus.

It became accepted, literally, by some as actual historical reality, which later, by the fourth century, became the basis for maintaining the Roman Catholic Church's power and authority within the Roman World. This was to become, as had always been in ancient times, the power of myth. It is the mystical understanding of religious experience that raises the inner core of literary tradition to the level of historical reality. It has been the so-called historical reality concerning the historical Jesus that is the major focus and concern of this study.

I would like to express my gratitude and appreciation also for all those who over the years have encouraged me in order for me to sustain my efforts and for their willingness to assist my efforts in the final preparation of this material. It has been under their scholarly guidance and direction that this study has been able to take its final form. They have allowed me to maintain a sense of humanity throughout the whole study. Without their kind support and academic encouragement, this study would never have been completed.

L. Ross Johns
Athens, Georgia
2 February 2016

INTRODUCTION

*Man must cling to his belief that the incomprehensible
is comprehensible, else he would cease to investigate.*
Goethe

The central purpose is to discover the contextual basis for
the development of early Christianity, within the structures of
socio-political activities that occurred during the development
and within the diversity of Jewish religiosity known as Middle
Judaism. This will enable us to identify the social matrix that led
to the historical formation of the nascent, Jewish christological
communities during the Second Temple period.[1] Religiosity can
be considered as the all-encompassing of the whole context of
human experiences; the ontological (ritualization, institutional
organization, and religious customs), and the epistemological
(the beliefs, theology, and religious expressions and conceptualizations)[2] in which the focus is on the interactive and systemic
relationships for cultural and religious existence.

---

1. It will be necessary to keep in mind the communal identity
of these early christological gatherings as being Jewish. They were
primarily the Gentile believers who had affiliated themselves with the
Mosaic tradition and its moral injunctions. They, even as Gentiles,
were educated in the Jewish scriptures as part of their Jewish acculturation into the faith community. These were those to whom Paul
ministered with such great success, the Gentiles as christological Jews
that had a revitalized hermeneutic and spirituality.

2. Given the historical contours of ancient cultural traditions,
Wells recognized in Paul's experience concerning the 'resurrection'
concept "that Egyptian ideas provided him with a 'resurrection theory'
that would more readily account for the experience than anything
available from Judaism or Hellenism." G. A. Wells, *Can We Trust the
New Testament?* (Chicago: Open Court, 2004), 18. Pharonic rule was
dependent on the ruling (political) priesthood of the upper classes.
Tcherikover, *Civilization*, 142, notes that "Hellenism, from its first

An analysis of the literature of this period will suggest a historical trajectory based on the use of symbolism, which reveals the conceptual development[3] of these faith gatherings that later developed into the Christian religion. Selected literary, mythological, and theological formulations,[4] which maintained an additional symbolic basis, will also reflect the communities' mystical and christological mind-set.[5] Thus, this socio-historical, methodological framework will encompass a wide range of Jewish apocalyptic and eschatological categories. It is Kerényi's approach to the study of mythology that understands *theokrasia*[6] as

---

appearance in Judaism, was internally bound up with one particular social class – with the wealthy families of the Jerusalem aristocracy."

3. The resurrection concept is a 'symbolic paradigm' for the early communal fellowship that was proclaimed by Paul and constituted a significant function in the early gatherings' understanding about new life by the Spirit of God within an anointed community (See 1 John). "It is a general principle in religious studies that associations among deities parallel similar associations in the symbolic meanings attached to their cults" by Edward A. Beach, "The Eleusinian Mysteries," in *The Potencies of God(s): Schelling's Philosophy of Mythology* (Albany, New York: State University of New York Press, 1994), 6.

4. An example is Rensberger's recognition of the symbolic role of the non-historical characters in the Gospel stories that were used to give instruction to the new faith communities. He refers to Nicodemus as "a communal symbolic figure" in the Gospel of John to represent the community to the surrounding religiosity, by David Rensberger, *Johannine Faith and Liberating Community* (Philadelphia: Westminster Press, 1988), 37.

5. Our current hermeneutic posture needs to be adjusted to the mind-set of the first Century. It needs to embody the mythological world in order to understand the vast array of symbolism for its interpretation. John Dominic Crossan, *The Birth of Christianity* (New York: HarperSanFrancisco Pub., 1998) cites an example of this process. Our eyebrows would not be raised with the suggestion that the dead could "return and interact with the living." It was a common understanding in "the Greco-Roman world, and neither pagans nor Jews would have asserted that it could not happen." Ibid., xvi.

6. Although Kerényi doesn't use the term '*theokrasia*' in his study, he certainly would agree in the cross-cultural commingling of

a substantive feature of developing religious traditions while using the Eleusinian festival as a prime example. His interpretation provides insight: the psyche of an initiate (*mystes*) took on the appearance of merging through the sacramental communion with the presence of the divinity.

This may have similar symbolic connections with the Eucharistic ceremony. He states that

> Mythology is understood at best as a coordinating and embellishing activity of the mind. Our [modern] way is opposed to this. It begins with the mythological ideas, which are easily recognized by their pristine *richness and many-sidedness.* Mythology is then understood as the mind's *creation* of gods in the sense that something real and valid is brought into the world, Realities that disclose themselves are stages in a process of (budlike) unfolding, and every unfolding tends ultimately toward dissolution.[7]

His approach, which provides a depth of psychological insight, has provided a vital factor in understanding an interpretation that uses a construction of a symbolic world-view within the context of communal myths. It also helps us to identify the emerging hermeneutic (Gk. *hermēneuein*, to explain, interpret), that which was used by the earliest Jewish christological gatherings. It reveals how these theological formulations developed into a distinctive mythological posture of pre-Christian faith. This posture formed a definite theological and philosophical basis for an emerging Jewish christology. This occurred along the lines of Hellenistic mysticism,[8] mythology, and metaphorical categories of religiosity.

---

spiritual categories, divinities, and mythic motifs that influenced much of socio-religious development as that term suggests.

7. Karoly Kerényi, "Kore," in C. G. Jung and C. Kerényi, *Essays on a Science of Mythology: The Myth of the Divine Child and the Mysteries of Eleusis* (Princeton: Princeton University Press, 1963), 125ff. Bracket is mine.

8. The use of '*christology*' without being capitalized, indicates that it refers to the early communities' understanding of being '*anointed*' by God; rather than having its later theological significance based on ideas about Jesus' divinity or messianic role. The following mystic

This new historic faith-understanding, within the Hellenistic, diaspora communities of the Jewish faith, was primarily within the geopolitical area of the Galilee[9] and generated a diverse christological, faith transformation. The new christological understanding of the traditional biblical religiosity became theologically particularized and became a new self-identity during Second Temple Judaism. This christological and socio-religious identity was perceived in apocalyptic terms in which they, the end time communities, saw themselves mystically and collectively as a resurrected fellowship, as the Son of God, the eschatological faithful servant of YHWH.

This apocalyptic perception became the accepted communal, socio-religious frame of reference for a theologically expanded understanding of the divine presence of God's Spirit and their religious existence.[10] These various christological commu-

---

terms were used in the Eleusinian mystery religion rituals and may add insight into the cultural milieu that influenced early Christianity. New initiates were called '*mystes*.' An experienced sponsor was a '*mystagogos*.' An '*epoptes*' was a mystes returned for higher esoteric knowledge. A '*hierphant*' oversaw the ritual enactments. A secret chamber was called an '*anaktoron*,' which contained the sacred objects, the '*hiera*.' The male torchbearer and second in command was the '*dadouchos*.' The ceremonies were held in the '*telesterion*' where the official herald, the '*hieorokeryx*,' would call initiates to order. These terms are based on Beach, "Eleusinian Mysteries," 238-44. Then cf., 1 Thess. 4:13-18, which may have possible Hebraic mystical and traditional, socio-religious connections with the *telesterion* enactment, as an adaptive theological interpretation.

9. The political figure of Judas the Galilean became prominent in this area. Martin Hengel, *The Zealots: Investigations into the Jewish Freedom Movements in the Period from Harod I until 70 A.D.* (Edinburgh: T & T Clark Ltd., 1989), xi, stated that, "the insurrectionary group appear then as principally relatively diffuse social revolutionaries who bound together only by hatred of the exploitative system of an unjust social order sanctioned by the Romans."

10. An interesting connection to the mystery religious ceremony and biblical exegetical hermeneutics is reflected in the three main components of the *Telesterion*: the *deiknymena* (things shown), the *legomena* (things said), and the *dromena* (things done) if applied to the

nities (Gk. *oikonomia*) within the Galilee came to understand their diaspora, Jewish faith existence as a divinely called people who were united with their Lord, YHWH, God of the universe. This became an acquired revelatory understanding that they had been anointed with the Spirit of YHWH. As an act of God, they were an eschatological people whose existence was then lived out in the Kingdom of God, a 'new" spiritual domain of existence,[11] in the age of Eternality. One significant purpose of the later Gospel narrative found in Mark was to persuade the christological gatherings that the Kingdom of God (as a spiritual reality) had come "from" the heavenly realm "into" the lower realm of earthly existence (Middle Platonism?).

Furthermore, the christological fellowship had accepted, symbolically, the new covenant relationship with YHWH in terms of a spiritually resurrected gathering,[12] as God's holy peo-

---

philosophical rhetoric in the Johannine prologue of I John 1:1-4 (that which we have *seen*, which we have *heard*, which our hands have *handled* concerning the 'word of life') which does not depict a historical person, but reveals a mystical experience of participatory salvation, an event that is communally enacted (both in I John and in the mystery religions that were celebrated by the initiates).

11. Maurice Goguel cites the ideas of Dupuis and Volney concerning the religious development from an essential spiritualism into cultic dogmatism when he quotes Volney: "... priests have deceived mankind in inventing dogmas which obscured the real religion, spiritual in its essence," in his *Jesus the Nazarene: Myth or History*, trans. Fredrick Stephens (London: T. Fisher Urwin, 1926), 3. Found on Peter Kirby's web site, *Christian Origins,* 2004, http://www.christianorigins .com/goguel/index.html (accessed February 6, 2008).

12. Cf., Ezekiel 37:1-14. Notice the theological categories that express communal life. Midrash on this particular passage was influential to communal identity as the new Israel within the early Jewish christological gatherings. In the formation of the new community, it was understood that Jesus' 'words' came from the scriptures (a revelatory experience); the words were not 'audible,' they provided 'understanding' when reading or hearing scripture. Thus, Doherty states that, "the Son is an expression of the wider philosophical concept -- primarily Platonic -- of an intermediary force who reveals and provides access to God, an agent in the divine scheme of salvation." In Earl

5

ple. They had become, by the divine power and presence,[13] a new spiritual creation, a body of the whole house of true Israel.[14] It is this specifically new christological religiosity, within the diaspora[15] and among a diversified Jewish mind-set that emerged as a Jewish socio-religious matrix within the Hellenistic culture.

Doherty's "Supplementary Article No. 7: Transfigured on the Holy mountain: The Beginnings of Christianity," *The Jesus Puzzle: Was There No Historical Jesus?* 3. http://www.jesuspuzzle.net/supp07. htm (accessed February 8, 2008). It is highly recommended as a site worthy of scholarly investigation.

13. The theological understanding of the early gatherings was that God's Spirit equates with his Son's spirit which equates with the divine presence of his anointing in the community; thus, Earl Doherty says "Christ is a spiritual medium through which God is revealing himself and doing his work in the world. He is a mystical force, part of and interacting with his believers, and he is God's agent of salvation," in "THE JESUS PUZZLE: Pieces in a Puzzle of Christian Origins." Part one, Pieces in the Puzzle, *The Jesus Puzzle: Was There No Historical Jesus?* 3. http://www.jesuspuzzle.net/jhcjp.htm (accessed February 8, 2009).

14. This socio-religious self-identification reflects and combines Ezekielian theology with the earliest christological fellowships understanding. It relates to the Son of Man concept and also the communities' sense of being anointed as Son of God. This was a testimony of socio-religious identity as "the faithful servant of YHWH" in an adulterous world of polytheism. G. B. Caird states that, "… the language of resurrection was used metaphorically of national recovery from disaster long before Israel had any belief in life after death (Hos. 6:1-2; Ezek.37:1-14)," in *The Language and Imagery of the Bible* (Philadelphia: Westminster Press, 1980), 246.

15. Based on his sociological propositions, Rodney Stark, *The Rise of Christianity* (New York: HarperCollins Publishers, 1997), considered that the early fellowships were "highly continuous with the Jewish heritage of diaspora Jews" and also "highly congruent with their Hellenic cultural elements," 138. Cf., where he is also in agreement with A. Harnack regarding the significance of Christian expansion based on the synagogues of the diaspora. Adolf von Harnack, *The Mission and Expansion of Christianity in the First Three Centuries*, trans. and ed. James Moffatt (New York: Harper & Row, Torchbooks, 1961).

It later became the historical foundation for the literalization of the Gospel of Mark.

These changes reflect the later Church's ritualization and the dogmatized theological formulations that we have come to know as the Christian Religion. This entire process is exemplified in the canonical literature of the expanded covenantal corpora (NT). The apocalyptic literature of the Second Temple period, which relates to the emerging christological, religious, and mystical concepts, also provided the literary, social context for the new Jewish christological fellowships. It was Paul's Apostolic preaching that sustained a religious mythological structure of mysticism and a socio-historical reference for an existential (morally imperative) understanding.

This theological frame of reference provided them with an understanding of their mystic relationship with the divine presence of the Christ event as God's revelation, the Spirit of his presence. The redemptive act of the Christ was perceived as having taken place outside the normal boundaries of time and space in the upper Platonic realm of divine (mythic and mystical) reality in the Heavenlies. These are mythological categories, which had their origins in contemporary Greek religious philosophy and were sustained in the biblical tradition[16] (midrashim) and were not historical realities. Myth is the religious overlay that provided a communal, hermeneutic of symbolism,[17] which then gave meaning to their mundane historical reality.

---

16. It is noted that, "Philo used a Platonic anthropological dichotomy as the model for his hermeneutical principle: the literal meaning of the sacred text is its body, the deeper spiritual and philosophical understanding is its soul." Karlfried Froehlich, Trans. and Ed., *Biblical Interpretation in the Early Church,* in the *Sources of Early Christian Thought Series,* Ed. by William G. Rusch (Philadelphia: Fortress Press, 1984), 7-8. Cf., Heb. 9:23-24 where an understanding is tied to "the same language to a Hellenistic, Platonic hermeneutics of copy [earthly] and original [heavenly], shadow [earthly] and reality [spiritually]." Ibid., 10. Brackets are mine.

17. Greek sophisticated philosophers regarded mythic stories involving the various salvation cults as allegorical interpretations, which by their symbolic expressions gave 'eternal meanings' that were

The newly formulated theological and apocalyptic categories were religiously related to the Hellenistic cultural milieu
of the developing Jewish communities, which added to their
christological expressions of self-identity in the diaspora. This
historical trajectory shows that these early conceptual developments for early Christian mystical religiosity were based on the
metaphorical and linguistic categories in the first century of the
Common Era. They became theologically fabricated into the later
gospel literature of the expanded covenantal text. The Gospel
narratives[18] found in Mark, by the mid-second century, functioned as 'historical documentation' for the later hierarchical
church authorities of Rome. They had been used to authenticate,
via a literary and creative imagination, a literal narrative life for a
fabricated historical Jesus.[19] Nevertheless, the Gospel narrative
of Mark can still be seen to attest to those earlier mythothematic
and apocalyptic expressions of a distinctive earlier, Jewish chris-

---

clothed in the myth. The evangelist, Mark, found established literary,
rhetorical categories readily available to accomplish his kerygmatic
intent that would reveal the mystical experiences of his communal
gatherings in a similar mythic fashion. Even Raymond E. Brown realized that the 'I am' sayings in the Gospel of John were made "chiefly
with a symbolic predicate" in *An Introduction to New Testament
Christology* (Mahwah, N.J.: Paulist Press, 1994), 23.

18. The evangelist employed elements of a historical backdrop
for the entire myth not real history and even the so-called Messianic
secret, found in Mark, is a literary devise. On the basis of the symbolic
nature found in myth, Wm. B. Smith adopted the idea of a divine pre-
Christian Jesus, who had been worshiped by the Nassene (or
Nazorenes) gnostic sect. Thus, for Smith, Jesus (the myth) was a God
who became progressively humanized by the Gospel narrative of Mark
in William B. Smith's, *Ecce Deus: Studies of Primitive Christianity*
(Chicago: Open Court, 1912).

19. See G. H. Wells, "Earliest Christianity," from *Internet Infidels, Inc.* 2000. Originally published in *The New Humanist,* Vol. 114,
No. 3 (Sept. 1999), 13-18. http://www.jesuspuzzle.humanists.net/
home.htm (accessed March 14, 2009).

tology that emerged along mystical, eschatological, and symbolic lines[20] during the Second Temple period.

In order to establish some semblance of a historical setting, out of which the various christological concepts emerged to form the symbolic religiosity of the Jewish gatherings, the following scheme of history will be used. The dates used to designate these historical periods are not critical and are used only to set the development and transformation of the early apocalyptic gatherings into an identifiable historical time frame. Shifting the dates in either direction or enlarging the time frame does not affect the significance of the historical and christological reflection of the Jesus myth by the Jewish fellowships. It is admitted that the labeling of periods of history is purely an arbitrary act of historiography by secular historians and biblical scholars alike.

The first historical setting is the period roughly from 200 BCE to 29 BCE that forms the background out of which the literary,[21] religious, and political infusion of ideas occurred. It was during this changing era of theological response, eschatological engagement, and mythological reformulations that the new socio-religious foundations were formulated. And it was their religious thoughts, as theologically constructed, that formed the christological basis on which the Jewish communities built their systemic mystical religiosity. Included in this time period was a cultural and religious disposition that was reflected by an anti-

---

20. Even in the mid-nineteenth century scholars recognized the significance of symbolism in religious views. Strauss in his *Life of Jesus* used the term '*Gottmenschlichkeit*' to mean that it was the essential idea that was important and not history. So, the Gospel narratives did not take place as history. They "express certain ideas by means of images and symbols, or ... by myths. What is important in the notion of the myth is not the idea of unreality, but that of a symbolical expression of a higher truth," as cited by M. Goguel, *Myth or History,* 4.

21. Beach correctly identifies the Greek cultural developments, when he states that, "this period saw the transition from the traditional polytheism of Homer and Hesiod, through the beginnings of scientific philosophy in Thales, Pythagoras, Anaxagoras, and others, to the pinnacles of philosophical monotheism represented by Plato, Aristotle and Plotinus." Beach, *Eleusinian Mysteries*, 9.

Hellenistic fervor by some groups within several of the gatherings of the diversified Judaisms.

In general, the origin of their eschatology may be placed somewhere around 170 BCE, and for apocalyptic origins, both religiously and theologically, occurred piecemeal and sporadic shortly after 200 BCE. There seems to have been an intellectual basis that developed along with deeply felt religious values that was, in part, responsible for the emergence of the Essene-style gatherings as a Jewish cultic identity at least by 135 BCE. It is certain that this religious intellectualization was both an anti-political endeavor as well as a demonstration of socio-political attitudes that formed the significant basis for the ideals of Zealotism. Zealotism was a loosely structured, organizational entity around 40 BCE, and it continued to influence and to consolidate many of the faithful devotees into its militant arena of influence.

The philosophical dynamics of this period also influenced the mystical basis of the christological communities' emerging theological posture, which cast them into the arena of cultural history. This was due to the religiosity of some of the diaspora, communities' leaders within its gathering who laid claim to Jewish Gnosticism, somewhere around 150 BCE together with its sporadic, mystical tendencies and Hellenistic religious influences (cf., especially Middle Platonism).

This particular overview of the early Christian Church's theological and mythical reflection, which is provided to account for the historical process, began roughly around 200 BCE. At this time, there existed no conceptual structure or theological frame of reference that could by any means be identifiable as substantive elements of the later Christian faith. Yet, there were Jewish, historical factors that were the foundational forces within the Greco-Roman world. These brought about what can be called the Jewish christological gatherings' religious posture. These historical categories were the socio-religious and theological mind-set that evolved and was nurtured by the mythical and mystic sensibilities of several Hellenistic, Jewish-Gentile communities in the diaspora as well as in the Galilee of Palestine.

The idea of a radical shift in socio-historical thinking and theory has led B. Mack to astutely suggest that

> A theory of religion is needed that can explain Christian origins as a thoughtful, collective human construction, instead of the result of human response to an overwhelming activity on the part of a god. Only a theory that gives the people their due, a theory firmly anchored in a social and cultural anthropology, capable of sustaining a conversation with the humanities, can do that.[22]

This whole dimension of the historical interaction of cultural mythothemes and religiosity became the basis for the historization of the Jesus Myth. It became formulated in all of the later Gospels and eventually, by the Fourth Century, gave rise to a systemic organization and religious liturgical forms. These also provided the systemic, theological posture of the orthodox "Christian" Church.

Also, at this time, there was political turmoil among the Jews in the land of Palestine under the rule of the Seleucid Kingdom and the reign of Antiochus IV Epiphanes. Many Jews became dishearten, disappointed, and viewed his political and military acts of religious insensibility, as a call to spiritual renewal within traditional Judaism. His defiance and desecration of the Holy of Holies was perceived especially as a socio-religious atrocity, which they called "the abomination of desolation." Many of them viewed these events as the beginning of their own separation from the traditional community of God's faithful people in Jerusalem. Even after victory by the Maccabees to establish the Hasmonean Kingdom, they continued to perceive those who occupied the office of the High Priest and the Jerusalem priesthood, as political appointees by the power of Rome.

They understood these events as religious contradictions that were being made against their Mosaic tradition, with religious disgust. A foreign power had deliberately brought about acts of abomination against their traditional, Jewish faith and against their God, YHWH. Many who left Jerusalem and other

---

22. Burton Mack, *The Christian Myth: Origins, Logic, and Legacy* (New York: Continuum, 2001), 67-8.

areas established a socio-religious community by the Dead Sea at Qumran. They maintained a separate priestly covenantal Essene style community, to await God's deliverance. The Essenes' were diverse gatherings that paralleled the Jewish christological communities within the diaspora. This was also reflected in the kerygmatic narrative of the Gospel literature of the Second Century.

Gnosticism, with its Jewish roots, seems to have developed out of Hellenism's philosophic concerns. Some of these ideas interacted with various long-standing mystery religions and were themselves influenced by them since there was a "tendency toward religious [symbolic] syncretism, or *theokrasia*,' the indiscriminate intermingling of ancient deities and their [mythic] characteristics."[23] These exchanges added to the syncretistic mood within the Hellenistic world. It is this period that we shall call the pre-nascent christological beginnings. Since the several Jewish gatherings in the diaspora were loosely organized religious associations, they lacked a formal social and religious structure at this time. Nevertheless, the synagogue, as a religious and social institution seems, to have existed in the diaspora and even in Judea as a focal point of Jewishness[24] in the Hellenistic

---

23. Beach, Ibid. 7. He adds that, "The specific cult of Demeter at Eleusis … [has] undeniable parallels with worship of grain goddesses in other parts of the eastern Mediterranean region" and "point to frequent contacts and the cross-fertilization of religious ideas," 2. Even Clement of Alexandria (*Stromata* VI.124.5-6) maintained that the "deeper knowledge (Gnōsis)," which is contained in the narrative text of the Gospels, was used "to open up the symbolic truth of biblical language to those capable of understanding." Froehlich, *Biblical Interpretation,* 16. And another Church Father, Origen also thought that humanity's "true home" resided "in the Platonic realm of 'intelligiblies,' the world of spiritual realities, compared with which the physical world is but a shadow or a material deformation." Ibid., 17.

24. Jewish identity whether in the diaspora or in Jerusalem found terms of commonality acceptable within their individual groups reminiscent of groups like the Essenes. Paul refers to the primary male circle in Jerusalem as 'brothers,' which was comparable to the Qumran community's usage as well. And religious leaders were called 'fathers.' This Essene-like commonality of a brotherhood also reflects

world. The social and religious formation, of the diversified christological gatherings, was encapsulated by theological, mythological, and eschatological expressions, and to some degree was dependent on the above developmental and historical factors within a diversified Hellenistic culture.

The next historical period, when the essence of the mythic understanding of the heavenly Christ was proclaimed by Paul in the mid-first century, began to be reflected in the mystic understandings of the then organized christological cults from 30 BCE to about 59 CE. It was probably during the earliest part of this period that the "seeds" for historization as a non-symbolic, literal understanding developed. "At the time of Paul neither the God nor the mystery had become historical. They were to become so in the period to follow the creative age, when it would be no longer possible to understand the high spirituality which had inspired the primitive faith."[25] This led to the acceptance of the mythic stories of the resurrected, heavenly Son that began to emerge as a part of the natural mystic relationships within the Jewish fellowships.[26] This occurred as the initiates learned and taught, within their own communal relationships, the new mythic and apocalyptic faith-understanding to the younger generation about their community's christological self-identity and their own eschatological existence, as the Son of God.[27]

---

eschatological and apocalyptic themes as part of their communal, theological posture.

25. Goguel, *Jesus the Nazarene,* 11.

26. M. P. Couchoud states a similar view that, "At the origin of Christianity there is ... not a personal biography, but a collective mystical experience, sustaining a divine history mystically revealed," as cited by Maurice Goguel, Ibid. In Paul's preaching, his Christ was perceived in a salvation drama; Christ had brought about subjugation of the demonic spirits of the air and thus had rendered their influence no longer affective on humanity because of the initiate's faith. This is a mythic drama of salvation similar in its theological concepts to the mystery religions of the Greco-Roman world.

27. Mythological adaptation used personification as a religious dynamic. The Jewish gatherings used it for self-identification among the diaspora communities. It became a collective symbol for them, as a faithful people, as a whole. "This mode of abstraction, representing a

Within the social structure of these Jewish gatherings, the children's religious perceptions of the new faith-understanding became the conservative posture for the next generations' theological concern and their hermeneutical posture in the emerging, faith community. This theological posture continued. It was safeguarded by the christological communities' own socio-religious existence. This entrenched point of view[28] was systemically maintained by the children together with a literalized perception and continued to be held when they had grown to adulthood. They perpetuated their conservative religious stance as a literal understanding of the kerygmatic sources throughout their later involvement in the leadership dynamics of the community's christological fellowship. This psychodynamic pattern of human development aided the process of historization as it was repeated from one generation to the next. The symbolic dynamics, which undergirded the gospel narrative of Mark, were being replaced by a historicized focus and were maintained by a theological literalism.

This whole process represents enough time and development of three or more generations to account for the accepted literal historization of a non-historical Jesus. The acceptance of a historical Jesus also furthered the theological acceptance of the

---

social entity in a single figure [*Yeshua*, Jesus], was a typical and very important intellectual pattern of thought in the ancient Near East." So that Jesus, as the community, while being used "in the singular could then be accounted for as the personified form of the collective abstraction." Mack, *Christian Myth*, 98-9.

28. The Jewish gatherings in Jerusalem had come to believe in the imminent arrival of the spiritual Christ at the 'End time.' With the demise of symbolic hermeneutic, they failed to theologically understand Mark's mystic Gospel as a literary and revelatory experience, in which 'the end had come' -- with the devastating events of 66-73 CE -- and that the eschatological community that remained were those who "had endured to the end" and "were saved" according to Mark's mythic narration. This is what the literalists failed to understand. The 'future' in Mark's literary work was not meant to be futuristic from their experiential present moment; but, was to be appreciated as a past significance which gave them hope for the future with the presence of Christ in their midst.

various other literary Gospels that became a part of the expanded covenantal literature of the Second Century. Members of the Jewish community interacted within the Hellenized world with Gnostic ideas, Cynic teachings, Stoicism, and the mystery religions' social appeal. It was the Jewish christological gatherings, which had earlier assembled a new array of mythological, symbolic, and ritualized forms (especially baptism and the Eucharist), that now considered it necessary to organize its fellowship on the basis of theological unity and a mystical relationship with their Lord.

Their eschatological posture had been formulated from the traditional apocalyptic understanding of the traditional Jewish, biblical writings[29] and the popular apocalyptic literature available. The renewed basis for a midrashic search for a metaphorical meaning from their established traditions had helped to determine the symbolic understanding of their eschatological existence in the Roman world. The Torah and the biblical tradition, as a whole, were foundational to their diaspora religiosity. It was their hermeneutical disposition that gave them concern and creative explorations into religious renewal. It was their disappointment in and distain for a corrupt and non-traditional priesthood (as Roman political functionaries) in the Jerusalem Temple that proved problematical. Another additional influence, regardless of its limitation, occurred as the Jewish christological members in the diaspora competed with the Essene-style communities, Hellenistic thought, gnostic ideas, and other diversified Jewish communities in their social struggle for religious accommodation within the Greco-Roman culture.

---

29. Paul's proclamation of his gospel based on revelation was not based on Jewish scriptural tradition as 'proof-texts;' but, his understanding of the 'Christ event' found its revelatory origin in scriptural 'source-texts.' Paul used midrashim methodologies to explicate his revelatory proclamation. Thus, Doherty states that, "New Testament scholarship in general, is guilty of reading into the early Christian mythological presentation of the divine Christ, the historical context derived from the later Gospels. The Christ myth as an interpretation of an historical event is a fantasy." Doherty, *The Jesus Puzzle,* Part One, 16.

This period reflects emerging ideas that were filtered through various gatherings of Jewish fellowships that sought out, through their diaspora faith, a revival of Jewish Spirituality for the 'end-times' in which they understood themselves to be living. They found in their traditional biblical text theological support for their eschatological religiosity by the use of midrashim. It was believed that God had sent his "Spirit of Truth" into their midst, the community of YHWH's people, and it had anointed them by his divine presence. They truly sensed that they had been elected by YHWH so that they perceived themselves, communally, as the Son of God, his faithful witness in the end times. Anointed with God's Spirit, they were given a mystical empowerment; they would be able to endure to the end of this evil age (cf., Gnosticism). God had ushered in the new age, the apocalyptic age of God's Kingdom.

Their salvation finally had been accomplished through the sacrifice of the Christ in the heavenlies; thus, the Christ had overcome the power of Satan and brought forgiveness (salvation, wholeness, new life ritualized within the new fellowship) along similar lines of other Hellenistic, mystery religions. They were to become God's anointed body of faithful followers (now resurrected), through their spiritual understanding and fellowship with God. *Yeshua*, his Son, the divine intermediary, was originally maintained with a Jewish christological, symbolic, and mystical understanding. Divine forgiveness and resurrection were inseparable theological categories that were expressed in the communal ritual of baptism and the holy Eucharist. In this way, they could live out their lives according to the Spirit's teachings about the divine 'way' that leads to life. They were saved by YHWH's presence within their community (again cf., Gnosticism and Greek mystery religious categories).

The apocalyptic literature and the eschatological social structure, which were the expressions of the times to explain existence and spiritual reality through Hellenistic and Jewish eyes, sustained and provided the Jewish christological community with its mystic and socio-religious equilibrium. Nevertheless, anti-Hellenistic attitudes remained during the Second Temple period. Much of divergent Judaism's consciousness was directed against

Rome's oppression and Rome's cultural attempts of moderniza-tion that was forced on them, their land, and their religiosity. Thus, this became a transitional period for the primitive Jewish gatherings. Many of these mystic and theological expressions of the early christological fellowships were based on apocalyptic thought and eschatological scenarios that reflect the sociological and political tensions of the times.[30] This scenario represents the earlier historical development and to a large extent a loss of its earlier mystic basis, which in time became the historical reality known as Christianity. Jesus, as a communal reality of spiritual self-identity for the christological gatherings, was changed by the literalists into a historical figure. The earlier, historic communal identity finally became a theological literary reality, which had been fabricated by cultural and historic forces over several gen-erations.

The period from about 60 CE to 115 CE will be called the time of formative Christianity when the process of historization of the Jesus myth continued to transform the symbolic interpreta-tion of the communities' myth of the Christ into the first literary narrative, the Gospel of Mark, and then later copied and rede-fined in the other synoptic Gospels. Mark, as literal history in the understanding of a historical Jesus, was taking hold by the end of the first Century.[31] During this period, the next generation of the

---

30. This would be similar to Peter L. Berger's "alienating as-pect of modernity" where the "reactionary" is "expressed theoretically in ideologies that look to the past in meaning while they perceive the present as a state of degeneration ... expressed as a sociopolitical prax-is ... to restore structures." [apocalyptic] And the "progressive" form, where "the present is also perceived as dehumanized and intolerable ... but ... is projected into the future," as redemptive [eschatological] in *The heretical Imperative* (New York: Anchor Press, 1979), 25.

31. Literary history is an ancient's tool of mythology that does not equate with actual history. Unfortunately, this has also influenced some biblical textual formations. For example: The book of Acts is "... highly tendentious and written for the purpose of creating a picture of an historical Jesus. Much of it is sheer fabrication, and highly incom-patible with information found in the letters of Paul. There is no attes-tation for Acts prior to the 170s." Doherty, *The Jesus Puzzle*, Part One, 7.

group's leadership fabricated the theological incarnation[32] of a historical Jesus. They also began to literalize Paul's mystical Christ proclamation of the gospel of God. During this formative period of early Christianity, when it was in competition with the Greco-Roman mystery cults, the Jewish gatherings maintained various geographic locals; and thus, they reacted differently to the surrounding cultural, historical, and religious influences.

The christological community in the Galilee seems to have been the center from which the Jewish christological members became known outwardly, socially and politically, to the Hellenized world as the people of 'the way' (cf., the Essene and the gnostic communal and social identifiers as well). Many of the political attitudes were based on the previous zealot tradition of Elijah's zeal. Hengel concludes that Judas' Galilean message also "had a similarly 'holy remnant' of eschatological Israel gathered around Judas. The members of this new sect founded by Judas, then, had an understanding of themselves as the 'true community of God' which they shared with other late Jewish groups."[33]

Hence, the inclusion and reformulation of the Christ theme (the anointed of God), which appears in the expanded covenant literature, will be seen as a later literalized adaptation[34]

---

32. The original symbolic understanding of myth, found in the First letter of John as the mystic personification of divine Wisdom (*ho logos*) of God, with the process of literary redaction, also went the way of literalism. In Greek philosophical works, categories of religious terms have a fluidity of expressions that tend to blend and assimilate a diversity of meanings. Hence: Wisdom (*hē sophia*), when personified in literary works, can also be expressed as Spirit (*to pneuma*), Word (*ho logos*), and God (*ho theos*); all of these share and intersect their nuances and literary basis to create a plethora of new mythological contexts.

33. Hengel, *The Zealots*, 140. In a note, 334, he points out that this was a common attitude maintained by several groups like the Essene communities: IQH 6.8; the idea of a remnant; CD 4, 3f and IQS 11, 16 the elect of the end time. And forms the biblical text, reflecting the early Jewish christological fellowships, their self-identity, Rom. 2:28f; 11:3 ff., Gal, 4:28; and Phil. 3:3.

34. Could this historical turnabout actually occur given Paul's and other early apostles' preaching about the divine Christ? Doherty

to the community's self-identity. This occurred at a time when the internal political climate of Jerusalem had disastrous affects for Roman-Jewish social relations (63-73 CE). It is from this historical perspective that the fabricated Jesus, his life and ministry, was depicted in terms of a Jewish Messianic prophet of Israel. Yet, it seems that Paul's Christ proclamation was devoid of any such theological 'messianic' scenario.[35] Both Tertullian and Theophilus mention this similar idea of an 'anointing' as it related to the idea of being 'Christian.'[36] Paul's gospel was based purely on

---

suggests an answer: "In an era of war and upheaval during which much of Palestine was laid waste, in a society which (compared to our own) possessed primitive communication, [poor] record-keeping, [little] scientific enlightenment and [lacked] skills of critical thinking, in an atmosphere of religious fanaticism fueled by sectarian expectations of mythic proportion, that question scarcely needs to be asked." Doherty, *The Jesus Puzzle,* Part One, 14.

35. Earl Doherty has suggested that the second century philosopher-apologists, who belonged to the '*Logos*' religion, perceived the Son "as an abstract heavenly force," and they would have "defined 'Christian' in terms of *anointing*, not any Messiah, spiritual or human." Doherty, "GakuseiDon," *The Jesus Puzzle: Was There No Historical Jesus?* 12. http://www.jesus puzzle.net/critiquesGDon.htm (accessed March 10, 2009). Original article posted as a critique on the *Internet Infidels Biblical Criticism and History* forum. http://www.jesus-puzzle.net/home.htm. Cf., I John 2:27. In fact, there is a Greek term, which could be used, to denote the idea of Messiah (*Messias*). Mack cites Merrill Miller's conclusion to his research on the Christian Origins Project with the Society of Biblical Literature while doing consultation on the topic "Ancient Myths and Modern Theories of Christian Origins," where he says "that the first use of the term [*christos*] in some 'pre-Pauline' Jesus school was not 'messianic,' could not have been 'messianic,' and makes no sense at all when pushed back into the life of the historical Jesus," in *The Christian Myth*, 210.

36. Tertullian remarks that, "the name Christian, however, so far as its meaning goes, bears the sense of anointing" in chapter 3 of the *Ad Nationes of Tertullian*, c217, and Theophilus says that "we are called Christians on this account, because we are anointed with the oil of God," in the *Ante-Nicene Fathers.* Vol. 3, 111-112. The *anointing* was prominent in early communities and only became connected to Messianic sensibilities after the appearance of the Gospel literature.

the Heavenly Son, the '*Christos*' event and was depicted as a mystic experience of revelatory forgiveness along with a moral imperative; Christ crucified for the forgiveness of sins (I Cor. 15).

Also at this time, there was opposition from the cult's Jerusalem members, as well as from the competing Essene groups, gnostics, and several Hellenistic, philosophical schools. Most of this opposition was basically terminated by 73 CE by Rome's military and political power, and thus, later took on a more literary and polemical form when it became involved in religious apologetics. It was also during this time that Rome continued to suppress local revolts. Thus it was that the Jewish christological communities came to understand their socio-religious role. It was an apocalyptic urgency to claim a victory with and by means of their faith, over the eschatological 'last days' and the 'end-times.' It was out of these socio-religious considerations that Mark's Gospel narrative occurred and to a large extent provided the basis to finalize the historization process of the Jesus myth.[37] It was probably not Mark's intention to aid a literalist hermeneutic. The earliest gatherings that had maintained a hermeneutic based on symbolism finally gave way to the historical pressures in which even the spirit of the gatherings now became socially different.

In order to 'understand' (its socio-religious symbolism), the death of Jesus in the fabricated Gospel of Mark (as myth), is to gain an insight into how the Jewish christological gatherings felt about Roman power (its political oppression, its economic exploitation, and its ability to forcibly shape their Jewish faith). This became a socio-religious consideration because of their involvement with and perception of the Second Temple priesthood,

---

37. I readily acknowledge my own philosophical perspective (atheism, bio-evolutionary science, and Marxism) as the source of my analytical frame of historical reference when doing historiography. "Historians who pretend to record nothing but pure facts while refusing to acknowledge their own presuppositions and theoretical perspectives succeed *only* in concealing from *themselves* the ideologies upon which their historiography is based." My emphasis added. Elizabeth Schüssler Fiorenza, *In Memory of Her: A Feminist Theological Reconstruction of Christian Origins* (New York: Crossroad, 1983), xvii.

as a dysfunctional, spiritual reality in Jerusalem. Dying by the hands of Rome via 'crucifixion' (for any of their people) offered a sense of outrage in true mythic fashion – it was the symbol of injustice that only God could change by his divine presence among their fellowship. Yet, within two or three generation after the historic events of 66-73 CE, these christological gatherings became known as the Christian church in contradistinction to the later reformulated historical faith of Rabbinic Judaism.

The last period, which has some significance to the understanding of historical Christianity's theologically reformulated basis and its historic origin in the diaspora, is from 116 CE to 325 CE. It was during this period that traditional Christianity completely historicized the symbolic interpretation and its mystical religiosity, which had been used in the earlier understanding of the Jesus myth. By this time, a purely historical Jesus had been accepted within the literary context of all the Gospel narratives by the Church's official hierarchy and the vast majority of its laity. The literary sources, which depicted the historical Jesus, had become the official accepted point of view by this time, even though the religious literature, especially Paul's letters, make no mention of an earthly, literal person as Jesus of Nazareth. Paul's proclamations were mystical in content, which focused on the Christ event, mythologically, as a revelatory, salvific experience together with its moral implications for human, communal behavior.

With regard to biblical scholarship, no evidence seems to be mentioned of a historical Jesus (outside of the canonical Gospels) until the Second Century. Within the official structure of the Christian church, the authorities accepted these narratives as literal, actual history. This became the biblical literary tradition, as well as other non-canonical apocalyptic literature, continued for a time to be the various sources for religious literature, inspiration, and was used by the formative Christian Churches for their theological education. Christianity also began, via the systemic authority of Rome, to formulate its institutionalized dogma and continued to broaden its apologetic endeavors. It is well known that the Jewish Wars were based on Rome's oppressive political demands. This also included its exploitive economic policies toward its subjugated peoples as well as the Jews. Thus it was the political and military engagements between Rome and the Jews that led to the later socio-religious conflicts of 115-17 CE and in 132-35 CE, the second Jewish (Bar Kochba) political and social revolt.

This period reflects the attempt to resolve the controversial issues, which emerged out of formative Christianity, into an official structure of religious authority. Official Christianity has seen the formation of Catholic and Orthodox denominations (325 CE to 500 CE) each with its own line of historical development and theological reformulations. Thus, the later organized Roman Church sought to establish its official theology, authority, and set forth its official apologetics (the rational defense of Christianity) against any and all religious and philosophical systems, beliefs, and gatherings. History at this point in time has no way of knowing what was contained in the literally thousands of volumes of literature in the great library at Alexandria in Egypt that was destroyed, burned by the authority of the Roman Church in the fourth century.[38] The various church councils became the vehicle of authority through which the church now finalized the revelation of God, the Canon, its religious rites, religious ceremonies, the church's polity, and its internal political structure. Out of this historical process came traditional Christianity that became the official religion of the Roman world.[39] Then from 500 CE until

---

38. An excellent historical assessment of the Roman Catholic Church's response toward the Jews and its destructive activities historically can be found in James Carroll's *Constantine's Sword: The Church and the Jews, A History* (New York: Houghton Mifflin), 2001.

39. The power of Rome influenced the orthodox church's theological formulations as seen in the Christian Trinitarian concept. Roman religious 'authority' was, like most ancient cultures, embedded in myth and symbolism. Trinitarian motifs are encountered not as spiritual realities; but, they summon a socio-religious focus on categories and expressions of socio-religious authority. Ancient Egypt had a triadic trinity of deities; the Ennead was their council of nine divinities. "The Romans recognized a triad consisting of Ceres, Liber, and Libera; where Ceres corresponds to Demeter, Liber to Dionysos, and Libera to Persephone." Jung and Kerenyi, *Essays on a Science of My-*

1500 CE to the period of modern times, Christianity became the major, unitary religious culture in Western Europe. It has continually maintained this religious understanding (tradition); that a historical Jesus was its spiritual founder.

Christianity, from the 1500s to the 1900s, has become theologically diverse again and differentiated into its various mainstream Protestant, Orthodox, Catholic, and the multi-marginalized forms of the faith. Christianity has theologically and officially accepted a historical Jesus as a literal fact of human existence[40] within the developmental context of an orthodox 'Faith.' It is hoped that a different socio-religious restructuring of the early church's christological and a historical analysis will offer some new sociological possibilities for a reasonable historical trajectory. This historical perspective should not be based on a mythological figure (the Gospel Jesus) of religious imagination. This process of historical assessment should clarify the religious history through which several early Jewish, christological communities became transformed into various distinctive, Christian gatherings (the church), which today is known as the Christian Religion.

The Orthodox Christian Church, by the fourth century, emerged triumphant within the Greco-Roman world during the

---

thology, 148. Marx's insight that "religion is the opiate of the people" makes good sense.

40. In order to accomplish this feat of scholarly magic, a lot of ancient historical source materials which depict a mythological literary past must be jettisoned from current considerations even though most biblical scholars know of them. In regard to 'the resurrection' of Jesus as a historical reality: Eduard Schweizer says "As soon as we seek to penetrate more closely and find out details, our sources fail us." It was Joachim Jeremias who said that "... the picture is quite a varied one" and refers it as "secondary elaborations." Han Kung says: "The history of the resurrection tradition reveals problematical *expansion, elaboration*, and occasionally even gaps." Add to this a list of several pages of mythological figures and a few historical ones who also died and were resurrected makes orthodoxy hard to maintain. All these are found in Pinchas Lapide's *The Resurrection of Jesus: A Jewish Perspective*, intro. by Carl E. Braaten (Minneapolis: Augsburg Publishing House, 1983), 34-43.

Second Temple period; but, this was accomplished without a real, historical person undergirding its foundational theological posture. The revision of mythothemes into a later historical literalism remains embedded in the historicized, Christian tradition (the expanded covenantal literature), the NT. When historical research into the biblical arena of the historic Jesus myth is demonstrated; we will be able to maintain a socio-religious focus on the historical issues and their emerging religious and mythical construct. It will also uncover the christological development of Jewish communities within the diaspora of Judaism's Second Temple period. A historical analysis reveals the transformation of theological and philosophical ideas concerning the historicity of Jesus.

Thus, a historical scenario, which is based on a socio-anthropological inquiry as developed within this study, provides adequate historical documentation for a critical analysis and assessment of Christian origins without a "historical Jesus," as a real flesh and blood person in actual history In order to accomplish this, we shall make a sociological excursion back to that actual historical period before Christianity had emerged on the religious scene as a separate religion distinct from Judaism. References to apocalyptic literature will be used to identify the social location of Jewish thought that provided the theological and philosophical foundation for a Jewish *christology*. This early christological formulation will not be a consideration of Jewish messianic expectations.

That perception only became a literalist concern with the appearance of the Gospel narratives,[41] which depicted a fabricated life of a literary character, Jesus. This type of social and religious analysis will take us back to a time before there was any

---

41. Biblical scholars recognize that beginning with Mark's Gospel all the biographical details about Jesus' life and ministry are the result of a large midrashic exercise by all the evangelists. Even the concept of the incarnation found in the gospel narratives has its comparable mythic relational ties, when seen as a thematic personification, in other Jewish literature. Cf., Baruch 3:37 where we find: "Thereupon Wisdom appeared on earth and lived among men." Even in the Mosaic tradition, angels (as messengers of YHWH) were called "sons of God."

sense of a literal and historical Jesus, back to Christianity's earliest historical beginnings. It has become difficult and yet necessary to argue the issues concerning Jesus' historicity, the biblical tradition's perception, the canonical posture that he is the Son of God, and the Christ of the Christian faith. The significant reason for this difficulty is that the historical Jesus, in the biblical tradition of the second century, must be separated from the divine Christ of the communities' earliest faith. The '*Christos*' also became a hermeneutical facet of biblical literalism by the historization of the earlier historic tradition. The acceptance of Jesus, as a so-called historical, real person, has come to be the essence of official Christian religiosity and is now embedded within the theological structures of modern church dogma.

Modern Christian scholarship has revealed the problematic nature of identifying historical evidence for the historical Jesus as well as other references to related theological issues within the expanded covenantal corpora. The use of an interpretation based on a symbolic hermeneutic will allows us to focus on the sociological,[42] historical, and christological understandings of the cultural, mystic, and religious origin of the Jewish gatherings. Thus, it offers a different perspective so that we can now understand how the earliest christological communities identified themselves, collectively, as *Yeshua*, Jesus. The name, Jesus, was used in the cult, with a Jewish eschatological and apocalyptic understanding of their deity's spiritual presence within the community. This interpretation provides a theological explanation of Christianity's expansion under the cultural, social, and political forces of the Roman world. The Hellenized, christological communities

---

42. The sociological beginnings of early Christianity were anything but a unified effort; there was no overall singular social structure. Doherty states that biblical scholars "… have failed to appreciate the chaotic, fragmentary nature of the entire movement, different streams from different places flowing at different times into the ultimate Christian river." Doherty, "GakuseiDon," *The Jesus Puzzle,* 4. Many conceptual and cultural understandings, that maintained mystical beliefs, were 'in the air' ready to be selected either in whole or in part for use and alteration if necessary according to communal, religious, and theological needs.

provided a theological understanding that was used to develop a distinctive Christian literature, a structured liturgical form, and a later distinctive non-Jewish religiosity. It is the later formulated historization (a theological literalism) that is now reflected in the canonical biblical tradition, especially in the Gospels. Myth has now finally become historical reality.

The canonical Gospels have been the focal point of traditional Christian thought that represents a distinctive orthodox Christian point of view, which still maintains a historical Jesus. It is a view that has lost the central eschatological essence of the earlier, Jewish christological covenantal understanding of Second Temple, Jewish apocalyptic and mystic religiosity. Hence, the Gospels, historically, have come to be perceived as the actual and factual account of the life and ministry of the historical Jesus. When speaking of the historical, mystical, and social events recorded in the biblical tradition, a further consideration of the later Gospel narratives, and a socio-historical distinction should be considered in order to establish the parameters for a historical and theological analysis.

Even though events considered as 'historic' are based on the hermeneutical perceptions of religiosity, these perceptions are considered to be revelatory (mystical) in the interpretation of religious experiences; hence, symbolic. They are understood in an anthropomorphic fashion because, as religious, mystic, spiritual, and theological interpretations of myth, they provide the meaning and spiritual understanding of human physical existence for religiously minded persons.[43] Thus, the metaphorical understanding of these historic experiences is the proper domain of religion. The development of the Christian Church's theology became necessary for later spiritual formation and religious dogma. It is within the literary construct of this 'historic' domain and its religious connections, within the biblical tradition, that this study focuses its application of a symbolic hermeneutic and its socio-

---

43. Indicative of this is Evelyn Underhill's classic study of the religious experience in her *Mysticism: The Pre-eminent Study in the Nature and Development of Spiritual Consciousness,* Foreword by Ira Progoff, Ph.D. (New York: Doubleday, Image Books, 1990).

historical analysis.[44] The historic, literary experiences embedded within the literary biblical tradition are part and parcel to the mentational structures of psychology, religion, and the creative human spirit, which is our ability for mythic imagination.

They are used to express the religiously oriented theological categories, the literary formulations, and a new pedagogical perspective for faith and moral instruction within the parameters of a metaphysical epistemology. On the other hand, experiential happenings considered as 'historical' are events that are based in actuality, in the physical reality of existence. They have the significance of being temporal and spatial in nature, and they are rightly the domain of 'history' proper.

The Jesus of traditional Christianity has been accepted as a historical person along with the literary biblical accounts of his life and ministry within a historical context based on the Gospel tradition. He has been embraced by Christian faith as a literal historical figure. His literary human existence, based only in the Gospels, has been elevated to a theological level within the context of actual historical reality. This denigrates and misconstrues the essential differences between real history and aspects of history that are 'historic' as psychodynamic understandings for human and physical existence.[45] Just because we can formulate an

---

44. To suggest that Jesus' death follows the historical examples of those who died with nobility only seeks to justify his historicity. His death by 'crucifixion' is a mythic and symbolic scenario, which has theological import, and expressed a mystical (*Christos*) event in the spirit realm that provided a 'redemptive death' (historic and religious not historical) that was a diaspora way of maintaining Jewish sacrificial integrity in the face of a Jerusalem, corrupted priesthood. Palestinian Judaism also reconsidered its theological base for a sacrificial system without a priesthood years after the conflagration of 66-73 CE with Rome, which became modern Rabbinic Judaism. Besides, for them, the Rabbis found this new formulated literary tradition to be based on a faithful rendering of the older 'prophetic' tradition of their faith.

45. Historical studies, including an understanding of biblical issues, use cross-disciplinary language and findings from general science, sociology, and linguistics (even neuroscience and evolutionary anthropology) to enlighten us today. Biblical scholarship needs to rec-

27

idea and describe it with words does not necessarily mean that it really exists in physical reality. Yet, Christianity continues to perceive its religiosity in this same literal manner upholding a high regard for historical facticity, even though biblical scholarship has found the factual significance of the historical Jesus to be more than suspect and the Gospels highly problematic, as actual history.

It is time to realize for some biblical historians, that a historical Jesus is an untenable position to support,[46] given modern humanity's understanding of physical existence, the nature of religious faith, and the psycho-dynamics of ontological experiences. Physical and historical experiences can always withstand the ardent scrutiny of the modern scientific community even by current historians and biblical scholars. Historical experiences can be maintained because they have a sense of verifiability, facticity, and ontological concreteness. But, the literary construct of the historical Jesus and all those events that occurred in the Gospel narratives are beyond the scrutiny of historians, they are purely mythological. In order to secure a more reasonable semblance of historicity, modern biblical scholarship concerns itself with uncovering past cultural and social artifacts in their quest for "historical" reconstructions in which they place the "life" of

---

ognize our species' adaptation and the use of symbolism in historical studies. Deacon states that, "symbolic adaptation has infected us," so that we "turn everything we encounter … into symbols." Terrence W. Deacon, *The symbolic Species: The co-evolution of language and the brain* (New York: W. W. Norton, 1997), 436.

46. Some biblical scholars who maintain a mystic view toward the origins of Christianity are Earl Doherty, G. H. Wells, William B. Smith, Jenkins, J. M. Robertson, Paul-Louis Couchoud, and Arthur Drews. These scholars represent just the tip of the iceberg, which has paved the way for the 'new atheism' by scholars that reject all aspects of faith and religiosity. Highly recommended is Dan Barker's *godless: How an Evangelical Preacher Became One of America's Leading Atheists* (Berkeley, CA: Ulysses Press) 2008. Also cf., Victor J. Stenger *The New Atheism: Taking a Stand for SCIENCE and REASON* (New York: Prometheus Books) 2009.

the historical Jesus.[47] What all this amounts to is comparable to the literary components of a modern historical novel. The narrative "background" of historical events maybe factual; but, the characters within the plot of the novel and the unfolding story are fictitious, purely literary constructs, which may have informational, inspirational, revelatory, and vicarious mystic significance for the reader. But the story unfolded, interesting as it might be, is not actual, factual history.

It is the modern mind-set, its analytical focus, its concern for details of conformity, and its power to provide 'revision' in order to accommodate the designated outcome of its institutionalized theology that relates to the modern study of a historical Jesus. Yet, this mind-set is not so modern after all. The socio-religious institution that developed in the late third and fourth centuries, in fact, also utilized this kind of revisionist process to fabricate its own developing theology, internal political structure, and spiritual authority into an official creed and religious dogma of the Roman Catholic Church. Literalists fail to recognize the mythological context of religious writings (at least their own). The idea of the divine 'coming into the world' is a mythological concept along with the scriptural idea 'coming in flesh.' Literalists also fail to recognize Platonic religious sensibilities that have influenced Christian thought, in which the higher realm of spirit consisted of the 'true' reality and was the counterpart to the material things below on earth. Thus for Paul, just as we (the earthy) can put on the Christ (the spiritual); Christ (the spiritual), while in the true reality of the Heavenlies, put on our humanity (flesh). This is mystical, mythic, and biblical (a historic and existential meaning, a religious understanding) and not history (part of our actual material reality).

It will be shown that the historical Jesus was not a real person in history. There was a lack of mystic understanding of the revelatory dynamics that fabricated a literary Gospel Jesus. The earlier perception of a mystical union with YHWH, which is similar to gnostic thought and the mystery religions in the Hel-

---

47. Cf., the current scholarly works of John Dominic Crossan, Burton Mack, John P. Meier, E. P. Sanders and N. T. Wright to cite a few historical Jesus scholars.

lenistic age, became a theological reformulation. It was no longer metaphorically understood as a 'life' being symbolically based in mythological expressions. The earliest, Jewish fellowships understood their own mystic relationships, christological religiosity, and the theological symbolism, which was used to empower them. The christological community understood its 'anointed' existence because of a midrash hermeneutic. They perceived that God spoke to them[48] (by the Christ or by the Spirit) through the Mosaic tradition and raised them out of death (the domain of Satan) into new life (the domain of God's Son).[49] The later Gospels' historicized narrative accounts still reflect that underlying 'historic' understanding of the Jewish fellowships and their apocalyptic, eschatological world-view. Nevertheless, the canonical texts, within the biblical tradition of the later Church, which are based on the historization by later Christianity, distort the

---

48. I agree with Doherty when he states that "Perhaps Mack is right in postulating a cosmopolitan Galilee, a strong Hellenistic environment in which certain Jewish circles began preaching the Kingdom. … and the sect may originally have regarded itself as spokespersons for the Wisdom of God." Thus, in the Gospels, Doherty points-out that in Luke 11:49 "That is why the Wisdom of God said …" Instead of "Jesus said" since at the earlier stages of the Q source, it may have been "Wisdom said." Doherty, *The Jesus Puzzle,* Part One: Pieces in the Puzzle, 23. Also note the close similarity between Wisdom and John's use of the *Logos* (Word) in John 1:1-4.

49. An example of this 'mystical presence' of the divine in their midst that was based on scripture can be found in Psalm 39 LXX: "That is why, at his coming [the mystic presence of God] into the world, he says: Sacrifice and offering you did not desire, but you have prepared a body [the christological community] for me. Whole-offerings and sin-offerings you did not delight in. Then I said; "Here am I [Jesus, as the body of the anointed gathering]: as it is written of me in the scroll. I have come, O God, to do your will." This is a source-text which could justify their understanding that the Son took on or entered into 'flesh' (the realm of humanity). Hence; the spirit realm of Platonic religious categories reflects the historical reality of the Jewish, christological communities (which were the 'flesh') in this mythological scenario.

original symbolic and christological understanding by its literalist meaning, by postulating a so-called real historical Jesus.

The above frame of historical reference is well established in eschatological terms and the literary influences of Apocalypticism within the social and religious culture of Hellenistic Judaism of the diaspora. It takes into account the religiously conceptualized world-view (Platonic conceptions) of the christological Jewish community in relationship to other Jewish literary mythothemes. It seeks to understand the cultural and historical milieu within which the Middle Judaisms of the diaspora reinstituted the religious rites of baptism and the Eucharist as basic Christological sacraments. It was these ritualized forms, derived from socio-religious ideas that reflected the mystical experience of resurrection (baptism), and memorialized the mystical union with the heavenly Son of their communal existence (the Eucharist).

This method of historical analysis employs a hermeneutic of symbolism and provides a socio-religious direction. It maintains that these early mythological and metaphorical categories are embedded within the sacred literary text and reflect the earliest historical reality of the christological communities; yet, it does all this without a historical Jesus. It allows us to maintain a focus on the significance of a revitalized Jewish community that was being transformed by its own theological self-identification. This new faith community as the body of the Christ, during the Second Temple period, expresses a historical nuance that demonstrates a facet of Jewish christological development that also became reflected in the later Christian biblical tradition (Mark's Gospel).

A socio-religious assessment of history does not concentrate its scientific methodology simply on the understanding of past events and personalities. Sociologists, anthropologists, and historians alike will admit that real, authentic history begins and ends with humanity in the present moment of our physical existence. It is within this context of that vast array of existential meanings that we are presented with definite, systemic considerations and understandings of our physical experiences. It is also within this social construct that we encounter history and our own selves. It is, by the use of a hermeneutic of symbolism, and by metaphorical religious expressions that one can recapture the socio-historical religiosity and the historic meaning of mystical existence for early Christianity.[50] This methodology preserves an understanding of the historic origin for the Jesus myth out of which emerges a historically based theological posture of the Jewish, christological assemblies during the Second Temple period.

In light of the psychodynamics of a literary constructed religiosity, the early Jewish christological existence will be reconstructed with a socio-historical methodology that makes no reference to a historical Jesus in order to explain the christological development of early Christianity. The results of this analysis provide us with a historical trajectory and represent the unfolding religious and social dimensions[51] of the early christological communities. For example, it will show how the concept of resurrection is interconnected with the apocalyptic understanding of the fellowships' self-identity as the Son, the Christ, the anointed of God. By sacramental rituals, they envisioned themselves as an anointed cult, united and given a communal spiritual life and a collective body, metaphorically symbolized, as God's Spirit, (*Yeshua*) Jesus.[52] The mythological base for the resurrection was

---

50. Symbolism is essential even in the modern study of the gnostic tradition, which is maintained by several groups today. Cf., G. R. S. Mead's classic work *Echoes from the Gnosis* ed. John Algeo with Biographical and Explanatory Introduction by Robert A. Gilbert and Stephen A. Hoeller (Wheaton, Ill.: Quest Books, Theosophical Pub., 2006).

51. Scholars who hold to a mystic evaluation of first century social and religious history realize that "the entire body of Christian documentation outside the Gospels … has nothing to say about a historical Jesus, but preaches a *logos*-style spiritual Son and cultic redeemer." For example: "the *logos* idea existed in Gnosticism [well] before an historical Jesus was added to it." Doherty, "GakuseiDon," *The Jesus Puzzle,* 16-17. Cf., Rom. 16:25-26 with Titus 1:3. Emphasis is mine.

52. The symbolic understanding even goes to the theological nature of the Eucharist as a ritualized worship formulation for salvation, where Rensberger states that, "the issue is not … one of the mate-

understood as their christological acceptance, by baptism, into the new eternal life of the early, Jewish communities throughout the diaspora.

This anointing, by the Spirit of YHWH's presence, directed the reformulation of theological categories within their community and provided them with a new self-identity, as Spiritual Israel. This new metaphorical basis was used symbolically to theologically emphasize an apocalyptic posture concerning their eschatological existence as the Son of Man, the faithful servant of YHWH. Thus, the historic name, *Yeshua* of the cult, was an eschatological interpretation and self-identification for the christological community. Consequently, it is still possible to detect, within the literary text of the Gospels, the early Jewish gathering's use of a symbolic interpretation to enrich these christological, metaphorical, and mystic understandings.

The idea of Spirit equates with the human inner psychodynamics of rational religiosity, which uses natural neurological structures, religious modalities, and a full range of mentational abilities and imaginative possibilities. An apocalyptic understanding of what 'Spirit' means by the Jewish christological group held an essential metaphorical and symbolic focus in their theological reformulations. Spirit (as used by the earliest Jewish, christological communities within the diaspora) is the psychodynamic means by which they grasped the significance of their communal existence (an 'understanding') that reached into the heavenly realm above and encapsulated their earthly existence in spiritual categories (similar to Neo-Platonism, and Gnosticism). The heavenly arena was where the power of the Spirit of God's Son wins the victory over the forces of Satan and provides a constant communal salvation.

The religious community equated the presence and power of the Holy Spirit, as the divine revelatory understanding. It was an eschatological perception of their new faith-understanding (Platonic in structural categories) and its mission was used to proclaim monotheistic universalism within the world of Hellen-

---

rial reality of the Eucharist but rather the claim that the Eucharist as the *Son of Man's* flesh and blood is true, reliable food and drink ..." for the communicates. Rensberger, *Johannine Community,* 73.

ism. The Spirit, understood symbolically, included the rituals and ceremonies of the cult as well as the missionary propaganda that proclaimed the salvation of the one true deity, YHWH. This recognition of YHWH as the anointed christological presence of Wisdom, Spirit, and Logos, and its metaphorical understanding for their religiosity became a mystical new faith-understanding for the Jewish community within the diaspora of the Hellenistic world. Paul was one of the primary examples of the early communities' missionary apostles that brought Israel's 'expanded' salvation to the world of humanity. It was God's saving activity by the power of his Spirit, the Christ, the Heavenly Son that was revealed and this perception empowered the fellowship to bring about religious healing to the polytheistic world of Hellenism.

By the use of a symbolic interpretation, as a methodology of socio-religious analysis of the biblical literary materials, it is possible to reconstruct the historic origin of the Jewish, christological gatherings. The Apostle Paul[53] and the biblical tradition

---

53. It is plain to see that Paul's apostolic ministry among the various gatherings of diaspora Jews and the God-fearers (Gentiles), which constituted his mission field, was encapsulated with Hellenistic cultural, religious, and philosophical modalities. It is a radical statement to make; but, Paul's religious and theological posture was definitely not Christian; it was Hellenistic, Jewish, and christological. The apostle Paul was never a Christian (if one defines Christian in the literalist orthodox fashion in the sense of the second to the fourth centuries, CE). It would seem that: He was Greek born into a Hebraic family on Greek soil. He was educated in the Greek Philosophical and religious traditions, after an early education in Judaism. He probably was involved in a Mithraic mystery cult at some time (possibly as a *hierophant*) at least as an initiate (*mystes*) in his youth. He also expressed interest in Judaism as a young adult (involved with the Temple priesthood and its conservative posture). He persecuted (being influenced by Zealotism) the followers of the 'way.' He participated with the Essene (Nazarene sect or Jewish Gnostic Ebonite group) of Qumran for a while. He became disillusioned by their conservative intolerance as an adult. He later received a divine call to apostolic ministry by exposure to a Jewish, christological community's faith and acquired their religious and moral posture (Essenes?). He blended Jewish and Greek religiosity to maintain a mystical and mythological posture as a diaspora

that has preserved his letters will clearly demonstrate that there was no historical Jesus known to exist within the earliest, Jewish communities of the first century. There was no historical Jesus, even though he is depicted as such in the Gospel, biblical tradition; at least, not one that ever existed as an actual real-life, flesh and blood person. The biblical tradition, from its historization perspective, shows the growth and development of pre-Christian beginnings, from a small Jewish, eschatological sect founded on a mystical relationship with YHWH, to an institutional organized 'Christian Church' that maintained a socially secured position in the Greco-Roman world. That construction is not actual history; it is religiously constructed historic biblical tradition.

Thus, the mystic symbolism, which reflected the earliest, christological gatherings' apocalyptic understanding, depicted their eschatological societal role and their sense of historic mission in apocalyptic terms. It used theological categories,[54] and it continues to be a consideration for a socio-religious and historical analysis. This historical analysis that takes symbolism, metaphorical religious language, and mysticism, as a perspective of ancient mythological religious development, represents a more

---

Jew. Within the atmosphere of Hellenistic syncretism of the first century, he absorbed, adapted, and assimilated Hellenistic religious ideas into his Jewish traditional beliefs to formulate a new 'Jewish mystery religion,' which later emerged culturally and religiously into early Christianity. Thus, he became, from an Orthodox perspective, a Jewish heretic and was a forerunner of a pre-Christian understanding. See Pamela Eisenbaum's thesis in *Paul Was Not A Christian: The Original Message of a Misunderstood Apostle* (New York: HarperCollins, 2009).

54. Resurrection was just one sacred concept that had communal significance for the early cultic gatherings in the diaspora. The *'dromena'* in the mystery ceremonies was a ritualized reenactment of the story of Demeter and Persephone based on Persephone's resurrection. When these "festivities wound down, the participants would dedicate special services in honor of the dead." Beach, *The Eleusinian Mysteries*, 6. Is it possible that these kinds of social proclivities of mystical concern solicited those questions that were raised by Paul's supporters (1 Thess.5:1-14)? Those questions may have had religious significance for their understanding of Greek communal religiosity.

reliable understanding of the actual historical development of early Christian origins.

What remains is an attempt to flesh out the historical, socio-religious dynamics in the theological developments within the context of the christological experience without a historical Jesus. Yet, a non-historical Jesus is still defended as a historical person and continues to be part and parcel to the faith structure of countless millions of modern biblical literalists.[55] We can understand why the communal gatherings' metaphorical, symbolic, and christological understanding ultimately became the theological reformulations of the later Orthodox faith. And, in time, this finally became the orthodox Christian tradition. We can identify this process of historization through which the creative christological faith, by some Jewish members of Middle Judaism in the Second Temple period, transformed and developed the Gospel narratives into the Christian faith. This process can be viewed as a historical, religious, and social process that led to a literalized, historicized, and later when the biblical tradition became canonical, dogmatized orthodoxy.

Consequently, a historical account of early Christianity cannot be achieved if the biblical tradition is the only document that is considered for historical analysis. B. Mack's idea of a radical shift in socio-historical thinking and theory bears repeating

---

55. Modern day biblical literalists constitute the vast majority of institutional memberships in all the major mainstream Christian denominations and close to full membership in most other denominations, cults, and religious fellowships, which maintain a historical, Christian theological posture. In general, they are probably numbered among the religious fundamentalists, conservative right-wingers, many evangelicals, and tend to be the most vocal with their opposition to modern critical biblical scholarship. This socio-religious situation in our American culture has led an Episcopalian Bishop, John S. Spong, to write a book based on his ministry experiences called: *Why Christianity Must Change or Die: A Bishop Speaks to believers in Exile* (New York: HarperSanFrancisco, 1998). Also, some biblical scholars are attempting to enlighten the general public with historical studies that could help to shake off the effects of literalism. See Bart D. Ehrman, *Misquoting Jesus: The Story Behind Who Changed the Bible and Why* (New York: HarperSanFrancisco, 2005).

at this juncture. "Only a theory that gives the people their due, a theory firmly anchored in a social and cultural anthropology, capable of maintaining a conversation with the humanities, can do that.[56] It is ultimately incumbent upon sociologists, historians, classical linguists, archaeologists, theologians, and NT biblical scholars to broaden the basis of scientific inquiry.[57] Only with such a cooperative spirit, which searches for historical truth that is based upon rationality, can we hope to understand the historical process involved in early Christian origins and its development into the Christian religion.

It would seem that religiously-minded peoples maintain an anthropological arrogance when seeking a divine, human relationship with a deity. Gribbin and Cherfas have remarked that,

The church, too, is one of the great bastions of anthropocentrism; did not God, after all, make man, and only man, in His image, and did He not give man dominion over all His other creations? One can fault [Darwin's] the *Origin* for sidestepping the evolution of *Homo Sapiens;* but, one cannot fault Darwin's good sense in doing so, nor find this any reason to doubt his own belief in the evolution of man.[58]

---

56. Mack, *Christian Myth,* 67-8. An excellent historical analysis that presents the intellectual development of Platonic mentors' 'schools,' together with their philosophic ideas, is John Dillon's *The Middle Platonists: 80 B.C. to A.D. 220* (Ithaca, New York: Cornell University Press, 1996).

57. Any modern, historical appraisal of Christianity and its faith traditions must deal seriously with scholars, whose scientific views of a materialistic reality lead to atheism, since they consider rationality and free-thinking as components to a proper, honest, and realistic understanding of religious conceptualizations. Such authors as: Richard Dawkins, Christopher Hitchens, Sam Harris, Michael Martin, David Mills, George H. Smith, and Victor J. Stenger have made available their rational influence in literary tomes to a wide public audience.

58. John Gribbin and Jeremy Cherfas, *The First Chimpanzee: In Search of Human Origins* (New York: Barnes & Noble Books, 2001), 153.

PART ONE

Foundational Era: *Preparation* 200 BCE to 29 BCE
The nascent christological communities are established

1

Nothing ever becomes real until it is experienced.
John Keats

This is a socio-historical reconstruction that recovers the symbolic interpretation used by the original Jewish christological communities and represents the underlying theological reflection that is now found in the biblical tradition.[1] This methodology best accounts for the historic origin and the historical development of the pre-Christian faith. The conceptual formulations that depict the religious development of early Christianity will be based on the research of modern literary, historical, and critical scholarship within the context of the Christian literary tradition. The fiber around which this view is woven is the new faith understanding of the Jewish christological fellowships in the diaspora of the Hellenistic period. It depicts, via symbolism, the new monotheistic categories of faith, in opposition to the traditional faith of other Jews in Judea. This has also been seen in contrast to the perceived false faith of the polytheistic world of Hellenism[2] (perceived as pagan Gentiles).

It is to be noted at this point that the historical and cultural influences that went into the theological formations of the christological communities, were decisive for the Jewish christological gatherings' religiosity. It was the Roman persecution and oppressive policies that brought to the forefront both the apocalyptic literary categories and the eschatological hope for the new

---

1. Martin Dibelius, *From Tradition to Gospel*, trans. Bertram Lee Wolf (New York: Scribner's Son, 1935). Also, see Frederick C. Grant, *Introduction to New Testament Thought (Nashville: Abingdon, 1950)*, 27ff. Cf., Vincent Taylor, *The Formation of the Gospel Tradition* (London: Macmillan, 1933).
2. See William. B. Smith's *Ecce Deus.*

41

emerging christological communities. It is necessary to recognize that the expanded covenantal literature (the NT) has preserved, albeit in its historicized form together with its distinctive apocalyptic mythothemes, the early symbolically based kerygma as proclaimed by the earliest christological fellowships. The best example of this is Paul's letters to the various christological communities. The literary sources and their conceptual development,[3] within the stream of later Christian thought, can ultimately be placed in a proper historical perspective.

Our ability to discern and handle the sources within the biblical tradition should cause us to realize the significance of the theological and socio-historical development of religiosity within the early Jewish christological groups, before they became identified as primitive Christianity. Usually when historical sects died off their scriptures were buried with them. Later Christian scriptures exhibited a kind of textual infection in the form of literalism. This was because of an orthodox perception that saw some of the earlier christological groups' literature as heretical texts within the diversified scriptures of the early gatherings. Walker states:

> We only know that the surviving text of the Pauline letters is the text promoted by the historical winners in the theological and ecclesiastical struggles of the second and third centuries. Marcion's text disappeared … it appears likely that the emerging Catholic leadership in the churches "standardized" the text of the Pauline corpus in the light of "orthodox" views and practices, suppressing

---

3. Religious concepts, which occur within history, usually have their basis in reification. This phenomenon of the mind creates from the religious ideas a reality of its own, which becomes embedded in the historical literary documents; but, the contents are not descriptive of actual ontological existence. Reification, like symbols and metaphors, is an autonomous reality with a psychodynamic life of its own. When doing historical research and even in science we should keep in mind Mayr's advice that "the most important objective of a historical narrative is to discover causal factors that contributed to the occurrence of later events in a historical sequence." Ernst Mayr, *This is Biology: The Science of the Living World* (Cambridge, Mass.: Harvard Press, 1997), 65.

and even destroying all deviant texts and manuscripts. Thus it is that we have no manuscripts dating from earlier than the third century.[4]

The direction presented here is to offer a socio-religious analysis of the theological concepts of the early Jewish christological communities. This analysis will then shed additional understanding on the later historicized tradition, which depicts a particular orthodox theology. This newly reformulated theology made a transition from primitive beginnings to the normative and somewhat official, orthodox, and authoritative doctrines of later Christian creeds, confessions, hymns, and prayers. Thus, for the most part, the findings of the modern historical and critical school of analysis will be utilized as a presupposition underlying this historical excursion.[5] In general, the critical methodological approach to the interpretation of biblical concepts and theological hermeneutics[6] is well established and accepted by a majority

---

4. William O. Walker, Jr. "The Burden of Proof in Identifying Interpolations in the Pauline Letters," *NTS* 33 (1987) 614. Robert Price adds that "One cannot help but wonder if text-critical theories" of some modern biblical scholars "are simply contemporary attempts to safeguard that official sanitized textual tradition in the interest of the same ecclesiastical establishment that produced the text they so jealously guard" in "The Evolution of the Pauline Canon," 28. *Institute for Higher Critical Studies*, Madison, Drew University, electronic version, http://www.depts.drew.edu/jhs/RPcanon.hthl (accessed May 21, 2004). Also note James Carroll's *Constantine's Sword,* which references the historical destruction of the Ancient Library in Alexandria, by the Church in the fourth century.

5. An excellent and concise introduction to the form-critical method can be found in Rudolf Bultmann and Karl Kundsin, *Form Criticism: Two Essays on New Testament Research*, trans. Frederick C. Grant (New York: Harper & Row, Harper Torchbooks, 1962). Also, see Gerhard Ebling, "The Significance of the Critical Historical Method for Church and Theology in Protestantism," in *Word and Faith*, trans. James W. Leitch (Philadelphia: Fortress, 1963).

6. Marvin R. Vincent, *A History of the Textual Criticism of the New Testament* (New York: Macmillan, 1903). Also, see Morris Goldstein, *Jesus in the Jewish Tradition* (New York: Macmillan, 1953).

of modern, mainstream biblical scholarship. Such a study must keep in mind that the newly reformulated theological categories of the earliest, Jewish faith community were not directed toward a historical person, such as Jesus of the Gospel texts.

For example, Paul's Platonic proclamations were a revelatory response[7] to, a confidence in, and a grasping of the symbolic understanding of the christological groups' mythothematic religiosity. This represented for the christological gatherings a religious experience that was seen as a mystical union with YHWH. These gatherings conceived their communal life as 'a return to the beginning' in which the in-gathering of the faithful had become a new end-time community, and they referred to themselves as being a 'resurrected' people.[8] This hermeneutical posture was a dynamic metaphor for understanding that the community was experiencing the divine presence and anointing of God. This aspect of resurrection was their realization that the community had been gathered, raised up, and united by the spirit of God's power and presence.

This revelation was encapsulated, theologically, in the concept of atonement (forgiveness, 'the cross of the Son mythology') that formed the essential elements of the kerygma. It is this

---

7. In ancient mythologies, primordial time was a time 'outside' of actual history and Platonism transferred this religious category to the upper part of a dualistic universe as part of his religious philosophy. Doherty points out that "both Christian and non-Christian myth of the period ... suggests that the standard placement was in a parallel upper spirit world rather than in a distant, past primordial time." "The spiritual [was] more 'real' and primary than the material." And for Paul, "the Jewish scriptures presented a revelatory window onto that higher reality." E. Doherty, "Reader Feedback," No. 22-24, in *The Jesus Puzzle: Was There No Historical Jesus?* 2 at http://www.jesus puzzle.net (accessed April 7, 2008).

8. Mitchell G. Reddish, ed. *Apocalyptic Literature: A Reader* (Peabody, Massachusetts: Hendrickson, 1995), Cf., I Enoch 90:33 which states that "all those which had been destroyed and scattered" were gathered together, apparently is implying a resurrection. 43. Also, note the reference to being 'born from above,' 'born again' as literary indicators of a new (resurrected) life within the anointed community. Cf., Ezekiel 37:1-14 and 1 John 1:1-4.

theological and mystical understanding that gave to these Hellenistic Jews its *christological* character. Compare the resurrection idea of communal restoration found in Ezekiel, 37:1-14. The spiritual birth (resurrection) was reflected in the communal baptism rite, and by its socio-religious ritual, symbolized the divine 'gathering' of the community into a spiritual existence by the presence of YHWH's Spirit. For Paul, their life "in Christ" was a communal and religious existence that Platonically reflected and combined the heavenly and the earthly realms where they could work out their salvation by their faith and overcome the power of Satan (the ruler of this evil age).

This mystical union with YHWH also provided them with a new apocalyptic self-identity, the mystic mythotheme of the heavenly Son. This new perspective gave them a different self-awareness as an eschatological community, the renewed Israel of the last days. Thus in this fashion, some writers identified the new communities of YHWH as a collective body, spiritual Israel or the Son of God, his faithful servant. The Son of Man identification with regard to the Heavenly man is also found in Greek and Babylonian thought.

These revelatory experiences were seen as a mystic revelation (*gnōsis?*) from YHWH to his people. The Jesus myth,[9] which was the earthly gathering of God's anointed people of faith, was understood, believed, and proclaimed, as a universal monotheism. The divinely established gathering of christological Jews was also perceived as the Kingdom of YHWH encompassing "the new heavens and the new earth." It united the 'heavenly' realm of divine and spiritual activities, where the divine acts of salvation brought about a new creation, with the 'earthly' fellowships (in neo-Platonic fashion).[10] This mystical realm above con-

---

9. C. H. Dodd, *History and the Gospel* (New York: Scribner's Sons, 1938). And cf., Erich Kahler, *The Meaning of History* (New York: World, Meridian Books, 1964). Cf. Robert Henry Lightfoot, *History and Interpretation in the Gospels* (New York: Privately Printed, Bampton Lectures, 1934).

10. This was understood as symbolic, which represents salvation in metaphor. The salvation myths in Greek religion represent an array of symbolic and metaphorical interpretations of stories that did not

tained the religiosity of the unifying principle of the universe, namely the new revelation of the divine presence of YHWH in their anointed fellowship, their socio-religious self-identity, as the body of Christ (God's anointed). The Kingdom of YHWH (God, the Kingdom of Heaven) equates with the earliest historical spirituality of the Kingdom of the Lord Jesus, the heavenly Christ, as proclaimed by Paul.

Out of this Essene-style community, the Apostle Paul proclaimed the gospel of the heavenly Christ. It was God's revelation of forgiveness through a mystical union with the Divine Presence, which was reflected as Jesus, the body of God's anointing, the faith community. It was based on Paul's midrashic, scriptural hermeneutic. Paul absorbed the community's understanding (that was symbolically represented as the Holy Spirit) through a revelation, a visionary experience, the *Christos* event, which had emerged out of his earlier persecution of those christological gatherings. Paul and they knew that according to the fellowship's self-identification, they were being anointed by YHWH's presence. This constituted theologically their christological understanding and their communal existence as *Yeshua*, Jesus (God's son). Thus, Paul lived his life with the community and became an apostle proclaiming this mystical presence and power (symbolized by the communal resurrection concept) as the gospel of the Heavenly Christ, The community on earth was a 'reflection' of the heavenly Christ, the eternal reality compatible with the mythology of Middle Platonism.

The later Gospel tradition can be seen as a reflection of the altered Jewish theology of early christological thought.[11] In

---

ontologically happen. Plutarch says that these myths are allegorical not literal. Indicating that probably a portion of the population believed they *were* literal. Plutarch, "Isis and Osiris," found in Plutarch's "Moralia," trans. by F. C. Babbit, *Loeb Classical Library*, Vol. 5 (London: Heinemann, 1993).

11. Historically, there was a 'parting of the ways' between the christological groups and those within the synagogues of traditional Judaism. Some historians have tried to answer what led to this split (ca. 85-95 CE). The mysticists' scenario provides an excellent historical answer in that this occurred when the early 'spiritual Christ,' as

fact, the early Jewish gatherings in the diaspora absorbed a strong Gentile religious element that was based on Greek, philosophical categories and mystery religious mythothemes. Even though, as a community of faith, they were still anchored to the Jewish Mosaic heritage that was based on traditional scriptural theology. Some biblical scholars seem confused or even baffled by Paul's utter lack of referring to the so-called historical Jesus' ministry or teachings.

Paul commented on significant issues, where he might have made a significant point to validate his arguments by referring to some aspect of Jesus' ministry or teachings; yet he made no attempt to do so.[12] In Paul's preaching, he always "assumed a common culture with his audience. Whether Judahist or Gentile, this audience was talked to in the vocabulary of the Tanakh, of popular late Second Temple motifs, and in Judahized forms of allegory.[13] This also included the sacrificial aspects of its traditional religiosity. These religious mythothemes brought together, with the later fabrication of a literary Gospel Jesus,[14] a definitely

proclaimed by Paul (a mystic), became embedded in the literary Gospel as a literal historical person (the religious symbolism of social personification was misunderstood by 'literalists' who failed to grasp the metaphorical significance).

12. Graham Stanton, *Gospel Truth? New Light on Jesus and the Gospels* (London: Harper Collins, 1995). Cf., F. J. Foakes-Jackson, and et. al., *The Beginning of Christianity*, 5 Vols. (London: Macmillan, 1920-33). Harnack, *Mission and Expansion of Christianity* (1961). See Luke 22:29, 30; and John 18:36: cf. with Eph. 5:5 and Col. 1:13.

13. Donald Harman Akenson, *Saint Paul: A Skeleton Key to the Historical Jesus* (New York: Oxford Press, 2000), 252. For example: some intriguing proximities of thought given Paul's "emphasis upon movement between earth and heaven, it is interesting that Judahist speculation of his era had fastened on the idea that Wisdom was an ascending and descending figure." Ibid., 307. See Wisdom of Solomon 7:24-30; Proverbs 8:27-31; Ecclesiasticus 24:1-7; and Enoch 42:1-3. These are Hellenistic patterns of expression even when used by Judean and Diaspora, religiously minded people. Cf., I Cor. 7:19f.

14. Several critical biblical scholars (Doherty, Mack, and LiDonnici) also maintain that "indeed, it is possible to argue that much, if not most, of the symbolism and details of the Jesus story was gener-

eschatological and apocalyptic interpretation of the faith of the new end-time community, as the new Israel.[15] The apostle Paul proclaims, by merging midrashim and Greek mystery categories, a Jesus who, christologically, is derived solely from the Hebrew Scriptures.

History does not exist simply as past events regardless of their facticity that seeks its own validation by the historical evidence. History is an experiential happening, an interpretation of contemporary existence. History is not to be used as a proscription for social-political change; but is a description of previous social-political changes that have resulted from the historic forces of social, political, and economic production. It determines an individual's consciousness and his/her historic mind-set. Any encounter with history is the moment of historic meaning for one's our existence. It is the ongoing necessity that requires one to act upon existence with meaning within the structured values by identifying those of a particularized Weltanschauung (world view).[16] Herein, an unavoidable question arises: Where do we draw that line that separates the historic (the significant meaning, its epistemology) from the historical (the actual reality, its ontology)? This question would not even be necessary if neo-Platonic categories and religious structures had not been used to formulate a socio-religious world-view foundational to earliest Christianity, which for many remains with them today.

---

ated from this preexisting stock of Greco-Roman expectations about what saviors were like," which is based on these mythothemes noticed in Ross S. Kraemer and Mary R. D'Angelo, Eds., *Women & Christian Origins* (New York: Oxford Press, 1999), 97.

15. Carl E. Braaten, *History and Hermeneutics,* Vol. II of *New Directions in Theology Today*, ed. W. Hordern, 7 Vols. (Philadelphia: Westminster, 1966), 49.

16. See Geddes MacGregor, *Introduction to Religious Philosophy* (Boston: Houghton Mifflin, 1959); Paul Tillich, *Christianity and the Encounter of the World Religions* (New York: Columbia University, 1963); also compare with H. A. Wolfson, *Philo: Foundations of Religious Philosophy in Judaism, Christianity, and Islam*, 2 Vols. 3d rev. ed. (Cambridge, Mass.: Harvard, 1962).

By the later part of the Second Century and a few generations removed from the kerygmatic missionary proclamations of Paul, some followers began to view their faith as based on a literal historical figure rather than on the original symbolic, mystical, and mythological understanding that had been their earlier understanding of YHWH's 'anointed' presence. Then as a result of the Great Jewish Revolt of 66-73 CE, someone in response to the historical conflation brought about by Rome, who was of a literalist persuasion within the Jewish christological community, wrote the Gospel of Mark. It may even have gone through a minor revision during the Jewish Revolt of 114-115 CE as a means to provide continuous encouragement to faith in a historical Jesus. It was probably by the time of the Bar Kochba Revolt of 132-35 CE that it was finally re-edited to sustain the faith of the emerging Christian community. Mark's Gospel can be seen as a religious explanation and theological interpretation of how the various communities, by their faith, came through the 'end times' and continued to interact with God's presence in the fellowships, as an act of God's salvation.

The overall thought patterns of the traditional biblical world-view are essentially mythological and create disharmony with the psychodynamic structures of modernity. What principles then should guide us to identify those ancient parameters of the symbolic, metaphorical, and mythological frame of reference with those of actual history? Modern Christian scholarship has edged cautiously around the issue when it comes to seeking evidence for the so-called historical Jesus in the biblical tradition. Some have even skirted the philosophic and linguistic avenues leading away from; but, stop short of, in order to keep within the Christian parameters (cf., Paul Tillich, Rudolph Bultmann, etc.), because of their faith and their connection to a specific denominational church organization (i.e., authorized financial support), and/or their integrity for the orthodox, Christian tradition.

The later formative Christian communities by the Second Century,[17] which had already accepted a historicized perspective,

---

17. By this time, the gospel tradition had completed its literary development. Crossan, *The Birth of Christianity,* 251 has cited J. Kloppenborg, who "proposed three main strata in the gospel: a sapien-

knew full well that any assertion about their divinely established community could not "at the same time be theologically true and historically false."[18] Religion, with its mythological categories and spiritual rationale as epistemological speculation, is used seemingly all too often to assert self-validation and legitimization, as ontological postulates in logic by orthodox Christian scholars. The mythological attachment of the resurrection concept to the Gospel Jesus in the formative church's Christology also grew out of this same process of historization. This can be seen as a loss of the earliest gatherings' symbolic, metaphorical, and mystical focus.

Thusly, it became the conservative theological posture, since it was based on a literalist understanding of the kerygmatic texts[19] to enable a traditionalist perspective. Formative Christianity based its decision of faith on the kerygma as it accepted the Jesus figure within the Gospel narratives, as a historical person. It established its religious scheme of thought precisely within the new historicized and mythological perspective. This was to a large extent part and parcel to their socio-religious outlook (orthodoxy), and it became the religious categories of an official reformulated, historical, and theological understanding (dogma)

---

tial layer (Q1), an apocalyptic layer (Q2), and a biographical layer (Q3) combined in that sequence." With regard to Mark's Gospel, I agree with Doherty that it is "chiefly as an allegorical and 'lesson'-oriented piece of writing, heavenly employing midrash on scripture, to embody certain outlooks and practices within a sect centered somewhere in the Galilean/Syrian region." Earl Doherty, "Comments on Carrier's Review of 'The Jesus Puzzle: Did Christianity Begin with a Mystical Christ?'" in *The Jesus Puzzle: Was There No Historical Jesus?* 2. http://www.jesus puzzle.net/CarrierComment.htm (accessed April 7, 2008).

18. Braaten, *History and Hermeneutics*, 92. This religious, historical reification seems to explain how and why Luke develops his early history of Peter and Paul in the life of the developing church. Acts was probably written sometime after the Jewish revolt against Rome in 134-5 CE and just before 150 CE.

19. See F. V. Filson, *Jesus Christ: The Risen Lord* (Nashville: Abingdon, 1941), where he uses arguments to show the fragmentariness of the resurrection appearance narratives.

by Roman church authorities. This process from the second through the fourth or fifth century took many generations to unfold and did so in sporadic, socio-religious fashion.[20]

Israel's traditional religiosity (in Judea and in the diaspora) began to unravel. This was especially due to political and anti-religious sentiments. There were many who regarded the religious functionaries of the Jerusalem priesthood, and their lack of moral integrity, with disfavor. Thus, many Jews reflected upon their own unfolding historical events and their relationship to the whole mystical schema of religiosity. This was perceived as a renewal of the divine visitation within the socio-historical development of Second Temple Judaisms. Their repeated attempts to curtail political domination by foreign powers, in time, lead them to consider new historical perspectives of apocalyptic thought. Apocalypticism was never a well-organized or consistent pattern of socio-religious expectations. Robinson strongly agrees with the assessment that descriptive elements, within the framework of apocalyptic literature, are mythological. He states that, "they are purely supernatural occurrences ... described in the language of the categories of history. But they are not part of the natural fabric of history."[21]

In this way, theological categories could refer to one or the other 'realms' of existence, interchangeably, without really identifying which realm to which they were referring, since both

20. Based on Ramsay Mac Mullen's historical analysis in *Christianizing the Roman Empire A.D. 100-400* (New Haven: Yale Press, 1986), 93, Philip Jenkins indicated that "in the mid-fourth century, perhaps half of all Christians belonged to some group that the Great Church regarded as heretical or schismatic, and new splits continued to form" from his *Jesus Wars: How Four Patriarch, Three Queens, and Two Emperors Decided What Christians Would Believe for the Next 1,500 Years* (New York: HarperOne, 2010), 12.

21. John A. T. Robinson, *Jesus and His Coming* (London: SCM, 1957), 96. Evolutionary scholarship has long recognized in biological science the astute comment of Dobzhansky, who said, "Nothing in biology makes sense except in the light of evolution." Mayr, *Biology*, 178. Maybe we could adapt it to the historical analysis of biblical narratives by saying that "nothing in theology makes sense except in the light of ancient mythology."

realms constituted the interconnected mystic (spiritual) realities of existence. The Heavenly Son was the divine intermediary of revelation who suffered death for them in the Heavenly realm, which manifested God's forgiveness of sin, an expression of deliverance from guilt (cf., the Platonic categories and religious structures of Hellenistic mythology). This was the mythothematic basis for their mystical union with their Lord of Heaven, the All of eternity. These terms were used for similar categories for their mystic union. It is most interesting why Paul thought that this mystic expression of the *Christos* event (a heavenly sacrifice) would be a 'scandal' amongst his Jewish brethren. It is not difficult to understand when we realize that the 'forgiveness of sins' was the special domain of the sacrificial rituals carried out by the priesthood in the Temple in Jerusalem under specific biblical mandates (Levitical demands) that were religiously instituted and provided by God for Israel.

The so-called 'supernatural occurrences' assessed by the historian are not a vital aspect of, nor a necessary part of, the historical argument used for a consideration of religious, historical reality. Since they are mythologically based in contradistinction to physical reality, they are not set within the parameters of historical occurrences. Even the apocalyptists, via the biblical tradition, have inserted these descriptive mythothematic categories into a literary, literal history within the text of the expanded covenantal corpora (Mark 13), which served the religious purposes and basis of historization for later Christian theology. This process was repeated generously during the formative years of Christianity. It facilitated a literalist acceptance of YHWH's sovereignty and power over history within the structure of myth and mysticism, which are now contained in the Christian canonical texts.

The concept of the divine presence maintained its sociological, religious, and unitary essence for the early Jewish christological fellowships. These Hellenized Jews, in the diaspora, desired to worship YHWH by equating their cultic existence and mystic religiosity with the 'divine presence' of the Spirit. They personified the divine spirit communally as *Yeshua*, Jesus, and anchored this perception within the same religiosity, as spiritual

Israel, whose roots had existed in the older tradition of Judaism.[22] This became a socio-theological perspective as part of their self-identity, when they based their new experiences on the former biblical tradition (by midrashim). Christ, the living and Spirit Son of God, as a revelatory experience within the community, within a dynamic mythothematic structure, was perceived as acting on their behalf, to bring about their communal anointing and salvation. This Eternal All, the God of Glory, was establishing a new viable gathering called 'the elect' that embodied the divine presence (*tēn ekklēsian*), God's end-time community. As the mystical embodiment of God's presence, the body of God's Son, they understood that their 'anointing' was by the Spirit of the Lord; and thus, they identified their communal gathering as the faithful servant of YHWH, his divine Son. It was not a difficult transition from a faithful servant (a son) to be identified corporately as 'son of God' as had also appeared in some traditional text of Judaism. Later, this became fused with the eschatological Son of Man with all its literary and thematic, apocalyptic ramifications.[23]

YHWH, theologically stated, is Spirit, and the Spirit's presence was known by the name of *Yeshua* (Jesus) by the community. Jesus was the community that was encapsulated by God's Spirit, in which they became a bodily entity to serve hu-

---

22. The Jewish scholar Davis Fusser in studying the various traditions of Second Temple lore, states that "we could easily construct a whole gospel without using a single word that originated with [the historical] Jesus." Bracket is mine. As cited by Akenson, *Paul,* 238, from David Fusser, *Jesus* trans. from the German by Ronald Walls (London: Herder and Herder, 1969, orig. ed., 1968), 72.

23. Cf. Ezekiel 37:1-14 which depicts a 'resurrected' corporate identity of a newly constructed social and religious body by the power of God's spirit, the whole house of Israel. In fact, most biblical scholars mention the blurring of divine roles and personality between Jesus in the literary narratives and God. This is "understandable once one accepts that Jesus is not a distinct historical person whom people had experienced and remembered, but was a theoretical spiritual entity, someone derived from scripture under the influence of ideas current in religious philosophy." Doherty, "Reader Feedback," No. 23, 5 (accessed April 7, 2008).

manity. This was used to designate their mystical union with God and their fellowship with God as his elect people. They lived 'in the Christ,' with his power of spiritual healing and deliverance from the power of sin. Historically, the sacred name of the Jewish deity, YHWH, had not been spoken for some time (which carried with it, a threat of death). The Jewish eschatological gatherings' mystical experience of the Jesus myth provided the socio-religious context that allowed them to worship him (as the divine presence); but, it also, epistemologically, enabled them to speak his name symbolically (now as *Yeshua*, Jesus: YHWH saves).[24] This mysticism unfolded within a socio-religious context and on a personal level within the cultic experiences of their new religiosity. It provided a spiritual 'union' significantly similar to concepts of union found in other Hellenistic, mystery religions' categories of union with their deity.

Furthermore, the significance of the 'name,' *Yeshua*, legitimized the communal metaphorical understanding that the divine presence and power was present as God's Son in their midst.[25] Thus, to call upon his name in baptism was to effectively

---

24. See Matthew 1:21 and 23 which the author felt it fulfilled a prophecy (Isa. 8:8, 10 LXX) that depicted ontologically and historically that God was, in fact, united by his Spirit presence in the end-time community (hence: the name Immanuel, which Matthew states means "God is with us."). Platonic categories often allowed them to merge 'heavenly' states with 'earthly' realities without signifying a theological contradiction.

25. This idea (God's communal presence) was later included in a Gospel text, which presents the words of Jesus: "For where two or three are gathered in my name, I am there among them" (Matthew 18:20). John Baillie, *God Was in Christ* (New York: Scribner's Sons, 1948). Cf., G. A. Wells, *The Jesus Myth* (Chicago: Open Court, 1998). He also mentions that "Pagan Platonists who held that God is incorporeal, passionless and unchanging did not want to hear of a God who took human form and suffered humiliation on earth," p. 2 in an article, *Earliest Christianity*, electronic version 2000. Especially for Paul, the spiritual divine presence, the anointing, even when applied to the Christ, the anointed one, had no messianic significance. The concept of Messiah "was at most a minor notion in Judaism around the time of [the historicized Gospel] *Yeshua* of Nazareth. Most of the Chosen Peo-

become encompassed by his anointed presence. This understanding also merged in the Eucharist to become a spiritual empowerment as the salvation of the Lord. Thus, Jesus was a symbolic reference for their mystic experience of spiritual union with YHWH (epistemologically), not a historical being (ontologically). The historic reality expressed by their ingathering into a faith community as depicted in Mark's Gospel was their symbolic dying, being buried, and resurrected into a new life (through baptism) with the Christ (the anointing of the community) with the divine presence.

This was the metaphorical language of religious experience (similar to Platonic structures) and not historical, actual occurrences. Thus, Doherty states, that

> It was possible for the devotees of the mysteries to base their faith and salvation hopes on the 'myths' of the savior gods – who were not regarded as having performed those acts in identifiable historical time – it would seem to be the case that the earliest cultic Christians, like Paul, envisioned the myth of Christ Jesus in the same way. And ... the placement of such myths, both pagan and Christian, was in this period located in the upper, heavenly world, following Platonic principles, rather than in a primordial or distant past on earth. The mythic Christ was indeed 'spiritual' and not material.[26]

It is unfortunate that Orthodox Christianity has accepted these mythologies, these literary narrative events within the kerygmatic corpus of the Gospels, as historical reality.

---

ple were not awaiting the Messiah." Bracket is mine. Akenson, *Paul*, 41.

26. Doherty, "Comments on Carrier Review," 3. Although Doherty admits that he 'can't' think mystically, I am sure that he means he cannot embrace this ancient mythology as part of his modern world view and as an understanding of reality. Yet, many Christians today, because of their biblical literalist beliefs, have transported this ancient mythological world view into their mind-set and have disregarded the contradictions, which their understanding of a scientific and material world of reality has taught them.

The metaphorical understanding became changed during the time of formative Christianity. Their perception of socio-historical, literalized religious categories maintained a futuristic perspective because of a continued emphasis of the historicized literal reading and understanding of the sacred literature of the church: especially the Gospels. This was a circular process of self-fulfilled expectation based on the literalist understanding of the biblical texts. That is, their attention was directed to the future apocalyptic resurrection event of Jesus' (second?) coming. The earliest Pauline communities did not share this expectation of a returning historical figure.[27] There is no exegetical foundation within Paul's literary compositions that reflect this type of eschatological understanding. The theological changes that occurred in the apocalyptic segments of the later historicized texts (Gospels) simply removed the earlier Jewish christological gatherings' mystic understanding of their spiritual and symbolic perspective of 'resurrection' reality. In its futuristic and literalistic form, formative Christianity lessened its appreciation for and mystical involvement in its metaphorical religious perspective. Experiential empowerment for building moral character became simply an expectation that asserted a theological belief about life after death.

Thus, Christianity's historicized religiosity negated the mythic resurrection, as a metaphor of God' creative power to bring into existence his new faith community (being raised with the Christ, as the socio-religious basis for their fellowship). Instead, later Christianity's primarily theological understanding of a literal resurrection of Jesus in the Gospels continued a theological interpretation of future immortality for believers that had

---

27. Robinson, *Jesus and His Coming*, 10-24. Cf., the mysticists' interpretation found in Earl Doherty's web site, *The Jesus Puzzle,* www.jesuspuzzle.com. The orthodox rivalry that developed in the mid-second century was not present in Paul. Its onslaught of opposition only developed as the historical and literalized, theological fabrication in the Gospels became accepted as real history by Church authorities within the Roman world. Earlier and Hellenistic religious categories were easily assimilated and exchanged as expressions of religious experiences among diversified faith groups.

been part of the traditional Jewish end-time eschatology.[28] The so-called historical events in the anticipated mythical drama of eschatological redemption were symbolized by the cross and Jesus' death as preached by Paul and other Apostles as mystical symbolism for "the forgiveness of sin" within the canonical texts. All this hinged now upon the significance of Jesus' literal bodily resurrection, which encouraged, soteriologically, a futuristic expectation. This non-historical interpretation can only occur by reading back into Pauline letters the metaphorical images of the Gospel Jesus.

Some modern scholars are divided on the question of Jesus' resurrection[29] as a fact of history or a symbol of religious communal understanding. The literalist and traditional approach, represented by the statement of Conzelmann, is typical of orthodox Christians, literalist thinking today. His point, with regard to formative 'historical' Christianity, is well taken. "The resurrection was an event in time and space and the appearances of the risen Christ were such that the ordinary physical senses of the witnesses were used to behold him."[30] For modern day Christians to be able, in their view, to justify historical reality and validate spiritual realities with this same kind of logic (mythological) reveals a lack of historical understanding, a lack of understanding religious, metaphorical language, and a lack of scientific rationality. The acceptance of Conzelmann's logic is to beg the ques-

---

28. A conservative work, chiefly polemic which discusses immortality within the scheme of redemption, can be found in James Orr, *The Christian View of God and the world*, Kerr Lecture Series, I, 9th. ed. (New York: Scribner's sons, 1908), Lecture IV, Part III, 150-161 and Lecture V, Part V, 196-199.

29. Scholarly division over the facticity of the resurrection, conceptually, can be seen in the theologies of Bultmann and Tillich; cf. the selected bibliography at the end of this study.

30. Hans Conzelmann, "Jesus Von Nazareth und der Glaube an den auferstandenen," *Der Historische Jesus und der Kerygmatische Christus*, ed. by Helmut Ristow and Karl Matthial (Berlin: Evangelische Verlagsanstalt, 1960), as quoted by Braaten, *History & Hermeneutics*, 80.

tion, tautologically; and therefore, it can only function without scientific rationality or historical facticity.

Wedderburn states, that "… the result of a historical investigation into the traditions of Jesus' resurrection seems to yield very little that is of much use for Christian faith." And suggests that we cannot know "whether anything in fact happened at Easter above and beyond what went on in the minds of the followers of Jesus."[31] Any investigation, into the Gospel narratives, lacks any rational sensibility that can be used for historical validation of Jesus' existence. Also, we cannot say what really went on inside peoples' minds. It was the earliest Jewish christological fellowships that would have understood this kind of mystical and mentational symbolism, which expressed and applied their metaphorical and mystical insights onto their spiritual, historical, and socio-religious existence.[32] To conclude the Gospel narratives as history would reflect a total negation and corruption of the mystical basis upon which their communal response to the divine presence, *Yeshua*, the Christ of God was experienced and symbolically understood.

This earliest period of theological formation was preparatory to the christological response that had taken place, since the apostolic proclamations would be based on a mystical revelatory understanding that could, in their minds, be validated through

---

31. See G. A. well, *The New Humanist,* Vol. 114 no. 3, 14 where he cites A. J. M. Wedderburn in *Beyond Resurrection* (London: SCM, 1999).

32. Once that the symbolic nature of the Gospel of Mark is considered, it is easy to recognize that it reflects the spiritual experiences of the religious community. Doherty states that "even the death and resurrection could conceivably symbolize what Mark considered to be the destiny of the Kingdom of God community." in "Reader Feedback," 8. One should not fail to consider the communal rituals; both in form and in the theological constructs that formulated a religious personification of the gatherings' ministry experiences. These reflected the 'anointing' within the gathering by God's Spirit. This would also include the symbolic understanding of baptism and the Eucharistic elements.

"scriptural evidence" in the process of midrashim.[33] Later, during formative Christianity's development, salvation theology would become the historicized proclamations of Christ's resurrection (as a reality in history) based on a literalist understanding within the biblical tradition of the later Gospels. Nevertheless, the earlier faith-understanding had been interpreted symbolically and mystically through the cultic forms and rituals[34] (e.g., baptism and the Eucharist) within the early church's worship. For example, in baptism they understood that they had been crucified symbolically with the Christ (an existential metaphor). They were 'raised' out of the water into newness of life (their communal existence), into a symbolic resurrected, eternal life[35] by the Spirit, as part of the Jewish end-time christological community.

This gathering of a new spiritual life, within the presence and power of God's anointing by his Spirit, began with their acceptance into the new fellowship via baptism and continued with their spiritual participation in the Eucharist. They were given guidance by the cult's spiritual instructions (the divine Spirit, the *logos*) and received the power of God's Wisdom (*Gnosis*). The cult's social interaction formed the basis for their communal meals as part of the salvation experience. Paul's discussion of the communal meal seems to indicate that early Jewish christological gatherings regarded the bread and wine as a 'participation' (i.e., an inheritance) in the body and blood of Christ, which now they experienced as the Kingdom of God.

The whole sacramental significance of the meal, given the cultic atmosphere of the time, was part of Paul's gospel proc-

---

33. See Paul's "according to the scriptures' in I Cor. 15:1-4, which referred to the divine sanctioned act of 'forgiveness' that had been established by God for his people by the Temple sacrificial system in Jerusalem: but, now completed and made available to the world through the Christ in the kerygma.

34. Rudolf Bultmann, "New Testament and Mythology," *Kerygma and Myth*, Ed. H. W. Bartsch, Trans. Reginald H. Fuller (London: S.P.C.K., 1954).

35. Samuel Angus, *The Mystery Religions and Christianity* (New York: Scribner's Sons, 1925).

lamation.[36] Even though the communal meal of the early Jewish gatherings had close affinities with the Greek mystery meals and similarities with the Essenes' sacred meal; yet, Paul compared the Pagan meals in the Greek temples by referring to them as the "table of demons."

Hellenism's affect at this time upon the varied Jewish religious mentality, especially in Galilee, is difficult to assess.[37] But, the richness of thought, the diversity of ideas both Jewish and Hellenistic, the several enigmatic mystery religions, and tendencies were all part of the religious and spiritual forces that molded the new faith-understanding of the Jewish christological fellowships and their socio-historical development.[38] The rich religious milieu of the other dynamic cultures of the Hellenistic world (especially Egypt) also offered additional intellectual connections for the development of early Christianity, especially through early Jewish Gnosticism and Iranian religious thought (dualism). It was only after the Gospel of Mark was written that a historical Jesus became a consideration from which anyone could draw intimations of theological reflection and doctrinal formulations.[39] Compare this with the extensive use of the resurrection concept that was produced in the earlier writings of the Apostle Paul that had no theological connection with any historical person known as Jesus. His Jesus was the mystical and mythical cosmic Christ.

The earliest socio-religious concept of resurrection was symbolically understood in the communal experience by these gatherings, metaphorically, as an act of God to call-out a special

---

36. Cf., 1 Corinthians 10:16, 21 and 11:23. Paul and his entourage moved in highly sophisticated, Hellenistic circles, which from his correspondence seemed to be well familiar with the religious philosophy of the day, both Jewish and Greek philosophies, which demonstrated a historical appreciation for mystical and religious symbolism.

37. Cf., this theological theme as expressed in John's Gospel with the synoptic tradition that maintains a greater emphasis on the historicized tradition for its mythological content.

38. G. Ernest Wright, *God Who Acts: Biblical Theology as Recital* (London: SCM, 1952).

39. Cf., Psalms 16:8-11 and 73:23-26.

people in the end time to be his faithful servant (God's Son). This seems only natural since the dominant force of symbolic interpretation, in the newly found religiosity of the Jewish christological assemblies, was the *symbolic* resurrection of Jesus. This mystic identification by the faith gatherings should not invalidate the religious significance of the long-standing, traditional resurrection concept.[40] Rather, it should clarify its symbolic nature and reveal its earlier metaphor and developing historic theology.

Thus, not only was the earlier mystical Christ preached by Paul as having been "raised from the dead,"[41] but formative Christianity reified this mystical basis; and thus, Paul's kerygmatic proclamations of the earlier mystic resurrection came to be perceived as a literal so-called historical fact. Even though the literal concept of a physical (bodily) resurrection developed as later dogma, it was primarily based on the literary, Gospel Jesus. The definite symbolic meaning of resurrection that was part of the social-historical setting of the earlier communal gatherings, which reflected the mystical union of initiates with God, can still be detected in the canonical, Christian biblical tradition (the Pauline texts and even in Mark's Gospel) when read symbolically.

---

40. Consider its ancient roots in the Egyptian culture that had embraced a socio-religious matrix, which was based on a symbolic and metaphorical understanding in which Pharonic, political power and religious authority were exerted over the Egyptian people. The Pharaoh was both political ruler and the high priest over the land and all the people. Therefore, resurrection was used as a political, social, and religious symbol to grant communal continuity of authority.

41. Acts 2:32, Rom. 1:4 and cf., (Rom. 6, cf., I Cor. 15:1-58 where Paul's purpose was to counter those who seemed to have denied the resurrection based on a materialistic understanding, a bodily resurrection; an idea that the Greeks rejected as repugnant) where 'resurrection' was used with reference to new Christians having been 'raised,' meaning that they had entered into the faith community with new life (a new mystic state of human existence), Col. 3:1-3. Paul understood that Christ's resurrection was 'in' a spiritual form in which Jesus' appeared in a 'vision,' a revelatory understanding. For Paul it was not a physical, bodily resurrection. His Christ was a non-physical 'heavenly man.'

Therefore, the mythological significance of how it was interpreted (a basic hermeneutic of symbolism) historically, is vital to our understanding of its social entrance into the theological stream of a later religious tradition.[42] A consideration of the resurrection concept, in the primitive kerygma, takes on hermeneutical dimensions that endeavor to stress the spiritual and mystical dynamics of the early christological religiosity. A symbolic interpretation of the resurrection of Jesus was held by the early Jewish christological fellowships. It reassured them, as the end-time (eschatological) socio-religious communities, that YHWH had delivered them "out of" the devastating war-torn calamities of 66-73 CE and later in 114-15 CE and finally out of the revolts of 134-35 CE against Rome. Redactional efforts are evidenced both in Pauline literary works and the Gospels during these historical periods.

The earlier gatherings and their mythological foundation in the diaspora experience formed a spiritual protest against the older Mosaic biblical tradition and the priesthood in Jerusalem.[43] An attitude of Jewish renewal (Spiritual rebirth) was a long time in the making. It was diverse and uneven in its development, and some of its outcomes could not have been predicted. One aspect of Jewish renewal also developed as an insurrection of new faith understanding, within a context of universal monotheism. It was developed in opposition to the diversity of religious idolatry of the Hellenistic world of polytheistic religiosity, as least as they perceived it. Paul was a major player in this effort. There was

---

42. Edwin Hatch, *The Influence of Greek Ideas and Usages upon the Christian Church*, ed. A. M. Fairbairn (London: Norgate, 1907). In time, based on historical 'evidence' and its interpretation, the impact of mythology on the formation of the Christian faith will become fact as in biology where the "evidence has become so overwhelming that biologists no longer speak of evolution as a theory but consider it a fact, as a well-established fact … ." Mayr, *Biology*, 178.

43. Hangel, *The Zealots,* 67 maintains that the early attitude of religious zeal was politicized: "These 'Zealots' presumably aimed to restore the purity of Israel, the people's faith, and the Temple." In a note, 341, he cites Kahler, *JE,* 639, that "a statue evidently of the Maccabean time"…"equates the 'Zealots' with the Hasidim." 68.

literally an offering of the grace of YHWH's salvation to the whole of humanity (Gentiles). This socio-religious "opening up" of traditional Judaism occurred by the Jewish christological proclamations of Pauline mysticism. This diversity of mind-set and philosophical concerns can also be recognized in the later biblical tradition in the mystical and conceptual formulations. These are reflected in the midrashic narrative of Mark's Gospel, in the Pauline literature, and in other expanded covenantal literary materials (e.g., James, 1 John, and Hebrews).

The historicized understanding of a bodily resurrection event as interpreted from the kerygma in the Gospel of Mark was a later, literal understanding; thus, it became a theological necessity to override the earlier theology of the mystical Christ event in the preaching of Paul. For Paul and the early christological fellowships, there simply was no historical earthly Jesus. Theologically and religiously, there was no conceptual need for one. Since the mid-second century on, we have learned by religious and cultural experience to read a historical Jesus into the Pauline texts of the canonical expanded covenantal literature. Thus, we have come to see a historical Jesus rather than the mystical Christ Jesus of Pauline thought. Hence, the Christian theological formulation of the Jesus myth and its historization into the later biblical tradition has become the traditional Christology of the Christian canonical text.

It is necessary to keep in mind that Paul's literary works "represented only one version of what was already a multiple-version *Yeshua*-faith, within the complex of multiple Judaisms."[44] Furthermore, it is Paul's gospel that is precisely a Jewish universalism that reflected the original religious response by the Jewish eschatological community to God's divine presence, their anointing by the Holy Spirit. It is also evident that Paul recognized the significant difference in theological perspective that he had, based on Platonic sensibilities, with those traditionalists within Judaism whose belief was dependent on the well-established and conservative, Mosaic tradition.

---

44. Akenson, *Paul*, 121.

For Paul, the preaching of another Jesus,[45] that made any kind of divine incarnation materialize into physical reality; and thus, made the Gospel Jesus a part of religious history, was unacceptable. Paul's mysticism reflects the original historic metaphorical meanings that had been associated with the original symbolic and mythothematic interpretations.[46] Thus, Paul used those mythological concepts, which were on his own familiar Hellenistic soil, to express the historic significance of this newly expanded and revitalized form of Jewish faith. Nevertheless, being based on the ancient biblical tradition, it was expanded to bring the Gentiles into a new Israel. Paul's proclamation was more faithful to the primitive eschatological community's theological posture, even though historically, it was different from what we know in the later formative Christian literary tradition, which has not escaped 'redaction' over the years.

Paul's letters were set into Hellenistic religious literary forms that reflect a very close connection with the mystery religions of his times, not to mention the prevalent categories of

---

45. For Paul, 'another Jesus' was any reference that one made to a historical and material person. Paul's 'heavenly man' was mystical and had apocalyptic expectational categories (for example: the 'anointed one'). "Paul's heavenly man is a resident of the spiritual world and incorporeal, not made of matter. Like the related Platonic concept, he is pre-existent and provides a pattern, the substance of what Christians will become when they are resurrected" (reborn, an act accomplished by the *'parousiatic'* Spirit of Christ, life in the communal gathering, their fellowship with the divine presence of God.). Doherty, "Supplementary Article No. 8: Christ as 'Man:' Does Paul Speak of Jesus as an Historical Person?" *The Jesus Puzzle: Was There No Historical Jesus?* 25. http://www.jesuspuzzle.humanists.net/supp08. htm (accessed May 11, 2005).

46. Cf., 1 Cor. 15:44-49; Where in Paul's argument he refers to 'the first man' (Gk. the Primal Man, the celestial man, the Heavenly Man, and the Babylonian first-born of Iranian myth) who in thought becomes the Redeemer descending to earth (the realm of the flesh, humanity to show the 'way' back to heaven). This concept of a first man was part of the ancient world's religious and mythological world view. Paul seems to use this same philosophical category again in his argument in Romans 5:12-21.

thought. Some of his gospel proclamations were historically compatible with the new faith-understanding of several of the early eschatological sects (the Enochian Jewish communities, the Essenes, and the Qumran community). His mystical message of the Christ of God in his gospel was not in conflict with the cultic divine presence[47] of the divine *Logos* of the mystery religions, neo-Platonic thought, and the religious categories of Gnosticism. All of which Paul certainly had more than a passive familiarity.

The inner kerygmatic stories in the Gospels are historic symbolic events. They are not historical in terms of modern historiography. They are interpreted as mystical understandings in order to explain their spiritual meanings as historic religiosity. Therefore, the core of existential response of faith-understanding (via symbolism) was the essence of the Jewish, christological communities' religiosity (i.e., mysticism, mythology, and spiritual existence). It made possible the objective, socio-historical situation, a verifiable religious reference in history. The several intrusions of other concepts, such as the myth of the 'dying and rising god,' the heavenly Christ of Paul's proclamation, and the original Jesus myth, were all fused together with the conceptual forms found in the Hellenistic literary milieu.[48] To this could be

---

47. Even though some terms reflect human-sounding categories (blood, man, born of woman, flesh, etc.) within the narrative gospel myth, in religious Platonic fashion, they may simply refer to the mystical understanding of salvation's divine activities taking place (or having taken place) in the Heavenlies, the sublunar sphere where mythical reality was considered the 'true' reality. Most ancient myths found no problem with this kind of socio-religious scenario as expressed in their communal and ritualized celebrations.

48. Inanna, a deity that also died, was buried and rose on the third day was known as the Queen of Heaven. She was a significant goddess of the Sumerian pantheon in ancient Mesopotamia and the Akkadians called her Ishtar. Being 'raised' (resurrected) on the third day seems to be a commonality even among the original covenantal literature and the later Rabbinic texts; cf., 1 Kings 17:17-24; 2 Kings 4:18-21, 32-37; Hosea 6:1-2; Ezekiel 37:1-14; and is also stated in the *Thirteen Articles of Faith of Maimonides* and in the *Eighteen Benedictions*. Being 'raised' is indicative of divine approval, vindication, and acceptance of a divine event.

added mythothemes such as the neo-Platonic idea of the cruci-fied 'Just' and the vicariously suffering Servant of YHWH in the book of Isaiah in the Jewish tradition. It would seem that four hundred years (200 BCE to 200 CE) of dynamic social, political, and religious changes, during the Hellenistic period, not only fostered cultural diversity but aided the infusion of diverse cul-tural and religious sensibilities.

We need to keep in mind the function of midrashim used by the early evangelists that made possible a fabricated literary figure in the Gospels. The literary matrix, mystic and symbolic, unified the socio-dynamic and hermeneutical patterns of the ear-liest christological response within the religious diversity in the Second Temple period. Also attached to these apocalyptic cate-gories was their eschatological relationship with YHWH, within the encapsulating ideas of Hellenism, as diaspora Jews. Thus, a formative period of christological thought, earlier than what ap-pears in the expanded covenantal literature, especially the Gos-pels, is suggested as a necessary historical occurrence. This is required for a historical analysis in order to account for the socio-religious emergence of a defining Jewish, christological posture within the various Jewish, eschatological and apocalyptic com-munities.

All of the conceptual categories were 'in the cultural air' along with many other Hellenistic religious and philosophical ideas. They were available for anyone who desired to use them. Anyone could expand the symbolic, metaphorical, and mythothe-matic meanings, and they could adapt them to and for their own theological posture. Those who accepted the Jesus myth were transformed by these cultural and historical forces, which neces-sitated the textual reformulation by the later Christian church. It was a redaction pressured by the historical forces that an authori-tative Church in Rome found favorable to its inner program of power, religious politics, and social control. This reformulation in language, religious culture, and its penetration into the Juda-ism of Palestine from the diaspora, is reflected only in the Gospel tradition by the literary creation of a historical Jesus.

It was the Gospel narrative that became the means by which the conservative, christological faction could anchor its existence to the ancient Mosaic (Jewish) past. This would then render their social presence with political validation and religious acceptance in the eyes of Roman authority. A historical Jesus is nowhere to be found in Paul's literary activities or in any other expanded covenantal literature. The Gospel narratives are seen as fabricated tomes that 'create' a historical Jesus. It was out of this socio-religious context; the influences by the expansion of oriental cults, the mystery religions, and Gnosticism throughout the Roman Empire, that religious syncretism provided, historically, a favorable climate and the soil on which the Jewish christological fellowships could plant the seed of its new faith-understanding of a monotheistic religion and ethical universalism.

All theology is political. Theological issues have always had definite social consequences. These relate to the ethical concerns of humanity rather than just any mythological basis, a particular religious stance, or theological understanding. The determination of biological reality and for all the sciences is the evidential physicality of the hypothesis that is tested, verified, and authenticated by countless others, which accounts for its facticity and progressive knowledge. The determination of historical reality must also, in its analysis, be accountable to the evidential physicality for its facticity, hermeneutical posture, and its theological sensibilities. Thus, myth must always be extrapolated from historical reality and explained for its part in biblical and historical investigations, if progressive, religious knowledge is to be obtained.

2

Biblical theology is incomplete without an understanding
of ancient mythology.
L. R. Johns

The dualistic thought of the Iranian religion so influenced the various Judaisms, that it transformed them differently and unevenly to such a high level that these later Judaisms' eschatology "... reveals a more extreme form of dualism than that of Persia."[1] The several Judaisms' apocalyptic hopes, such as the resurrection and its eschatology in general, "... have drawn their ultimate inspiration from the religions of Babylonia and Persia."[2] Robinson cites McCown to support the idea that Jesus' language in the biblical

---

1. Sigmund Mowinckel, *He That Cometh*, trans. G. W. Anderson (New York: Abingdon Press, 1954), n., 23; quoted by R. M. Grant, *Gnosticism and Early Christianity*, rev. ed. (New York: Harper & Row, Pub., Harper Torchbooks, 1966), 114. The Mandaean liturgies for the dead relate this concept as a standard formula that is derived from the canon (i.e., Avesta) of Zoroastrian writings as redacted in the Sassanian period. Also, see note 1 for the Hellenistic view of the Persian religion (Zoroastrianism's ultimate dualism), Ibid., 205-207.

2. Wilfred L. Knox, *St. Paul and the Church of the Gentiles* (Cambridge: University Press, 1961), 3. Cf., C. H. Dodd, *The Parables of the Kingdom* (New York: Charles Scribner's Sons, 1961), 24-25. He presents a good argument for the limits to the influence of the Iranian religion upon Judaic thought. Also, see Walter Bauer, *Orthodoxy and Heresy in Earliest Christianity* (Philadelphia: Fortress Press, 1971) where he remarks that "a Gnostic Christianity was more original than 'orthodoxy.' The latter was initially just one current among others and established itself through Rome. To exaggerate: 'orthodoxy' was the 'heresy' " is historically valid; as cited in a note by Gerd Theissen, *The Religion of the Earliest Churches: Creating a Symbolic World* (Minneapolis: Fortress Press, 1999), 368, n3.

tradition was also definitely apocalyptic, and that to the multitudes which heard him, "... he would have seemed to the people to use the language of Apocalypticism, for the prophets were [also] interpreted in an 'historic' apocalyptic sense."[3] These words that Jesus spoke were the narrative words within the literary Gospels and do not in any way authenticate apocalyptic speech by a historical person. Apocalyptic categories were the benchmark of symbolism when used in the context of socio-political revolt in Palestine and in the diaspora. The language of Apocalypticism also had definite implications for the development of the resurrection concept that was metaphorically anchored to the rite of baptism as God's divine process enabling a person to enter into the community of the end times. This was expressed in their socio-religious theology[4] as a mystical resurrection of communal significance and especially for its symbolic interpretation within the Jewish christological community.

In this manner, dualistic thought has made its profoundest contribution through the dualism of the Persian religion into the religious concepts of Israel, deposited in the various Jewish sects

---

3. Robinson, *Jesus and His Coming*, 97. See A. V. W. Jackson's concluding remarks concerning the relationship of the religion of Zoroaster to Judaism during Israel's prophetic period in his book, *Zoroaster: The Prophet of Ancient Iran* (New York: The Macmillan Co., 1899), 140-143. "The word 'historic' has here a double meaning: it means 'of major importance', and it also means 'forward chronology' as opposed to backward," which is applicable to science as well as to historical analysis. Richard Dawkins, *The Ancestor's Tale: A Pilgrimage to The Dawn of Evolution* (New York: Houghton Mifflin, 2004), 536.

4. The interrelation of 'language event,' 'hermeneutic,' and 'theology of the word of God' has emerged between both the European and American biblical scholars. The interpretation of language as a basis for historical illumination of the biblical message, the gospel, can be seen in Amos N. Wilder, *The Language of the Gospel: Early Christian Rhetoric* (New York: Harper & Row, Pub., 1964); See Braaten, *History and Hermeneutics,* Vol. II for a general survey. Hazen's astute observation that "Nature is not governed by our metaphors, however cherished they may be" is justly applicable to the study and use of a historical analysis. Robert M. Hazen, *Gen•e•sis: The Scientific Quest for Life's Origin* (Washington, DC: Joseph Henry Press, 2005), 106.

(Qumran, the Essenes, etc.),[5] and influenced Jewish and Christian Gnosticism as well. This type of conceptual intrusion and dualistic religiosity is part and parcel of the eschatological hermeneutic of the many diversified communities within the various Judaism's development that existed prior to the rise of Christianity. There were other forms of dualism available within the Hellenistic, religious culture of the times. Thus, a Platonic duality is well recognized even by traditional biblical scholars such as Marcus Dods when he states: Platonism represents "the contrast of this world and heaven, between that of the merely material and transient, and the ideal and abiding. Things of this world are material, unreal, transient; those of heaven are ideal, true, eternal. Heaven is the world of realities, of things themselves, of which the things here are but copies."[6]

These theological reformulations were a mixture of midrashic forms and Greek mystical symbolism. They emerged out of their traditionalist Jewish beliefs within the diaspora. And, at the same time, they expanded these beliefs within their new eschatological communities. They perceived these in Platonic fashion as christological and as religious reality that occurred interactively between the heavenly or spiritual realm and the earthly realm of

---

5. Etienne Nodet and Justin Taylor indicate that this view, as the self-designation of the 'brotherhood' groups, was concerned with their daily life, ritualization, common meals together, and the special deliberations of the 'rabbim' (1 QS 6:2f.) in *The Origins of Christianity: An Exploration* (Collegeville, Minn.: The Liturgical Press, a Michael Glazier book, 1998), 395. Cf., 1 John as fellowship in terms of a spiritual (anointed) brotherhood.

6. Marcus Dods, *Expositor's Greek Testament* (London: 1910), 271 as quoted in E. Doherty, "Supplementary Article No. 9; A Sacrifice in Heaven: The Son in the Epistle to the Hebrews," *The Jesus Puzzle: Was There No Historical Jesus?* 12. Supplement 9; http.// www. Jesuspuzzle. com/supp09.htm (accessed May 23, 2005). Many scholars would agree with this appraisal of Paul's religious posture: "Paul is a mystic. He thinks mystically, teaches mystically, and lives mystically. He also expects other Christians to do likewise." John Dominic Crossan and Jonathan L. Reed *In Search of Paul: How Jesus' Apostle Opposed Rome's Empire with God's Kingdom* (New York: HarperSanFrancisco, 2004), 283.

human existence. Their apocalyptic perceptions and theological self-identity assisted them socially to become also interactive and accommodating to the larger Hellenistic world. Within this cultural and religious context of diverse Middle Judaisms, these fellowships emerged as new communities of christological Jewish thought. They maintained a close affinity with the general movement known as Essenism. Therefore, many of these christological communities readily adapted to an apocalyptic eschatology, as they lived out their religious posture in the diaspora. They were also influenced by the literary corpora and religious devotion of Enochic Judaism. This overall development in no way suggests, during this time, that these particular christological Jews maintained a religious posture that could be called 'Christian.' They were Jewish, renewal gatherings within the Second Temple period. What we have come to identify as Christian, in its later theological formulations and socio-religious ritualization, emerged at a much later time in the formative period of the Christian Church's history.

Historicity involves a criterion used in socio-historical research to validate past events according to their religious actualities. The only substantial so-called proofs or evidences which lay hold of the Jewish christological and theological formulations are those sources that are products of the formative Christian witnesses' faith. This is the testimony of the biblical tradition, Scripture, as a revelation by the Spirit for the Christian believers. We know that historical research can uncover factual data as physical evidence concerning the faith interpretation within the christological community through their religious proclamations as perceived by them as a historical event. But, even these scholarly endeavors are limited, due to the nature of religious, metaphorical, and symbolic language. "It is important to realize that, in early Jewish thought, a personified abstraction could be storied as an individual without losing its generic or social significance."[7] As referents, the conceptual and spiritual events come to rely on the kerygmatic intention

---

7. Burton Mack, *Who Wrote the New Testament? The Making of the Christian Myth* (New York: HarperSanFrancisco, 1995), 37. Cf., Richard A. Burridge, *What are the Gospels? A Comparison with Greco-Roman Biography* (Cambridge: Cambridge University, 1992).

of the later literary corpora. This seems to be the conclusion of most modern Christian and non-Christian biblical scholars.[8] The entire metaphorical scheme, via its symbolic hermeneutic, has expressed the historic religiosity of the original Jewish christological assemblies which then became reshaped (historically distorted?) in the later development of formative Christianity. It took time and several generations to unpack the symbolic categories and the metaphorical language and to restructure a different literalist framework that theologically could express in literary fashion a life of a historical Jesus.

The original interpretation of their self-identity and eschatological existence made a theological statement embedded in symbolism about their new spiritual life within the community (the '*Yahad*') of faith. It expressed their new life within the spiritual anointing of the christological community, symbolically, as an eternal resurrected life (cf., Mark's Gospel)[9]. Most scholars involved in the study of the historical Jesus issue admit to the identification of Jesus with the Son of Man in apocalyptic literature.[10]

---

8. I am in full agreement with a historical view that is based on an understanding of the mythicist analysis of early Christian origins. In summary: "The mythicist theory does provide the better explanation for the beginnings of Christianity as reflected in the record, and it is incumbent upon the 'orthodox' side to discredit it or come up with something better -- something they have not yet done, or perhaps even attempted." E. Doherty, "Challenging Doherty: Critiquing the Mythicist Case," in *The Jesus Puzzle: Was There No Historical Jesus?* 5. http.//www.Jesus puzzle.com (accessed May 14, 2003). This first appeared in *JHC* (fall, 1997), published by the Institute for Higher Critical Studies, Drew University, Madison, New Jersey.

9. In all probability, the final destruction of the Temple prompted the writing of the Gospel of Mark. Theissen suggested that "the Gospel of Mark not only describes the end of the Jewish sacrificial cult, but at the same time provides a basis for the new rites of the first Christians, baptism and Eucharist. ... In the Gospel of Mark, Jesus' public activity begins with his baptism. His last action is the institution of the Eucharist." Theissen, *Earliest Churches,* 173.

10. Cf., F. H. Borsch, *The Son of Man in Myth and History* (Philadelphia: The Westminster Press, 1967) for a general bibliographic study of the historical Jesus literature. Two recent analyses which note

Some scholars connect these references to the mythical concept of the three days when he would arise from the dead (Mark 9:31; cf. Hosea 6:2). Mead thought that Jesus was probably an Essene[11] who had a similar ministry as the Therapeutae, in the Essene communities. Some perceive all of these socio-religious themes as a theological unity (e.g., death, burial, resurrection, and the *parousia*).[12] The historization process applied to the Jesus myth also finds a comparable phenomenon in the later liturgical tradition. It would seem that the earliest Eucharist had been intensely eschatological. But, it had become transformed within the liturgy of the earlier christological fellowships. Why this occurred is most difficult to ascertain. We know that the biblical tradition reflects this development, but without explanation. This early development

---

the understanding of the Bible as theological hermeneutics are Heinz Kimmerle, "Hermeneutical Theory or Ontological Hermeneutics," trans. by Friedrich Seifert; and Wolfhart Pannenberg's, "Hermeneutics and Universal History," trans. by Paul J. Achtemeier, both in *History and Hermeneutic*, Vol. IV of the *Journal for Theology and the Church,* ed. Robert W. Funk (New York: Harper & Row, Pub., Harper Torchbooks, 1967), 107-152.

11. G. R. S. Mead, *Did Jesus Live 100 B.C.?* (London: Theosophical Publishing Society, 1903). Alvar Ellegard also pointed out that both Christian and Essene communities used similar names for the members of their fellowships (examples are: saints, fathers, elect, the poor, those of the way, and assemblies of God to mention just a few), in *Jesus One Hundred Years Before Christ* (London: Century Press, 1999).

12. Cf., L. S. Thornton, *The Common Life in the Body of Christ*, 2d ed. (London: The Dacre Press, 1944). For additional comments by M. Buber on the concept of Spirit as dynamic religiosity, see *Israel and the World*, trans. Maurice Friedman and others (New York: Schocken Books, 1963). In the early gatherings, *parousia* was a term that applied to communal realities (the divine presence of YHWH in the community) and only later when literalism infected theological hermeneutics in the second century did it emphasize its futuristic aspect. *Parousia* (*parousia*) has three aspects or nuances: expectation that anticipated an arrival, an arrival that necessitated a celebration, an event or presence that allowed for communal festivities to celebrate the honor of the dignitary's *presence* (*parousia*) with them.

reveals the historical process and its transformative power over primitive spirituality and mythical conceptualizations.[13]

Regardless of the symbolic and metaphorical nature of the early traditional religiosity, modern Christians tend to believe that they will be raised from the dead (literally) to a potential eternal life (spiritual existence?), heaven bound, which is established by their belief. These same religious, Jewish categories of the earlier tradition were interpreted symbolically by the earlier christological believers so that metaphorically, they could be raised "in Christ," to a 'newness of spiritual life' in the christological community of the end time, which was their *contemporary* existence. Wright makes note that the past religious focus was in the Temple, which was now resided symbolically in the new spiritual, christological community.[14] The historicity of the resurrection's spiritual power rested within a mythological context as an expression of their faith understanding.

The resurrection concept provided the basic rationale for the early Christian tradition in that it gave, through its total scheme of divine, mythical redemption in the kerygma, a living spiritual hope for the early christological gatherings. This hope was anchored to their moral discipline that was to be lived out in this world: not to a future expectation of dying and going to a heaven above, even though that former idea was prevalent within the Hel-

---

13. The problem of God in the modern world is examined by Buber in an essay, "Gottesfinsternis," (1953). It appears in English translation, *Eclipse of God*, trans. Maurice Friedman and others (New York: Harper & Row, Pub., Harper Torchbooks, 1957). Cf., W. Bowman, *Prophetic Realism and the Gospel* (Philadelphia: Westminster Press, 1955); and cf., Ernst Kasemann, *Jesus Means Freedom* (Philadelphia: Fortress Press, 1969).

14. He also noted: "It was standard Jewish belief, rooted in Scripture and celebrated in regular festivals and liturgy, that the Temple was the place where heaven and earth actually interlocked, where the living God had promised to be present with his people." And that "Judaism had two incarnational symbols: Temple and Torah." N. T. Wright, *The Challenge of Jesus: Rediscovering Who Jesus Was and Is* (Downers Grove, Ill.: InterVarsity Press, 1999), 110 and 120.

lenistic culture. The apostle[15] Paul received his 'gospel' as a reve-latory experience and relied upon its midrashic function to explain the literary tradition and proclaimed it with religious reverence.

The early Jewish communities' religiosity was based on the symbolic christological understanding of YHWH's power and presence to create a people via resurrection for his service in the world. The new faith-understanding (their *contemporaneous* resurrection) was the essential apocalyptic and eschatological core of their fellowship because it centered on the gathering's anointing by YHWH's Spirit. Symbolism was the religious hermeneutic that explains so naturally the metaphorical dynamic, the theological freshness, and the cultural vitality of the Jesus myth with which the Jewish community had its christological beginnings.

The *parousia* was a dynamic and symbolic expression of the newly anointed community. Crossan and Reed note that

> The *parousia* metaphor means that Christians do not ascend to stay with Christ in heaven, but to return with him to this transformed world. ... The metaphor of *parousia* as state visit would presume that those going out to greet the approaching ruler would return with him for festive rejoicing within their city. ... The *parousia* of the Lord was not about destruction of the earth and relocation to heaven, but about a world in which violence and injustice are transformed into purity and holiness.[16]

In fact, it is evident from all of Paul's genuine letters that the 'cosmic Christ,' who he proclaimed as the Son of God and Savior in his gospel, is never mentioned or referred to as a historical person, a man named Jesus of Nazareth. Nor is there reference to Jesus being put to death by the Roman authorities in Judea. To relegate the biblical Christ, the anointed deity of the community, *Yeshua*, into a historical persona and thereby mitigating a purely

---

15. Paul's 'apostleship' is evidence of early christological terminology. G. H. Wells states that "no extant document before the gospels is Peter or anyone else called a 'disciple' in the sense of a companion during a ministry. The term used in the earliest documents is 'apostle' and it there means missionary," in "Earliest Christianity," 14.

16. Crossan and Reed, *Paul*, 170. Note especially their general comments on the *parousia*, 167-174.

human Jesus, is to render his historic literary existence as beyond historical verifiability. This has led some scholars, based on the biblical tradition, to adopt the extreme but a correct historical view that Jesus was in all actuality a non-historical person. His existence, perceived, as the anointed divine presence of YHWH which encapsulated the eschatological cult, had become the new faith-understanding of the early Jewish christological assemblies, referred to as Spiritual Israel.

Even the thoughts of Egyptian religious ideas are never far from apocalyptic forms and imageries. They can be seen in the symbolic and kerygmatic intention recognized by Brandon. He relates this to the emendations of the biblical tradition, especially in the Gospel accounts. He makes this important observation: that "Jesus was not thought to have been resurrected to resume his life on earth..." to a mundane historical reality, but "was rather of the order of that ascribed to the ancient Egyptian mortuary God, Osiris ... to become the ruler of the *Duat*, the realm of the dead."[17] In Pauline religious thought, Jesus ascended to the heavenly realm to be at the right hand of God immediately after his resurrection (death/sacrifice). He makes no mention of any sojourn on the earth prior to his ascension. For early gnostic Christians, this world was the realm of Satan's rule out of which resurrection delivered a believer into the mystical body of Christ, the new creation, the new community. Hence, they were in the world but not of this world. Wright's perception of this is very astute:

And yet the very earliest church declared roundly not only that Jesus was raised from the dead but that "the resurrection of the dead" had already occurred (Acts 4:2). What is more, they busily set about re-designing their whole world-view – their characteristic praxis, their controlling stories, their symbolic universe and their basic theology –

---

17. S. G. F. Brandon, *Jesus and the Zealots* (New York: Charles Scribner's Sons, 1967), 178-9. Also see C. K. Barrett, Ed., *The New Testament Background: Selected Documents*, intro. C. K. Barrett (New York: Harper & Row, Pub., Harper Torchbooks, The Cloister Library, 1961), 231. And cf., Frank Morison, *Who Moved the Stone?* (New York: Barnes & Noble, 1922). See Richard R. Niebuhr, *Resurrection and Historical Reason* (New York: Charles Scribner's Sons, 1957).

around this new fixed point. They behaved, in other words, as though the new age had already arrived.[18]

The full metaphorical scope of this type of interpretation is reflected in Paul's Corinthian letter, chapter fifteen on the resurrection in which a *metaphorical* understanding is more historically exacting of the spiritual dynamics, which are reflected in an understanding of Christ's resurrection.[19] This is definitely reflective of their communal experience. Paul transmits this Jewish christological understanding of how God's community of faith is to be gathered as a socio-religious entity through their faith acceptance of his gospel proclaimed as the 'forgiveness of sin.'[20] The spiritual power of God's presence to forgive sins is equated with Christ being raised from the dead. Thus, not to accept God's salvation based

---

18. Wright, *Challenge of Jesus,* 136.

19. Paul's response to the questions of resurrection reflect his grave concerns and his inner anxiety to convince the Corinthians that people can be resurrected from death (life without faith) through poetic religious language: from mortality to immortality, from 'flesh' to 'spirit,' from earthly under the law to heavenly, freedom in Christ. Nowhere in his declaration of his gospel does he make reference to any historical tradition to indicate that Jesus resurrected several people from the grave or refer to "all of those in the graves in Jerusalem were resurrected" when Jesus was crucified. Paul is not referring to historical (physical) realities but to spiritual (mythological) realities. Theissen notes that these concepts have definite Hellenistic influence. "Moreover the notion of vicarious dying entered the biblical world from its pagan environment. It is characteristic that in the few passages in which it occurs, it is always bound up with the hopes of a new life." Theissen, *Earliest Churches,* 149.

20. Cf., I Cor. 15 for the full impact of Pauline theological perspective as it relates to the newly formed faith community as the body of the risen Christ and the believers entrance into that 'body' via baptism into Christ death on the cross (the forgiveness of their sins), see 1 John. The initiates were believed to have been 'transported' from death to life. This probably occurred ceremonially at the time when they entered into the new faith community through baptism, which was the beginning of their communal faith journey.

on the mythic and heavenly sacrificial act,[21] the crucifixion and the resurrection symbolically understood, is not to receive forgiveness of one's sins. Paul believed that the religious effect of this divine act within the kerygma would be perceived by his Jewish brethren as a 'sandal' since 'divine forgiveness' was now made available to the whole world without Judaism's sacrificial and priestly religious system.

The presence of 'the kingdom' (the historical reality and presence of *Yeshua* as the faithful Jewish christological people of God) stood between a rejection by the Jewish traditional religiosity and its acceptance by those involved in the Hellenistic, Gentile religious and Platonic categories, as mystically formulated in the revitalized Jewish communities. This was precisely the view maintained by the evangelists in the historicized form of the biblical tradition (Mark's Gospel). Thus, the theological implications of Paul's conceptualizations, his metaphorical proclamations, and his mystical *christology* found religious significance through Hellenistic language forms. Paul could easily proclaim, in Platonic fashion, a divine Christ with clarity of understanding among the Hellenistic believers in the synagogues of the diaspora. "The synagogue was a

---

21. Some scholars outside the mystic tradition have recognized the Platonic world view in the formation of biblical literature, especially in the book of Hebrews. J. Moffat in the *International Critical Commentary, Hebrews,* xlii states, "For the complete sacrifice has been offered in the realm of the spirit." And in xliii that it "had been offered in the spirit -- as we might say -- in the eternal order of things ... it belonged essentially to the higher order of absolute reality." And, Dods in *Expositor's Greek Testament,* 332 suggests a greater significance is given to Christ's sacrifice since it was "exercised in a more perfect tabernacle and with a truer sacrifice" in the Heavenlies. Doherty, a biblical scholar of rationality, says: "In other words, they recognize Jesus' sacrifice as an event which in some way takes place in the world of Platonic-type myth, in the higher world of the spirit." The others are quoted by Doherty in his "Supplementary Article No. 9," (accessed May 23, 2005). Even if you acknowledge that those traditional scholars simply are following a conservative, literalist perspective; it, out of necessity, indicates that modern day conservative, 'literalist' Christianity has taken over the ancient Platonic world view as a statement of reality for them in contradistinction of a secular, scientific 'materialist' world view of physical reality.

publicly visible place serving as the religious, political, legal, social, and economic center of Jewish life in the Roman cities of the diaspora."[22] Paul received his mystic, experiential revelation when his hermeneutical understanding of scripture enabled his consciousness to identify and comprehend the mythological basis for the renewed, Jewish gathering's communal identity, which he had persecuted for so long. Doherty is correct to point out that "Paul believes 'in' Jesus the same way many people believe in God: they postulate his existence, not from having seen him bodily, or from talking to those who knew him on earth, but through religious faith."[23] This faith was also based on scriptural testimony within a faith community.

Thus, when considering a socio-historical methodology that is based on a scientific rationality, contemporary Christianity might conclude in agreement with Kahler's remarks as quoted by Braaten:

> Either faith and theology receive the Jesus of history [and the resurrection] through the tradition of apostolic preaching, namely, the kerygmatic Christ of the primitive community; or the historian must resume the quest of the historical Jesus, by going behind the post-Easter witness of the church (of which we do not possess any sources which the historian can accept as reliable and adequate according to the standards of contemporary and secular, historical science). ... Revelation in history simply eludes the grasp of the historian qua his-

---

22. Crossan and Reed, *Paul*, 35. Also see Berger's treatment of a religious and philosophical discussion concerning 'theodicy,' which existed for many centuries in the ancient world. It was out of this concern that the theological posture of the early gatherings was formed in the Second Temple period. Cf., Peter L. Berger, *The Sacred Canopy: Elements of a Sociological Theory of Religion* (New York: Doubleday, 1967), 53-80.

23. Doherty, "Critiquing the Mythicist Case," 11-12. For an excellent bibliography of scholarly works on Middle Judaism from the first century to modern times, see Gabriele Boccaccini, *Middle Judaism: Jewish Thought, 300 B.C.E. to 200 C.E.* (Minneapolis: Fortress Press, 1991), Chapter 2, "Toward a Bibliography of Middle Judaism," 26-74.

torian. ... From non-theological perspectives there are no visible trac-es of revelation in history.[24]

The historical Jesus escapes detection by the historian when attempting to find evidence of his earthly existence precisely because that so-called physical entity, Jesus, in the biblical tradi-tion, did not exist as a historical person in reality. Historically, he did exist symbolically when referring to the Jewish christological gathering and existed metaphorically in the mystical relationship, as the anointed body of God's presence within the community. It would seem that contemporary biblical scholarship of early Chris-tian origins distance themselves, at least theologically, from a mythothematic perspective because its hermeneutical basis and the mystical experience that was ritualized within the early christolog-ical community suggests an unacceptable form of Gnosticism and/or a form of the ancient mystery religions for them.

The idea of the dying and rising of the divinity was certain-ly part of the religious milieu of the Greco-Roman world. This can be detected in some forms of Gnosticism and the various mystery religions of the Hellenistic world. It is not a new observation, to be sure, that Paul's epistles abound in the patterns of thought familiar to Gnosticism.[25] These ideas also expressed Christ's function as

---

24. Martin Kahler, *The So-called Historical Jesus and the His-torical Biblical Christ*, Seminar Editions, Theodore G. Tappert, Gen. Ed., trans. and ed. by Carl E. Braaten, Foreword by Paul Tillich (Phila-delphia: Fortress Press, 1964), 35-36. Developing a good methodology for a historical analysis should keep Karl Popper's dictum in mind. "Theories, to be theories at all in the scientific sense, must make testable predictions that might be proved false by empirical tests. ... By the same token, the more precise (and, therefore, the more falsifiable) its predic-tions, the more believable a theory becomes when it survives scrutiny." Cited by Hazen, *Gen.e.sis,* 111.

25. E.g., I Cor. 15:8; cf. Gal. 1:15-17. The mythological world was altered drastically by the end of the first century after the appear-ance of Mark's Gospel. Literalism became the theological focus for the developing Christian communities. Doherty comments that "The only difference in conditions that could exist between the first and the fourth centuries, which makes any sense, is that the historical Jesus and a ca-reer on earth did not exist in people's minds in the first century, but had

Creator, as the *Logos* and his role as Savior, as the fellowships' divine presence of union with YHWH. Most of these terms were very familiar to those who held spiritual and philosophical interests within Hellenistic religiosity. Thus, it is not difficult to understand that several literary tomes in the ancient Hellenistic world could utilize Platonic categories. In the *Testament of Levi,* third part of the *Testament of the Twelve Patriarchs* we have an example of Platonism where we see 'sacrifices' being offered to God in a heavenly temple that is located in the third heaven (cf., Hebrews). Recall Paul's out of body experience in the third heaven? "In this multi-layered universe, the third heaven contains an archetypal sanctuary whose copy is the earthy temple. Here the archangels 'offer propitiatory sacrifices to the Lord in behalf of all the sins of ignorance of the righteous ones' (as in the earthly rite on the Day of Atonement). ... Such sacrifices are declared to be 'bloodless', although sacrifices in heaven involving blood are to be found in later Kabbalistic thinking."[26] Also, these early Jewish communities identified their own christological communal existence as *Yeshua*, Jesus, in terms of the divine function of the Spirit of YHWH in their midst.

These faith-understandings are mystical, mythological, and Platonically structured in the Hellenistic language of religious categories. This was similarly done in various forms of Gnosticism. It was not uncommon for the general religiosity of the times. As Smith states:

> The very early identification of the Jesus with YHWH is found in the regular application to him of the term *Kyrios* (Lord), which is the uniform Septuagint rendering of the divine name, the tetragram YHWH, in *the original covenantal literature* (i.e., the Old Testament) ... when used with the article and without specification, as in

---

established itself in Christian consciousness by the third and fourth centuries." In "Critics of the Mystic Case," 19 (accessed May 13, 2003). The mystic and gnostic traditions continued and still have adherents today. Scholarly tomes in print today are: Evelyn Underhill, *Mysticism: Development of Spiritual Consciousness* (1990) and G. R. S. Mead, *ECHOES* (2006).

26. Doherty, "Supplementary Article No. 9," 16.

the Lord ..., it is perfectly unambiguous, and means YHWH, God. So too, in *the expanded covenantal literature*: Lord, the Lord, the Lord Jesus, the Lord Christ, all mean one thing; namely, the Supreme being, the YHWH of the Hebrews, the God of the Greeks.[27]

It is our familiarity with the religiosity of the Judaeo-Greco-Roman world that suggests a common agreement that this was a historical era of vast and intense religious activity. These infusions and influences occurred outwardly and internally and are recognized by biblical scholars who study the socio-religious literature of the diverse traditions.[28] There are many personalities that are preserved in the literature[29] of these periods who are noble in their humanity, excellent by their virtue, and superb in their moral integrity. They represent the persona of a cultural hero. It was not difficult to add Jesus to this list and along with the several historic religious sentimentalities.

The tremendous influx of new converts to the Jewish christological communities' faith was in general by people of human goodness and virtue, honest in their moral integrity, whether they

---

27. Smith, *Ecce Deus*, 135. Smith's overall theme of symbolic hermeneutic suggests that a conceptual interaction of cultural religiosity was operative during Christianity's quest for its earliest religious survival. Italicized remarks are mine.

28. Cf., Stark's fundamental thesis, in *The Rise of Christianity*, for a sociological perspective of Christianity's historical development along similar lines of other cult movements, in which he considers it as a movement "based on the more privileged classes," 33.

29. Note the sociological perspective of Clyde Kluckhohn in "Common Humanity and Diverse Cultures," *The Human Meaning of the Social Sciences*, Ed. Daniel Lerner (New York: Meridian Books, 1959). Also, see Gustaf Dalman, *Jesus-Jeshua*, Trans. Paul P. Levertoff (New York: The Macmillan Co., 1929) for a wide range of names and titles that designate the early understanding of *Yeshua* for primitive Christianity. In contrast to the biblical names for divinity see the religious impact of divinity for the Imperial Roman authorities where "Imperial divinity was, quite simply, the ideology that held the Roman Empire together and the theology that allowed Greek pride and tradition gracefully to accept Roman law and order." Crossan and Reed, *Paul*, 160.

be God-fearing pagans or former people of Israel,[30] the chosen of God. Paul and many others attempted to broaden the focus of God's grace by reaching outward to the Gentiles (all of humanity, God's creation as universalism). Thus they were all "not far from YHWH's Kingdom," as we learn in the book of Acts. These are indicative of some people who hungered and thirsted for spiritual truth (moral integrity?). They were "fed the bread of life" a textual metaphor, midrashic relationship with the manna of Moses. This continued to be the christological communities' bases for their moral instruction.[31] Thus, it is in the Gospel of John that Jesus reflects the pedagogical experience within the fellowship, who says, "I am the bread." They, in the older Mosaic tradition, "drank from the well of living water." In midrashic literary form, this type of hermeneutic reflects the baptismal and resurrected understanding that brought them into the Kingdom of Christ, the new community of the end-times. And, they found the 'truth,' which set them forever free. It was Jesus, the embodiment of God's wisdom (Gnosis) that instructed the christological fellowship in the new 'way' and 'life' of the eschatological community,[32] as the historical biblical tradition testifies.

We can validate socio-historical reality by the evidence of the tradition and its transmission. But, we cannot validate the inner consciousness, its psychodynamic content, such as the historic Je-

---

30. Cf. the 'devout women' and the 'God-worshippers' in Luke 2:25 and Acts 2:5; 10:2), in Barrett, *New Testament Background*, 231ff.

31. Paul extrapolates a thanksgiving meal based on Jewish origin for the basis of his hermeneutical posture. Thanksgiving meals were also common among the Greco-Roman, pagan cults. Most of the mystery religions had them. They were regarded mythically as having been established the God's divine presence. This made a spiritual 'union' with the deity a mystical reality within the cult. These were foundation myths, which were meant to explain by symbolism and justify the socio-religious practices of the cult, their metaphorical experience, and the cultic rituals of the mystery celebrations. Note John 6-33, 35, 41, 48 (John 4:10-15).

32. Hence; in the Gospel of John 4 we find the mystical conversation in the literary story (myth) of Jesus and the woman at the well (myth and midrash), which invites a hermeneutical response, not a quasi-news report of an actual historical event.

sus myth, which is reflected in the historical biblical tradition. One can reach out for the concrete, physical, reality of historical ideas, forces, and events of the times that existed. But, we must be reminded that when you extrapolate ontological categories from the epistemological dynamics, irrationality and contradictions, while present, become acceptable as theological paradoxes (minimally) and theological truth (maximally). These then generates into religious categories that are accepted by faith as authoritative dogma of the religious institution. This process can be used to reconstruct the historic encounter and the socio-religious building blocks on which the theological parameters of the Jewish christological communities existed.

These mystical ideas must have conveyed, within the early gathering of believers, some kind of theological language in order to be meaningful. Wells made an astute observation concerning these linguistic exchanges of theological concepts, when he said:

> The essential ambiguities of language, combined with different capacities for abstraction in the persons who use it, are bound to lead to different interpretations of the same formulae; and this distortion will result in religious change, or at least affect the uniformity of belief even in a small community. In this way, complicated and sophisticated ideas become degraded into more tangible concretes.[33]

More importantly, since much of the ancient Jewish religiosity and its mythological basis had maintained a high level of symbolism, it would seem quite natural for the early Jewish christological people of God to express its faith symbolically and metaphorically.[34] YHWH, as the hope of Israel and the nations, was

---

33. Wells, *The New Humanists*, 1999, 18. In terms of historical methodologies, see Davis S. Pacini, *The Cunning of Modern Religious Thought* (Philadelphia: Fortress Press, 1987).

34. A Symbolic reference to mythothemes includes various aspects and nuances. For example: when discussing Wisdom as a divine aspect of God, some regard "the Wisdom of the Jewish literature not as an actual being in God's service, but as a mere personification of some of his attributes." There is no escape from mythological arguments even in this perception. Larry W. Hurtado, *One God, One Lord* (Edinburgh: Clark, 1998).

proclaimed as the christological basis for universal, monotheism along similar symbolic lines, using metaphorical religious language, Platonic categories, and given an apocalyptic and eschatological interpretation.

This psychodynamic and natural process, within ancient human existence, has not changed over the eons of bio-evolutionary time. It functions today as well as it did during the times of the historic origin of the Jew's christological faith. Let me venture to say, that, if we were privy to the inner mind-set of the early members of the Jewish gatherings and were also christologically aware of the vast variety of oral and literary ideas that impacted those contemporary times; and, if we had a real sense and feel for their perceived mission as the new Israel of YHWH who were led by the Spirit of the divine presence (as the secret cult theologized its faith out of the body of sacred literature, their traditional Jewish Scriptures); we today, and the whole of Christendom, would probably understand more fully the need for a symbolic interpretation of their mystic experience with the *Christos* event. There would be, in general, somewhat of an agreement about the historic origin of the earliest christological followers, as they lived out their Jewish, religious experience of the divine spiritual presence, its way, its truth, and its life[35] that was made available to others in the Hellenistic world.

The earliest kerygma proclaimed the Jesus myth to which the later biblical tradition ascribed a certain earthly historicized career. This christological mythology was understood originally, and symbolically, as a Jewish mystic metaphor for the early christological community; but, it later became quasi-historical as the literalized persona of the Jesus figure in the Gospel narratives. Brandon suggests that "... this apparent lack of concern about the historical Jesus is paralleled by an equally remarkable evaluation of the death [and resurrection of Jesus which lifts the events] ...

---

35. Reddish, *Apocalyptic Literature*, 224 makes reference to the Essence Community Rule (1QS) 3-4 that they moved to the Dead Sea because of dissatisfaction with the High Priest, the sacrificial practices in Jerusalem in order to practice what they considered to be the 'pure form of Judaism.' Paul and the early christological communities were of a more liberal persuasion in their practices of the true faith.

completely out of its historical setting."[36] It was the historic faith understanding of religious symbolism that was also significant to Paul's metaphorical beliefs, theology, and use of mystical religious language. He identifies the heavenly 'Lord of Glory' with Jesus as the divine spiritual *presence* whose power in this world, the evil domain of Satan, acts through the christological gathering (cf., similar gnostic categories and religious constructs). Therefore, the secret eschatological Jewish cultus, within the context of myth, perceived itself as being against "the demonic rulers of the present evil age."[37]

In all of this can be seen the earlier Yahwistic thought of ancient Israel that underwent profound religious changes in its mythic, Jewish religiosity by the efforts of these christological fellowships within the diaspora.[38] Nevertheless, to some extent, the revised (redacted) biblical tradition, at least by the fourth Century, held to some conceptual expressions that also reflected the earlier socio-religious ideas of Hellenistic religiosity. And likewise, the

---

36. Brandon, *Jesus and the Zealots*, 22. Cf., the symbolic world constructed from myth and history in Theissen, *Earliest Churches,* 286, where he states that "This mythicizing of history and historicizing of myth begins with Jesus' proclamation of the Kingdom of God, a mythical dramatization of the basic monotheistic conviction of Judaism. Since then a unity of myth and history has stamped the narrative sign-world of primitive Christianity."

37. I Corinthians 2:6-8; also cf. the influence of Gnosticism. These ideas highly impacted the Essene communities at Qumran in their spiritual struggles with the moral sensibility, which speaks of the 'darkness' as evil. The various literary works in Hellenistic Judaism also reflect the dominant religious philosophy of the age. There was a fluidity of ideas that could morph from one religiosity to another and merge theological and philosophical categories together with a kind of linguistic mortar. There was the Jewish personification of Wisdom that was associated with the divine *Logos* within gnostic ideas and Greek philosophy that also dealt with the Cosmic Son as an expression of divinity having salvific significance.

38. The missionary efforts in the diaspora were the primary work of Paul, it would seem. Yet, it is difficult to really know if that is so, since the Orthodox Church in the fourth century destroyed all the evidence of other missionary efforts that had a different point of view.

Jesus myth, in the cult of the christological gatherings, underwent profound changes. They also reformulated the Yahwistic religious forms of the old Mosaic tradition.[39] The christological gatherings retained the idea of the kingdom of God as the spiritual sphere of YHWH's rule, and the divine presence that gave them 'life,' through fellowship with him.

Bultmann, as previously suggested, has indicated the levels of tradition that existed in the development of the 'Gospel' records.[40] A similar development of tradition, as expressed in the whole of the expanded covenantal thought, was seen in the early christological proclamation by the renewed Jewish communities. Thus, the theological perspectives of the older tradition that were preserved in the Christian scriptures as midrashim, while demanding our close attention, does not seek an equal demand for spiritual authority.[41] These ascriptions were not taken literally by the earliest Jewish gatherings, but were understood correctly as symbolic, christological, mystical, and mythological. They were comparable to the various religious interpretations that were commonly in vogue with the Hellenistic religiosity that used spiritual and mystic concepts to describe 'divinity.' These concepts and interpretations were representative of the religious age[42] and cultural milieu. For the metaphorical understandings by these early Jewish fellowships within the Jesus myth, there was nothing that was not generally comprehended in this christological way. William B. Smith, who represents this position, speaks to the issue of the dilemma: "On the contrary, we substitute for [the historicized dilemma] a single lemma: We affirm and maintain that the real Jesus is the Jesus of

---

39. Cf., I Kings 21; I Samuel 8-15.

40. Rudolf Bultmann and Karl Kundsin consider some of these effects of the early church's life upon the transmission of its tradition in *Form Criticism: A New Method of New Testament Research,* Trans. F. C. Grant (New York: Willett, Clark & Co., 1934). Note Chap. IX, 86-95.

41. Gospel of John 2:22; 10:35, and II Timothy 3:16.

42. There are definite limitations to cultural influences. G. A. Wells notes that "pagan Platonists … did not want to hear of a God who took human form and suffered humiliation on earth," *The New Humanist*, 13.

the Evangelists, the purely divine Jesus who in the Gospels has "cast about him the shining semblance of a reverend man."[43]

When the christological communities had openly propagandized the Jesus myth, it became successful on a conceptual level, due to the historical forces (as myth and mystic revelatory experiences) already in the minds of the peoples who populated the Hellenistic world. This was also the essence of the Jesus myth, the divine Jesus. The anointed one, *Yeshua*, was the name for YHWH's Spirit without human form.[44] It was so understood by the Jewish christological communities via their symbolism and only later, when the process of historization had humanized YHWH's Spirit, into a historical Jesus, with a divine persona, that a historical and scholarly problem occurred. This problem, together with the later gnostic influences, remained as theological confrontations within the ranks of the formative Church's apologists, and their theological handiwork can still be detected in the later church's literary interpolations.[45]

It seems to have been Paul's desire to know him (in the gnostic sense of mystical union), not the historical, earthy Jesus; but the resurrected heavenly Christ (a revelatory experience for Paul united in common 'fellowship,' life with) Jesus the Lord, as the anointed authority and the divine presence. Paul's desire was to know the 'power' of Christ's resurrection as an abiding spiritual reality indicative of the forgiveness of sins. Paul's desire had an abiding moral integrity (honesty) and a truly personal passion and concern for others. Hence, the kerygmatic tradition of the early church became the basis for Paul's own proclamation of his gos-

---

43. Smith, *Ecce Deus*, 40. Also, Ernst Kasemann began a new 'quest' within the Bultmannian School. He grapples significantly with the text, interpreting the historical significance of Jesus to the disciples in "The Problem of the Historical Jesus," *Essays on New Testament Themes*, trans. W. J. Montague (London: SCM Press, Ltd., 1964), 15-47.

44. Edwyn Bevan, *Symbolism and Belief* (Boston: Beacon Press, 1957), 254. Cf., John 2:22; 10:35, and II Timothy 3:16. Resurrection for Paul always had an aspect of 'authentication' and 'validation' of an initiate's spiritual development anchored within the conceptual understanding of the deity's presence.

45. See additional insights in Ehrman, *Misquoting Jesus*, 2005.

pel, and it can be seen in the theological development of his own *christology*. The Berlin fragment that is known as the Acts of Paul recently substantiated this point.[46] It was through Paul's preaching that he proclaimed spiritual redemption (baptized) for all believers so that their lives could be mystically transformed (resurrected) due to God's divine presence (*parousia*) uniting them in communal existence (the Eucharist), which was all based upon their faith response. These thought patterns used by Paul are not very far from the religious mystical patterns used in the Hellenistic mystery cults to express their communal union with the Divine.[47] In this regard, he could say that, "... we preach and through such preaching you have become Christians," anointed ones with life eternal in Christ (I Cor. 15:11). In view of the natural socioreligious process of the humanization of the divine presence, YHWH's Spirit and by its literary historization, it has now become embedded within the Christian tradition. Thus, we can understand that the earlier mystic experience has historically evolved and a "... strictly rectilinear development we may not in reason expect, but any imagined evolution from an original doctrine of the humanity of the Jesus seems highly un-natural and improbable."[48]

---

46. Dibelius, *From Tradition to Gospel*, n. 1, p. 23; and J. Gesham Machen, *The Origin of Paul's Religion* (New York: The Macmillan Co., 1921). Cf., Burton Scott Easton, *The Gospel before the Gospels* (New York: Charles Scribner's Sons, 1928); and B. P. W. Stather Hunt, *Primitive Gospel Sources* (New York: Philosophic Library, Inc., 1951).

47. This theological and mystical process began as a revelatory experience in which Paul found a midrashim-like methodology that gave substance to his new socio-religious understanding. The salvific voice of God's Son was a linguistic symbol for Paul's method of scriptural interpretation. For Paul the scriptures, which now illuminate a new spiritual understanding, were a window into the Platonic, religious world-view that gave insight to the Jewish gatherings' systemic faith and communal self-identity. Hence, revelation always brings forth a new understanding.

48. Smith, *Ecce Deus*, 139-40. Theissen, *Earliest Churches,* 25, states that "The historicizing of myth works with the possibilities of mythical thought itself, even if it breaks through the separation of mythical and profane time and seeks to proclaim a 'mythical' event from the qualitatively different time as a 'historical' event in the midst of this time."

Given this developmental and symbolic perspective (based on mythological, mystical, and religious categories), we can appreciate the Hellenistic philosophical basis (Platonism), regarding the significance of temporality that entered into the arena of myth making during the Second Temple period. This provided the socio-religious structure for a symbolic understanding of the divine presence among the early christological gatherings and their Jewish self-identity, as the body of the anointed one. "In more enlightened gnostic [Jewish christological] circles the original symbolic sense of the Gospel narratives was long recognized; and, as we have seen, traces of it may be found even in Jerome and Augustine."[49] In the long history of religious mythology, symbolism is a hermeneutical factor that is not easily dismissed. Even the church father, Jerome[50] did not fail to see the significance of symbolism in his own metaphorical interpretation of the biblical text. It is difficult at times to understand why so many modern biblical scholars are so keen on dismissing symbolism as a historical hermeneutic and as a socio-religious methodology, which could enhance and clarify everyone's understanding of early Christian origins.

---

49. Smith, Ibid. Paul's entire proclamation of the Christ in his gospel was a polemic to bring about a new understanding of the traditional sacrificial system without the Jerusalem priesthood. This was the finalization of rethinking about the revitalization of Hellenistic Judaism that could embrace the 'prophetic' idealism found in the original covenantal scriptures. Many decades had pasted in which resentment over the rightful and scriptural priestly appointments and divinely sanctioned functions of their office had taken hold among diaspora Jews and by some Judean groups (the Essene communities at and around Qumran). Paul merged Hellenistic Platonism (with its mythology and mystical ideas) with Hellenistic Judaism (with its gnostic sensibilities) to reconfigure a *christological* understanding of sacrifice (the forgiveness of sin) with the Christ as the main mythological symbol that accomplished salvation without Jerusalem's tainted, religious officials.

50. Smith, Ibid., 31. In the original covenantal scriptures, it was stated, "thus saith the Lord." For Paul, God's voice of revelation was "thus says his Son" (cf., Mark 1:9-13, and 9:7). The revelatory basis was, in both cases, the scriptures that provided the 'voice;' and for Paul, the revelation was the disclosure of new meanings and the symbols for a christological understanding.

3

The evidence suggests that the New Testament is not a history of actual events, but a history of the evolution of Christian mythology.
Freke and Gandy

The canonical tradition presents Jesus in the Gospel narratives as a truly divine incarnation within the context of a physical world reality (i.e., the ancient Palestinian world). A vast majority of modern Christianity has embraced that ancient mythological world-view, as a current mind-set, which has established its theological posture as an aspect of spiritual formation and religiosity (the present era of biblical literalism). That ancient world-view is a socio-religious, reality construct that is in contradiction to a basically modern scientific mind-set (without a mythological focus in its ontology) by people throughout the world in the twenty-first century. That ancient world-view, by means of the biblical tradition, has continued to assert its mythological basis through the centuries into the present.

The reformulation of myth into reality takes time. For example: the deep roots of Gnosticism within the fabric of early Christianity took a great deal of time to develop and merge with the developing conceptions of the Christian tradition. "Moreover, gnostic ideas were not so far from the popular philosophies of the time, such as Neo-Platonism and Neo-Stoicism."[1] Religionists often fail to recognize or admit for that matter that their biblical analysis is based on an essential mystic epistemological construct that has been anchored in the mythological categories of understanding within the ancient world.

Doherty admits to this essential mystic epistemological construct. He points out quite clearly the vast literary silence (the Gospels are the primary exception) in the apostolic references to a

---

1. Ellegård, *Jesus -- One Hundred Years Before Christ*, 253.

historical Jesus in the writings of the New Testament scriptures. "The kind of pervasive silence on the Gospel character and events found in the early Christian record would, in any other discipline or field of research, inevitably produce a self-evident conclusion." Doherty's assessment reveals the enormity of this literary silence when he also states:

That a dozen different writers in over two dozen documents, representing Christian communities spread over half an empire and more than half a century, concerned with describing and defending their faith, ethics and practices, their christology and soteriology, engaged in disputes on a variety of issues that were critical to the success and survival of the movement, would nevertheless fail to mention–even by chance–a single element which would enable us to clearly identify the beginnings of their religion and the object of their worship with the man and events recounted in the Gospels, is a situation that allows for only one deduction: that early Christianity knows of no such man [a historical Jesus] or events.[2]

The mythological and literary basis, which also applies to 'miracles,' does occur as literary constructs within several religious narratives of the ancient biblical tradition.[3] Biblicists should

---

2. E. Doherty, "Postscript: The Sound of Silence" 200 Missing References to the Gospel Jesus in the New Testament Epistles, *The Jesus Puzzle: Was There No Historical Jesus?* 1. http.//www.Jesus puzzle.com.htm (accessed April 16, 2005). This preliminary statement by Doherty is precisely the reason for this study. It is to provide an explanation for early Christian origins that began without a real flesh and blood person called Jesus. Even Thomas L. Thompson in *The Messiah Myth: The Near Eastern Roots of Jesus and David* (New York: Basic Books, 2005), 24, states that "oral tradition is not needed to explain the development of a [historical] figure embodying a tradition of ancient wisdom." Bracket is mine.

3. No biblical scholar really believes in miracles, if they attempt to explain them by the use of rationality, which seeks to provide scientific and factual evidence that describes 'how' it could have occurred, as part of physical and historical reality. They may even suggest that the divine power suspends, by supernatural means, those physical laws; since, he/she was the deity that created them (pure irrational arrogance). Miracles are accepted by believers as a faith commitment that uses the

94

recognize that miracles are purely a 'literary device,' mythic in their basic form that is used to make a spiritual point among religious believers regarding the 'power and authority' of their god(s). Thus, miracles are a certain aspect of myth (a part of the story in which they occur), which purports to validate the mythotheme of divine purpose, which is clearly exemplified in and by the biblical story. Countless millions of believers today still hold to the ancient Christian biblical tradition that continues to reflect a mythological reality. The divine myth of the early Jewish communities and the entire christological range of their cultic titles emerged from their historicized theology.

Myths were first perceived metaphorically and interpreted symbolically; then, later were ignored as part of the historic process of conceptual reformulation by later generations of believers. Even though history has lost most of this ancient, symbolic and hermeneutical posture, as well as its metaphorical focus because of the age of science and our current understanding of modernity and physicality, it has continued to be subverted by a current biblical literalism that is wrapped around the language of mythology. Modern historiographers (including the disciplines of science, sociology, and history) admit that their writings reflect their own cultural bias.[4] Biblical historians should also follow this transparency, openness, and scholarly integrity.

It was the acceptance of the literalization of the kerygma by later formative Christianity that originally provided a historical Jesus in the Gospel tradition. Hence, this reformulated tradition had replaced the original symbolic hermeneutic and its mystic understanding of the earlier christological fellowships with a new

---

literary tradition to give them 'understanding' and 'purpose' to their religious faith, as they engage the biblical story (*mythos*). This is an example of the reality of religious symbolism and metaphorical usage that is used to maintain theological dogma by literalist believers.

4. Michael Shermer, *Science Friction: Where the Known Meets the Unknown* (New York: Times Books, 2005), 114 where he cites Greg Dening's approach and artistic views from his 1992 narrative history, *Mr. Bligh's Bad Language* that "at bottom history is nothing more than an echo of the historian's times, an 'illusion,' he calls it, of a past that can only ever be a reflection of our present."

historical perspective based on a non-symbolic interpretation.[5] Thus, a new theological hermeneutic by formative Christianity has restructured the mythological basis of the narrative Gospel, beginning with Mark. It has discarded the symbolic meaning that had been a socio-religious dynamic for the christological communities' self-identity and mystical union, as life in and with the heavenly Christ. The mystic, historic, and religious dynamic had fallen victim to the historical perspective in formative Christianity's attempt to understand the essence of divinity as part of human existence.

The Gospels, which had become accepted as historical biographic presentations, were a rejection of the epistemological structure of myth (a position maintained by most modern Christian scholars who do not want to admit that mythology is a part of their Christian faith). This historical posture of interpretation became the non-metaphorical basis for a non-Jewish literalist religiosity by later formative Christianity. This was an attempt that unfolded over several generations to validate and authenticate the Church's religious life and its authoritative structure by the power of Rome. It turned the communal persona, the designated name, *Yeshua*, Jesus, into a historicized Jesus by a later conservative generation within formative Christianity. We understand that all written history is subject to revisionism including the history of Christianity's origin. By the second century the literary Gospels had provided the impetus for historical revision. They were turned from allegory into history and by a literalist hermeneutic brought a purely literary personality (Jesus) into the arena of actual history; myth became historical reality and was embraced as a dynamic of the formative church's faith.

This process occurred because of a variety of theological issues, apocalyptic categories, and eschatological considerations within formative Palestinian Christianity on the one hand and Jewish Gnosticism and Hellenistic religious categories within the di-

---

5. The ancient intellectuals' approach was that the revered myths should be symbolically interpreted as allegories by ignoring the literal sense in order to reconcile the myths with their sophisticated values while at the same time concealing the essential truth from the masses. Even in the mystery religions, disclosure of the cult's inner secrets carried a threat of grave bodily harm (cf., Mark 1:44).

aspora on the other.[6] And as usual, this polarized, historically, into the divergent socio-religious and theological tensions that eventually brought about a theological and religious dogmatization by the fourth century Imperial councils, which later became the only acceptable historicized biblical tradition. Theologians have noted that

> In the process, traditional orthodoxy emerged -- a distinctive historical phenomenon, characterized by the fatal tendency to attach an absolute value to dogmatic formulas, to consider faith and assent to creed as virtually one and the same thing, to harp upon the language of confession or catechism without at each point getting back behind the form of sound words to truth as truth is in Jesus.[7]

The early Jewish cult's hope had been strengthened christologically by a symbolic understanding of resurrection perceived as Yahweh's gathering; God's calling of his people to be unified in and by his Spirit. 'The elect,' who were followers of God's 'way' within his established community, were being saved by the heav-

---

6. Much literature of the times employed theological categories in eschatological and apocalyptic themes in which these themes were applied to their own communal existence. See Leonard L. Thompson, *The Book of Revelation: Apocalypse and Empire* (New York: Oxford University Press, 1990), 63. Much of Jewish wisdom literature depicts the role of Wisdom as delivering the righteous Jew from the evil that is present in the evil world. For example: John M. G. Barclay, *Jews in the Mediterranean Diaspora: From Alexander to Trajan (323 BCE – 117 CE)* (Edinburgh: T & T Clark, 1996), 191 where he notes that "the *Wisdom of Solomon* fosters a cultural antagonism in which Jews under stress are encouraged to trust that God will vindicate their righteousness and confound their enemies."

7. See H. R. Mackintosh, *Types of Modern Theology* (London; Nesbet & Co., Ltd., 1937), 8-9. Most if not all that the Gospel narratives disclose was part and parcel to the Hellenistic world's conceptualization of moral sensitivity. Nevertheless, James H. Charlesworth admits in his *Jesus' Jewishness: Exploring the Place of Jesus in Early Judaism* (New York: Crossroad Pub., Co., 1991), 171 that "from early Jewish writings, we could easily construct a whole gospel without using a single word that originated with [a so-called historical] Jesus," Bracket is mine.

enly Christ (all of which are also familiar gnostic, religious ideas). They saw themselves as the eschatological community who had survived the tumultuous war-torn years of Rome's destructive military campaigns (from 66 to 73 CE). It was their mystic faith and endurance that enabled them to survive until 'the end,' so that they saw themselves as participants in God's Kingdom (an anointed life and united, mystically, in the eternal sphere with their heavenly Father).

This was one of Mark's midrashic purposes in his Gospel. He wrote his narrative in order to reflect the Jewish communal experiences of the Christ cult as depicted in terms of their own ancient biblical tradition.[8] They were actively engaged in working out their spiritual redemption as the true and spiritual Israel, the primitive church with its revised and newly reformulated monotheistic faith-understanding. As diaspora Jews, they perceived themselves, collectively, as God's faithful end-time servant (son of God?) who would carry out the ancient Mosaic traditions of their forefathers in order to bring 'the knowledge of the LORD' to the entire world, which, for them, had always included the Gentiles. Paul was their principle missionary apostle (prophet?) of this end-time scenario. But, this meant a radical departure from observing (ceremoniously) their current Mosaic traditions in order to make the 'renewed faith of spiritual Israel' acceptable to the Hellenistic world.

As a representative of the communities and a proclaimer of the christological gospel, Paul accomplished this project masterfully. He spoke of the resurrection as a matter of faith. So that "The resurrection is not only the product of faith, it is in Paul's mind, as the Jesus Seminar has rightly perceived, envisioned simply as a 'spiritual awakening,' not a bodily emergence from the grave, something that came later to formative Christians' con-

---

8. Reddish, *Apocalyptic Literature*, 291-2. In reference to a 3rd Century text that parallels Paul's 2 Corinthians 12:2-4 passage about being caught up into the third heavens (Paradise?), a 'land of Promise,' as the place to be inhabited by the righteous during Christ's millennial reign is an elaborate hermeneutic of spiritual interaction on a mystical level, a parody of the new life in Christ by the early Jewish fellowship.

sciousness only with the appearance of the Gospels."[9] When interpreting the corpus of the expanded covenantal literature, a primary
focus must rest on the ethical themes, its metaphorical religious
language, and the total scope of Hellenistic, moral values within
that body of literary materials.

The expanded covenantal literature had also become a part
of the systemic Church tradition, regardless of the internal textual
changes, emendations, interpolations, and editorializing (its redaction) by later orthodox Christianity.[10] The life of the Spirit, the
way of God's anointing, the resurrected life as God's power to establish the community of faith, were all seen between the tension
of this life (the contemporary life) and living out its moral responsibilities as a newly resurrected creation, the mystical body of
Christ. Dying and going to a heaven to receive God's blessings did
not constitute any religious or christological significance for the
earliest Jewish groups who were certainly not literalists in their
theological posture. The religious perspective, maintained by the
early followers of Paul and the community from which he
emerged, was an indication that the promised kingdom, as a meta-

9. Earl Doherty, "A Review of the Jesus Puzzle: Did Christianity
begin with a mythical Christ?" *The Jesus Puzzle: Was There No Historical Jesus?* 8. http.//www.Jesuspuzzle.humanists.net/rfJHbkrv. htm (accessed January 10, 2003). Barclay, *Jews in the Diaspora,* 8, suggests that
"Diaspora Jews defined their identity in many different ways, some national and political, some ethical, philosophical or even mystical." At the
historical level, especially for Mark's Gospel, the narrative factors represent a hermeneutical view of the larger christological movement of the
first century even though it also reflects the communal experience of his
own faith gathering. See Ben Witherington III, *The Gospel of Mark: A
Socio-Rhetorical Commentary* (Grand Rapids, Mich.: Wm. B. Eerdmans
Pub., 2001), 1-62.

10. Brandon, *Jesus and the Zealots*, 187ff. Most if not all the
Gospel narrative events are fiction and most of them have been constructed from passages in the Jewish scriptures. Most critical scholars
today recognize this fact and would agree (depending on their theological
and institutional connections) that there is nothing left to be 'history remembered' to use Crossan's terms. Even the words of Jesus (even if not
in red print), as the Heavenly Son, are derived, directly and word for
word at times, from the sacred scriptures of Judaism.

phorical understanding, was actualized in this (resurrected) life on earth; even though it was perceived on a mystical, communal level. Resurrection was a viable historic concept that was perceived by the fellowships as their ingathering by YHWH, as his end-time community.

It was a mystical experience of being taken out of the kingdom of darkness, the rule of Satanic powers and the evil influences from which they were constantly being defeated, and were 'transported' (via baptism) into the light of God's kingdom (the christological fellowship). These new christological gatherings became, through a mystical union with God, his anointed body, encapsulating his spiritual presence (*parousia*) in flesh (their earthly humanity). This was occurring in order to bring about the transmutation (God's reconciliation) of this world. This mythic scenario was accomplished with metaphors without ascribing to them any physicality (as later biblical literalists have done). "On the one hand, a metaphor isn't literally true, and yet on the other hand a well turned metaphor seems to strike like lightening, revealing the truth more deeply or directly than a drab, literal statement."[11] It was Paul's gnostic tendencies that employed Platonic categories that merged heaven and earth into a unified moral and theological arena of God's activities.

The one dimension (physical, the earthly) was transformed into a new creative dimension (spiritual, metaphorical, heavenly) based on the symbolism of a morally systemic and mythological world-view. Even in Ephesians, it "supports the conclusion that the Christians of Paul's time had experienced Jesus exclusively as a heavenly figure, appearing to them in visions."[12] And for Paul, the

---

11. V. S. Ramachandran, *The Tell -- Tale Brain: A neuroscientist's Quest for What Makes Us Human* (New York: Norton & Co., 2011), 106.

12. Ellegård, *Jesus,* 106. Thus, Essene and gnostic patterns of social and political as well as apocalyptic sensibilities could influence the early christological movement. Kurt Rudolph, *GNOSIS: The Nature and History of Gnosticism,* Trans. and Ed. Robert M. Wilson (New York: HarperSanFrancisco, 1984), 54 notes that the gnostic tradition frequently draws its materials from the most varied existing traditions, attaches itself to it, and at the same time sets it in a new frame by which this mate-

resurrection concept would still be, as a metaphor, acceptable theologically, morally, and philosophically by the Greco-Roman world.

For Crossan, this is a form of social radicalism as "the attempt to live out of an alternative reality."[13] Even the word of God as personified Wisdom, as Spirit, or as the cosmic *Logos*, all communicated in and through various aspects of the early kerygma, did not convey the meaning of a historical report, but rather, it was a *revelatory* call to a mystic experience in which past mythic events in their biblical tradition become contemporized.[14] Thus, Robinson states that, "... the proclamation of the kerygma itself: The act of proclaiming Jesus' death and resurrection [within a mystic union with the divine presence] becomes God's act calling upon me to accept my death and receive resurrected life."[15] This was precisely the early Jewish communities' metaphorical and christological understanding. It is also the gnostic and pagan understanding that served many of the mystery religion's initiates' participation in their communal rituals in the Hellenistic world.

These concepts were part and parcel to a cultural matrix available to most peoples around the Mediterranean world at the

---

rial takes on a new character and a completely new significance. Gnosis ... is a product of Hellenistic syncretism."

13. Crossan, *The Birth of Christianity*, 269 where he states that social radicalism "is practical, not just theoretical; physical, not just mental; material, not just intellectual. It is of the body and not just of the mind. It touches society not just as an idea but as an action."

14. Smith, *Ecce Deus*, where he has restated the moral basis from other sources which were utilized by the cult's propaganda in "The Didactic Element," 125-131. This is a very modern point of view with regard to the concept of history. Some conceive history as only the present moment of actual historic experience. The past and future are only words that describe contemporary mentational linguistics of the present experience of existence.

15. J. A. T. Robinson, *A New Quest of the Historical Jesus: Studies in Biblical Theology*, No. 25 (London: SCM Press Ltd., 1966), 42. The kerygmatic effects (i.e., its central contents, the death and resurrection) can be seen illustrated in the basic method of the 'new quest' where it seeks a new level of theological meaning and existential significance to the faith understanding of the primitive community's faith.

time. The previous statement, by Robinson, depicts precisely the theologized format of the christological gathering's spiritual, symbolic, and mystic understanding that gave rise to those historic socio-religious meanings. Nevertheless, they later became embodied (attempting to reject the earlier mythological themes of symbolic perception) into the later expanded literary corpora with the fabrication of the 'Gospels' as a type of religious 'history' that depicted mythothematic events in the life of a so-called historical Jesus. As Goodenough has stated, "Jews in the diaspora were less concerned with theological orthodoxy than with the social requirement that members of the community be 'propagating Jews' (Goodenough 2.290), raising the next generation as practicing Jews who in turn would do the same for their offspring."[16]

At first, the primitive Jewish christological community's life in the Christ (i.e., the mystical embodiment of the anointed presence (*parousia*) and power of the Spirit of truth, the *Logos*, the heavenly Son) held firm to the new mystic religiosity, as an existential experience, which maintained a symbolic meaning. Their "whole present being" was at stake in which they were "... personally wrestling as for life or death"[17] with the mythological perception of "this present evil age." This occurred historically at a time when the oppressive powers, both foreign and domestic, radically disrupted the socio-economic and religious life of the Jews and brought down the final curtain through confrontation with Rome's military and political conflicts (66-73 C.E.).

Thus, a deliberate effort was made (primarily because of the militant times) to incorporate apocalyptic thought into their eschatological experience as a new hermeneutic for their theological posture. This only added a new aspect of mythology to the total scope of divine, revelatory redemption and the further mystical basis for their new religiosity. Thus, the events which unfold in Mark's Gospel narrative must be understood as the unfolding of the communal experiences of the early believers (the christological community) that lived 'life' in fellowship with the anointing of

---

16. As quoted by Barclay, in *Jews in the Diaspora,* 413 from E. R. Goodenough, *Jewish Symbols in the Graeco-Roman Period,* 13 vols. (New York: Pantheon Press, 1953-68).

17. Mackintosh, *Modern Theology*, 220.

God in their gathering. They were truly God's Son, resurrected and united with a divine, spiritual (communal) life, living in the new age of Christ's Kingdom. Their communal 'earthy' experience, in Platonic fashion, reflected the 'heavenly realities' of the Christ event. To speak of one sphere was to speak with the understanding of the other sphere. Both spheres were inseparable. This provided spiritual meanings in the metaphorical structure of their theology that was full of symbolic, religious categories, and mythological nuances.[18]

The Christian biblical tradition, which had incorporated the earlier Jewish tradition of primitive christological thought, is representative of a form of Christianity that developed after the ruin of the Jewish nation, 66-73 CE, and the demise of the Jewish religious and political assembly at Jerusalem, the Temple. With the process of historization in the Gospel narratives in mind, we should consider these historical and important events and the changes that had occurred in the biblical tradition as a result of that history. Brandon remarks, concerning the biblical tradition of Paul's proclamation, that "... we may notice here the remarkable absence of reference to Jesus as a historical person that is manifest in every letter."[19] He also admits his surprise that Paul, who dealt with detailed Jewish issues that arose in the several christological

---

18. Paul was a philosophical apostle and missionary of the christological movement. He adopted or at least was influenced by Platonic categories of knowledge. This can also be seen in Philo, whose exegetical purposes adapted the Alexandrian Platonism of his day, which was influenced by Stoicism and Pythagoreanism. He utilized a methodology that was "simply the hermeneutical correlate of his Platonic dualism." Barclay, *Jews in the Diaspora*, 166.

19. Brandon, *Jesus and the Zealots*, 150. Cf., Bowman, *Prophetic Realism* (1955) and Kasemann, *Jesus Means Freedom* (1969). Cultural themes could be easily adopted and fitted into the developing narrative of the Gospels without any real connection to an actual person in history. Witherington III, *Mark,* 70, mentions that "the birthday of the emperor was celebrated throughout the empire and was the occasion of festivals called *evangels.*" An imaginative and creative mind among the christological community could easily have latched onto this theme in order to present the gospel narrative within a historical structure as a literary work having a wider social connection.

communities, failed to mention the events of Jesus' life, and he neglected also to mention Jesus' teachings, which appear later in the Gospel tradition.[20] There is no difficulty of a socio-religious misunderstanding here, especially when the Jewish gatherings' christological theology, concerning the mystical nature of the Christ event, has been considered in its non-historicized original symbolic formulation.

It would seem that the kerygmatic terms used in the narrative Gospel accounts were originally used to facilitate the continuance of the former mystic understanding of the christological communities. Then, after the historical pressures (to live through the oppressive political and economic tensions of the Roman world) were apocalyptically evaluated as the various literary sources suggest, the communal propaganda (the gospel of the Kingdom) became more fully historicized by the Gospel evangelists. Most biblical historians would agree that the early Christian movement's development became an effort of socio-political unification.

---

20. Archibald M. Hunter in his, *The Gospel According to St. Paul*, rev. ed. of "Interpreting Paul's Gospel" (Philadelphia: The Westminster Press, 1966), 80-82, presents a well-defined pattern of the earliest kerygma that has been reconstructed by modern scholarship. This explanation for the difference in form (i.e., internal theological structure) between the apostles' kerygma and Jesus' proclamation is the events of Easter and Pentecost. In Frederick C. Grant, *The Earliest Gospel* (Nashville: Abingdon Press, 1943), this distinction reached its full height for some 19th Century liberals who, like Adolf Harnack, felt that we should worship God 'with' Jesus (i.e., in a similar manner or fashion) rather than 'through' Jesus as an object of our faith. The religion of a human Jesus and its antithesis exhibit this dilemma of the early church's faith. For further significance and the symbolism of this theme, see Mark 1:17 and Matthew 4:19 and 13:47. Two important historical studies that relate this difference in the kerygmatic structure are Johannes Weiss, *The History of Primitive Christianity* (New York: Wilson-Frickson, 1937), I, 14-31; and Maurice Goguel, *The Birth of Christianity*, trans. H. C. Snape (New York: The Macmillan Co., 1953), 29-86. Volume number I is now out of print. Although old, it still remains as one of the many standard works for New Testament scholarship because many of his judgments still present live options.

Ellegård and others agree that, "The development of Christianity was not from unity to diversity, but on the contrary, from diversity which existed all along within the Essene movement, and naturally also between the individual apostles, to the very deliberate attempts to establish a Christian orthodoxy towards the end of the second century CE."[21] Given the nature of the times and the religious philosophies, which abounded, I seriously doubt that the Gospel of Mark was ever intended to represent history. It was symbolic and relied on its internal metaphors in the story (*mythos*) to inspire the community of faithful believers to understand their socio-religious existence having lived through the devastation of the Jewish-Roman war.[22]

Grant, grappling with the historical changes in the theology of the Gospel narratives, states that there was no such distinction drawn by the apostolic preaching "... between the gospel of Jesus and the gospel about Jesus. That is a modern distinction!"[23] This

---

21. Ellegård, *Jesus,* 45. Ellegård's "hypothesis is that earliest Christian communities may have grown out of Essene ones, they were of course Jewish" to which some Gentiles were also connected, among whom the Apostle Paul ministered.

22. Doherty sees the Gospel of Mark as a symbolic representation of the gospel which two different expressions of time were promulgating: the gospel about the coming Kingdom of God [that expressed the gatherings' diaspora allegiance to their biblical tradition], and the gospel about the redeeming savior-god, Christ Jesus [expressed by Hellenistic Jews who bought into Greek mythothemes] preached by the apostle Paul. Mark combined the two for the first time in a creative way, but no one for perhaps a couple of decades would have regarded it as history." Brackets are mine. Doherty, "A Review of the Jesus Puzzle" 31. Rudolph, *GNOSIS,* 25 also points out that "the gnostics had produced the first Christian theological literature of all. ... This holds not only for theological works ... but also for poetry and the literature of simple piety, as shown by the remains of hymns and the numerous apocryphal stories about Jesus and the apostles."

23. Grant, *The Earliest Gospel,* 81. This distinction reached its full height for some 19th Century liberals like Adolf Harnack who felt that we should worship God 'with' Jesus (i.e., in a similar manner or fashion) rather than 'through' Jesus as an object of our faith. The religion of a human Jesus and its antithesis exhibit this dilemma of the early

modern theological polarity finds similar expression, when you consider the historic narratives with their original mythic understanding by the symbolic method of interpretation that fully accounts for metaphorical religious language. This distinction came about because of its later historical formulation within the Gospels by the writers within formative Christianity in the second century. The gospel of the kingdom had been proclaimed as a mystical relationship originally; but then, it came to be understood by the apocalyptic significance of Jesus, as a historical consideration.

God had established the kingdom with the coming of the Spirit (retaining the original mystic sense of an anointing), the coming of his Son, the anointed one and faithful prophet like unto Moses,[24] the Son of Man (a blending of the historical process with newly formed literalist history from the gospel tradition).[25] The evangelists' kerygmatic intention was not to declare historical accuracy, but was to transmit the gospel, the message of salvation, in the historical figure of Jesus as 'the Son of Man,' the apocalyptic intermediary, a divine entity. Religiously, philosophically, and theologically he was perceived within these early communities as the incarnate *Logos* of John's Gospel.

The eschatological Jewish gatherings living in the diaspora attempted to identify their christological fellowship (regardless of geographic locations) as a socio-religious reality. It was this apocalyptic aspect of their existence, based on the historical and

---

church's faith. For further significance and the symbolism of this theme, see Mark 1:17 and Matthew 4:19 and 13:47.

24. Thompson, *Myth*, 57 where he contrasts Jesus on the holy mountain with three disciples (Mt. 17:1) with Moses also on the holy mountain with three men (Ex. 24:1) and righty states "this close, creative association of events in Jesus' stories with similar events in the stories of Elijah and Moses is not merely implicit. The association is conscious, explicit and significant." This scriptural connectivity is a good example of hermeneutical midrashim.

25. From the preaching of Paul and the early christological propaganda, Charlesworth, *Jesus' Jewishness*, 225 states that "the Church maintained that Jesus' resurrection was the beginning of the apocalyptic end time." The symbolic nature of the resurrection concept was overshadowed by the growing historization process of the second and third century CE.

cultural forces, which allowed a symbolic and mythic understanding to transform their mystical religiosity into a persona cult, along the typical lines of the Hellenistic forms of religiosity. This newly formed historical basis was acted upon by the christological communities, with momentous force, as a creative historic development in primitive Christian thought. Again, such a theological summation does not purport to validate itself. Any rational defense in this historical appraisal only suggests a more or less probable hypothesis.

It does dramatically set the tone for understanding the direction of the historical and material forces as well as the cultural influences that brought about changes in these early communities. The theological basis in the socio-religious tradition sheds some light on the religiosity of the times that helped to determine the historic origin of the Jesus myth. The process of midrashim was well established in the socio-dynamic period of the Second Temple by the christological communities. It developed along with the kerygma within the gospel corpora prior to and along with the historization of the theological concepts that became accepted by formative Christianity.[26]

The spiritual and christological expressions of the Jewish gatherings were as diverse as their geographic and cultural influences. This diversity lent itself to the particular local style and

---

26. Even though the conceptual term 'resurrection' appears rarely in the Jewish Scriptures, we must allow its evolution to add significant religious expression by later generations' cultural adaptation to refocus sometimes in drastic form. Note that in Jewish Scriptures, that Elijah, Enoch, Moses and Melchizedek were translated (also, cf., Hercules) and in the earliest version of Mark and in Paul's letters, Jesus was transformed (raised up, translated; note: 1 John 3:14 transported, "we have passed out of death," *metabebēkamen ek tou thanatou*) and from a purely religious and cultural infusion, Matthew and Luke present it as a physical resurrection, which would not be very compatible with the Greco-Roman's rejection of a bodily resurrection. Even though in Ezekiel and in the pseudepigraphic literature (1 Enoch, Jubilees, 2 and 4 Maccabees) mention is made of a general resurrection, it does not refer to an individual resurrection. Judaism had and christological early believers had been influenced by Zoroastrianism so that one can say that the idea of physical resurrection most probably was derived from Zoroastrianism.

107

forms of interpretation for the religious experience of faith. This new christological faith-understanding of the Jesus myth and its symbolism was a distinctive aspect of religious existence within the early Jewish gatherings. The overall distinctive spiritual unity, running through all of this is the kerygmatic theology concerning the mystic presence (*parousia*) of the divine *Logos*, *Yeshua*, Jesus. This was the self-identity of the cultic gathering as the people of Yahweh.

The later historicized biblical tradition in its entirety still reflects this singular mythological fact -- Jesus the Christ is the divine presence of the cult's existence. God gave (sent, revealed) his Spirit, his Son, which was their 'anointing' by Yahweh so that they perceived themselves as the divine body of God's heavenly Son (on earth as it is in heaven). Thus, the later testimony, within the formative church that dealt with the comparative essence of the Christ as God's Son, is indicative of the merging together of the historical development of the christological communities' mystic theology[27] with the historic religious and theological reformulations, as the new Israel of God in the end times without reference to an actual, historical Jesus. This mystical understanding was accomplished while they still grasped the eschatological and apocalyptic significance of their religious and mystical experiences in the 'last day.'

The dynamic, christological myth and religiosity of the Jewish fellowship relative to the eschatological significance of the last day, which had been so significant in apocalyptic thought, was later lost to the process of literalism as a perspective of future expectation in the historicized Gospels. Thus, a very distinctive element of futurity has crept into the biblical traditions' theology.

---

27. John 11:24, 20:30; I Tim. 3:16. Also, note: Harry Emerson Fosdick, *A Guide to Understanding the Gospel* (New York: Harper & Brothers Pub., Harper Torchlight Books 1938). Also, cf. C. F. D. Moule, *The Phenomenon of the New Testament, Studies in Biblical Theology*, Second Series, I, (Naperville. Ill.: Alec R. Allenson, 1967), 45-46. Note his discussion on the Jesus of history [the Lord of faith argument] where he recognizes the apostolic kerygma and presents a positive justification for the apostolic confessions. See Acts 6:12; 7:55; 8:29; 9:31; 10:19, and 11:12, 28.

Even though some apocalyptic imagery was maintained, this marked the demise of any symbolic interpretation by later Christianity. The Jesus myth of the Jewish christological communities had been its spiritual vitality to express that former religiosity in terms of earthly mystic existence, service, and spiritual union with their heavenly Father. And this was eschatologically accomplished while the oppressive world around them included the heavenly and earthly domain of Satan, was perceived as conquered by the Christ[28] (the body of believers who overcame the world by faith). They also perceived the fellowships' mystic union, as being in the grasp of YHWH's power and redemptive Spirit (*Logos*) during the last days.

The traditional mythic idea of the 'last days' was an eschatological reminder of that apocalyptic hope that the primitive communities held in common. It was at first mystical and symbolic that provided a metaphorical understanding. For Philo and Paul, the essential aspect of understanding apocalyptic concerns was embedded foremost in the human condition as it related to moral integrity.[29] But, it had become embedded in the later tradition's process of historization and then became understood as a literal and futuristic perception by formative Christianity. This meant that now the final mythological act of YHWH's redemption in the world would be brought to its completion by their resurrection at the return (the second coming?) of the Lord from Glory.[30] This

---

28. Stark, *Rise of Christianity,* offers a sociological conclusion to the extent of their involvement as an "intense community ... who invited their friends, relatives, and neighbors to share the 'good news,'" 208, which is his explanation for the growth and success of the early church within the Hellenistic world. Growth was sporadic, diverse, and uneven. Ellegård, *Jesus,* 196 states that "It is essential to keep in mind that the Christians ... were not, and had never been, a homogeneous group."

29. Barclay, *Jews in the Diaspora,* 170 notes that "for Philo there is only one sort of truth worth discovering [as a lover of wisdom and virtue, it is philosophy] and that is truth about ourselves." Bracket is mine. Cf. I Cor. 1:18-25.

30. For additional discussion on this subject see George Arthur Buttrick, and others, ed., *The Interpreter's Dictionary of the Bible*, Vol. K-Q (New York: Abingdon Press, 1962), 187ff. Also for an assessment

hope, now part of the church's historicity, was 'in him' the literal historical Jesus of the end-time community, whom to know was 'life eternal' having been baptized into the life of the institutionalized Roman Catholic Church.

As an example of traditional Christian scholarship, Dodd has rightly stated the spiritual values of a modern, literalist Christian perspective that were directed toward a historical movement:

> Every crisis is a thing by itself, unique and non-recurrent. Consequently, we need not try to reduce all events, great and small, to the same scale, as elements in a uniform process, governed by general laws, and driving its significance from the remote goal to which it tends. Events in their particularity have value, and value in different degrees. Thus, we are at liberty to recognize in one particular series of events a crisis of supreme significance, and to interpret other events and situations with reference to it. Christian thought finds this supreme crisis in the ministry and death of Jesus Christ with the immediate sequel [resurrection, ascension, exaltation, and events of the Spirit]. Its supreme significance lies in the fact that here history became the field within which God confronted men in a decisive way, and placed before them a moral challenge that could not be evaded... Thus, history is molded by the spirit.[31]

The ideas of mysticism, symbolism, and mythology, out of which Christianity historically emerged, have all vaporized from modern theology when evaluated by a literalist kind of hermeneutic. Let us seek a historical perspective that, never-the-less, acknowledges these ancient categories of religiosity (*mythos*) and attempt to evaluate the how and why there was no historical Jesus, as the extraordinary founding personality of the Christian faith. This means that the mythothematic categories of the ascension and exaltation, like the symbolic event of the resurrection, must be understood in their religious significance, interpretively, as a historic religious experience (i.e., as an act of YHWH, a revelation, the

---

on Luke 23:34; see William Barclay, *The First Three Gospels* (Philadelphia: The Westminster Press, 1966), 245-295.

31. Dodd, *Parable of the Kingdom*, 167-8. Brackets are mine. Also cf., C. H. Dodd, *The Authority of the Bible*, rev. ed. (New York: Harper & Row, Pub., Harper Torchbooks, 1960), 261-264.

spiritual discernment by the believer). It is noted that none of the earliest first century authors presents a time-frame reference for when the resurrection occurred.

For Paul, this is precisely what functions as 'the grace of God,' the posture of interpretive acceptance, which was based on readings of the Mosaic scriptural tradition. In this mythical manner, the early Jewish community also found itself proclaiming, through the symbolic and christological content of the kerygma, the power of Yahweh's Spirit to become victorious (resurrected?) in the believer's life. The symbolic hermeneutic, foundational to the proper consideration of the origin of Christianity, explains quite naturally the unparalleled enthusiasm, by Paul and the other mystics who preached this faith-understanding, yet without any consideration for a real, historical Jesus.[32] Their divine obligation and affection was for the Christ as a *revelatory* and mystical experience in their religious lives.

The deity's power and presence, within the Jewish community, became their christological salvation through a moral commitment of faith. And, along similar lines of religiosity, with an enthusiasm by Hellenistic paganism,[33] they understood the mythological origin of their own eschatological existence within the parameters of actual history. Metaphorical language was all they needed to validate and authenticate their mystic and religious experiences. Literalism (as we perceive it in the modern world) was of no concern and was of no religious necessity within a

---

32. Scholars for centuries have noticed many of the similarities between Paul and the central myth of Gnosticism. Rudolph, *GNOSIS*, offers a brief sketch of the dualistic world view akin to middle Platonic categories of which Paul seemed to be at home with his gospel. Rudolph suggests the following connections to the gnostic central myth: the presence in man of a divine spark, which fallen from the heavenly realm to the earth below and the necessity to be re-awakened by the divine entity (often called *Sophia* or *Ennoia*) to recover the divine spark (often designated as *pneuma*, "spirit), 57.

33. See V. Taylor's *The Formation of the Gospel Tradition* where he discusses these themes. Cf., Matthew 19:29; Mark 10:30, and Luke 10:25. Cf., John 3:16, 6:47, and 12:50 with Galatians 6:8; I Timothy 1:16, and 1 John 5:20.

world of ancient mythological existence. The real question that concerned the religiously minded person was not: is it factually true? But, does it have spiritual meaning for my relationship with the divine presence in my life? Theirs was not a spiritual imagination that needed a literal, wonderful human personality in order to contribute spiritual meaning to their eschatological religiosity. The early christological faith and devotion did not create the historical objectification of a divine persona.[34] That was a later process of formative Christianity's historization by later generations who accepted the Gospel narrative stories as literary history.

In those Gospel accounts, Jesus was presented as the superhuman God-man of biblical Christianity and not as the mystical *Christos* event preached by Paul, not as the Spirit of the Lord who, by YHWH's holy presence, anointed the christological gatherings of the last days with a divine revelatory experience, which was in reality the actual historical experience of the community. The community's christological mysticism was perceived as God's union with his faithful servant, the son of man. This was understood symbolically in the original Jesus myth[35] as the Jewish christological fellowship. These are the elements out of which mythology and religiosity have always been made. Thus, theology has always been and continues to be a basically speculative and creative activity.

Hence, the words of Charles Darwin from his *Descent of Man,* at this juncture, are most appropriate: "False facts are highly injurious to the progress of science [and humanity], for they often endure long; but false views, if supported by some evidence, do little harm, for everyone takes a salutary pleasure in proving their falseness; and when this is done, one path towards errors is closed and the road to truth is often at the same time opened."[36] With this in mind, our venture into a reliable historical enquiry of the origins of the Christian faith is given its speculative direction and leads to critically fine-tuned assessments. Thus, we may conclude at this

---

34. David E. Forrest, *The Christ of History and of Experience* (Edinburgh: T. & T. Clark, 1897).

35. Albert Schweitzer, *The Mysticism of Paul the Apostle* (New York: Seabury Press, 1968), 68 ff.

36. As quoted by Ramachandran, *Brain,* 244. Bracket is mine.

juncture that the later canonical biblical tradition, including the Gospels and Acts,[37] do not provide an accurate, historical picture of the historic origin of the Jewish christological communities nor the origins of Christianity.

The historical Jesus and the biblical Christ of the proclamation are essentially one and the same, the Spirit as a persona of the early Jewish fellowships. Later generations of biblical literalists maintained that the essential aspect of divinity revealed in the person of Jesus was a historical actuality. The theological validity, of which the historicity of Jesus was authenticated, was only to be found in the literary, fabricated narrative of the Gospels. The expanded covenantal texts continued to enable orthodox Christianity, as did the early kerygma, to proclaim the salvific and mythological, redemptive act of Yahweh. This is indicative of the purpose for the writing of the Gospels by the early evangelists. It is "... their purpose to awaken faith in Jesus through a clear proclamation of his saving activity [i.e., his life, death, and resurrection]."[38] It is the nature of the kerygmatic purpose that is found in the entire expanded covenantal literary corpora as myth.

It is not really necessary to propose a real historical Jesus to validate the literary message, since the intent of the kerygmatic mythology remains intact. The results are the same without having

---

37. The speeches in Acts are considered by critical biblical scholars as a type of religious history not actual history. Unfortunately, even Eusebius' so-called history of the early Church's development is well recognized as an editorialized piece of literature and is generally untrustworthy. See Marion L. Soards, *The Speeches in Acts: Their Content, Context, and Concerns* (Louisville, K.Y.: John Knox Press, 1994).

38. Martin Kahler, *Historical Jesus-Biblical Christ*, 127. It is still difficult to maintain that Paul, given his religious conceptualizations, was Christian in any 'orthodox' way of understanding. The Dalton's remarks are generally accepted among biblical scholars who maintain an interpretation based on mysticism. "Paul's religion was a kaleidoscope, reflecting many syncretic elements of the Greco-Roman world; it was not an identical copy of any particular pagan religious phenomenon." Paul fused ideas from the "mystery cult with Gnosticism and Stoic Cynicism, and added a Jewish veneer." Excerpts from Laurence E. and Shirley S. Dalton, *Jesus: Pagan Christ or Jewish Messiah?* (March 14, 2004) at http//www.jesusquest.com/ 41, (accessed May 20, 2005).

to deny the symbolic basis and its mystic theological point of view. Ever since the post-exilic period, a radical shift over time developed in Jewish perceptions of historical events (Apocalypticism) as to how they related to God's actions on behalf of his people, Israel.[39]

Significantly, Jewish apocalyptic themes permeate the narrative structure of the canonical Gospels. Even so, this does not in any way validate the historicity of Jesus. It only validates the historical and literary modality for religious valuation. The reality of the spiritual life, for all practical purposes as the early believers realized, is the acceptance into the communities' spiritual life (*logos*) as "the anointing" (*charisma*) by YHWH's Spirit. Even without a real historical Jesus, the religious and theological basis for the Christian religion, given the philosophical, religious, and mythological categories within the Hellenistic world, still accounts for the historical factors that were used to formulate the later Christian Gospels.

The historicized scenario has always been problematic for the serious student of the biblical tradition. If these religious possibilities were accepted as historical reality, that would strain the imagination of the modern, rational and scientific mind. Yet, these religious concepts, metaphorically based, become understandable, especially when they are understood symbolically. As the biologist Peter Medawar has indicated, "All good science [historical and theological insight] emerges from an imaginative conception of what *might* be true."[40] These kind of speculative insights (educated

---

39. Charlesworth, *Jesus' Jewishness,* 74 asserts that "the apocalyptic fervor in Early Judaism was pervasive; it tore apart the nation and eventually contributed to the two massive revolts against Rome."

40. Ramachandran, *Brain,* xvii also adds insight to this *speculative* process. He unashamedly says, that "Every virgin area of scientific [and historical] inquiry must first be explored in this way. It is a fundamental element of the scientific process [and historical and theological inquiry] that when data are scarce or sketchy and existing theories are anemic, scientists [and biblical theologians] must brainstorm. We need to roll out our best hypothesis, hunches, and hair-brained, half-baked intuitions, and then rack our brains for ways to test them [that is formed by

guess-work and intuition) maintain a very meaningful theological base, as religious mythology, when considered by the symbolic interpretation. They also reveal the historical and christological basis of the Jesus myth by which the historic and primitive Jewish cult evolved, and in later years, emerged into the Christian Church under the imperial authority of Rome.

The Hellenistic world was an integrated system of shared intellectual diversity. The religious, social, philosophic and political arenas were not isolated from the emerging theological and cultural systems of religious speculation. Thompson captures this ongoing intellectual configuration of cultural adoption, adaptation, transformation, and transmission with this summation: "Common bonds of technique, rhetoric, function and sentiment imply a relationship that is well beyond the sharing of phrases, metaphors, motifs and themes, or even entire segments of a story or a song. ... They shared and transmitted a common Near Eastern intellectual and cultural world created by Egyptian, Mesopotamian, Syrian, Persian and Greek writers."[41]

The symbolic interpretation used by the Jewish christological gatherings becomes clear, precise, and natural (when myth is understood metaphorically) in that it discloses, the distinctive activity of the revitalized Jewish gatherings' communal experiences as they had been casting out demons (in the literary context). To cast out demons was to bring about the demise of polytheism (a false faith), which to the early diaspora Jews, polytheism was demonic. And, to a large extent, this was Paul's motivation. This was accomplished by their communal presence with the divine anointing as an eschatological fellowship in the Kingdom of God. This original perception provided a theological basis and was viewed mystically as a constant fulfillment of God's purposes for the redemption of humanity through the Kerygma.[42]

---

evidentiality]. You see this all the time in the history of science." Brackets are mine.

41. Thompson, *Myth*, 25. Paul was born into this world and navigated both philosophically and religiously throughout its geo-political space without any difficulty.

42. Cf. Acts 2:32; 3:15; 4:10; 5:30-32; and 13:30f. Within the early-formed faith communities, the kerygma was viewed as the Spirit's

The conversion of humanity was their spiritual goal, a call that would unite humanity to the spiritual worship and presence of their heavenly Father. They were called to bear witness to the knowledge of the LORD to the whole world of humanity,[43] and to bear witness of this new faith-understanding through the proclamation of the gospel. Out of this theological structure, the anointed one (the Christ as the faithful community) was understood as the Spiritual presence of YHWH in the christological fellowship. By their anointing, it was YHWH's spirit that empowered them to carry out the divine mission of universal salvation. In fact, much of the expanded covenantal literature, even though its Orthodox Christology came later, echoes the commonly accepted morality of the contemporary Greek literature, philosophers, sages, and prophets of the period.[44] It is well to remember that "the tendency to evoke oral tradition [in order] to transmit the sayings from [a historical] event to the writing of the gospels is required only by the assumption that the text is about a historical Jesus."[45]

The biblical tradition, as it now stands, represents a theological fabrication (the historicity of Jesus) and continues to form the theological posture for modern Christian religiosity, which is based on that historization by formative Christianity. As a result of such theological tenacity, a real global threat with a lack of real moral, human integrity faces the world of modernity. Religion, historically, as it has usually been, continues to separate and keeps apart our diverse humanity from becoming a world community on this planet. In a real sense and to some degree, modern Christianity, in its diverse forms, is becoming a global religion of sorts.

---

instruction within the fellowship; their anointing that was perceived as the presence of Yahweh as the 'living Torah' in their gatherings.

43. Matt. 10:27; Mark 16:15. Also cf., Joel 2:32.

44. Karl Marx and Friedrich Engels, *On Religion*, Intro. Reinhold Niebuhr (New York: Schocken Books, 1964), 323-326.

45. Thompson, *Myth,* 11. Brackets are mine. A close consideration of the intellectual world that was shared in Hellenistic times is a necessary prerequisite to good biblical and historical research. "Before we write the history behind the text, we must first understand the literary world of which a text is but a single, historical example." Ibid., 8.

It is precisely because of its literal understanding by most of Christian believers that religion has become fuel for world conflict. Is it possible that the opposing 'literalists of fundamentalism,' of the different faiths in our twenty-first century, might bring about wars of mass destruction and even the possibility of global annihilation of our humanity?[46]

---

46. J. Carroll unfolds some prospects for world peace based on his historical evidence which he has gathered with regard to the functionality of the Church in this world. See especially, "Agenda Item 4: The Holiness of Democracy," in *Constantine's Sword*, 588-598.

PART TWO

Transitional Era: *Revelation* 30 BCE to 59 CE
The primitive christological fellowships expand in the Diaspora.

4

"You see; but, you do not observe."
Sherlock Holmes

The problem of our theological understanding of the origin of Christianity is usually found in accounting for the embellishment of apocalyptic language within an eschatological drama of early, so-called Messianism.[1] Yet, this understanding continues not to reflect the historical, socio-religious, and cultural factors evidenced by historical research. The predominance of an early Christian Messianic expectation has more to do with scholars' theological agenda in the handling of early Christian materials than with the evidence provided in historical studies. Any explanation must probe deeper into the inner christological core of the Jewish communities' mystic understanding and beyond to recognize their symbolic interpretation and to focus on that historical point-in-time that a new faith-understanding was born, blossomed, and then later was transformed into its orthodox, creedal posture.

This will determine its grounding in the christological understanding that reflects their '*anointing*' as a people of God,

---

1. Some pertinent works which relate the eschatological significance to Jesus' proclamation of the Kingdom are: Joachim Jeremias, *The Parable of Jesus*, rev. ed., trans. S. H. Hooker, *Scribner Studies in Biblical Interpretation* (New York: Charles Scribner's Sons, Pub., 1963), W. G. Kummel, *Promise and Fulfillment*, trans. Dorothea M. Barton (London: SCM Press, Ltd., 1957), and Oscar Cullmann, *Christ and Time*, trans. Floyd V. Filson (Philadelphia: The Westminster Press, 1950). There are socio-religious implications to Messianism. Also, cf., in Jewish religious history, it was Joshua () who was blessed by Yahweh and allowed to enter the promised land (i.e., Yahweh's house, his earthly Kingdom through which he offered Israel's deliverance, their salvation).

rather than a messianic expectation. As Horsley states,[2] "… it is an over-simplification and a historical misconception to say that the Jews expected a 'national' or 'political' messiah" in contradistinction of the spiritualized concept among the progressive, early christological communities. It is this kind of systemic thought that has been found by critical biblical scholarship when the kerygma in Paul's earliest writings is considered in the light of the symbolism of the resurrection[3] and the metaphorical understanding of the biblical, Mosaic tradition of the earliest Jewish communities. The vast array of Wisdom literature transformed the nature and use of metaphors to develop the Gospel story (*myth*) as seen in Matthew. Scholars have noted that much of the feminine aspects of wisdom personification were absorbed into the literary figure of a historical Jesus.

This also can be seen in I Enoch whose apocalyptic Son of Man persona has been associated also with Wisdom. Deutsch claimed that in Matthew's Gospel, "the redactor perceives that Jesus is who Wisdom is, does what Wisdom does."[4] This process

---

2. Richard A. Horsley with John S. Hanson, *Bandits, Prophets, and Messiahs: Popular Movements in the Time of Jesus* (Harrisburg, Penn.: Trinity Press International, 1999), 90. When considering any of the cultural themes in early Christianity's history by exegetical scholarship, Fiorenza's words should be taken more seriously: "Students of early Christianity … must begin their investigations with the assumption that women actively shaped cultural traditions in general and the early Christian traditions in particular, unless scholars can prove otherwise." Elisabeth Schüssler Fiorenza, *JESUS Miriam's Child, Sophia's Prophet: Critical Issues in Feminist Christology* (New York: Continuum, 1994), 122.

3. The nature of resurrection becomes understood symbolically. The initiates' empowerment was their share of living in Christ's resurrection: as 'their own resurrection.' It was God's activity within the gathering that via his spirit they were being conformed to his image (a new creation) so that the Christ would be formed in them; thus, they became a part of him and he was a part of them, the community of God's 'glory,' the *kavod*.

4. Celia M. Deutsch, *Lady Wisdom, Jesus, and the Sages: Metaphor and Social Context in Matthew's Gospel* (Valley Forge, Penn.: Trinity Press International, 1996), 78, also notes that "in the

was widely used in the Hellenistic world where literary and epigraphical sources were used to deify various virtues.

The historical existence of the Jesus myth was developed on a literary level[5] and was accepted within the christological cult as the understanding (gnosis) of their relationship to God. The anointed presence and authority of YHWH was reflected in the socio-religious development of the cult's eschatological religiosity. This theological process is still detectable within the biblical, Christian tradition even with its various layers of secondary emendations and recognized interpolations. A modern critical scholar, who recognizes this theological process, within the Christian tradition and maintains a textual integrity with his historical and biblical research, is Bart Ehrman. An example he cites is:

> It is important to know that for ancient Jews the term "Son of God" could mean a wide range of things. ... The son of God was someone specially chosen by God to perform his work and mediate his will on earth. And for Mark, Jesus was certainly all that. ... It is

---

Greco-Roman world, deified virtues were sometimes identified with charismatic leaders, especially the monarch ... deified virtues such as Pax, Justisia, Concordia and Providentia had their earthly manifestations in Caesar Augustus." Ibid. Also, see Morton Scott Enslin, *The Prophet from Nazareth* (New York: Schocken Books, 1961). He maintains that Jesus saw himself simply as a *Nabi*, a prophet in the long line of Hebrew prophets and aspired to give leadership to Israel.

5. The phrase 'the Jesus Myth' will be used in this study to refer to the 'historical Jesus' as depicted in the Gospel accounts and will be used interchangeably. In the process of historization, it was the ontological 'literary narratives' that determined their epistemological 'historical perceptions' that fall within the insights of an epiphenomenon. "An epiphenomenon ... is a collective and unitary-seeming outcome of many small, often invisible or unperceived, quite possibly utterly unsuspected events [the divine nature of Jesus in the Gospel narratives]. In other words, an epiphenomenon could be said to be a large-scale *illusion* created by the collusion of many small and indisputably non-illusory events [the cultural and historic significance of the times]." Douglas Hofstadter, *I Am A Strange Loop* (New York: Basic Books, 2007), 93.

123

striking, though, in the Gospel of Mark, that Jesus never refers to himself as a divine being, as someone who preexisted, as someone who was in any sense equal with God. In Mark, he is not God and he does not claim to be.[6]

He has revealed through his work an intellectual honesty that is refreshing in biblical and historical studies. Thus, an exegetical methodology (a hermeneutic of symbolism), when used with this kind of integrity, should provide the evidentiary basis for the modern historian with verifiability, authenticity, and a sense of the biblical traditions historicity for understanding the origin and christological, faith development of the various Jewish communities.[7] Therefore, it will be necessary to explicate the symbolic function of the sources as they were interpreted metaphorically from the early biblical tradition within the Greco-Roman socio-religious milieu.[8]

---

6. Bart D. Ehrman, *Jesus, Interrupted: Revealing the Hidden Contradictions in the Bible (and Why We Don't Know About Them)* (New York: HarperOne, 2009), 79. Cf., in the Hebrew Bible, Hosea 11:1 and 1 Samuel 7:14. Unfortunately he did not maintain this integrity in his later treatment of the historical Jesus.

7. According to Sid Green, "We cannot speak of Christianity in any meaningful way prior to the visions, as described by Paul and which mark the point of the resurrection for Christians. Prior to this, we have only Judaism, regardless of what messianic belief a particular group of Jews might hold, and afterwards we have a Jewish heresy on its way to becoming Christianity." *Qumran and Early Christianity*, from "Qumran and the Dead Sea Scrolls," revised (October 23, 2001), www.christian origins.com/qumran.html, 8 (accessed November 18, 2004). Therefore, from a historical perspective, the gospel of Mark represents the real beginnings of the Christian faith with Paul being no more than an apostle of a cynic type of mystery faith, a heretical Jew.

8. See Paul Veyne in *Did the Greeks Believe in Their Myths?* (Chicago: University of Chicago Press, 1988) suggests that the various postures between belief and skepticism toward mythical stories are indicative of "the ingenuousness of the people," "the educated classes," and "the learned." 42-43. In regard to the prevalence of metaphor in biblical and other Hellenistic sources, see Deutsch, *Lady Wisdom,* 10 where he states: "Beginning with Ben Sira, Jewish authors identify

The oscillating argument, whether 'reason,' as the perception of the actuality of the resurrection as an historical fact in reality, precedes 'faith,' as the response of believing that which is perceived in the historic experience. Or, on the other hand, does 'faith,' which arises and projects its own basis and content out of its conceptual formulations and inner religiosity, precede 'reason?' This has led most Christian biblical scholarship into a dilemma over the resurrection as a historical event in the biblical tradition in relation to its historicity and its authenticity. Our suggested resolution of this dilemma is the consideration that reason and faith "are not separate acts, following a chronological or psychological sequence but are actually co-essential [mentational] dimensions of a total act of a person."[9] Thus, symbolism and metaphor are the cultural forces that have played into these kinds of theological issues. Gail P. Corrington has examined "female savior figures and the experience of salvation in the Jewish and Greco-Roman worlds of formative Christianity. She recognizes that symbolic language not only expresses but also shapes 'reality' and 'the way things are.'"[10]

Hence, in the early kerygma, we find that the resurrection was a symbolic interpretative dimension that was responded to by faith. Myth was an epistemological narrative within the context of historic experience and was not an ontological aspect of history. Doherty elaborates on mythological categories when citing the Daltons:

---

divine Wisdom with Torah. Other Second Temple authors associate her with apocalyptic mysteries."

9. Braaten, *History and Hermeneutics,* 49. Cf., Paul Badham's astute reply to this is "a faith which claims that something which happened in the past is important, cannot evade historical scrutiny of that claim." In *Christian Beliefs about Life after Death* (London, 1978), 19 as cited by G. A. Wells in *A Resurrection Debate: The New Testament Evidence in Evangelical and in Critical Perspective,* rev. ed. originally pub. 1988 by the (Rationalist Press Association, 2000), http://www.internet.infidels.org/infidels/html, 12 (accessed June 17, 2007).

10. Cited by Fiorenza, *Jesus: Sophia's Prophet,* 77-8 from Gail P. Corrington, *Her Image of Salvation: Female Saviors and Formative Christianity* (Louisville: John Knox Press, 1992), 33.

Ancient pagans, too, believed in secrecy. 'Myths have been used by inspired poets, by the best of philosophers, by those who established the mysteries, and by the gods themselves in oracles.' The Pythagoreans taught their disciples to keep secret the 'divine mysteries and methods of instruction...' After communicating a magical formula, a pagan magician says, 'Share this great mystery with no one [else], but conceal it, by Helios, since you have been deemed worthy by the lord.' (cf. Mk 1.44). Many pagans thought that the wise person interprets myths allegorically, i.e., symbolically, ignoring the literal sense, thus concealing the truth from the masses. Sallustius writes that only 'the ignorant Egyptians' and others would believe that earth is Isis, moisture is Osiris, water Kronos, and so on. He asserts that various myths are suitable for philosophers and poets. Some are suitable for '... religious initiations, since every initiation aims at uniting us with the world and the gods.' For Sallustius the revered myths and literature must be symbolically interpreted in order to reconcile them with sophisticated values and thought. Similarly, using symbolic interpretation, writers of the Christian Scriptures sought to harmonize the Jewish Scriptures with Christian beliefs.[11]

The theologian Keith Elliott has said: "There is no independent witness to the Easter events outside the New Testament." And, "Jesus in his resurrected state is visible only to those who have faith [as a *revelatory* 'understanding']," which was also maintained in the second century Book of Acts following this perception that only those "who were chosen by God as witnesses" (Acts 10:40-1).[12] It was, in all significance, a psychodynamic faith-understanding of the Jewish christological gathering's self-

11. The following was excerpted from Laurence E. and Shirley Strutton Dalton, *Jesus: Pagan Christ or Jewish Messiah? A Skeptic's Search for the Historical Jesus,* 2nd revised edition (March 14, 2004), 2-5. Earl Doherty, *Who was Jesus?* www.jesusquest.com (accessed 11 April 2014).

12. Wells, *Resurrection Debate,* 12 where he cites n. 26, J. K. Elliott, *Questioning Christian Origins* (London, 1982), 86. Brackets are mine.

identity. It was a historic revelation[13] that was created by the internalization of the gatherings' religious interpretive posture. The christological fellowship understood that their religious existence had come about as a divine act of God (a mystical event) as a resurrection (the in-gathering of God's people by the presence and power of his Spirit). It had gathered them into the body of the Lord's *presence*, the Christ event that was proclaimed in the kerygma. "For Paul, the Lord, if not identical with, is at least equivalent to the Spirit.[14]

At this juncture, it is time to re-assert the basic underlying historical situation that makes possible an understanding of the historic christological origin of the Jewish communities.[15] All theological concepts that religiously convey *mythos* as the non-reality of historical existence, but generate those spiritual aspects

---

13. Immanuel Kant offers three options -- these do not exclude other possible schemes of thought -- on the question of revelation: a) naturalism, which is a denial of all supernatural revelations of God, b) rationalism, which accepts historical revelation, but only in the sense that it is a transitional stage on the way to a religion of reason, and c) supernaturalism, which accepts the supernatural and its superiority over natural religion, in his book, *Religion Within the Limits of Reason Alone*, trans. T. M. Greene and H. H. Hudson (New York: Harper & Row, Pub., Harper Torchbooks, 1960), 143.

14. Krister, Stendahl, Ed., with James H. Charlesworth, *The Scrolls and the New Testament* (New York: Crossroad, 1992), 182. See the significance of the proclamation for the early church as it relates to the ideas of revelation through history in Paul Althaus, *Fact and Faith in the Kerygma of Today*, trans. David Cairns (Philadelphia: Muhlenberg Press, 1959). Also cf., H. Wheeler Robinson offers a significant understanding of this aspect in its development in, *Inspiration and Revelation in the Old Testament*, Part III, "God and History," chap. VIII, "Time and Eternity" (Oxford: The Carendon Press, 1962), 106-122.

15. Cf. C. K. Barrett, *The Holy Spirit in the Gospel Tradition* (London: Privately Printed, 1947). For a detailed study of this tension, see Rudolf Bultmann, "Jesus and Paul," *Existence and Faith*, trans. Schubert M. Ogden (Cleveland: The World Publishing Co., Meridian Books, 1960), 183-201; and John Knox, *Chapters in a Life of Paul* (Nashville: Abingdon Press, 1950).

(mysticism) for the meaning of physical existence, determine the central theological perspective of historical development (mythology).[16] From a new socio-dynamic and historical perspective, these types of theological concepts are accepted together with their symbolic significance for a mystic understanding of early christological issues and faith response.[17] This will place the Jewish christological communities' natural limitations within the scope of historical integrity and socio-religious investigation. It is no wonder that present day commitments to such a mythological and historicized tradition have been modern Christianity's most tenacious dilemma. It is an aspect of contemporary faith, orthodox theology, and the current mainstream 'biblical' and literalist religiosity. Russell has rightly reflected on a remedy: "A habit of basing convictions upon evidence, and of giving to them only that degree of certainty which the evidence warrants, would, if it became general, cure most of the ills from which the world is suffering [due to the mythological foundations of religiosity]."[18]

---

16. Wells, *Resurrection Debate*, relates, Dennis McDonald's interesting appraisal, with his remarks that the Gospel of Mark's story line "was modeled on a Homeric pattern, as were most Greek literary works at the time, and with much material transposed or adapted from the '*Odyssey*' and '*Iliad*,'" as cited in note 25, www.christianorigins.com/qumran.html, 13 (accessed November 18, 2004).

17. Historical and biblical exegetes are beginning to recognize the cultural determining factors with greater clarity. For example: Stendahl, *Scrolls and New Testament*, 30 notes that "… both forms of Christianity [the Johannine and the Palestinian due to Hellenism] existed from the beginning, because both found their roots in forms of Judaism present in Palestine." Bracket is mine.

18. Bertrand Russell, *Why I Am Not a Christian: and other essays on religion and related subjects*, ed. Paul Edwards (New York: Simon & Schuster Inc., A Touchstone Book, 1957), vi-vii. Bracket is mine. Fiorenza adds a very important note of consideration: "A theology that is silent about the sociopolitical causes of Jesus' execution and stylizes him as the paradigmatic sacrificial victim whose death was either willed by God or was necessary to propitiate God continues the kyriarchal cycle of violence and victimization instead of empowering believers to resist and transform it." Fiorenza, *Sophia's Prophet,* 106.

If this were applied to the modern biblical, Christian tradition and modern biblical research, the mythological basis that existed in the primitive christological cult, that was also part and parcel to the whole Greco-Roman world religiosities, would be noticed and validated without much argument. It was an eschatological faith-understanding that was symbolically maintained. It directed their perception of themselves as the end-time apocalyptic, christological community. It provided an existential and a metaphorical understanding of their communal existence (a mystical life in Christ) as proclaimed by Paul. It was the cultic significance of their spiritual encounter within YHWH's activities through the primitive fellowship that was ultimately responsible for their personal (revelatory, mystical, and ritualized) survival. This historical perspective captures the post 66-73 CE events and reflects the communal situation as it relates to their spiritual salvation, which was symbolically depicted accordingly in Mark's Gospel point of view.

An analysis of the tradition of early primitive Christianity and its direct and indirect connections to the original covenantal, biblical tradition will uncover and reflect the early kerygma that proclaimed the original symbolic interpretation by the Jewish christological fellowships. Their proclamation took on a two-fold directive. Inwardly, it formed its significant religious function (mystically) as part of the cultic worship of the primitive sect within the religious construct of Greco-Roman, mythological religiosities. At the heart of religion is metaphor, which activates the symbolic world-view. We see that "metaphor brings together words, phrases, fields of meaning in such a way as to create new meaning. It is a form of symbol, pointing to a reality beyond itself."[19] This reality does not necessarily have an ontological foundation; it finds adequate expression as a religious reality, epistemologically based.

Outwardly, the proclamation was then developed systematically along with the later formative church's Christology to function as a literal, historicized account of a historical Jesus. In fact, "... in the sermon [which reflected the earlier symbolic ba-

---

19. Deutsch, *Lady Wisdom*, 142.

sis], everything was linked with the eschatological message of salvation."[20] With this in mind, formative Christianity was constantly and intentionally showing that YHWH had entered into history as well as having entered, by faith, into the believer's own personal historic experience of salvation. The ritualized hermeneutic of this experience is seen both in baptism and in the Eucharist, which was also their socio-religious perception of the original symbolic understanding,[21] the indwelling Spirit, as YHWH's gift of salvation via the cult's religious and moral development.

A historical Jesus is not what was seen in the primitive propaganda of the early christological gatherings' kerygma proclaimed by Paul. What actually became part of their religious formulations, historically transmitted and symbolically understood in the early preaching, is the heavenly 'crucified and resurrected Christ' of the kerygma. Even though the death of the Christ occurred in the heavens (before the foundations of the world?), in the Spirit realm, its primary focus was symbolic. In reference to Jesus' burial, Wells remarks that, "He was actually buried is important theologically for Paul, who regarded the death, burial and resurrection as reflected symbolically in Christian baptism of total immersion: into the water constitutes death; under the water, burial; and out of the water, resurrection (cf., Romans 6:3-4 and Colossians 2:12, where references to Jesus' burial are explicit)."[22] This was a new metaphorical spirituality (*mythos*), and was also a testimonial of the Jewish gatherings' eschatological communal and christological existence (symboli-

---

20. Martin Dibelius, *Tradition to Gospel*, 132. Brackets are mine. For the New Testament atmosphere and life situation, see F. C. Grant, *Economic Background of the Gospels* (New York: Oxford University Press, 1926), Charles Guignebert, *The Jewish world in the Time of Jesus*, trans., S. H. Hooke (New York: E. P. Dutton & Co., 1939), and S. Angus, *Mystery Religions and Christianity,* (1925).

21. Mack, *Who Wrote New Testament*, 37 where he states that "It is important to realize that, in early Jewish thought, a personified abstraction could be storied [mythologized] as an individual without losing its generic or social significance." Bracket is mine.

22. Wells, *Resurrection Debate*, 19.

cally understood), which was worked out along Greek philosophical categories of religious, Platonic thought.[23] This new spiritual power (without the actual necessity of a historical Jesus) was revealed (perceived) by the divine presence of YHWH, in the 'anointed' resurrected life of the cultic fellowship.

As metaphor, the Jesus cult perceived themselves, as the body of YHWH's Spirit, chosen, called, and resurrected into the Kingdom of God. They were to bear 'witness' to YHWH's divine inclusive salvation of reconciliation to the world.[24] The resurrection, symbolically understood, was propagandized openly to the Hellenistic world, comparable to other mystery religions and as religious education it was given to their initiates in terms of a resurrected cultic way, truth, and life. It is interesting to note that as Christian writings emerged, the figure of the Divine or Lady Wisdom seemed to disappear. Actually, the idea of Wisdom entered the arena of Christian theology[25] in order to elaborate the theological significance of Jesus in the Gospel narratives (myth).

Moreover, the concept of resurrection in the kerygma was interpreted as God's redemptive act, which had brought the old age (the evil age of 'Satanic' power and influence, according to

---

23. E. Doherty, B. Smith, and other mysticists recognize the thought world of Platonism that was available to the diaspora Jews who desired to revitalize their tradition along Hellenistic lines of religiosity and rituals. In addition, symbols within the Hellenistic religions were used to enrich and vitalize a moral and virtuous life. With a similarity to the Gospel narrative, Athena counsels Achilles against Agamemnon "if you will follow me," in order to check his rage, he by 'self-control' obeys. Myth, through divine intervention, reveals virtue's true course and moral prudence in life. Walter Burkert, *Greek Religion,* Trans. John Raffan (Cambridge, Mass.: Harvard University Press, 1985), 142.

24. As an example, cf. the cult's propaganda, cf., I John 6; III John 1; Rev. 1:5, and 3:10-13. "The metaphor, the hypostasis of Lady Wisdom, bears an implied narrative. [Thus ...] we can speak of a Wisdom myth [which] provided a vehicle for reflection on questions of crucial to Israel's existence, particularly after the Exile, during the suffering of the Maccabean era and that of the first century, culminating in the fall of the Second Temple." Deutsch, *Lady Wisdom,* 21.

25. Fiorenza, *Sophia's Prophet,* 139.

the flesh) to a close. As the Israel of the last days, God had inaugurated the new age, the age of the Spirit,[26] the age of Christ's kingdom. This redemptive understanding, within the context of literary formulations, was mythologically based as christological and theological expressions. I accept Stendahl's assessment of these literary formulations as being historically accurate: "… there existed on the edge of Judaism, a sort of Jewish Gnosticism, which judged externally, must be considered the cradle of earliest Christianity."[27] These texts underwent a further theological and religious alteration, by later Christian generations within the authority of the Roman Church, as a historicized and canonical, biblical tradition.

It was the conservative expression (a literalist hermeneutic) that was used to encapsulate a historicized life of Jesus in the theology of the later Roman Church. It was clothed in conceptual mythic elements that were part of an essentially eschatological proclamation that had been embellished with the apocalyptic language descriptive of the Jewish-Roman War (66-73 CE). Even though these events had taken place by the time Mark wrote his Gospel, later readers ignored the time significance of the narrative. Thus, the coming events, depicted in the narrative of Mark's Gospel, were viewed by the later formative Christian Church differently and were considered within the contextual scheme of the historic and the supernatural, as events yet to be fulfilled in history. This allowed a literalist scenario to push the end-times and a

---

26. An excellent presentation which discusses the interpretation of the resurrection to the new age of the Spirit, within the context of '*Heilsgeschicte*,' can be found in Oscar Cullmann's discussion, "Immortality of the Soul or Resurrection of the Dead," the Ingersoll lecture for 1955, *Immortality and Resurrection*, ed. and intro, by Krister Stendahl (New York: The Macmillan Co., 1965), 9-53. The reader is greatly encouraged to consult the entire works of the Ingersoll lectureship, from 1896 to the present, which was established at Harvard University and deals with the specific topics, 'the immortality of man,' on a yearly basis.

27. Stendahl, *Scrolls,* 19. Thus, he concludes that "there was a Jewish Gnosticism before there was a Christian Gnosticism, as there was a Jewish Hellenism before there was a Christian Hellenism." Ibid.

literal coming of Jesus into an unspecified future expectation in a future time.

Symbolism was now historically embedded within the process of literary historization and glossed over. Yet, it could not be totally eradicated from the literature of Apostolic Christianity. The concept of resurrection in its original theological setting of symbolism cannot be studied in isolation from the Jewish christological community's social, political, and economic spheres of life prior to its literary transformation in the Gospels of the later church. The main presupposition of symbolic understanding, an act of new emerging faith-understanding by the diaspora Jewish cults in which we see its christological affect upon the later church as a process of historization, will allow us to proceed with a socio-historical methodology. The mythological concept of resurrection, that was christologically, symbolically, and mystically understood, depicted the new communal 'spiritual life' within the Jewish gatherings. It came to be expressed in non-symbolic form, as a literal hermeneutic, especially in the later Gospels, which appeared after Mark.[28]

The concept of resurrection was seen in contra-distinction to Greek thought, immortality through the survival of the soul. There is no point in trying to reconstruct the symbolism, which is embedded in the christological proclamations of Paul, without recognizing the 'power of faith' in the metaphor of resurrection attached to their perception of being 'anointed' by God. This was a charismatic and communal force that had unified them to the socio-religious presence of God's Spirit. Miyahara has pointed out that

Charisma is a collective illusion, indicative of group alienation that enables the 'charismatic community' to ascribe a quality to some

---

28. Cf., F. W. Beare, *The Earliest Records of Jesus* (Oxford, 1964), 13 where it is reasonable and probable to admit that the church leaders in the second century made "guesses that gave the gospels their names by which we now know them." There doesn't seem to be any tradition extending back to the first century. "Originally, they [were] 'anonymous documents,' of whose authors nothing is known." As cited by Wells n.10 in *Resurrection Debate,* 5. Bracket is mine.

person or object regardless of their actual condition, and endow that quality with superhuman factuality. There can be no distinction between authentic and inauthentic charisma since all charisma is illusory; the only distinction to be found is that among the groups imputing it.[29]

From Paul, we understand that the fellowships became the cultic 'body' of the anointed one, the indwelling Spirit, *Yeshua*; and thus, they perceived themselves as the new Spiritual Israel.[30] This theological posture helped to shape the gatherings eschatology, as the new community of Israel living in the new (eternal) age of the Spirit. It was a new apocalyptic understanding that was based within the earliest kerygma of the fellowships' perceived mystic relationship (union) with YHWH.

A new relationship was emerging historically out of the old literary tradition (midrashim) based on a revelatory experience with the divine intermediary of heaven, the Son of Man, the *Christos*. It was becoming clear in their minds that they were the living cult chosen by YHWH to propagate the universal monotheistic salvation for humanity.[31] Herein lies the significance of "casting out demons" so pronounced in the Gospel of Mark. It was the power of God's Spirit granted to the fellowship as a divine, spiritual presence and understanding that empowered them to cast out demons (the false faith of polytheism) by their anoint-

29. Cited by Bruce J. Malina, *The Social World of Jesus and the Gospels* (New York: Routledge, 1996), 125-6 from Kojiro Miyahara's summary report, "Charisma: From Weber to Contemporary Sociology," in *Sociological Inquiry* (1983), 53:368-88.

30. Cf. Barrett, *Holy Spirit in Gospel Tradition.* An extensive study of the book of Acts in relation to the rise of Christianity is found in Foakes-Jackson, *The Beginning of Christianity,* (1920-33).

31. Cf. the old and the new wine in the Gospel narratives as symbolic of this historical transition. Also see Fiorenza, *Sophia's Prophet*, where she identifies Lady Wisdom as a source in the adaption to a christological theology, 131-162. This type of reflection in which gnostic and early christological themes are identified (cf., 1 Enoch 42, 1-2 Vgl. Sir., 24, 3-7) also finds similar expressions in the Gospel texts and Jewish apocalyptic literature where Wisdom is sent down to earth, found no place to dwell, and returned to dwell in the heavens.

ed ministry. This still retains the Jewish christological cult's symbolic understanding. It was by the power of God's Spirit that allowed them to overthrow and cast out the heathen gods of Hellenistic polytheism and any other deity opposed to YHWH.

This was the universal monotheism of the Jesus myth.[32] It is in this sense that Jesus, the communal identity of God's presence, is similar to the Greek legendary heroes who also maintain a religious connection for communal solidarity. Since Achaeans' earliest time when most of the Homeric figures were heroes *en masse,* myth enriched the religiosity of the Greek world. Burkert reminds us that "Great gods are no longer born, but new heroes can always be raised up from the army of the dead whenever a family, cult association, or a city passes an appropriate resolution to accord heroic honors."[33] It seems, at this stage of modern historical research, to deny the details of symbolism and mysticism in Paul's proclamation, which does not depict an earthly life and ministry of a historical Jesus, is to deny the spiritual impact of the preserved christological tradition for the sake of historical authenticity. Such a denial does not grasp the significance or the historical impact of these relational and analogous interactions. Symbolism, mysticism, metaphorical religious language, personifications, and first century Hellenistic religiosity all shaped the minds of the Jewish christological membership in their understanding by way of analogy of the divine presence of YHWH.[34]

These literary Gospels were very much dependent on a focused understanding of the narrative so that the meaning as always would come from the analogies of the myth. Realizing

---

32. I give credit to William B. Smith, *Ecce Deus*, for his initial insight into the symbolic themes of the biblical text. That insight has now become my own point of view, and it is now the crucial methodology that has been used in this study as a symbolic hermeneutic to disclose biblical historiography (cf. Mark 1:24).

33. Burkert, *Greek Religion,* 206. "In Hellenistic times the heroicizing, *apheroizein*, of a deceased person becomes almost a routine event. Ibid.

34. Cf., Paul's theological concepts with those religious expressions on the Mystery Religions.

this method of rationality, Hofstadter clarifies the essence of deriving meaning from analogies:

> Well, once again, it's all thanks to the power of analogy; it's the same game as in a *roman á clef,* where a novelist speaks, not so secretly, about people in real life by ostensible speaking solely about fictional characters, but were savvy readers [who understood symbolism, metaphor, and analogy] who know precisely who stands for whom, thanks to analogies so compelling and so glaring that, taken in their cultural context, they cannot be missed by anyone sufficiently sophisticated.[35]

That spiritual presence was the encapsulating authority of God's calling them out as a new resurrected people, the eschatological end-time community. They were working out their mythothematic understanding for their own existence while developing new liturgical forms such as baptism and the Eucharist, as an eschatological religiosity. This is an analogous ritualization process that was significant for their 'end-time' existence and deliverance.[36]

The Gospel of Mark reflects the inner symbolic meaning of the Jesus myth and represents the early process of historization. We can detect this process, which is seen in the revelatory accounts of the early witnesses in the Gospel's narrative. We can note and maybe appreciate the historic role of symbolism and the metaphorical categories that generate these kinds of historic revelations. These revelations provide the spiritual and mystical meanings for the theological interpretations and also provided a socio-religious understanding of physical existence for those who live by faith.

Mircea states that, "The revelation brought by the faith did not destroy the pre-Christian meanings of symbols; it simply added a new value to them. True enough, for the believer this new meaning [which bore the seeds of literalism] eclipsed all the others; it <u>alone</u> valorized the symbol, transfigured it into revela-

---

35. Burkert, *Greek Religion*, 158.
36. See Ernest F. Scott, *The Spirit in the New Testament* (London: Hodder & Stoughton, 1923); and Henry Barclay Swete, *The Holy Spirit in the New Testament* (London: Macmillan & Co., 1910).

tion."[37] Even though this spiritual scenario is accomplished in the biblical tradition by the kerygmatic intention of the Gospel authors, the various conceptualizations of spirituality, beyond the purely physical, was not the religious conclusion that the christological communities encountered. Their faith response enabled them to understand the symbolic nature of their own spiritual existence on a metaphorical level as mythology, which empowered them with a sense of social and moral integrity (1 John).[38] The religious scenario that developed out of this theological context was the historicized fabrication of later, Orthodox Christianity.

It was an attempt to explicate the earlier non-literal religiosity and to establish the tradition on a new historical basis. It is considered historic for its religious faith; but, it is non-historical when the origin of Christianity and its socio-religious endeavors are based on the personality of Jesus, as a historical reality. It shall be shown, repeatedly, that any resemblance of a humanity ascribed to the figure of Jesus is the evangelists' kerygmatic attempts to reveal a purely human essence in Jesus' divine character[39] because of a literalist hermeneutical endeavor. The biblical

---

37. Eliade Mircea, *The Sacred and the Profane: The Nature of Religion,* trans. by Willard R. Trask (New York: Harper & Row, Pub., Harper Torchbooks, The Cloister Library, 1959), 137. Brackets are mine.

38. This concept of 'faith-understanding,' as it relates to the response of the revelation of God through the resurrection will be expanded in greater detail throughout this study. This faith understanding is related hermeneutically to 1 John 3:21-24 where the "divine name contained mystical, magical properties. Revelation of that name gave access to the deity's attention and powers. Through access to the name, they became intimate with him, protected and blessed by him. Such language best fits the community's belief in Jesus as a spiritual force, a deity beside God in Heaven, who has acted entirely in that supernatural world, as God himself does and every other mythical deity believed in at that time." Doherty, *Sound of Silence*, 7-8.

39. Most of the insight, with reference to the biblical text and the explanations as to their symbolic form, has been based on the excellent work of William B. Smith. His understanding of this biblical material that appears in *Ecce Deus* is difficult to separate throughout this study. His work is a piece of brilliant scholarship, philosophic in-

sources have preserved the essential fact of the mythothemes contained therein even though the kerygmatic intent and its symbolic hermeneutic was deleted by later generations. This also demonstrates, from the later church's historicized Christology, why there became a revised theological proclamation of the literal bodily resurrection of Jesus.[40] The Gospels were perceived as literal, historical accounts, which sought to strengthen each believer in their faith-understanding (John 20). This became the new official dogma of orthodox Christianity.

These earlier literary forms sought to convert the unbeliever, the Jews, and the Hellenistic followers of polytheism, to a faith in the heavenly Son, the Christ by their faith in a renewed and revitalized Judaism, as Spiritual Israel. The later historicized tradition transmits *some* of the original christological vitality and assurance of the Jewish communities' faith. This involves the historicized perspective of the resurrection concept even though it was later proclaimed as literal history based on the Gospel narratives. It eventually became the indispensable interpretation, the hermeneutic of a historic '*fact*' as it related to the Christian Church's later dogma. Westcott's words are typical of Christian, literalist sagacity when he states that: "We know so little of the laws of the spiritual world, and of the conditions which beings of another order are revealed to men, that it is idle to urge as a final inconsistency the diversity of visions which, while truly objective, may still have depended, in a manner which may be faintly conceived, on the character of the witnesses to whom they were

---

quiry, and rich in religious interpretations. Others who have maintained this similar symbolic point of view are Arthur Drews and Paul Jensen.

40. Brooke F. Westcott offers a good historical, critical, and explanatory note to this argument, *Introduction to the Study of the Gospels* (New York: Macmillan and Co., 1887), chap. VI, "The Differences in Detail of the Synoptic Evangelists." Note especially sec. VI, "The Resurrection," 309-342. The Jews, who had 'Moses and the prophets,' were now offered spiritual redemption by Jesus, (i.e., the fellowship of Yahweh's salvation).

given."[41] Is it really necessary that we revert to such a calamity of irrationality in order to justify the objectification of the myth of the deity, Jesus, just in order to maintain a literalist, theological posture?

We need to recognize the symbolic nature and underlying mythology that is derived from this type of research and supplemented by the criticism of modern, secular scholars of history. They have provided a new socio-religious methodological approach to New Testament biblical studies. This approach would seem to be more acceptable for people of modernity, science, and rationality.

The original covenantal literature, used by the early community of believers, prior to its canonical acceptance, was derived from a dynamic, living body of literary traditions that was in circulation, rather than a product of a private or isolated literary form. The circulation of this body of tradition, which found its later midrashic expression in a definite literary form, the Gospel of Mark, has come to be viewed as 'the Church's book.' Mark's Gospel is accepted as the earliest of the apostolic traditions,[42] which also contains a well selected array of apocalyptic and eschatological sources. This Gospel may have been circulated among the various christological gatherings. More than likely, it reflected the mystical and mythical concepts that had been identified according to a symbolic hermeneutic via the Jewish fellowship's earliest christological preaching.

---

41. Westcott, Ibid., 327. Cf. Hunter's pattern, n. 7, in his *Gospel According to Paul* (1966).

42. A concise account stating the priority of Mark's position, the evangelic tradition, and the nature of the early apostolic preaching is found in Grant, *The Earliest Gospel*. Note especially Chapters III and IV, 58-88. His summary outline of the main features of the apostolic message (kerygma), 82-83, has generally been accepted by modern scholarship today. Also, Paul most likely would have learned at Damascus several essentials of Jewish Essenism. The Essenes spoke of a 'new covenant,' they were a baptizing sect whose ritual symbolized the cleansing of sins, and they had a communal meal, which used bread and wine.

It finally brought the theological and moral dimensions of Paul's preaching in the diaspora back to Palestine and its Jewish roots. The earliest proclamations, of which Paul is but a representative apostle, were interpreted along Jewish apocalyptic lines and developed a definite eschatological *christology* that was used by Paul in his missionary activities. The alternative approach to this problem suggests that the reformulated biblical tradition, as seen in the Gospels, depicts a process of historization in which the use of Jesus as a literary 'character' is made to reveal, within the context of the literary narrative, what the mystical understanding of the new faith experience should be. Mark's Gospel still reflects within the biblical text some degree of this literary characterization, mythical symbolism, and some surviving christological elements of the Jewish cult's eschatological faith in YHWH.

Keep in mind that the *only* Jesus of most people in modern Christianity is the literalists' divine Jesus (Son of God, Son of Man) whose humanity is supernally depicted in the Gospel tradition. In this regard, to use the symbolic methodology would preserve the historical integrity, as religious mythology. It would also restore the symbolic and metaphorical bases of the dynamic, mystical religiosity of the early christological gatherings. While at the same time, it would demand a re-evaluation in the faith experience of most modern Christians with regard to their literalist foundation. Thus, it would demonstrate within the biblical tradition that the historic origin of the christological fellowships has now been identified by a more reliable, socio-historical methodology. It would also finally reveal the actual socio-religious basis for the historical and authentic development of primitive Christianity.

The proclamation of the early christological kerygma, as proclaimed by their apostle/missionary, Paul, revealed additional symbolic insights into the primitive community's interpretation of the 'life' (the initiates' communal existence) and the ministry of a heavenly Christ Jesus (the Son of God). The reformulated biblical tradition, as historicized in the Gospel of Mark, can be seen as a theological reflection of the communities' religious experiences. The early fellowships interpreted Jesus' activities (as the Son of Man) symbolically and eschatologically as the divine activities of YHWH's Spirit in the communal life of the cult. How would pagan converts perceive the christological categories of Jesus' narrative life? For example, Ehrman reminds us of the possible comparisons of such a conversion experience:

> In pagan mythologies there were lots of people thought to be sons of God. These people were thought to be half human and half divine because they had one mortal parent and one immortal one. These groups would make comparisons between Jesus and their pagan traditions. Examples include the Greek demigod Heracles (the Roman Hercules; compare Luke's version of Jesus' birth). These semi-divine figures were often thought capable of great miracles (compare the Gospel stories of Jesus' ministry), and at the end of their lives they went to live with the gods in heaven (compare the story of Jesus ascension). Anyone who came into the Christian faith with this understanding of what it meant to be the son of God could easily have thought of Jesus as a semi-divine being, not like the traditional 'Jewish' son of God, who was completely human.[43]

They used eschatological and apocalyptic concepts like the Son of Man within the range of Hellenistic and Judaic thought to reflect their communal 'anointing' as a mystic union with God's divine presence, which also had similar gnostic religious significance. Thus, Jesus' life and ministry, found in the Gospel narrative, was originally a symbolic reflection of the life and ministry of the christological community as God's faithful servant, the Son of Man.[44] We shall try to find formative theological categories that are based on historical grounds for indicating the nature of the believer's faith as expressed in the biblical kerygmatic tradition.

This objective is reached by stripping off the historicized layer of later Christian interpolations and its corresponding liter-

---

43. Ehrman, *Jesus, Interrupted*, 252.

44. Cf., Dan. 7:13. Also cf., F. V. Filson, *The New Testament against Its Environment* (London: SCM Press, 1950), for some pertinent background information. Cf., Ezekiel 34:1-14 and son of man declarations.

alism. Then, by indicating the original symbolic interpretation of the early Jewish gatherings,[45] we can identify and realize that the Jesus myth was their christological, communal self-identity. The mystical centrality, even for the christological fellowship, was an adaptation to a socio-religious philosophy (Platonism?). This generated the metaphorical bases for an interpretation that expressed a theological and symbolical frame of reference, which reflected their cultic life and existence. This socio-cultural religiosity served as the common religious basis for their acceptance of God's call, a revelatory experience to bring all of humanity into the original Abrahamic Covenant. This is expressed by the relevant symbols of existential understanding and the idea of spiritual unity by God's grace through faith within the historical and social dynamics of the christological community.

Smith rightly describes this process of interpreting the religious christological experiences, by the early Jewish communities of the Jesus myth, as a struggle to secure monotheism (an anthropological unity) in the ancient Roman world. He fits this christological perception of the Jewish gathering's monotheism within the essential context of its mystical religiosity. He provides insight to the rich symbolism and metaphorical nature when he states that: "The heart and soul of primal Christianity was an impassioned, sustained, and well-reasoned protest against the prevailing idolatry, as degrading, immoral, irrational, and wholly unworthy of man; ... and it was precisely this plea for monotheism that won for the new religion its sudden and surprising victory."[46] The environmental context that provided for this spiritual development was, in part, due to the turbulent and changing cultural milieu of the Greco-Roman world and the established intellectual, mythological, and syncretistic unity around

_____

45. In 1 John 5:9-11, the tradition reflects the symbolic nature of their communal 'revelatory' experiences. Thus, God bears witness through the 'spirit' in their anointing, the 'water' in their baptism into the community, and the 'blood' in their remembrance of Christ's sacrifice in their Eucharist service.

46. Smith, *Ecce Deus*, 68. One can easily detect in Paul's letters the fundamental concern he had for moral integrity in the spiritual life of the believers from his preaching and pastoral comments.

the Mediterranean world. This had been virtually accomplished by the conquests of Alexander the Great as a political and cultural endeavor.

The spread of Hellenistic thought, culture, religions, and speech, later sustained by Rome, was a unifying historical force that helped to determine the emergence of the earliest Jewish christological communities as well as the later development of formative Christianity[47] and its reformulated theology. The extensive geographic areas that espoused a mystic religious posture within the diaspora were all familiar with a great many of the contemporary Greek philosophies (pre-Socratics, Plato, Aristotle, the Stoics, the Pythagoreans, the Cynics, and the Epicureans). These Greek socio-religious interactive forces had all played a part in the liberation of the mind of ancient humanity[48] and helped to bring about a moral basis and virtuous life. Yet, the significantly new religious mediator and liberator of the world, according to Mark 16:15,[49] soon literarily appeared. Another evangelist followed the tradition of Mark's Gospel and embodied the Wisdom of God (Gnosis), as a mythotheme in the persona of the historicized Jesus figure. Many biblical scholars have recog-

---

47. Cecil John Cadoux, *The Early Church in the World* (New York: Charles Scribner's Sons, 1925); and Will Durant, *Caesar and Christ*, 11 Vols., *The Story of Civilization*, Part III (New York: Simon and Schuster, 1944).

48. Stenger's criticism is well founded from a historical perspective when considering Christianity's moral development: "Religious liberty and diversity were core values of classical polytheism. When one nation defeated another in war, the losers were expected to worship the conquerors' gods but were still allowed to continue to worship their own. Polytheism did not have holy wars, inquisition, and crusades. These were all the products of monotheism." Stenger, *New Atheism*, 107.

49. See Matt. 28:19 and cf. Romans 8:19-21. Also, note the views of the analytic and linguistic philosophy known as the 'Wittgensteinian method of analysis' reveal the empirical attitudes in confrontation with apocalyptic thought in Paul Van Buren, *The Secular Meaning of the Gospel* (New York: The Macmillan Co., 1963). Note Braaten's concise interpretation in the study of this debate, Chapter IV, "The Historical Event of the Resurrection" in *History and Hermeneutic*, 78-102.

nized that the evangelist Matthew perceived Jesus as the personification of, the embodiment of the eternal 'divine Wisdom' of God, in his mythic narrative in the extended biblical tradition, the Gospel of Matthew.

The mystical words "I am the resurrection and the life" of John 11:25, meet with equal symbolic and christological understanding when these concepts are applied to the early Jewish communities' self-identity. It had historic meaning in its original symbolic form for the eschatological religiosity of the christological sect. It is not representative of any actual historical, real speech by a real person such as a historical Jesus. Its apocalyptic usage, taken from the Jesus myth, demonstrated the christological cult's belief in the ongoing power of YHWH as a soul-quickening teacher (the power of resurrection) via his Spirit (the *logos* that gave 'eternal life') through the cult's anointing. God had created within them, by the power of his Spirit, a new communal person. God had delivered them from the 'flesh,'[50] which was the sphere of 'Satanic' power and influence over their lives that had previously been their moral undoing.

Divine salvation was achieved by the mystical religious activities of worship and ritualization (baptism and the holy Eucharist) within the early christological gatherings of Jewish and Gentile initiates. This communal process was identical in many respects with the Hellenistic, mystery religions' practices. Historical research further concludes that the kerygmatic Christ of faith[51] had been the major religious focus and authority for the

---

50. Many scholars would agree with Stendahl's remarks: "In the Qumran texts man is called 'flesh.' Man is 'flesh' in so much as he sins and stands under ungodly power." "In the Qumran setting, the 'I' represents the human existence as 'flesh' in the sense of man's belong to the sphere of the power of the ungodly." And finally, "Both in Paul and at Qumran, the 'neutral' use of 'flesh' is completely embedded and overshadowed by the loaded meaning. 'Flesh' is the sphere, the realm where ungodliness and sin have effective power." Stendahl, *Scrolls,* 94-113.

51. The Christ of the Kerygma was a hermeneutical adaptation to similar cultic, mythological themes within the Hellenistic world. Cf., the Essenes and the diversity of their mystical beliefs. The Essenes

earliest christological sects. For Paul and the other apostles, this religious focus was not the canonical, biblical historical Jesus, as depicted in the Gospel texts as the Messiah.[52] Historical research cannot authenticate or identify a truly historical person known as Jesus. It has reached a dead-end with the fabrication of the Jesus of the biblical literary history (the Gospel texts). His historical existence was based on a mythic and literary fabrication of an ancient symbolic, mystical, and metaphorical religiosity. This has been, in the development of Judaeo-Christian religious thought, encapsulated by the dogma of literalism. This had occurred by the third and fourth century within the Christian Church together with its literalist, hermeneutical posture. Nevertheless, it was still based on an ancient mythology.

---

had disappeared as an organized major sect by the time of Josephus' literary corpora. Historically, there is a good probability that they adapted to a stronger apocalyptic outlook, demonstrated extremism in an effort to fight against Rome and lost out with the rest of the Jews.

52. Ehrman presents a concluding remark about messianic considerations: "Before Christianity there were no Jews that we know of who anticipated a Messiah who would suffer and die for the sins of others and then be raised from the dead." Ehrman, *Jesus Interrupted,* 229.

5

Every man is a creature of the age in which he lives;
few are able to rise above the ideas of the times.
                              Voltaire

There is no other existence beyond the parameters of the physical universe that is known by our experiences, ontologically. This also includes the spiritual domain that encompasses that part of our physical encounter that we call religious existence, an epistemological posture.[1] Maintaining this perspective is a natural rational process, based on the neurological structure of the human species' brain function and development. This is most natural as a perceptive posture because of the millions of bio-evolutionary eons that have historically transformed humanity into the Homo sapien sapiens of the modern world. Therefore, the linguistic forms descriptive of religiosity and the conceptual, symbolic, and metaphorical understandings that convey religious meanings are all perceived mythologically. Historical actuality, which is based on real physical experiences, is ontological; while religiosity together with its cultural and mythological context is epistemological within a systemic ontological structure.

These aspects of existence are embedded in the historical religious texts and must also reflect this natural, cultural, and historical process of human rationality, also within the context of physical existence. Rationality as a tool of historiography is necessary for modern, biblical scholarship. Detering puts it this way:

---

1. In other words, even though we can 'think' of fantasies with a creative imagination and create images in our minds, in print or on the digital screen, there is a vast difference in the results and what someone might conclude as 'real' in an external physical (molecular) sense. Fantasies are 'real' fantasies but their *contents* do not depict reality (actual physical reality, ontological existence).

147

"A theology that has learned to ask for the historical truth in a neutral way and without taking ecclesiastical interests into account will also be prepared to do historical justice to the 'heretics'"[2] Seen by this modality, as a psychodynamic understanding of humanity, the mythological term, such as Spirit, can be understood in both contexts: the religious and the secular in a symbolic manner. It can be used as the symbol for a supernatural mythology and spiritual religiosity. It can also be used to describe the modern mind-set of scientific humanism as well as the formation and basis of an atheistic posture.

When we are exposed to various forms of knowledge by our physical experiences, they are interpreted for us by those who already have committed themselves to a set pattern of cultural valuation; for example: the Christian system of faith and its religiosity. We then process these perceptions via the given interpretations as our own reflective thoughts. Out of this mental process, we make a commitment to the concept or knowledge that explains or gives meaning to our own existence. On a relational level, we thereby establish, internally as a neural structure of the brain and the potential for mental processing, the essence of evaluation, which is described as the essence of spirit. Out of this comes the array of all human behavior, both religious and secular. This becomes a behavioral aspect of humanity that has the same rational and foundational basis for all human, global experiences in a physical world.

---

2. Hermann Detering, "The Dutch Radical Approach to the Pauline Epistles," *JHC* 3/2 fall, 1996), 171. Copyrighted by the Institute for Higher Critical Studies, 1996 at http://depts.drew.edu/jhc/detering.html (accessed February 13, 2006). He also recognized, as many scholars also do today, that "the first definite traces of Paulinism are to be found among the circles of the gnostics and heretical Christianity," which prior to the later Church Councils constituted a vast number of early 'Christian' communities that are based on Hellenistic philosophical concerns. Ibid. Also note especially, Elaine H. Pagels, *The Gnostic Paul: Exegesis of the Pauline Letters* (Philadelphia: Trinity Press International, 1975), 175f; and cf., Bauer, *Orthodoxy and Heresy,* (1971).

Given this data, it is understandable that the early Jewish christological assemblies did not internalize perceptions that they received from an objectified historical reality, such as an actual historical Jesus. For us today and for them from the first century on, it is not necessary to encounter a real physical person, Jesus, in order to have a faith commitment (John 20). In a religious sense, they focused their faith-perceptions, which were based on inner religious mentational values, on those socio-religious interpretations that had been taught to them via metaphor, symbolism, and communal narrative (i.e., a mythic savior, Jesus in Mark's Gospel). That instruction (mythological in its scope) became a reflection of and the basis for their mystical communal experience. It was their faith-understanding of the previously held symbolic[3] interpretation. This same process and mental modality was continued by later generations of believers and was used to formulate the later historicized kerygmatic events.

Hence, the early cultus preached universal monotheism, the proclamation of the original Jesus myth as its mission to win over the world to the acceptance of the divine presence of YHWH together with his salvation based on the older tradition of the Abrahamic Covenant (Matt. 28:18-20). The Jewish communities' christological mission in the world was perceived symbolically and metaphorically as casting out the demons of false polytheistic deities. This was dependent on an interpretation from the older tradition "for all the Gods of the heathen are demons"[4] and

---

3. All symbols, besides pointing to a specific meaning, stand for a so-called spiritual reality in which they also participate. Accordingly, Tillich states that, "... the main function of symbols -- namely, the opening up of levels of reality which otherwise are hidden and cannot be grasped in any other way," is a necessary component to faith. Paul Tillich, *Theology of Culture* (London: Oxford University Press, 1959), 56.

4. Hengel, *The Zealots*, 83 maintains that this religious zeal was acted out in a militant fashion where the "Sicarii clung to the thesis of the 'sole rule of God' even under torture." He stated "Judas' message was inseparable from active revolt against foreign rule" and "presupposed the formation of an organized community." Cf. Psalms 96:5, and the gospels, Luke 10:17-20; Matt. 10:1 and Mark 3:14, 15.

was connected with the later Gospel tradition where Jesus (who reflects the christological cult's activities) also casts out demons.

Again, this is a historical reference to the socio-religious activity of the christological fellowships. The later objectification of the deity's persona (YHWH's Spirit, as *Yeshua*, Jesus) was re-transformed into a historical figure (that was still divine in the Gospel narratives) only later to lose its symbolic basis[5] when it became historicized. This historization was a hermeneutical and theological dogmatization within the Imperial church's Roman, hierarchal structure. Nevertheless, it retained its mythical import and has continued to be the theological dogma under consideration for biblical research in modern times.[6] The early christological communities' new religious dynamic of social commitment and valuation also represents the old religious tradition and basis for spiritual and moral knowledge (*gnosis*, wisdom). This was religiously perceived as a 'spiritual revelation,' that reflects the

_____

5. See Wells comment, in *The New Humanist*, 13-18 citing A. Ellegard's perspective on the 'heavenly figure' proclaimed by Paul, as "an idea reinforced by the Wisdom literature, which told of a supernatural personage who had sought an abode on earth, and, rejected, and returned to heaven. The visions gave an assurance that this heavenly figure was now preparing to descend to Earth for the last judgment." Based on the personification of wisdom, it is well to keep in mind Jon Whitman's remarks in *Allegory: The Dynamics of an Ancient and Medieval Technique* (Cambridge, Mass.: 1987), 272 that "it is only when the 'personality' a literary fiction separate from the actual condition that we have a personification." As cited by Daniel Boyarin, *Intertextuality and the Reading of Midrash* (Bloomington, Indianapolis: Indiana University Press, 1990), 97.

6. Arthur Drews' astute comment is well taken: "Thus, there is no hope for the denial of historicity [of Jesus] to find a general public acceptance for a long time, as it would violate the interests of the supporting columns of the established society. Only a complete change of the socio-psychological constitution may someday permit the truth to be accepted broadly." Bracket is mine. Cited by Arthur Drews, "The Denial of the Historicity of Jesus in Past and Present," (Original article, "Karlsruhe," 1926), *Radical Kritik*, Klaus Schilling, Trans. Ed. Michael Hoffman at http://www.radicalkritik.de/leuggnung.html 22 (accessed October 18, 2004).

same historical process and/or socio-religious movement that we understand by the phrase 'metaphorical theology.' This is the fundamental, communal hermeneutic that we find in the ancient biblical tradition.

It is the religious communal experiences in the physical world of reality that are understood as the presence of the Holy Spirit.[7] The divine revelation, which is a historical encounter with a perceived spiritual entity (mysticism), is the biblical tradition's dimension of a perceived aspect of the religious, the supernatural, and the mythological. These all comprised a common cultural core of social and religious philosophical categories. "Yet Judaism, Christianity, and the mysteries were equally parts of the religious milieu of the Greco-Roman world, and this explains why there are many similarities. As Greco-Roman religions, they sometimes faced similar challenges, proposed similar ways of salvation, and shared similar visions of the way to light and life."[8] It is precisely this same natural, psychodynamic process within the context of physical reality and human experiences that functions, metaphorically, as the presence of God's Spirit.

In fact, one aspect of the divine anointing and the presence of the deity cannot be separated from the other aspects of the earliest kerygma, the resurrection, and the spiritual life within the Jesus cult, without destroying the earliest, Jewish community's religious symbolism. Thus, the idea of resurrection was a vital theological and christological necessity (for a mystical union) in the proclamation of the kerygma, which expressed the spiritual interpretation and symbolic explanation for religious existence by the early christological assemblies. Hence; it was based on a mythological, mystical, and epistemological structure.

---

7. The idea of 'Spirit' within the Christological gathering was identified as communal instruction, divine guidance as wisdom's role in the instruction and fulfillment of Torah.

8. Marvin W. Meyer, Ed., *The Ancient Mysteries: A Sourcebook of Sacred Texts* (Philadelphia: University of Pennsylvania Press, 1987), 226.

History and theology have been transmitted to us in the form of language;[9] and thus, language predetermines the various modes of our observations and interpretations of the events and ideas within the context of our physical experiences. Theology, as hermeneutic, is a facet of the biblical language that has become increasingly problematic for modern humanity.[10] It has been noted previously, that the symbolic principle of interpreting history and the use of religious language concepts, metaphorically, provided a mystical reality. "The authors of apocalyptic literature commonly conveyed this type of meaning by portraying contemporary history in symbolic form and continuing the symbolic narrative so as to include the supernatural events which they believed to be [eschatologically and metaphorically] close at hand."[11] A messianic, Judean atmosphere was not prominent in the early part of the first century, and "there was little evidence that expectations of an eschatological prophet were very prominent in Jewish society"[12] as well.

The formative Christian Church, and thereby theological patterns of systematic thought from the second and third centuries on, that derived its theology from an early christological religiosity, has produced and accepted the historicized Jesus of the emerging biblical tradition, the canonical Gospels. Jesus was the mythic divine being, a deity on the conceptual level that was

---

9. Mackintosh suggests three forms of the word of God: a) a proclamation in the church, b) a written witness to the revelation in Christ by the church, and c) a revelation which illuminates the proclamation of the biblical witness. He develops these as a criticism of Barth's 'Word of God' concept in his, *Types of Modern Theology*, 287-298.

10. H. A. A. Kennedy, *The Theology of the Epistles*, Studies in Theology Series (London: Duckworth Pub., 1934).

11. Barrett, *New Testament Background*, 231. Bracket is mine. It must be re-emphasized that Mark's Gospel is a symbolic mythotheme, not historical biography of the life of Jesus. It expresses the communal religiosity and their *christological* existence (as God's anointed people of the last days) whose initiation into a 'new life' in the *Christos* event by faith established their end time salvation, the Kingdom of God and his Christ.

12. Richard A. Horsley, *Bandits, Prophets & Messiahs*, 149.

152

made human on the historic literary level through the Gospel tradition. Even though modern Christianity accepts the biblical or so-called kerygmatic Christ as a historical actual personality (who was in essence, the Spirit deity [YHWH] of the original Jesus cult), it does not accept the mythological foundation on which the history and tradition is based. Thereby, the narrative myth and the faith of the primitive community of believers have come to be historically validated by religious objectification.[13] Faith and theology are both intricately bound historically together in the early gatherings' christological understanding. It is the former that gives believers access to the latter; but, unfortunately this has developed into religious dogmatism.

It would seem reasonable that the events narrated in the kerygma, even if they represent a process of historization as an interpretation of Jesus' life and ministry, could historically only be accessible by faith. In fact, as Richardson so boldly states, "Christian theology has never suggested that the 'fact' of Christ's resurrection could be known apart from faith."[14] Since the later formative Christian community awaited the *parousia* of the Christ (the conservative traditionalists, a historicized, theological posture), any temporal consideration concerning the interval between his resurrection and his *parousia* in the Gospel tradition (a hermeneutical, fabricated historicity), must either distinguish psychologically, in terms of religious values, between the resur-

---

13. Robert E. Wood, *Martin Buber's Ontology: An Analysis of "I and Thou"* (Evanston, Ill.: Northwestern University Press, 1969), 107. Such an approach may also be found in Walter Kunneth, *The Theology of the Resurrection*, trans. James W. Leitch (London: SCM Press, Ltd., 1965), where he demonstrates his conviction that the new theological direction must be achieved by comprehending the basis of the reality of the Lord's resurrection rather than the essential problem of Christology (i.e., the witnesses to the resurrection of Jesus).

14. See Moule, *Phenomenon of New Testament*, note 3, 5 where he cites A. Richardson, *History Scared and Profane* (1964), 206. Faith also allowed the process of historization to take place, as in A. N. Wilson, *Paul: The Mind of the Apostle* (New York: Norton & Company, 1997) notes: "The genius of Paul and the collective genius of the 'early church' ... were to mythologize Jesus." 72.

rection and ascension in the evangelist's perception of the historic experience, or apply a symbolic interpretation to spiritualize the ascension with the exaltation, and thus, extend the whole metaphorical process to the interpretation of the Gospel's theological construction of Jesus' resurrection and his *parousia* as purely spiritual, (mystical) factors of the Kingdom of God[15] understanding. This does not mean that any of these theological concepts cannot be spiritualized, analogously so stated, when expressing technical religious meanings in certain mystic contexts (cf., Gnosticism in general). This they do cannot seriously be denied. It does mean though that we must take the different historical and symbolic interpretations that understand a mythological reality as socio-religious perceptions by an individual's faith-understanding[16] with a more serious consideration within an understanding of physicality (ontological and historical reality).

The mystic experiences of those who accepted the Jesus myth were the historic reality that the christological cults found essential for their symbolic interpretation and survival in the Greco-Roman world. The practicality of a *christological* faith had a definite moral component that was also part of the Hellenistic cultural and religious fabric of the Greco-Roman society. Wilson notes that "Judaism certainly offered both the austerity of a strict moral code and the simplicities of a monotheistic philosophy; but then, so did Stoicism, which was in a sense the most popular form of 'personal religion' at this date, and which could

---

15. Crossan, *Birth of Christianity*, 314 where he states, that "the problem is not to await its future arrival but to recognize its actual presence."

16. Cf. the Gospel interpretation in the article by John Fenton, "Raise the Dead," *The Expository Times* London: T & T Clark (November, 1968), 50-51. For example, see Eph. 2:1, 5, 6; and Col. 3:1. Meyer, *Ancient Mysteries, 200* states that "The Mithraic rituals were intended to bring about the salvation and transformation [resurrection?] of the initiates. ... The salvific transformation is described as rebirth and creation (or re-creation)." This suggests "that the new life of the initiate was experienced in an ascent of the soul to the realm of the divine." Bracket is mine.

be practiced without danger of mutilation" (circumcision?).[17] The fellowship expressed its mystical encounter with YHWH, as *Yeshua*, Jesus the divine, *Spiritual* presence. They signified the same; as Paul declared, "God was in Christ reconciling the world to himself, God sent his spirit, and God sent (revealed, manifested) his son." These were revelatory and communal experiences. Keep in mind that which was originally a descriptive function of the deity, YHWH, became over the years, equally applied to the Gospel character, Jesus.[18]

There are two decisive elements, within the historicized scheme of the salvation event, that were not considered as a significant aspect of the argument. They are precisely the essential symbolic interpretation and the religious facts of the mythology expressed through their communal life. These aspects of their communal understanding make the mystic resurrection theology, the symbol within the myth in the kerygma, a historical and socio-religious necessity. This was primarily intended to suggest religious and conceptual connections for their group's existence. When, such a communal consciousness regularly used the theological term, Lord, which was used by Paul in his proclamation of the divine heavenly Son to refer to the Jesus (*Yeshua* of the Jewish christological gatherings), the conclusion is quite inescapable: it would thereby identify Jesus as 'the Divine Presence,' YHWH's Spirit within the fellowship.

As a result, some religious and cultural confusion may have been experienced due to the terms used for the Imperial

---

17. Wilson, *Paul*, 105.

18. A. Drews has pointed out the significant scholarship done in the 19th century on the Gospels. In general, he states: "The Jesus of scripture is an ideal person, symbolizing the essence of the people of Israel that sacrificed itself in the wars against the Romans, and was revived spiritually in the shape of the Christian community. The whole Gospel story is thus a purely symbolic one." And in reference to Bolland on the Gospel of Matthew, he further said, "Christ is interpreted as the symbolic representation of the celestial community that overcomes the earthly hegemony of the Caesars and the pagan deities. The original Jerusalem mother community is of course mere fiction." Found in Drew, "Denial of Historicity of Jesus," 5-6.

characterization of the official Roman head of state, Augustus. Borg and Crossan indicate that,

> Augustus was Divine, Son of God, God, and God from God. He was Lord, Liberator, Redeemer, and Savior of the World – not just of Italy or the Mediterranean, mind you, but of the entire inhabited earth. Words like "justice" and "peace," "epiphany" and "gospel," "grace" and "salvation" were already associated with him. Even "sin" and "atonement" were connected to him as well.[19]

Within the earliest gatherings, the Divine Presence was known as the Savior (a functional salvific title, not a designated person), whose Spirit indwelled and christologically *empowered* the early, Jewish communities of the Jesus myth.

Hence, the Lord, the divine Savior, the heavenly Redeemer, the Anointed one, and so many other theological concepts, were the cultic christological names for the socio-religious vitality of the Jewish communities' mystical experience. These were born out of the eschatological perceptions and apocalyptic thinking of the Hellenistic Jewish gatherings in the diaspora. Drews reaffirmed what modern, mysticists' scholarship has validated through historical analysis that "there's absolutely no reliable witness whatsoever on the life of Jesus or the apostles."[20] The early tradition, within the community and proclaimed by Paul in his gospel, was reformulated by the efforts of historization within the fellowship of the primitive community by later generations. This produced a positive result at least from the view of traditional, orthodox Christianity, in which, it provided the historical fabric of theological unity and spiritual meaning for Christianity's religious existence.

---

19. Marcus J. Borg and John Dominic Crossan, *The First Paul: Reclaiming the Radical Visionary behind the Church's Conservative Icon* (New York: HarperOne, 2009), 93.

20. His summation is that "Christianity evolved from a quietist Jewish diaspora movement named previously *Hagioi*. They represented a liberal, spiritualized view of the Torah, with deeper moral attachments, but relaxed exterior signs of Judaism, while still sticking to the selected role of the people of Israel." Drew, "Denial of the Historicity of Jesus," 7.

The symbolic and mythic tradition was selected, reformulated, interpreted, and remolded within the later religious community, which had emerged from the earlier Jewish christological fellowships. The eschatological significance, which is contained in this type of historical trajectory as an interpretation, can also be seen in the historicized contents in the midrashic Gospel narratives. The salvific coming of the Son of Man was a typical cultic expression for the divine presence as an apocalyptic act of God. This identification, the son of man, was not used by Paul who declared his gospel to Hellenized believers in the diaspora. The Jewishness of Jesus, by his historic presence in the narrative Gospel, provided an eschatological understanding to the symbolism and metaphor of the resurrection narrative. This had been the significant theological connection to Paul's idea of communal 'new life' in Christ's body (a communal mythic experience). Thus, a spiritual reconciliation of humanity by God's grace was perceived along eschatological lines to extend to the whole of the Roman world: "God was in Christ reconciling the world unto himself."[21]

The symbolic significance of the resurrection, for the early Jewish gatherings and for the faith of later Orthodox Christians, had developed in part out of Hellenistic influences and an understanding of Jesus as the divine presence of YHWH. As a "sociopolitical" category of religion, the idea of resurrection goes back thousands of years to the Pharonic religious sensibilities in Egypt's cultural and religious history. This idea of resurrection influenced not only Judaism (from Babylonian Zoroaster's religious categories) and the Hellenistic world, but contributed to the earliest christological understanding as well. God had provided spiritual redemption, divine healing, and religious salvation to

---

21. Second Corinthians 5:19. The use of these kinds of symbolic, moral, and philosophical considerations should have come easily to Paul if he had come from Tarsus. A prominent intellectual life style and Stoic center was located there, and they practiced a "Stoic tradition of allegorical interpretation in which they saw natural forces personified in the form of gods and heroes." David Ulansey, *The Origins of the Mithraic Mysteries: Cosmology & Salvation in the Ancient World* (New York: Oxford University Press, 1989), 76.

the primitive community (as a deeply felt moral and spiritual re-birth), and through Paul's gospel, it was also offered to the wider world of humanity, the Gentiles.[22] Biblical scholars indicate that eschatological modes of thought were being theologically realigned along with its companion, apocalyptic language. This can be seen in the fourth Gospel's later historical application of the idea of 'eternal life.'[23] This may have been an attempt to regain the historic and religious integrity of the original symbolic interpretation. Or, it may simply be that the so-called later fourth Gospel really depicts an earlier and more 'historical' perception of the theological and philosophical ideas maintained by the earlier christological tradition.

The verification of the resurrection as an actual event, historically, cannot be made possible any more than the verification of God's existence, which would consist of the same mythological structure and theological interpretation. To maintain that a historical Jesus could be resurrected in a physical realm while at the same time maintaining that God exists in a heavenly spiritual realm is far more than a contradistinction of cultural religiosity: it is a rational misunderstanding (contradiction?) of the mystic and symbolic realities and logical religious conceptualities that form the basis of religious myth, a biblical world-view, and all of those various mythothemes that are generated by this line of religious and theological argumentation.[24] God's existence cannot be

---

22. Cf., Paul's argumentation in most of his literary works that deal with faith in relationship to the whole of humanity (Gentiles) is the acceptance into God's fold, along the lines of the Abrahamic covenant.

23. See C. H. Dodd, *The Interpretation of the Fourth Gospel* (Cambridge: The Cambridge University Press, 1968). Compare his views on the dating of the biblical tradition as set therein. Dodd also provides some summary remarks concerning this change that was expressed by the New Testament writers in the outlook of liberation from the disabling fear of bodily death in his, *Authority of the Bible*, 205-8.

24. Cf., Fred Adams, *Origins of Existence* (New York: The Free Press, 2002), T. W. Deacon, *Symbolic Species,* (1997), and Joseph LeDoux, *Synaptic Self* (New York: Penguin Books, 2002) which deal with symbols and physicality. A scientific understanding and a traditional biblical world view provides modernity with its manifold

historically verified by physical evidence nor can Jesus be historically verified by physical evidence. To deny historical physical
evidence for one is to deny it for the other as atheism properly
does.

There was a historical sense to the primitive church's
symbolic and metaphorical interpretation within the kerygma that
is affirmed historically in the biblical tradition (the literary evidence) and also seen in the early christological propaganda of the
eschatological Jewish communities. This does not mean that a
messianic movement or even a general expectation preoccupied
the religious and political landscape at that time. In fact, we note
that,

> Far from being uniform, Jewish messianic expectations in the early
> Roman period were diverse and fluid. It is not even certain that the
> term *messiah* was used as a title in any literature of the time. There
> was no uniform expectation of "the messiah" until well after the
> destruction of Jerusalem in 70 C.E., when it became standardized
> as a result of scholarly rabbinic reflection. ... Thus it is an over
> simplification and a historical misconception to say that the Jews
> expected a "national" or "political" messiah, whereas early Chris-
> tianity centered on a "spiritual" messiah.[25]

These religious sensibilities all have become part and
parcel to a communal life of 'faith.' The literary mythothemes,
which are epistemological considerations, can be historically verified by historians, biblical or secular, or by social scientists or
modern literary critics. But, the ontological reality to which these
literary historical forms refer (due to their conceptual nature)
cannot be historically verified by historians, biblical or secular,
or by social scientists or modern literary critics.

---

tensions today. White suggests that ancient religious tensions also reflect "the growth of a new religious outlook that combines resistance
to Hellenism with influences from Hellenistic thought and culture to
form a new Jewish [and Christian] world view we call *apocalyptic*." L.
Michael White, *From Jesus To Christianity* (New York: HarperSan-
Francisco, 2004), 69.
   25. Horsley, *Bandits,* 90-91.

A religious attitude arose, which was based on theological conceptualizations within a cultic *christology*, that was similarly found in the Israelites' relationship to their king, historically. It also was expressed in the same conceptual terms, YHWH's *anointed* (I Sam. 10:6-9), in which the king receives a new name. In the Jewish christological gatherings, *Yeshua* (Jesus) as Lord, is the new name of YHWH (the LORD, Adonai), which for some gnostic Christians and even later formative Christianity, is the only name that provides spiritual salvation.[26] Even the biblical tradition, which has gone through a theological reformulation, maintained the unity of the Jesus myth. Quite probably, Mark's Gospel was penned in order to provide the ever watchful eye of Imperial Rome with an opportunity to assess the emerging, early christological faith as having a connection with Judaism and its long religious tradition as an ancient 'faith.'

The unity of the Jesus myth also became a historical unity based upon its religious, mystical, and mythological connections. Wilson clearly discerned that,

> In both his gospel and the book of Acts, Luke was writing for a Roman audience, trying to empress upon them that the movement was a religion fit for the Roman Empire. But he had a problem. There was a new religion on the scene, bereft of noble ancestry. But a noble ancestry is precisely what the religion needed if it were to succeed on the Roman stage. In linking the Gentile Christ movement through the Jesus movement back to Jesus and biblical Judaism, he was creating an impeccable heritage for the new religion. It had the virtue of antiquity, a prized Roman virtue. With this historical legitimacy, the author of the Book of Acts positioned the new religion as one that possessed an impressive pedigree, go-

---

26. Those who quote John 14-16, the 'only way' passage misinterpret and do not understand the moral reference to the two ways in Rabbinic Judaism and early Christianity; see Joshua Rudder's brief study in his *Two Ways: A Lost Christian Manual of Personal and Communal Ethics, Discipline and Morality* (Los Angeles: Native Language, 2009). Unfortunately, Christianity today fosters faith (Greek, *pistis*) as a 'belief system' about doctrinal substance rather than its morally based understanding as a total dedication and lifestyle commitment. See, Borg and Crossan, *First Paul,* 168.

ing back into the history of Israel, back to David, Moses, Abraham – even back to the first human, Adam.[27]

The theological unity that was so close to Paul's heart is the divinity of *Yeshua's* presence, the heavenly Son (i.e., as the Spirit of YHWH) and was propagated as universal monotheism. This mystic christological unity, the deity as the Savior of the renewed Jewish people of God, can be seen clearly in the cult's eschatological missionary endeavors, which brought about confrontational religious encounters with the Hellenistic world of polytheism. And through that world encounter, their religiosity became a socio-religious adaptation, so that later Christianity was maintained as a multicultural product. The earliest christological gatherings predate the canonical Gospels and they were a communal mixture of Diaspora Judaism, Hellenistic philosophic religiosity, and Roman cultural forms of socio-religious interaction. Thus, we see that the use of a symbolic hermeneutic maintains the historical integrity of the expanded covenantal literature (the New Testament accounts) and validates the actual historical development of the earliest christological gatherings (Romans 9: 1-11).

It is significant to note that in the discourse of Jesus to his disciples, in Mark's Gospel, the author connects the passion (i.e., the events, historicized), which lead to the cross, with the event of the '*parousia*' (the coming of the Son of Man), an eschatological connection. Since the early church's symbolic interpretation of the proclamation was based on the similarity of eschatological perspectives, it became historicized and spoke of Jesus' advent, resurrection, and the *parousia* in connection with 'the consummation of the Age.'[28] These contrasting schemes of eschatology

27. Barrie Wilson, *How Jesus Became Christian* (New York: St. Martin's Press, 2008), 146.

28. Mark's Gospel incorporates these mythothemes in his apocalyptic section of his narrative, which is connected with his use of the Son of Man identification and the end times perspective. Furthermore, an eschatological figure, the idea of a messiah was redefined according to geopolitical circumstances, and "there was no coherent picture, 'no paradigm or checklist by which to discern whether a man

and apocalyptic thought, which have come to be theologically interpreted literally in the later Christian tradition, place these theological categories sequentially within a historicized tradition, and, thus are impossible to understand without the historicized, mythic resurrection attached. It is the Apostle Paul who is the best historical example of one who proclaimed a mystical basis in his gospel of the *Christos* event. The mythic heavenly Son is an essential aspect of Paul's proclamation that validates the earliest tradition[29] of eschatological sayings to the self-identity of the christological fellowship (the body of the Christ, the *anointed* one of God).

This symbolism was also applied to their own (e.g., Jewish, pre-Christian) particular inner experience of faith responses (the communal life in Christ) and to the interpretive faith response in the kerygma. The lasting mystic significance for faith is that the spiritual language that conveys the 'Word of God' (the divine *Logos*) in the kerygma had entered, as a religious perception for them, into the arena of history once again.[30] This has formed a written testimony to the historic proclamation and pro-

---

was the Messiah'" from J. H. Charlesworth, Ed., *The Messiah: Developments in Earliest Judaism and Christianity* (Minneapolis: Fortress Press, 1992), 14; as cited by Wells, *Jesus Myth,* 108-9.

29. Cf. Robinson, *Jesus Coming*, 43-52. Also, contrast Luke 17: 22 with Luke 17:26. The foundational theme from the Old Testament had definite symbolic application for the Jesus cult and remained a significant theological theme in Paul's writings (cf. Deuteronomy 21:22-23 with the direction of the Jesus cult's new spirituality based on the law, embracing the Gentiles, the advent of the Spirit, and their deliverance by faith. Cf. also Galatians 3:10-14.

30. The relationship of salvation history to world history is discussed by E. C. Rust, *The Christian Understanding of History* (London: Lutterworth Press, 1947). Also, class divisions within a society can foster sociopolitical and economic tensions so that, in the first century, these erupted into a literary flurry of eschatological and apocalyptic thought. Horsley, *Bandits,* 28 records that "within a generation or two of the Maccabean popular rebellion against aristocratically-led Hellenization, there emerged the same old class division between the wealthy aristocracy and the bulk of the people whom the former dominated."

ceeds in and through the historic crisis of God's preparatory stage (the traditional Jewish covenantal tradition, the Old Testament)[31] in the divine drama of humanity's (including Gentile's) redemption. Midrashim, as a hermeneutical methodology, played its part in the emerging literary development and theological reformulation by the christological communities. Consequently, some biblical scholars have noted this historic development: "The doctrine of the church was steadily increasing in extent, as the original 'Kerygma' (or proclamation of the gospel) became settled 'didache' of the church's teachers and pastors and was enshrined in its growing liturgy, catechetical instruction, and the collection of sacred books."[32]

This historical development enabled the later congregation of believers to express their religious convictions through the acceptance of the historicized literary creations (the canonical Gospels). It also helped to establish the transmitted proclamation in the non-historical speeches by the several apostles in the book of Acts. The effect of this was that the sermons that appear in Acts have a contrived unity of viewpoint (a historical Jesus as divine and the power of the Holy Spirit's role in the development of the church, just to mention a few). This also reflects a very early form of Christian proclamation (e.g., the deity's presence within the Jewish cult, Jesus, [Yeshua as symbolically and christologically understood] as a mystic communal experience, the body of Christ). Even though these formulated sermons in Acts may be regarded as artificial (as literary inventions of the later Christian church's Christology based on the Gospel tradition), they should not be dismissed as non-authentic in their symbolic representation of the 'mythic content of the kerygma' for the primitive community.

---

31. Hunt, *Gospel Sources,* (1951) stresses the importance of Old Testament interpretation (midrashim?) as the initial stage in the production of the Gospels.

32. Grant, *Introduction to New Testament Thought,* 44. And for a skeptical analysis, see Martin Dibelius, "The Speeches in Acts and Ancient Historiography," *Studies in the Acts of the Apostles* (London: S.C.M. Press, 1956).

The earliest Christian writings (Paul's and other apostolic epistles) depict the Christ experience essentially as the transcendental, spiritual revelatory force within the early fellowships. The mood of these gatherings was in all probability eschatological. Their socio-religious existence was expressed in apocalyptic terms; and thus, the events that they awaited were expected to bring forth something cataclysmically new.[33] It was the kerygmatic proclamation that re-entered the religious experience of each local fellowship, it generated faith among its hearers, it sustained and edified the believers, it called forth a decision for salvation, and it attested to the fact that YHWH, the LORD has acted decisively in their personal history[34] and has acted decisively for those who continued to respond to God's Word (the *logos*, the living mythological and mystic heavenly Son).

Paul's mystic and revelatory experience of God's heavenly Son being 'revealed' to him is perceived by some Christian literalist as a modality that "... is of a different order from the resurrection appearances that were witnessed by the early disci-

---

33. Mark's Gospel was an interpretation and explanation that 'the something new' was that the end-time had arrived with the 66-73 CE Jewish-Roman military catastrophe. God's Kingdom had come in the form of the 'revitalized' and 'anointed' community, the body of the Cosmic Christ, God's Son. The older theology saw resurrection as an end-time 'hope;' but, the *christological* gatherings saw resurrection (Mark's symbolic mythotheme) now as a present experience of divine union with YHWH. They were born into the fellowship (baptized) and now resurrected (post-baptism), which constituted themselves as Jesus, the body of the Christ, God's faithful servant in the end times. They lived out this new divine fellowship as eternal life in mystical union (eucharistically) with God's presence and each other.

34. Robinson points out this liberation of the Word of God along functional lines. It was a familiar phenomenon -- the ancient attitude to the spoken word that sought a sense of objectivity. So, "Once spoken and current," it then "enters upon its own independent history." Robinson, *Inspiration and Revelation*, 170. See Rudolf Bultmann, *Theology of the New Testament*, Scribner Studies in Contemporary Theology, trans. Kendrick Grobel, 2 Vols. (New York: Charles Scribner's Sons, I, 1951, II, 1955), Vol. I, 306-308.

ples."[35] This is an example of the way Christian scholars tend to differentiate between the spiritual (mythical) and conceptual forms of religiosity (as history). Thus, to preserve the historical aspect of an actual reality, as a 'different order' is suggested in order to accommodate the tradition's integrity. The symbolic interpretation of the resurrection (understood mythologically) on the other hand is far more reasonable for the historic religiosity of the original Jewish christological communities; because, it is an unforced exegesis, and it is representative of the historical situation in light of the social and religious essence of physical reality.[36] The proportionate difference in Paul's mystical thought is one of spiritual reflection along similar symbolic lines that was also expressed mythologically in the Hellenistic mystery religions.

---

35. Knox, *Life of Paul*, 27. We should always take note of the theological language used. The different ways it affects believers is suggested by Wells: "The essential ambiguities of language, combined with different capacities for abstraction in the persons who use it, are bound to lead to different interpretations of the same formulae; and this distortion will result in religious change, or at least affect the uniformity of belief even in a small community. In this way, complicated and sophisticated ideas become degraded into more tangible concretes." Wells, *New Humanists*, 17.

36. When considering Paul's gnostic accommodations, it is not really necessary to impose a docetic Christology of gnostic origin for his theology, which would only seem to reflect a later second century Church controversy. Even though they (doceticists) taught that Jesus was not a real flesh and blood human being, the influence of Platonic categories and expressions used by Paul indicate a different theological consideration. Why not, in Platonic fashion, take a concept, a 'symbol' that can be personified as the 'earthly' community, the divine presence is a reflection of the 'spiritual essence' of the Heavenly, the Cosmic Christ. This would denote the integration of spiritual conceptualities with our materiality (of the flesh) as a new humanity, as moral creatures (from the heavenly to the earthly) from the domain of God to the domain of Satan. It would signify not material objectification (as incarnation); but, spiritual identification, a revelatory experience of communal 'understanding.'

Wells speculates as to Paul's Jewish, religious, and philosophical focus on Wisdom's personification. He states that it is plausible to accept that, "The Jesus of Paul was constructed largely from musing and reflecting on a supernatural 'Wisdom' figure (amply documented in earlier Jewish literature), who sought an abode on earth [as did Wisdom] but was there rejected [as was Wisdom], rather than from information concerning a recently deceased historical individual."[37]

Consideration of a 'different order,' as previously stated by Knox, is not actually so different after all. It really consists in a historical reality and the same basic psychological process of religious valuation that also produced the *christological* faith-understanding in the earliest kerygma of the Jewish cult. The Christ event and the faith response in Paul's religious experience (Gal. 1:15-16) was considered also as a spiritual revelation, a vision attested by scripture (1 Cor. 1:1-5; midrashim?). Some see midrash as a program that preserves the old by making it new.[38] The spiritual and mythological consideration of Christ's resurrection, mystically based, was a faith response to the spiritual revelation from God to Paul.[39] This was true in the religious experiences of the other witnesses (I Cor. 15).[40] They were understood

---

37. Wells, *Jesus Myth*, xviii. Brackets are mine.

38. Midrash has a liberating force to its style. Boyarin, *Intertextuality,* 37-8 suggests that the midrash "appeal to the postmodern sensibility is not so much for the way it liberates from cultural exemplars (that work really needs no buttressing in our culture!), but for the way that it preserves contact and context with the tradition while it is liberating. ...The midrash realizes its goal by means of a hermeneutic of recombining pieces of the canonized exemplar into a new discourse."

39. Kennedy offers a good discussion concerning this aspect of Paul's conversion experience in, *Theology*, 50-72. Also, cf. Knox, *Life of Paul*, especially Chap. VII, "The Initial Revelation," 111-127.

40. There existed historically a kind of theological fluidity with regard to end-time resurrection. Schilling indicated that while the Pharisees stuck "to legal scribalism, less conservative Jews like the Essenes and the Therapeutae established their own mysteries for assuring resurrection at the end of time. Philo performs the perfect fusion of the Tanakh and Hellenic, prevalently Stoic philosophy." I disagree

166

symbolically as revelations in the cultic experiences of primitive Christianity. Yet, the mystic nature of the two revelatory experiences (i.e., Paul's and the other witnesses) transmitted in literary form (the New Testament tradition) is somehow now perceived as being historically different due to the fabricated process of historization.

The idea of resurrection, while being a staple of the diverse Judaisms, was also amendable to various ideas within a Hellenistic world view. And thus, Paul could adapt it to the particular interpretation useful in the proclamation of his gospel that also had similarities to the mystery religions. This may be why gnostics accepted Paul's literary tomes so readily. The concept of resurrection was for Paul, a concept that was descriptive of the ingathering of God's elect into the end-time body of the Christ because of his apostleship and preaching. It referred primarily to a transformation of moral consciousness in order to see the Satanic world from a different perspective; one in which the believer could participate victoriously in new, eternal life and could act toward others with kindness, compassion, mercy, and justice (God's agapē, love).

In traditional 'generation gap' dynamics, the new generation of primitive Christian believers must have occupied, as adults, positions of cultic authority or at least positions of intellectual influence within the developing local churches. They in all probability proceeded, when necessary, to denounce the mystic adherents of the older view (i.e., symbolism and its Hellenistic, mythological basis), and in all probability referring to them as old fogies, heretics, and schismatics. This new generation of Christian literalists became the conservative element within authoritative, orthodox Christianity. Obviously, their offspring were taught this and would also perpetuate the new historicized orthodox faith with social, religious, and dogmatic vigor.

The biblical tradition reflects this stage of redactional development, wherein 1 John 4:2 attests to the fact that some held on to symbolism within the church. "Every spirit which confess-

with his political assessment of the two groups (Essenes and Therapeutae) that he mentioned. His comments are found in Drew, "Denial of Historicity of Jesus," 14.

es that Jesus Christ is come in the flesh is of God [e.g., the conservative historicized position]: and every spirit which confesses not Jesus [i.e., denounces that Jesus has not 'come in the flesh,' the earlier symbolic position and maintained by some] is not of God and this is the spirit [i.e., the religious mind-set] of the anti-Christ, whereof you [i.e., the younger generation] have heard [i.e., by the older conservative generation] that it comes; and now it is in the world already." The diversity of earlier thinking, which included docetic and gnostic ideas, became a primary threat to the developing formative church[41] structure of authority both from within the ranks of Christianity and beyond its borders by the later established Roman religiosity.

We are reminded that Gnosticism is an outgrowth of ancient intellectualization of mythological themes and as Drews so wisely has pointed out, "Gnosticism is undeniably pre-Christian, with both Jewish and Gentile roots."[42] It seems quite clear from the biblical text that their primary hermeneutical concern about the anti-christological view was not a denial of the *anointed* one of YHWH, the Christ, with regard to Jesus' essential divinity; but, the major offense was the rejection of the incarnation, his coming in the flesh (the historicity of Jesus' humanity), as a historical reality (as a religious fabrication). The biblical tradition reflects, even after the process of historization, the essence of the symbolic instruction of the cult via the Spirit of YHWH (Jesus, the sect's divine presence, the cosmic *Logos*). The christological gatherings' propaganda was taught by means of symbolism to the inner members (communal initiates), the new spiritual Israel within the Kingdom of God (cf. the Teacher of Righteousness in the Essenes' community at Qumran).[43]

---

41. Smith's overall theme of symbolic hermeneutic, *Ecce Deus*, suggests that a conceptual interaction of cultural religiosity was operative during Christianity's quest for its early religious survival.

42. As cited in Arthur Drew, "The Denial of the Historicity of Jesus in Past and Present," Trans. Klaus Schilling, Ed., Michael Hoffman, http://www.radikalkritik.de/leugnung.htm at *Radikal Kritik,*17 (accessed June 14, 2005).

43. Cf., Neil Asher Silberman, *The Hidden Scrolls: Christianity, Judaism, and the War for the Dead Sea Scrolls* (New York: A Put-

The language that expresses the concept of resurrection, once having lost its symbolic meaning, required a historical interpretation of the biblical, canonical Gospel narrative events. This was accomplished as a socio-religious hermeneutic by later generations of formative Christians and found a literary place in Mark's apocalyptic narrative.[44] The resurrection in the primitive kerygma not only became a historicized 'fact' for the church's interpretation of YHWH's eschatological event, but the reformulated historicized fact of Jesus' resurrection, now on the basis of historical interpretation, became a dogmatized revelation in the church's orthodox theology.

Revelation, as the interpretation of YHWH's acts in history (the resurrection as salvific), had been the new spiritual reality upon which the earlier Jewish christological congregation maintained its religiosity for faith and existence; but that all changed. With all of this in mind, one must conclude that there can be no historical verification for the 'historical' events of biblical revela-

---

nam Book, 1994), and Lawrence H. Schiffman, "The New Halakhic Letter (Q4MMT) and the Origins of the Dead Sea Sect," *Biblical Archaeologist* 53 (1990).

44. D. E. Nineham, *Saint Mark* (London: Harmondsworth, 1963), 352-4. Cf., Mark 13:14-16. Nineham "discusses the likelihood of this being a Jewish apocalypse from this date which was incorporated into the Gospel tradition and placed as a prophecy into the mouth of Jesus by the evangelists. Some commentators take this 'apocalypse' as a reference to the Roman siege of Jerusalem in 68-70. When Titus besieged the city in 68, he had already taken care to occupy the surrounding hill-country, and those who were caught in the siege had no possibility of fleeing to the hills. Besides, when Titus reached the sanctuary, he did not, as Caligula had wanted to do, set up a blasphemous idol therein. He set it on fire and gutted it. Much the likeliest date for this passage must be the period when there was an actual possibility of the Abomination of Desolation being set up in the temple. Since nearly all commentators believe that this passage started life as a piece of Jewish apocalyptic which has been incorporated into the Gospel narrative, it remains possible to believe in a 'late' date for the Gospel and an early date for the apocalypse, though there is no logical necessity for this." He cites Wilson, *Paul*, 90.

tion within the canonical Gospel narratives to a life of Jesus as interpreted in response to the kerygma.[45]

Furthermore; that which is historically verifiable is the faith-understanding of the early church that is preserved in the proclamation of the kerygma (the 'historic' event, the revelation of YHWH to his people by the metaphorical understanding of resurrection, the communal body of the Christ).[46] This all may be just more theological rhetoric, as it tends to lay stress on the kerygmatic intention of the proclamation. It was the historicized intention that hid the historic origin of the Jesus myth (perceived as the Jewish christological people of God). This has been its symbolic dynamic for religiosity for the world for hundreds of years by traditional Christianity. The mysticists' position by scholars today would support Schilling's appraisal in that "Paul is recklessly misunderstood by those who try to read anything historical Jesusish into" Paul's letters. He continues: "Paul is thus the strongest witness against the Historical Jesus hypothesis. The Gospels exhibit a historization of an originally mythical Jesus, performed for demagogical and dogmatic reasons."[47] Yet today,

---

45. It is one thing to recognize the quasi-political and religious connections that the biblical scholars have with orthodox institutions to which they must answer; but, it is not necessary to hold them in contempt. I find Schilling's words to be harsh; but, true, in which he states that "the reasons for theologians to insist on the historicity of Jesus proved not to be historical ones, but merely social and psychological ones. Theologians are shown as unworthy of being called researchers of history of religion." For it shows their "reckless intellectual dishonesty." As cited in Drew, "Denial of Historical Jesus," 16.

46. On this subject see A. Michael Ramsey, *The Resurrection of Christ* (Philadelphia: The Westminster Press, 1946). Cf. Matt. 8:11, 12, and the story of Lazarus who was raised from the dead in Luke 16:19-31.

47. Schilling also makes reference to H. Raschke's scholarship on Mark's Gospel where Raschke "emphasized the non-existence of the modern consciousness in ancient times. Rather, everything for them was understood magically and speculatively." (To which I would add; mythically, symbolically, and metaphorically) as cited in Drew, "Denial of Historical Jesus," 18.

this vital methodology of symbolism has remained lost in antiquity.

The revival of it, as an interpretive tool to understand the historic and mythic origin of Christianity, may also make it possible to revive a rational dynamic and assessment within the communal existence of those who experienced the Christ event. Thus, we might eventually understand the mythological base that was historically used for a symbolic interpretation of ancient religious conceptualities, which are still used by some within modern Christianity.

The present effort by modern biblical scholars to uncover the historical Jesus through a thorough historical analysis, enhanced by technical methodologies, which use various academic disciplines, has not made any real headway. Those scholars that recognize the ancient mind-set and its underlying mythologies have provided a better historical analysis, which provides rational and meaningful answers to more historical questions within the framework of modern scientific understanding; and yet, do so without a historical Jesus being the founding personage of the Christian faith. Let me summarize, in the words of Earl Doherty, the efforts that have transpired by these scholarly activities:

> The idea that Christianity may have begun without an historical Jesus was first floated near the end of the 18th century by certain philosophers of the French Revolution. In Germany a few decades later, D. F. Strauss and Bruno Bauer laid groundwork for the theory by labeling much of the story of Jesus "mythology" and the Gospels "literary inventions." Bauer came to doubt the historicity of Jesus. But it was at the turn of the 20th century that detailed examination of the issue began in earnest. Since then a handful of reputable scholars in each generation have denied outright any historical existence for the Gospel Jesus.[48]

---

48. E. Doherty, "Main Articles - Preamble." *THE JESUS PUZZLE: Was There No Historical Jesus?* 2, at http://www.jesuspuz zle.com/preamblc.htm (accessed June 22, 2005). Several of the scholars mentioned are: J. M. Robertson in Britain, Arthur Drews in Germany, Paul Louis Couchoud and Prosper Alfaric in France, followed by several others. Most recently, G. A. Wells, Professor of German at the University of London (now retired), has published six books on the

With this view in mind, one can see that the origins of Christianity blended into the ancient cultural socio-religious environment of the Hellenistic world. It, in essence, was really no different from other ancient religious expressions of religiosity. An appreciation of these facts allows us to understand the theological framework, mystical applications, and the mythological foundation out of which the apostle Paul (to use a biblical idea) lived and moved and had his being in the first century C.E. The Apostle Paul's faith in the Christ experience[49] was the faith of an acquired 'understanding' that he believed the Christ was sent (revealed, manifested) by God through his hermeneutical efforts in the handling of sacred scriptural tradition as a diaspora Jew. Borg and Crossan[50] realize that "all these images had their home in Paul's conviction that the 'new age' had begun" with his own proclamation of his gospel. It was not a messianic faith. It was a faith that provided a new understanding (revelation of moral imperatives), an anointing of God's Spirit and presence within the gatherings to whom Paul wrote and ministered.

Paul was just one of many other apostles that championed this new, Jewish revitalization movement, which eventually became the Christian faith. For Paul, the theological and mythical expressions that recognize the heavenly spirit realm was in no way discontinuous or detached from the socio-religious and cultural realities lived out within the historical, christological fel-

---

subject, a telling dissection of Christian literature, especially the Gospels, which reveals just how wispy and elusive is the historical basis that lies behind the story of Jesus of Nazareth.

49. Paul conceptualized his faith by seeing that the christological communities, as "the body of Christ," were animated by the 'Spirit of Christ/the Spirit of God.' Borg and Crossan, *Paul*, 186-191 indicate that these early faith communities had "their identity and their life together 'in the body' were grounded in Christ, in the Spirit, in the Spirit of God as known as faith communities in Christ, and not in 'this world.'"

50. Ibid., 187.

lowships of Jewish/Gentile believers.[51] There was a culturally engaged interaction of salvific understanding, which was employed in their ritualized forms that also provided a theological basis for describing 'the spiritual realities' of the Christ in the Heavenly realm.

This type of socio-religious interactivity is also seen in the Homeric literary works, the *Iliad* and the *Odyssey*. Thus, the Hellenistic world, out of which Christianity was born, provided a large and varied family tradition consisting of a multifaceted religious universe of gods and goddesses, popular mystery religions and mystical unions, and cultural diversity and philosophic vitality that allowed anyone to freely embrace, adapt, and expand a variety of religious and theological ideas into new dimensions of spiritual and salvific understanding. It was out of this historical process that the Christian Church emerged.

---

51. For those that express an interest in the modern evangelical spirit to revitalize Christian faith in the 21st century need to hear Tillich's advice with regard to symbols and the modern expression of a new theological posture. He says that, "the principle of evangelism must be to show to the people outside the Church that the symbols in which the life of the church expresses itself are answers to the questions implied in their very existence as human beings." See Tillich, *Theology of Culture*, 49. And when the Church's language ceases to be relevant, we should cast it aside and chose symbols, a humanistic theology, and religious language that makes sense and not in conflict with our rational, scientific mind-set.

6

All language about God is, in the end, symbolic.
Tom Harpur

To accept miracles as literal occurrences in reality, as a part of the flow of historical actuality, is to debase a rational understanding of religious existence, and as such, could not teach us the existential necessity of profound religious values.[1] Human consciousness is the real divinity.[2] No matter how hard we try, the meaning of our existence is not derived from supernatural external forces. Whatever meaning that exists personally for each of us has been born out of our own human experiences. In a real sense of human destiny, we individually give meaning to our

---

1. John Macquarrie, *An Existentialist Theology* (New York: Macmillan, 1955). Cf., Paul Tillich, *Biblical Religion and the Search for Ultimate Reality* (Chicago: University Press, 1955). Amos N. Wilder, *New Testament Faith for Today* (New York: Harper & Row, 1955) especially Chapter II, "The Language of Faith," 38-71 which was originally published under the title, "Myth and Symbol in the New Testament," Symbols and Values: An Initial Study (by the Conference on Science, Philosophy, and Religion in their Relation to the Democratic Way of Life, Inc., 1954).

2. Marx and Engels, *On Religion*, (1964). Clement of Alexandria employed conceptual and linguistic modes of philosophical dialogue that was acceptable to pagan as well as early Christian leaders that demonstrated a mythical and mystical commonality. Angus said that Clement wrote: "If anyone knows himself he shall know God, and by knowing God he shall be made like unto Him" ... and "the *Logos* of God became man that from man you might learn how man may become God." Angus remarks that Clement recognized the true (Christian) gnostic "has already become God." S. Angus, *Mystery Religions*, 106-7. Here God can be perceived as linguistically related to the 'divine' presence or eternal cosmic, moral force.

own personal, human existence. Humanity gives its own meta-phorical meaning, as well as the social and religious reasons for existence (from a bio-evolutionary and anthropological schema). We may search antiquity for answers; but, the inquiry must yield to our scientific modernity and sense of rationality. One should also add to this list scholarly integrity. "Thus, historical research is not faced with the simple alternative 'authentic' or 'inauthen-tic,' but with the question of how the extant tradition may receive the most satisfactory historical explanation, whether this is by tracing it back to Jesus or simply explaining it from some other historical context."[3] In his masterfully and scholarly way, Smith states the nature of such an inquiry as this:

> The inquiry should be pursued calmly, dispassionately, with scien-tific caution and accuracy, with no appeal to passion, with no re-spect to rhetoric, according to the rules of the syllogism and the formula for Inverse Probability, with firm resolution to accept whatever conclusions may eventually be recommended, and with absolute confidence not only that the truth will ultimately prevail, but that it should prevail, whatever it may be.[4]

The significance of this religious inquiry, seen in the christological proclamation of the early Jewish gatherings,[5] is

---

3. Gerd Thessien and Dagmar Winter, *The Quest for the Plausi-ble Jesus: The Question of Criteria,* trans. M. Eugene Boring (Louis-ville: Westminster, 2002), as cited by Willitts, in *Presuppositions and Procedures in the Study of the Historical Jesus,* 90 at http://www.online.sagepub.com/html (accessed April 14, 2006).

4. Smith, *Ecce Deus*, 8.

5. Jesus, the 'messenger' of the Kingdom, became the 'message of salvation' in the kerygma. Thus, some have proposed that Christian-ity was a complete transformation of the message '*of*' Jesus to a doc-trine '*about*' him. Cf. Adolf Harnack, *What is Christianity?* Trans. Thomas B. Saunders, Intro. Rudolf Bultmann (New York: Harper & Row, Pub., Harper Torchbooks, 1957). For the eschatological signifi-cance to Jesus' proclamation, see Albert Schweitzer, *The Quest of the Historical Jesus: A Critical Study of its Progress from Reimarus to Wrede* (New York: Macmillan, 1966) whose scholarship has set the stage for studies about the historical Jesus in modern scholarship.

justified by its symbolic understanding of the resurrection myth found in the early kerygma. Jesus was a metaphor, the symbolic basis for the divine presence of YHWH, among the various Jewish diaspora cults. He was declared later as the *christological* Son of Man, YHWH's salvation, the heavenly intermediary. And as such, he had been proclaimed, as the Heavenly Christ, by the early apostolic missionaries and especially Paul. This methodology of symbolism is not by any means new in the understanding of Christian theology. Nor is it new in the historical formulation of its Christian origins. It was part and parcel to the christological consciousness of early Jewish gatherings in the diaspora and is evidenced even in the biblical tradition that later emerged.

Keep in mind that the ancient mind-set did not place such a lofty precision or high regard for what modernity calls 'actual history.' So that, when we attempt to do biblical historiography as part of a historical analysis to uncover evidence for the origins of Christianity, we should be aware of our presuppositions that are brought to bear by our research and methodologies used to handle the evidence (religious, biblical, social, and historical). Everyone who is involved in providing a historical understanding of early Christianity, and especially references to a historical Jesus, need to be constantly aware of those presuppositions that are brought into the research. We all hold philosophical beliefs, theological concerns, and religious interactive postures that are based on our current culture, which influence our decisions concerning historical facticity.

History is not only the study of past events and ideas, people, or cultures. History is conscious experiencing, reflection, and commitment of data input so as to create a new introspection of our human existence. It provides a new understanding about us and of our inner selves. It is based on the ideals of that encountered experience, which so many call past events as actual experienced history. Thus, the historical persons or events in the literary, biblical tradition, mythologically based, were perceived by the ancient mind-set in terms of their religious significance, the ethical and moral import, and the historic meaning for the people's religious experience of their times. Thus, our historical research should not be based on an apologetic as a result of the basis of the evidence we are trying to analyze. Crossan does this when he states that "all Gospel texts contain three layers: *the earliest stratum* ('the voice of Jesus'): *the intermediate stratum* ('the anonymous voices of the community talking about Jesus'); and *the latest stratum* ('the voices of the Gospel authors').[6] Actually, these are just one sustained voice of hermeneutical, literary creativity by the early faith communities. Even some modern biblical scholars, who accept a historical Jesus as a real person, make allowances for Hellenistic influence on the Gospel claims. Shorto suggests that the 'wisdom' associated with the historical Jesus' ministry was degraded into a religious gathering based on the model of a Hellenistic mystery cult, which featured "a divine hero with all the attributes familiar to a Greek audience: a miraculous birth, miraculous powers, [and] a miraculous return from death."[7]

The historical dynamics within the christological community that determined a new hermeneutic for the early initiates, was understood by them metaphorically, so that the kerygma was interpreted symbolically. Literalism is the modern demon, which is intoxicating the world of Christianity today. Thus, Willitts' remarks, concerning the historical research into the biblical Jesus, that "there is no accessible Jesus of history who is distinct from faith,"[8] is based primarily on the historical texts of the Gospels.

---

6. Crossan, *Birth of Christianity*, 140.

7. Russell Shorto, *Gospel Truth: The New Image of Jesus Emerging from Science and history, and Why It matters* (New York: Riverhead Books, 1989), 153. Bracket is mine.

8. Willitts, *Presuppositions and Procedures,* 70. Literalism has always accepted the Jesus of the Gospels, the theological bases for the Christian faith, as being the same person as the Christ (even with its Gospel messianic interpretation); but, this places historical inquiry in a precarious position of accepting a Jesus 'remembered' (the literalists view). The major point of historical inquiry into the origins of Christianity is to determine if there really was an actual person, as indicated in the texts of faith that led to Christianity's development. Those scholars of the mystic tradition have shown otherwise, and that the literalists simply are using apologetics rather than maintaining historical methodologies when dealing with historical analysis. Cf., James G. D. Dunn, *Jesus Remembered: Christianity in the Making* (Grand Rap-

Scholars of the mystic tradition hold to a somewhat contrary view. For them, it was the symbolic, mystical experiences that those in the ancient world, who were involved in the various ceremonial experiences of the Greek mystery religions, found to be most appealing, spiritually satisfying, which became enormously and socially popular. Even the various designations of deity in Hellenistic culture were similar to the Jesus narratives in the Gospel texts (especially John's Gospel). Angus cites an Orphic verse: "Zeus was first, Zeus last, and Zeus head and middle." And recorded in Plutarch: "Isis appears as 'I am all that which has been, is, and shall be." And further, Serapis is "the beginning and the ends."[9] These were all expressions of divine eternality, metaphoric categories of inclusive religious, ontological existence.

The later conservative traditionalists interpreted the elements of a historicized Jesus' life and ministry no longer as the essential metaphorical experiences within the literary context; but, now they were perceived as literal, historical accounts. The next two or three generations saw the events of the Gospels' narrative through the prism of a literalist faith-understanding. Even today, the historical Jesus is understood as the Gospel Jesus; both are the 'one' religious and theological reality that is expressed as a hermeneutical bases for traditional Christianity's faith (dogma). The literary Gospels, which had been motivated by the symbolic event of the 'cosmic' resurrection event (and symbolized an initiate's moral transformation) and was originally understood by the christological community as such, were now proclaimed by later generations as literal history. These aspects of faith were given validation by formative Christianity through the political activities and religious influence of the Roman hierarchical authority of the Church throughout the Empire from the later second and third centuries on.

The evangelists fabricated the narrative myth, which was later transformed into the literalist tradition. It was accomplished

ids: Eerdmans, 2003) with Earl Doherty, *Jesus Neither God Nor Man: The Case for a Mystical Jesus* (Ottawa, Canada: The Age of Reason Publications, 2009).
9. As cited by Angus, *Mystery Religions,* 71.

by a second or third generation of believers who were removed from the symbolic propaganda of the original, Jewish christological cults in the diaspora. They had grown up 'in the faith' as part of the historical process through conservative theological reformulations[10] within the established, hierarchical church. The new conservative, evangelical generation of believers accepted the reformulated narrative life of Jesus in the literary tradition. It is even maintained, by most biblical scholars today (evidence to the contrary), that the most reliable sources for the evidence of Jesus is found in the Gospel tradition, regardless of how vast the revision to the text has been. These biblical scholars see the Gospel tradition as history and not as hermeneutical and theological enterprises within the early faith-communities, which reflected the communities' faith-perception of their missionary endeavors. Nevertheless, the early Jewish christological fellowships' objectified faith reformulation (based on the acceptance of a previous faith declaration) can be seen as becoming the new conservative element within the restructuring aspect (literalism) of formative Christianity.

As seen in Matthew's gospel, the changed metaphor, of the female nature of Wisdom, became absorbed and personified into the male figure of Jesus[11] in his gospel story (Christianized

---

10. History is constituted by both ontology (actual historical events) and epistemology (events that transmit imagery, poetic verse, imaginative myth [stories], and a host of conceptualizations) wherein lay the borders of fuzziness for a historical analysis. This has led Green to conclude that "events are chosen in light of the interests of the communities who formulated [fabricated, for the mystic scholars] their own histories and the historians who inscribe them into a historical narrative" in his article. J. B. Green, "In Quest of the Historical Jesus: Jesus, the Gospels, and Historicisms Old and New," *Christians Scholars Review* 28.4 (1999), 556. His emphasis is on historical selectivity in the biblical tradition.

11. Note: This shift in gender may also have been part of an earlier tradition that united Wisdom with the apocalyptic figure in I Enoch, the Heavenly Son of Man where he functions as revealer of 'Wisdom' and the apocalyptic judge, as maintained by Deutsch, *Lady Wisdom*, 78. Castelli citing Mack on wisdom's folly (Burton L. Mack, *The Lost Gospel: The Book of Q & Christian Origins* (New York:

myth). It was not an attempt to demythologize the earlier tradition, since the historicized tradition still remains with its mythological foundation intact. This process of historization was an internal psychodynamic process that was objectified in the literary forms (the Gospels of the expanded covenantal tradition). The overall gospel literature emerged as theological polemics. Jesus was not depicted as just another prophet or religious teacher. A hermeneutical and theological configuration occurred, so that he, in midrashic fashion, was portrayed a prophet working miracles in the 'last days.' His teachings became eschatological directives for the end-times scenario. When the Gospels appeared, this did not express the previous and essential religious nature of the early christological communities.

It became a hermeneutical task of re-orientation of existing contemporary theological categories within the several Judaisms. These several diverse, Jewish christological gatherings, in the wake of Alexander's conquests, saw the temple-states destroyed along with their cultural, supporting social structures. Hence, Mack indicated that, "The temple-state centered, defined, and maintained the society's myths, rituals, codes of recognition, the patterns of thought and behavior, social hierarchies, national boundaries, system of education, round of festivals, social ethics, laws, and the meaning of a people's labor, production, and exchange."[12] Within a cultural context, this was reflected in the existing communities' socio-religious need to re-think its own religious existence as an end time people.

Thus, the author of the Gospel of Mark provided a literary attempt to update this theological perspective through his communal end-time eschatology and with it he provided a sense of apocalyptic urgency. Wenham notes that, "It is easy to see how the atrocities that occurred in Jerusalem under the Roman

HarperSanFrancisco, 1993), 175.) says: "For the people of Q the destruction of the Temple was a monument to the failure of second-temple Judaism to construct a society worthy of wisdom's residence." Elizabeth A. Castelli and Hal Taussig, *Reimagining Christian Origins: A Coloquium Honoring Burton L. Mack* (Valley Forge, Penn.: Trinity Press International, 1996), 101.

12. Mack, *Ibid.,* 65.

governor Cumanus, as described by Josephus, might have been seen as the beginnings of a new desecration of the Temple like the earlier one under Antiochus."[13] From an eschatological point of view discernment of disastrous events could be misleading and open to several apocalyptic meanings. Nevertheless, the other Gospel authors followed this apocalyptic, eschatological, and hermeneutical posture. In part, this process was due to the social, religious, and political circumstances in the tumultuous lives of Jews and early Christians in and around Judea,[14] which brought their struggles to an end with the cataclysmic 66-73 CE historical and devastating events against Rome.

Modern biblical expositors, within the camp of the critical and historical school of thought, have repeatedly claimed that the original expanded covenantal literature (i.e., the New Testament Scriptures) have been compiled, revised, reworked, and interpolated by the same forces that were applied to any other historical body of literature.[15] The elaborate and deeply

---

13. David Wenham, *Paul: Followers of Jesus or Founder of Christianity?* (Grand Rapids, Mich.: William B. Eerdmans Pub., Co., 1995), 322, note 77. He further states that "to the modern historian the events of AD 49 may be seen as something like the beginning of the end, so far as Jerusalem was concerned; it was only a matter of time until the outbreak of the disastrous Jewish war of AD 66-70." Ibid.

14. Mack, *Who Wrote the New Testament*, 50, where he states that, "they addressed the question of how to keep the law in the absence of the sacrificial system. From them would eventually arise the academies of rabbinic Judaism, the Mishnaic codes of purity, and the regulation of liturgy for diaspora synagogues." Stanley K. Stowers, *Letter Writing in Greco-Roman Antiquity* (Philadelphia: Westminster Press, 1986), 41 conveys that "By the first century C.E., more Jews lived in cities of the Roman Empire outside of Galilee and Judea than within. Most of these Jews spoke Greek and were just as Greek in culture as Jews living in the United States are American in culture; they were also at least as diverse in their forms of Judaism."

15. A survey which presents historical attempts to explain the resurrection of Jesus on the basis of imported conceptions -- indeed the whole New Testament Christology -- can be found in James Orr, "Neo-Babylonian Theories Jewish and Apocryphal Ideas," in *The Resurrec-*

thought out symbolism of I Corinthians 10:14-22 gives evidence of the original purpose that existed in the symbolism of the Jesus myth. It was a testimony against the perceived false deities surrounding the Jesus cult within the Hellenistic world; hence, we read: "Wherefore, my beloved, flee from idolatry."[16] It is also maintained that the hermeneutical limitations of Christianity, its later formulated Christology, and the spiritual parameters of faith (the historical Jesus/the biblical Christ polarization) have ended in an enigma. This is because it has been historically based on a mythological and paradoxical foundation.

Hence: Freke and Gandy have been able to construct a biographic and mythic motif that related to Osiris-Dionysus of Hellenistic religiosity as follows:

> Osiris-Dionysus is God made flesh, the savior and "the Son of God." His father is God and his mother is a mortal virgin. He is born in a cave or humble cowshed on December 25 before three shepherds. He offers his followers to be born again through the rites of baptism. He miraculously turns water into wine at a marriage ceremony. He rides triumphantly into town on a donkey while people wave psalm leaves to welcome him. He dies at Eastertime for the sins of the world. After his death, he descends into hell; then on the third day he rises from the dead and ascends to heaven in glory. His followers wait his return as a judge during

---

tion of Jesus (Cincinnati: Jennings & Graham, Pub., n. d.), chap. IX, 235-261.

16. 1 Corinthians 10:14-22 and cf., 1 John 5:20. The personified figure of Wisdom was a female (in the earlier Hebrew tradition [Proverbs 8:1-36], Wisdom is feminine in gender and also in Greek religious tradition) and may have had some cultural pre-Exilic influence with a female consort to YHWH. Even in the Hebrew biblical text, personified Wisdom is indicative of the Near Eastern tendency to extract from the divine quality distinctive divine figures, which, although they expressed the divine qualities of the higher deity, they over time tended to take on a religious life and divine function of their own. Cf., Baruch 3:37, 1 Enoch 42:1-2 in contrast to John 1:1-4. Wisdom and the Greek *Logos* religious expression seemed to be combined. See the Wisdom of Solomon 7:22-30 and the pre-existent imagery of Colossians 1:15-20 (also 2 Cor. 4:4 and 1 Cor. 8:6).

the last days. His death and resurrection are celebrated by a ritual meal of bread and wine, which symbolize his body and blood.[17]

In part, this has also occurred when the various modes of Hellenistic thought and the linguistic, religious concepts, used to identify and explicate the Jesus myth, were transformed by the literalized religiosity of a later formative Christianity (thus, myth entered into history).

In the case of the biblical, expanded covenantal tradition, the historic myth of Jesus has become so embedded into the body of historical literary record, the Gospels, and in the theology of Orthodox Christianity and the creedal dogma that one has difficulty in separating the myth from historical reality. So most scholarship with reference to the historical Jesus studies in the modern period, to use Schweitzer's criticism, have merely constructed a Jesus who is nothing more than a reflection of our own theological biases. Even if most of the current historical Jesus work has done just that – their greatest achievement has uncovered the ancient cultural proclivities that impinge on the earliest christological communities.

Most of modern and even to some degree fundamentalist sermons, as well as the theological literature of modern Christianity, continues a meager attempt to psychologize the evangelical message and the biblical theology of the tradition. Hence, the biblical text is used to make spiritual application of the mythological message of an ancient world-view[18] into an acceptable religious and spiritual language, so that modern humanity can accept and understand it, even though, it reflects a contradictory world-view that is understood by most people who espouse a

---

17. Timothy Freke and Peter Gandy, *The Jesus Mysteries: Was the "Original Jesus" a Pagan God?* (New York: Harmony Books, 1999), 5.

18. "Origen understood this spiritual sense to refer to the fate of human souls who have their true home in the Platonic realm of 'intelligibles,' the world of spiritual realities, compared with which the physical world is but a shadow or a material deformation." K. Froehlich, *Biblical Interpretation*, (1984), 17. This kind of world view exists today only among biblical literalists.

modern, scientific rationality. Consensus is not synonymous with historical facticity. I am also reminded of Willitts' words that "a scholarly consensus is not a sure foundation on which to build a historical argument about [the historical] Jesus."[19]

We are taught, in a multitude of fashions both religious and secular, both about a particular spiritual religiosity and about the scientific understanding of the universe. It is this substantive knowledge and understanding that is processed through mental reflection, commitment, and valuation that becomes our human religious experience for our devotion and our behavior. Similar to this basic human spirituality and physical process are the biblical statements that reflect the essential core of what has been called 'the Spirit of God' among the early christological gatherings. These theological understandings on the mythological level are the reformulations (midrashim), which are based in part on the Israelite's religious scriptural traditions and were intermingled with Hellenistic, philosophical categories.

Doherty is always ready to point out that "the well-known 'love your neighbor,' originally from Leviticus, is quoted in James, the Didache, and three times in Paul; yet none of them points out that Jesus had made this centerpiece of his own teaching."[20] These theological categories were based on the synergistic tradition and redefined a cosmic persona (i.e., the Jesus myth) as a historical figure in formative Christianity's religious development. Mowinckel suggests in his comments on the idea of kingship in ancient Israel that this form of religiosity reflects the common 'pattern' of ancient near eastern religions. It had been the pattern of religious myth, spiritual ritualization, and the cultic socio-religious expression according to their ancient hermeneutic (mysticism).

---

19. Willitts, *Presuppositions and Procedures,* 68. Bracket is mine.

20. E. Doherty, "Main Articles -- Part One: A Conspiracy of Silence," *THE JESUS PUZZLE: Was There No Historical Jesus?* 4 at http://jesuspuzzle.com/htm (accessed June 22, 2005). Also see 1 John and 1 Thessalonians 4:9. Cf., Burton Mack, *A Myth of Innocence: Mark and Christian Origins* (Philadelphia: Fortress Press, 1988).

Thus: "At its center stands the king, himself divine, the offspring or the incarnation of the god, who in the cult is at the same time the god himself, so that in dramatic form he lives [who in the mystery religions also dies and is reborn, resurrected] or endures the entire 'myth' of the god, his deeds and his experience."[21] It is difficult not to see in these ancient religious ideas the theological fabrication of the biographic 'life of Jesus' as it appears in the Gospels' tradition. This had originally been the conceptual and mystical basis similar to the Hellenistic philosophies, which now were used for the symbolic understanding of the Jesus myth by the early Jewish gatherings in the diaspora. Doherty summarily notes that, "all the apologists came to the same Christian faith: a Platonic religious philosophy grounded in Hellenistic Judaism which failed to include any historical Jesus."[22] From a historical and biblical analysis, it is easy now to understand, given theses philosophical and religious underpinnings that Paul was not a Christian apostle; but was a Hellenistic Jew who shared his spiritual, revelatory insights and missionary endeavors to bring the Mosaic 'Knowledge of God' and divine forgiveness to the world of the Gentiles.

The idea of resurrection, the historic conceptual basis for the christological cult's understanding that YHWH had gathered them into a new life of the Spirit, the body of his presence, was also the central interpretive 'Christ event' in Paul's gospel and of the epistles in the expanded covenantal literature. The concept resurrection, itself a symbol, reflected their faith-understanding of God's eternal love and forgiveness, through a cosmic event. Thus, the methodology of handling the biblical text is of critical significance and religious importance for modern Form Criti-

---

21. Mowinckel, *He That Cometh*, 23. Bracket is mine. Also note, Smith, *Ecce Deus*, 267-289.

22. Earl Doherty, *Jesus Neither God Nor Man*, 491. There was an active Jewish community in Alexandria Egypt (Diaspora Judaism) exemplified by Philo (ca.20 B.C.E. to 50 C.E.). "Philo used a Platonic anthropological dichotomy as the model for his hermeneutical principle: the literal meaning of the sacred text is its body, the deeper spiritual and philosophical understanding is its soul." Froehlich, *Biblical Interpretation,* 7-8.

cism[23] that may help to capture the essential symbolic nature within the ancient literary tradition.

The so-called historical appearances of the risen Christ within the narrative text were in no way raised to a rational level of objective reality. They do not function as proofs of Jesus' historicity. They are not the objective validation of a risen Lord, even though a later formative Christianity perceived them in the literal fashion of actual historical reality. These christological and mythical perceptions of religiosity have been a distortion of physical reality by the passion of those who failed to grasp the spiritual significance and the metaphorical essence of the divine presence in the original symbolism of the Jewish, diaspora communities.

Thus, every essential theological concept, which emerged as orthodox Christological dogma by later Christianity, had its focus -- as did the earlier Jewish christological Gatherings -- in the intertextualization of the Jewish scriptures as midrashim.[24] This historization phase, within the gatherings' christological and religious development, although prominent in Mark's narratives, was to a larger extent reflective of the christological gatherings'

---

23. See Rudolf Bultmann and Karl Kundsin, *Form Criticism* (1934). Also, for a fascinating introduction and able analysis of form criticism, also see Dibelius, *From Tradition to Gospel* (1935). Additional material of scholarly taste, clarity of presentation, and representing the theology of the historical and critical methodology, can be found in Gerhard Ebeling, *Word and Faith*, (1963) and Richard R. Niebuhr, *Resurrection and Historical Reason* (1957).

24. Many scholars have identified early gnostic literary works that contain the name Jesus within their text so that the biblical historians have argued historical priority from gnostic to Christian and vice versa. Priority, although important, is not really the determining factor in historical Jesus research. Jesus was a very common name used at this time. The real significance is that an early gnostic group could identify the heavenly scenario (that also appears in later Christian theological terms) with the name of Jesus securely anchored in its mythological structure. The ancient mythological and cultural environment exchanged religious conceptualities without any difficulties. For some, this seems to cut across our modern sensibilities as irrational or minimally unnecessary.

faith-understanding. This historical perspective formed the mystic understanding and the basic christological theology of the communal experience and provided a social/religious meaning for their survival after 73 CE[25] from Roman military power and the political devastation that it caused.

Many of the eschatological narrations in the Gospels and in Paul's writings reflect the early gatherings' experiences with their Greco-Roman overlords' intrusions into the Jewish religiosity, their Temple programs, and the Jewish cultural and religious sensibilities. For example: Paul's comments about 'the lawless one' may have reference to Rome's Emperor, Caligula, who attempted to defile the Temple in 41 C.E., and was viewed eschatologically as a reoccurrence of a 'pagan desolating sacrilege' like that which had occurred under Antiochus Epiphanes in 167 B.C.E.[26] The apocalyptic idea that connects these events is just as '*then*;' so '*now*.' Historically, these perceptions became a driving force for literary socio-political productivity.

The above assumptions of the super-historic existence of the Jesus myth seeks only to explain the symbolic nature of the *christological* faith-understanding that was lived out in community by the primitive Jewish cults. These became historicized in general, and in particular, its understanding of the symbolic interpretation of their "called by God" existence, as a resurrected gathering, was reformulated as literal history by the later formative Christian Church, which served the political needs of Rome. Within this theological context, especially with an exegesis of the Gospels that uses a methodology that takes symbolism into serious account, we can identify the actual historical origin of the Jesus myth, which is the real basis for the christological development of the Jewish gatherings. The christological groups that

---

25. Even though Horsley, *Bandits*, 217 dates the origin of the Zealots to the winter of 67-68, according to Josephus' reports, when the Roman armies were reconquering Judea, the unorganized bands of anti-Roman forces are much earlier even though they are not called Zealots officially, they were identifiable with the same socio-religious and political characteristics.

26. Cf., Wenham's insightful comments regarding this, *Paul*, 305-326.

were intellectually engaged with the Hellenistic and Roman world owed some of their socio-religious impetus to the various Greek philosophical schools.

They owed a special debt to the Stoics, Pythagoreans, and Cynics who aided this development with their method of allegorical interpretation.[27] This was a syncretistic, religious process that tended to preserve the underlying mythological heritage of the Greco-Roman forms of religiosity. Much of the theological and socio-religious, contextual basis is found in the early Christian literature (especially in Paul and in the other apostolic epistles). Hence, it is not difficult to understand the influences of gnostic, mystic, and mythological constructs that are now embedded in the expanded covenantal texts. Given the nature of diaspora Jews' social and religious activities and the vast array of literary texts of a religious nature, it is not difficult to see how Alexandria in Egypt could easily have been the seed bed for the origins, at least intellectually, of Christianity. The Hellenistic Jews, both in Palestine and in the diaspora, became partakers of this mythological and thematic influence upon their own socio-historical development, and they developed their own various theological and rabbinic forms of mystical religiosity as a result.

The early Jewish communities in the diaspora were able to survive the historic influences while their christological theology interacted with the various cultural forces of Gnosticism and the various mystery religions of the time. In order to understand Paul's theology and his proclamation of his 'gospel,' the socio-religious contexts of the Hellenistic influences must be taken as a hermeneutical guide. Even the apocalyptic literary tradition impacted this process within the Galilean Jewish christological gatherings where their early cultic existence interacted with a volatile world of philosophical ideas and mystery religiosities. Mack's extensive studies into Christian origins have shown the religious and philosophical dynamics for "the motif of the ascent vision" as it appeared in Hellenistic Judaism, when he says: "In its fullest form it is a mythological 'pattern of structure and

---

27. G. MacGregor, *Introduction to Religious Philosophy,* (1959); P. Tillich, *Christianity Encounter of World Religions* (1963) and H. A. Wolfson, *Philo: Foundations of Religious Philosophy* (1962).

movement' involving descent of a heavenly figure to this world, a sojourn here to carry out the intentions of heaven, often fraught with struggle and frustration, and a return on high culminating in access to the divine presence or a vision of God."[28] From this systemic and eschatological relationship, we can obtain a slight glimpse of the essence of the emerging socio-religious christo-logical cults and their historic transformation. The mythological essence of Jewish communities in the diaspora was God's divine presence, Jesus, *Yeshua*, a mythic persona that was perceived metaphorically.[29] He was the divine presence of God's Spirit in the community. The diaspora gatherings were YHWH's anointed, the faithful servants of the Lord who were dwelling within the apocalyptic and eschatological existence of the last days.

The sphere of all physical reality has its own parameters out of which all religious myth must finally be cast. In order to understand the conceptual basis of any metaphysical or supernat-ural system of thought as historic, a thoroughgoing assessment of the historical milieu, out of which it sprang in the religious mind, is necessary for critical assessment. In order to understand the resurrection, which is a non-historical event and an impossible occurrence in physical reality, we need to identify its symbolic form (a mystical understanding) and its metaphorical signifi-cance. Interestingly, Freke and Gandy propose a suggestion of probability. They ask: "Could it be that the story of Jesus was actually yet another version of the myth of Osiris-Dionysus?[30] We have seen earlier the symbolic connection between the Gos-pel narratives and the myth of Osiris-Dionysus. Additionally, we need to understand the socio-historical, cultural milieu that was propagated by the christological hermeneutic of the Hellenistic Jewish gatherings in the diaspora.

---

28. Castelli and Taussig, *Christian Origins,* 185.

29. Metaphor "brings together words, phrases, fields of meaning in such a way as to create new meaning." C. M. Deutsch, *Lady Wis-dom*, 142. Thus, for the early christological community, personification and metaphor as a symbol of the new Heavenly Man became histori-cized as *Yeshua*, Jesus, the faithful community.

30. Freke and Gandy, *Jesus Mysteries,* 62.

We have seen that its later proclamation, having been historicized by formative Christianity, represents a firm literary foundation within the actual history of early Christian origins. This socio-religious reconstruction of the Jewish christological fellowships' existence provides the real historical bases together with its emerging eschatological mythology to understand the origin and historic development of primitive Christianity. It is necessary when we try to understand the historic religious value within the symbolic interpretation that emerged within the eschatological Jewish sect. This was clearly based on their mystic communal experience of salvation (accepted by faith in Paul's gospel proclamation) that was found embedded within the theological hermeneutic by the Jesus myth.

Some transformation of theological concepts becomes evident in this interpretive process. There are some examples in Paul's Thessalonian letters.[31] It is evident that the traditional 'day of the Lord' in the original covenantal literature (i.e., the Old Testament) expressed a Jewish religiosity of divine judgment. And the phrase, 'the day of the Lord Jesus' found in the expanded covenantal literature, the New Testament text of the primitive Christian faith has evidently been re-interpreted by the anointed, cultic body, the christological gatherings. This was perceived as the validation of their cultic, redemptive existence as it related to their forgiveness of sins (cf., 1 Cor. 15:1-3). The extensive use of midrashim by the early writers of non-canonical literature is well documented by most critical biblical scholars today.[32] This in effect on a practical and religious level, as well as on a conceptual and theological level, had equated *Yeshua* (Jesus) as being in the same position as YHWH, as the divine presence, the spiritual

---

31. Cf. I Thess. 4:15-5:11, and II Thess. 2:1. Note the range of Paul's mythothemes as a theological structure for faith in J. G. Machen, *Origin of Paul's Religion*, (1921).

32. See H. L. Strack and G. Stemberger, Trans. Markus Bockmuehl, Foreword Jacob Neusner, *Introduction to the Talmud and Midrash*, (Minneapolis: Fortress Press, 1991) and Hyam Maccoby, *The Mythmaker: Paul and the Invention of Christianity* (New York: HarperSanFrancisco, 1986).

anointing of the cult who brought salvation. This naturally has led some to certain interpretive positions.

Dodd astutely regards the early church's kerygma with its theme of salvation as being "... directed towards reconstituting in the experience of individuals the hour of decision which Jesus brought."[33] This historical consideration is also within the scope of eschatological considerations mentioned above. Consequently, the idea of resurrection, the ascension, and Christ's exaltation, within an apocalyptic tradition,[34] will also take on descriptive mythic connotations of an eschatological nature. Keeping in mind that theological postures within the early faith-communities are always reformulated (as metaphor?) according to the historical tensions affecting their lives and used by them to explain and mythically understand their own religious existence. I am always reminded of the closing words in First John to "keep yourselves from idols." This injunction is far more powerful as a moral imperative rather than advice not to customarily fool around with cultural graven images.

This spiritual and moral advice could have easily been stated by the Hellenistic mysteries as well.[35] To a large degree,

---

33. Dodd, *Parables of the Kingdom*, 165. Also, see C. H. Dodd, *The Coming Christ* (Cambridge: The University Press, 1954). Any eschatological consideration of the events in the life of Jesus should not overlook the masterful and scholarly work, now a classic, by A. Schweitzer, *Quest of Historical Jesus*, (1961). Also cf. Rudolf Bultmann's article, "The Primitive Christian Kerygma and the Historical Jesus," in his *History and Eschatology* (Edinburgh: The University Press, 1957).

34. Mackintosh, *Modern Theology*, 19. Freke and Gandy quote J. A. Stevenson, *The new Eusebius*, (London: SPCK, 1957) concerning Origen's views about mythical allegories. "I do not think anyone will doubt that these are figurative expressions which indicate certain Mysteries through a semblance of history and not through actual events." Freke and Gandy, *Jesus Mysteries*, 114.

35. This makes sense given the dualism of the times. In Hellenistic times pagans were taught that every person has a 'lower' material self, the *Eidolon* and an immortal, spiritual 'higher' self, the *Daemon*. Freke and Gandy, Ibid., 101 explain that "the eidolon is the embodied self, the physical body and personality. The *daemon* is the Spirit, the

the mythothemes involved in the Johannine literary form is somewhat a reflection of those gnostic stylistic categories found in Paul. It is Doresse's contention that Paul "who himself claimed to have had the benefit of heavenly revelations -- is yet nearer than that of John, to the speculations of our gnostics." And he recognizes a very close similarity of Gnosticism in Paul, when he appeals to "the Wisdom of God in a mystery, even the hidden wisdom which God ordained before the world."[36]

Even the traditional biblical texts[37] were redefined and interpreted christologically by the Jewish gatherings' mystic and symbolic outlook. They used current esoteric terms that were found in similar non-biblical traditions of the Hellenistic age. It was these christological gatherings, based on the christological mystic and communal experiences, interpreted the older biblical material that was significant to pending apocalyptic events, in midrashic terms. Their communal religiosity had used the ample oral/literary stories available within the culture to formulate its new tradition. They based the new mythic interpretations on the apocalyptic elements of the older structure of the supernatural.

---

true Self, which is each person's spiritual connection to God. The Mysteries were designed to help initiates realize that the *eidolon* is a false self and that their true identity is the immoral daemon."

36. Jean Doresse, *The Discovery of the Nag Hammadi Texts: A Firsthand Account of the Expedition That Shook the Foundations of Christianity,* (Rochester, Vermont: Inner Traditions, 1986), 233. According to Doresse, Gnosticism also influenced the Gospel mythothemes when they made 'the strange figure' of Jesus "by glossing upon the phrase 'the Son of Man,' our sectaries placed him in the higher world and made him the Son of the primordial Anthropos. For them, his incarnation was fictitious, and so was his crucifixion." Ibid., 231-232. Cf., 1 Corinthians 2:7-8, 1 Corinthians 15:44-47, and Ephesians 5:8, Colossians 1:15-20.

37. Many modern biblical scholars today see Jesus as an eschatological prophet. See Dale C. Allison, *Jesus of Nazareth: Millenarian Prophet* (Minneapolis: Fortress, 1998), 39-44. See the book of Daniel; also cf., Enoch and IV Ezra. Yet, given the mysticists' historical methodologies, the earliest biblical texts can still be seen as containing the socio-religious reflections of their communal, missional activities within what they viewed as a hostile world of Satanic influences.

Originally, the symbolic interpretation was applied to the older faith of Judaism with its established literary tradition, but in time this was changed to an acceptance of literalness by formative Christianity.

The Jewish gatherings in the diaspora had fused these elements together, the Jewish scriptures and a symbolic hermeneutic, in a process that for them was natural, non-problematic, and without any theological objections.[38] The cult's perceptions of this mystic material transformed the old hermeneutic of the original passage, the spiritual significance found in the prophetic literature, into a new eschatological, midrashic hermeneutic. The new spiritual significance, as part of the communal self-identity for the christological communities, was adapted to apocalyptic thought and their own eschatological existence. These theological categories could also be applied to a mystic understanding of God's presence within metaphorical and epistemological limits. "The embodiment of God in Judaism … implies an ontological investiture experienced concretely, albeit in human imagination." Hence: "Incarnation of the divine body in Judaism relates to theophanic images that are [also] localized in the imagination."[39] Over time, historization did not fully negate symbolism or its mythological content from its original eschatological religiosity. Hence; the early Jewish christological gatherings' Platonic mysticism and the Greek religiosity can still be identified in the canonical texts by the original theological categories that were used.

The primitive Christian communities re-used the original covenantal, theological categories, such as the original covenantal literature's concept of the advent of the Lord, for midrashic purposes. They served the socio-religious needs of the christo-

---

38. Cf., II Cor. 4:3; and Col. 1:28. For a complete discussion of Christian worship, see Oscar Cullmann, *Early Christian Worship* (Chicago: Henry Regnery Co., 1953). Cf. Buber's Jewish perspective of religiosity, in his *The Origin and Meaning of Hasidism*, ed. and trans. Maurice Friedman (New York: Harper & Row, Pub., Harper Torchbooks, 1960).

39. Tikva Fryer-Kensky, et al., *Christianity in Jewish Terms* (Boulder, Colorado: Westview Press, 2000), 240-241. Bracket is mine.

logical communities, and they became dogmatized by the process of historization to some degree by the second and third Centuries. They had transferred the mystic concept of the Lord, within the context of their faith-understanding, to refer metaphorically to the divine anointed one, Jesus, the cult's self-identity based on God's presence.[40] This type of historical transformation of older concepts by midrashim into freshly oriented historic patterns of faith is a very common, primitive and theological methodology. "Helmut Koester of Harvard University believes that all of these divine-birth stories, including that of Jesus, have one common ancestry: ancient Egyptian myth."[41] Shorto continues this idea, stating that,

> People looked to the then ancient tales of the strange gods of Egypt as a grab bag of mystery. The divine birth of Horus from his mother Isis had particular appeal; statues of the two gods were popular throughout the Mediterranean region. Of course no historian can prove that Christianity formed the myth of the virgin birth of Jesus under the influence of these stories, but the model of a god conjoining with a mortal to produce an extraordinary offspring was well established in the Greek world of the first century.[42]

It is the same kind of theological transformation, which used the terms 'Christ' as the heavenly anointed one and 'Lord,' (*Kyrios*) as the prominence of spiritual authority within the christological gatherings. These served the religious needs and the cultic titles of the community and stood for the divine presence, Jesus, *Yeshua*. It was through the process of historization by later formative Christianity that these titles became used, in a new sense, as proper names for the divine mythical being, the Lord Jesus Christ, Christ Jesus the Lord, etc. The apostle Paul and other early epistle authors make no reference to Jesus as the Son

---

40. For several brotherhoods a sectarian feature was to perceive their own community as the 'true Israel' a feature not only of early Christian fellowship, but also of other Jewish groups such as those known as Essenes, Tannaites, and the Qumran sect: Nodet and Taylor, *Origins*, viii, 123-125.

41. Shorto, *Gospel Truth,* 28.

42. Ibid.

of Man, even though the phrase appears repeatedly in the later Gospels' narratives.

This same apocalyptic figure (Daniel 7:13) also appears in several Jewish sectarian documents that denote an end-time scenario. From the mid second century BCE on, it had missional aspects that signified an end-time community (both collectively or individually; cf., the Book of Ezekiel). It was Ezekiel, as the son of man, in the narrative that could likely become a symbolic reference to God's resurrected people, Israel, and included the idea of God's Spirit within the newly created community, "the whole house of Israel" (Ezekiel 37:1-14).[43] Even though the concept, 'the Son of Man' predates the earliest christological gatherings' existence, it is well attested in the original covenantal literature and has the sense of "a representative" of YHWH amongst his people as a 'faithful servant' of the LORD. When the christological fellowships began to identify themselves (corporately) as the Son of God, the faithful community (servant) of YHWH in the end time, it was natural for the author of Mark's Gospel to exercise his own creativity and use it to describe the end-time community as the apocalyptic 'Son of Man.' This expressed the communal spirit (the Jesus myth) as their own self-identification, which was based on their perception of God's presence among them through his anointed Spirit.

Thus, several scholars agree that in the current cannon of fixed biblical tradition, there has been a historical process of 'pushing back' the historic theological concepts of the Christian faith in order to transform the religious myth into historical reality. The application of these titles, originally divine in essence as

---

43. Paul and the author of Mark's Gospel, being Hellenistic Jews of the diaspora, had no difficulty in identifying God's end-time people with terms that expressed the 'faithful servant' (son of man) idea and added terms of their own from their a cultural context. It is Wenham, *Paul,* 180 who notes that since the Gentiles were becoming part of Israel, "They are thus 'the saints' (i.e., holy ones) -- a term used in the OT of Israel, notably in Daniel 7 ('the saints of the most high'); they are the 'congregation of God,' the word *ekklēsia* [church] being used in the Septuagint of the people of Israel, though also in secular Greek of an assembly of citizens." Bracket is mine.

to their meanings, eschatological in their significance, and apocalyptic in their cultural religiosity, have become anchored in the biblical Gospels of Mark, Matthew, Luke, and John. They have been pushed back behind the resurrection as symbol, back behind the baptism of Jesus in historical narrative to the mythic narrative account of his historicized birth.[44] The historic, Jewish significance of these religious concepts, which were applied by the christological cult, objectified the meaning of the anointed one of YHWH, the Christ, onto the historical scene of socio-religious reality.

The developing theology of later formative Christianity was essentially the religious fabrication of the historic Jewish, religious, and biblical concepts of the earlier christological fellowships. It was a historically compelling process used to validate the earlier cult's new faith-understanding (symbolic of their religious experiences and existence). This was done within the context of other historical forces that were dynamically alive in the social and religious milieu of Hellenistic times. For instance, the Gospel evangelist, Mark sought to dramatize these faith-understandings of the Jesus myth of the primitive communities by presenting them with a literary, eschatological, and historical form. This was the historicized setting for the later biblical tradition. This tradition, based on the Jesus myth, identified the eschatological existence of the christological community, as the new Israel in the end-time. They developed, within a mythological understanding, a perceptual relationship of union (mysticism) with YHWH through an expanding theology that exegetically was based in the Jewish scriptures. Conceptually, Jesus' 'death'

---

44. When Matthew talks of Jesus (*Yeshua*) as the one who would, because of his name, save (heal, deliver) his people from their sins, we have an idealized reference to Joshua (*Yeshua*) in the original covenantal tradition (*ton biblion tou Iēsou*, the Book of Jesus, the Book of Joshua) of whom Goguel says was seen as "a national hero, the successor of Moses, and the continuator of his work. He [Joshua] was one of the most popular heroes in Israelite history." M. Goguel, *Jesus the Nazarene*, Chapter 3, 1.

was understood according to the Jewish scriptures, and his 'resurrection' was also understood according to the scriptures.[45]

Paul never identified that the Jewish original covenantal texts claim to prophesy about a historical Jesus, the divine Christ. The religious conviction, by Paul and other apostles, was to express (by revelatory means, a new hermeneutical posture) that the ancient ritualization of 'sacrifice' that had been necessary for the forgiveness of sins through the Jerusalem priesthood and attested to by the ancient writings, would be made available to the entire world (the Gentiles). These were the holy requirements of YHWH in sacred scripture. Paul simply was making this 'forgiveness' now available to the rest of humanity (the Gentiles) according to the revelatory understanding that he received from the LORD. Possibly, this is why he felt that opening the Grace of God through forgiveness to the Gentiles would be a 'scandal' for the Jewish religious leaders. The spiritual, revelatory symbolism is very clear, religiously understandable, and necessary for a better historical interpretation of the ancient biblical text.

The spiritual affirmation of these significant theological concepts for the religiosity of the Jewish gatherings do not depict actual matters of history per se; but, they do reflect the later religious categories that became dogma and appeared as articles of faith within the later Christian church.[46] It is not difficult to find in these conceptual and linguistic similarities the reason some

---

45. Cf., Romans 15:3, 4; and I Cor. 15. These reflect the essential content of which Paul proclaimed as the gospel of the cross, the forgiveness of sins and a proto-Christian paradigm reflecting the sacrifices in the Jewish Temple in Jerusalem by the official priests (according to Levitical legalities).

46. Cf. Gal. 1:16, 17 as represented earlier by the instruction of the Spirit, the knowledge [gnosis] in the propaganda of the Jesus cult. Even Goguel recognized in 'Simonian Gnosticism' that "it is an extremely valuable indication certain theorists ought not to lose sight of: the idea of a human being in whom a divine principle incarnated was not in any way a strange idea in the environment in which Christianity was born." Goguel, *Jesus the Nazarene,* 10. Add to this the symbolism and the mystical creativity of Mark's Gospel and we see how Jesus in the narrative (the *mythos*) became historical (historic) for the later Christian Church.

have concluded that Paul and other expanded covenantal literary writers were only speculators of Stoic, Epicurean, Cynic, or gnostic philosophies in contradistinction to an orthodox Christian religiosity.[47] Nevertheless, one should not be too cautious. That is not to say that the christological faith of the early Jewish communities or the later historical Christian tradition would not have been possible without these other social and religious historical influences. There were definitely several historical forces (including Platonism, mysticism, various cultural mythologies, and the Hellenistic cultural religiosities of the period) that interacted with the historical christological tradition.[48]

Thus, throughout its formative period, which continued to project a mythological structure, the primitive faith of spiritual

---

47. A detailed, analytical exposition of Stoic doctrine can be found in William L. Davidson, *The Stoic Creed, Religion in Literature and Life Series* (Edinburgh: T. & T. Clark Pub., 1907). Note especially chapter XI, "theology and Religion." Given the years of redactional forces at work in the authority structure of the Church under Roman domination from the second century on, it is most difficult to provide a linguistically based assessment of theological, socio-religious, and mystical concepts that were not part of a general view of Hellenistic mythology. It never was a question of who borrowed from whom; it has always been that these are the conceptual understandings for the religious minded, and one could choose from the vast assortment of ideas, to pick and merge, alter and expand, and relate contradictory themes, if necessary. The ancient religious mind-set, much like modern times, is a self-authenticating mystical experience, as a tool of religiosity. Just note the *Logos* theme with the concept of the 'image of God' in the Hellenistic period. Cf., 2 Cor. 4:4, 1 Cor. 8:6; Colossians 1:15-20, Galatians 4:5-7, Hebrews 1:2-3, and 1 John 2;1.

48. This Hellenistic syncretism of Jewish and Greek epistemological religiosities is detected readily; for example: in the heavenly Son where in Platonic fashion, the Son emerges out of the superior world of spirit (above, the heavenly) and interacts in the lower world of matter (below, the earthly) whose function is as an intermediate being, a mediator figure in terms of personified Wisdom (*Sophia*), the Spirit (*pneuma*), and the *Logos*. All were expressions of the divine presence, which brought union of the initiates with the deity, salvation and life eternal, as in the Greek mystery cults. Cf., Matt. 11:27-29, 1 Cor. 3-4.

Israel continued to be further influenced by Gnosticism, Stoicism, and the various forms of the mystery religions, which were never far from the heart of Paul and other apostles. Cultural religiosity had its roots deeply engrained in the ceremonial festivities of ancient Egypt. Herodotus noted in his travels to Egypt that "on the shores of a sacred lake in the Nile delta he witnessed an enormous festival, held every year, in which the Egyptians performed a dramatic spectacle before 'tens of thousands of men and women,' representing the death and resurrection of Osiris."[49]

The contents of the modern Christian tradition are purely religious in style and dogmatic in theological formulation. It is the former symbolism, within the faith-understanding of an earlier formative church that speaks through the later apostolic tradition. Faith brought forth spiritual knowledge (i.e., gnosis, the mystical instruction of the Jesus myth to the initiated members of the christological cult), and knowledge (gnosis) brought forth the spiritual wisdom of God. Doherty points out that,

Philo described the *Logos* as the "image" of God. It was God's "first-begotten," the primary of his emanations. For Philo, this emanation, this *Logos*, was not a separate divine being. Rather, it was the point of contact with God, just as the Sun's radiated light and heat is the part of the Sun we experience, the Sun itself being unreachable [as God was unknowable and indefinable].[50]

---

49. As cited by Freke and Gandy, *Jesus Mysteries,* 120 from Herodotus, *The Histories* (New York: Penguin Classics, 1954), 197, Book 2, 172.

50. Doherty, "Supplementary Article No. 5," *THE JESUS PUZZLE: Was There No Historical Jesus?* 5 at http://jesuspuzzle.com/htm (accessed September 16, 2006). Brackets reflect Doherty's words from the same page, but in a different location. It is Doherty's entire and unique biblical scholarship that utilizes his brilliant insights, which are based on his understanding of middle Platonism. "Platonism had certainly produced, as it were in outline, some of the themes we find in gnostic mythology [and Christian origins]." Even *The Republic* of Plato "elaborates the myth of the reincarnation of souls in the bodies of men or of animals; this takes place in a heaven where there are the 'ways of the right' which lead upward, and the 'ways of the left' leading downward, and where the spirits, before returning to our world, go

It is upon this similar symbolic and mythological foundation that Christianity was founded. The religious distortions that have been perpetuated throughout Christianity's history, which depict a non-physical realm of mythology, with the existence of divinity and spiritual beings as mythical entities, is demonic (in a symbolic, spiritual sense) because of its rejection of modernity, rationality, and a scientific world view for global humanity. And, these modern demons are just as needful of being cast out, as were the distortions by polytheism that was perceived by the early Jewish christological gatherings. It was the ancient prophet (characterized literary in the Jesus myth) who also cast out demons in the biblical Gospels' narratives.

In order to establish a closer proximity to the actual historical reality of a human Jesus, the evidence found in profane history certainly would be most helpful; yet, none seems to be forthcoming.[51] If that profound personality of the human Jesus actually existed (as depicted in the biblical tradition, the earliest Gospel, Mark), then certainly historians of profane history would have included some references in their chronicles, which would be substantial as evidence of that supreme earthly and human personality. It is safe to say that the historical references in Josephus and Tacitus, and other historiographical sources that purport to provide historical evidence for a historical Jesus are definitely later Christian interpolations.[52] The difficulty of profane historical collaboration, used to provide hard historical evidence of a human Jesus, is a fact attested to even by many Christian biblical

---

to drink the waters of Lethe." Doresse, *Nag Hammadi Texts,* 204. It doesn't take much to see a mythothematic relationship of these Platonic ideas to the 'two ways' of Rabbinic Judaism and those which were placed in a Gospel text and similar themes of commonality found in the Johannine literature.

51. Earl Doherty does a suburb and scholarly job in dealing with most of the arguments of a historical and literary focus on his internet web site: www.jesuspuzzle.com/html. His most recent book, no doubt will become a classic study in Historical Jesus research for decades to come, is *Jesus Neither God Nor Man,* (2009).

52. Smith, *Ecce Deus*, 229-265.

scholars. Compare the scope and extent of the search for the historical Jesus literature just in this century alone.[53]

This whole contention becomes unproblematic when we assume the present thesis of a symbolic interpretation as the foundational basis for a historical analysis in the origins of the Christian faith. Jesus was simply a myth that became historical. This perspective is justified through biblical exegesis and its religious validation has been authenticated by studies concerning the mysticism of the historic origin of the Jesus myth. It is Modern critical, biblical scholarship that provides a historical analysis of Christian origins through the use of social, religious, and scientific research. Mack also mentions with regard to early Christian origins that the early faith-communities found ways of evolving social adaptations to the cultural mythologies in which they were located. Most critical, biblical scholars would agree that,

> As for methods and means toward the creation of a mythic universe, the Jesus people also performed according to normal patterns. They assessed their social and cultural context with critical care, laid claim to the cultural traditions most relevant and ready at hand, sorted out the combinations most appropriate to their movement, and borrowed creatively from the mythologies current at the time.[54]

The socio-religious and cultural methodologies that were used by formative Christianity have shown how the early gatherings actively engaged in their own theological developments, and they also bring to light the mysticism of these early Jewish christological communities. "Mack's re-imagination of the origins of Christianity as multiple, non-miraculous, and tied fundamentally to the social history of the first Christian movements is truly a

---

53. A. Schweitzer, *Quest of the Historical Jesus*, presents an overview of the typical research by biblical scholars in this area. "Only if the fundamental concept of a heavenly intermediary between God and humanity was already part of the philosophical fabric of the time can we understand the genesis of the Christian movement, or the success, which apostles like Paul achieved." Doherty, "Supplementary Article No.5," 1.

54. Mack, *Lost Gospel,* 213.

breakthrough proposal that deserves serious and sustained discussion by New Testament scholars."[55] If the scholarly world of New Testament studies really wants to get serious, it needs to concentrate its historical and biblical analysis in the same manner as depicted by the scholarly work[56] of Earl Doherty, which presents his case for a mythical Jesus. His approach is a formidable and scholarly challenge to the existence of a historical Jesus. Given the vast array of scholarly, historical and biblical assessments, we certainly are now able to understand how early Christianity, when given its mythological and mystical contents and its ancient, cultural religious adaptations, could develop historically (as it did), yet without an actual historical person (Jesus as its religious and spiritual founder).

55. Castelli and Taussig, *Christian Origins,* 312. Some scholars who are concerned about the historical development of Christianity have already proposed some different trajectories. See James G. Crossley, *Why Christianity Happened: A Sociohistorical Account of Christian Origins (26-50 CE)* (London: John Knox Press, 2006).

56 Doherty's book, *Jesus Neither God Nor Man,* contains the elaborate arguments and scholarly findings of his biblical and historical research. His website, www.jesuspuzzle.com or www.jesuspuzzle. org, is a masterful work and can be accessed for further elucidation of his biblical, theological, and historical works.

PART THREE

Formative Era: *Demonstration* 60 CE to 115 CE
The christological groups reformulate a historicized kerygma.

7

*The real voyage of discovery consists not in seeking
new landscapes but in having new eyes.*
Marcel Proust

The divine name used by the christological cult to express
a relational, mystic experience with the divine presence, YHWH,
and its various forms of ritualized religiosity, was *Yeshua*, Jesus.
This name was the spiritualized, mythological name for the deity's functional presence (*Yeshua*, YHWH's deliverance)[1] as the
divine anointing within their Jewish, eschatological cult. Their
mythic, theological perceptions were also understood symbolically. The saving deities of the Greco-Roman mystery religions
were extremely popular and were regarded as entirely mythical[2]

---

1. See Vincent Taylor, *The Names of Jesus* (London: St. Martin's
Press, 1953); and Dalman, *Jesus-Jeshua*. In this study, we shall affirm
that the cultic worship of a Jewish eschatological, religious sect of the
One God, YHWH perceived him apocalyptically as Spirit (i.e., as a
teacher-healer and conceptualized him as the divine persona, namely
Yeshua, Jesus, the *anointed* one). *Yeshua* (Joshua, Jesus), means that
Yahweh saves, redeems, and delivers. And, by this holy name, *Yeshua*
(Jesus), universal and spiritual redemption would come to the world of
humanity.

2. Earl Doherty, A Reply to G. A. Wells' "Earliest Christianity,"
THE JESUS PUZZLE: Was There No Historical Jesus? Which was an
article that was written for the New Humanist (September 1999) 2, at
http://www.jesuspuzzle.com.htm (accessed October 26, 2006). Bracket
is mine. The significance of this mythical experience for a new initiate
'into Christ,' became a communal responsibility to re-evaluate the new
experience (born from above by God's Spirit) and its transformative
empowerment as a vital change from the initiate's previous life experiences. See Alan F. Segal, *Paul the Convert: The Apostolate and Apos-
tasy of Saul the Pharisee* (New Haven: Yale University Press, 1990),
20-30.

so that "Paul's concept of the Christ [the *anointed* one] as a supernatural divinity conforms to the dominant religious expression
within the Hellenistic culture of the day." After Paul's call (that is
perceived as a conversion by some scholars), the Hellenistic faith
community embraced him, and for three years he became ac-
quainted with their *christological* ideas. Brian Taylor suggests
the critical importance of this communal period in Paul's life.
The newly emerging christological experience ...

> is always mediated through the values of the convert's new com-
> munity, which defines what a conversion is and actually teaches
> the covert how to think of it. This emphasizes that the community
> has enormous influence on the interpretation of the emotional life
> of the believer, not only in the case of gradual conversions, where
> such control would be expected, but also in sudden conversions,
> where the social message must be more subtle and more quickly
> transmitted. [3]

Pauls' hermeneutical use of this methodology became
distinctively his own and evidenced his concern for its validity in
opposition to other community apostles, which are noted in his
several literary correspondences. In time all things change. Even
among the diversified, christological groups in the diaspora the
process of historization, by later generations of formative Christians, did not preserve their original mythic integrity[4] or the sym-

---

3. Segal, Ibid., 29. In all probably, it is a good possibility that
Paul acquired his hermeneutical methodology (a form of Jewish Midrashim and an intense understanding that God's 'revelation' of the
Christ emerges from the sacred text) from his communal activities during this time.

4. Timothy Freke and Peter Gandy, *Jesus and the Lost Goddess:
The Secret Teachings of the Original Christians* (New York: Harmony
Books, 2001), 12 indicate that myths by "the ancients regarded them as
profound allegories encoding mystical teachings." ... "Mythical motifs
represented philosophical principles." ... And especially for the gnostics, who reworked the "old myths and syncretizing them to create new
ones was a major preoccupation." With regard to the symbolic nature
of their early christology they also state that "... the image of the resurrected Christ, which represents the realization of Gnosis ..." wrote

bolic interpretation within the christological gatherings. This historical process also did not maintain the dynamic religiosity or the metaphorical essence of the earlier christological fellowships' mystic understanding. In a mythologically based cultural environment the christological gatherings emerged and focused their socio-religious concerns on eschatological expectations and became open to apocalyptic thought,[5] which was manifestly divergent within the Hellenistic, religious culture.

Thus, the various names, used to express the conceptual essence of religiosity in their mystic experiences with their deity, Jesus, were also many-fold. For example: the Nasaree, the Savior, the Lord, the Christ, Barnasha, Son of Man, Man from Heaven, Son of God, Second Adam, etc. are just a few of the cultic titles, some of which have been used by Paul and several canonical and non-canonical authors[6] during this volatile period. It would appear, based on the historical circumstances of the Jewish people's foreign occupation and subjection by several world

---

the word for resurrection, *anastasis*, which "also means 'awakening,' so the idea that resurrection represents spiritual awakening was obvious." Ibid., 76.

5. Filson, *New Testament against Its Environment*. The Hellenistic world and its religious culture provided the mythical context, for Paul and the early Jewish christological gatherings, to develop a mystical religiosity. In this sense, they fashioned an entirely spiritual figure (the Christ Jesus, the anointed savior) that was in keeping with the other savior deities of the times. This Christ was not an actual real person who lived on earth.

6. In the letters of the apostle Paul, he often speaks of the Christ as a person, a man ($\H{\alpha}\nu\theta\rho\omega\pi o\varsigma$). What he has in mind, typical of Platonic categories, is the heavenly man, an idealized concept whose intermediary function serves a religious purpose. This was "a widespread type of idea in the ancient world, including [in the writings of] Philo," where the "spiritual 'body' provides the prototype for the heavenly body Christians will receive at their resurrection." For Paul, "such higher world counterparts had as real an existence as flesh and blood human beings around them [had] on earth." E. Doherty, "Main Article -- Part Two: Who was Christ Jesus?" *THE JESUS PUZZLE: Was There No Historical Jesus?* 8, at http://www.jesuspuzzle.com/html (accessed June 22, 2005). Brackets added for clarification of text.

powers over a period of time, that the dominant concept and corresponding title (as the name of YHWH's divine activity for his people) would come to embrace the salvific idea and conform to *the* general religious term, Savior.

Some of these terms that had been used for spiritual redemption in the traditional faith of Israel,[7] had also been used considerably by the various mystery religions and the philosophic schools around the Mediterranean world. Even Alexander the Great sought his own divinity as 'the Son of God' and likened himself through his accomplishments as a kind of Savior for, at least, Mediterranean humanity.[8] And, in faraway Egypt, the Pharonic power of each ruling monarch (the name for Pharaoh) had been expressed also as the son of the God (e.g., Amun-Rā, as the religious power for the salvation of the Egyptian's socio-religious life). In this contextual sense, the political power of the Pharaoh was equal to the religious role he maintained (as the High Priest) by his Pharonic presence; hence, his religious role as savior of Egypt. Much of Egypt's religiosity had been deeply influential by their historical and political involvements in Palestinian affairs, which also is true in their religious influence in the Greco-Roman religious culture.

---

7. We should always keep in mind that the history of Judaism whose root had been in a variety of ancient polytheistic categories from its beginnings so that we do not think of it as a unitary system of ideas but rather as varied systems, which as "a genus composed of many species and developing in a plurality of branches -- can in fact be effectively described as a genealogical tree." Gabriele Boccaccini, *Roots of Rabbinic Judaism: An Intellectual History, from Ezekiel to Daniel* (Grand Rapids, Mich.: Wm. B. Eerdmans Pub., Co., 2002), 36.

8. For a general reference to this historical era, see Will Durant, *The Life of Greece*, Vol. II of *The Story of Civilization* (New York: Simon and Schuster, 1944), 548f. And, for the view that Alexander considered his own divinity, J. B, Bury, *A History of Greece* (New York: Random House, Inc., The Modern Library, n. d.), 814. Yet even historians are not above criticism. Jakob Burkardt remarked that Eusebius was "the first thoroughly dishonest historian of antiquity." Found in his Life of Constantine (Vita Constantini), *Leben Konstantins,* 2nd edition (1860), 307 at http://encyclopedia,stateuniversity.com/pages/7211/ EusebiusCaesaria.html (accessed August 18, 2009).

The early Jewish communities of the Jesus myth found adequate expression through the resurrection concept in the kerygma as a symbolic understanding of their new, mystical life in the *Christos* event. The cult, as a mystical fellowship with God, was the *anointing* of the fellowships by the *Spirit* of YHWH and his *presence* (*en tē(i) autou parousia(i)*).[9] Their salvific self-identification was 'Jesus,' the anointed community of faithful servants of the Lord, the body of the Christ. And later became associated with the conceptual name, son of man (also understood as God's faithful servant in the end-times). This idea was used by the author of Mark's Gospel so that the mythic Jesus speaks of himself with this same title.

The biblical tradition by the Apostle Paul stated that they had been baptized "into Christ" a mystical union (the historical faith-community with a close affinity to the mystery religions). And, they had been buried and raised "with Christ," the essence of their new redeemed life (a resurrected mystic experience) again with a close affinity to the mystery religions. They maintained a socio-religious epistemology, which expressed faith statements that explained the ritualization and ceremonies of the christological gatherings. This new faith, for Paul, was God's mystery revealed through a hermeneutical effort that he engaged in with the ancient Jewish biblical tradition.

Some biblical historians have recognized the intertextual role of faith in this type of theological reformulation. Thus, they conclude that "the historicity of Jesus is an article of faith."[10]

---

9. A recent inquiry into the implications of early Christianity is presented in C. F. D. Moule's, *Phenomenon*, 43-76. Tom Harpur, *The Pagan Christ: Recovering the Lost Light* (New York: Walker & Co., 2004), 12 is in agreement with the mysticists position when he says that "the Christian story itself … was turned into a form of history in which the Christ of the myth became a flesh-and-blood person identified with Jesus (*Yeshua* or Joshua) of Nazareth."

10. P. I. Couchoud, *The Creation of Christ,* Vol. 2 (London: Watts & Co., 1939), 447 as cited by Historicus, *Did Jesus Ever Live? Or Is Christianity Founded Upon a Myth?* 13 (the United Secularists of America, 1972) from an article that appeared on the Internet Infidels

This form of theological conceptualization expresses the historical enterprise of early primitive, christological religiosity. The earlier christological gatherings were aware of the symbolic and mystic relationship to YHWH, and they understood metaphorically his plans (receiving *gnosis*, God's wisdom) for spiritual healing, deliverance, wholeness, (the divine spiritual revelation of his Son from heaven). This mythical understanding was foundational to the bringing about of "divine action in historical events bearing an eschatological significance"[11] that would encompass all of humanity (the Gentiles).

It was the intent of these progressive Jewish communities in the diaspora to carry the knowledge of YHWH to the Gentile world. Obviously, some theological changes in the older Mosaic tradition were necessary in order to accommodate God's salvation to a Hellenistic culture. As historians would attest:

Stoics, Epicureans, Platonists and others offered new moral and intellectual ways of coping with life and the unpredictable world. Understanding the ultimate Deity and establishing personal ethics were central concerns of all these movements. Wandering philosophers became a kind of popular clergy, frequenting the market place and people's homes. Healing gods, Oriental mysticism, whole paraphernalia of magic and astrology were added to the pot to cope with another dimension to the world's distress: the vast panoply of unseen spirits and demons and forces of fate which were now believed to pervade the very atmosphere men and women moved in, harassing and crippling their lives. The buzzword was personal "salvation." And for the growing number who be-

---

1995-2009 web site http://www.infedels.org/library/historical/ historicus/html (accessed August 18, 2005).

11. Ernest F. Kevan, "The Principles of Interpretation," *Revelation and the Bible*, Ed. Carl F. Henry (Grand Rapids: Baker Book House, 1958), 293. Cf., George Halley Gilbert, *Jesus* (New York: The Macmillan Co., 1912), 23. In the spirit of form critical analysis, Gilbert regards the 'Logia' as the oldest source and indicative of the silence of Jesus' teaching concerning his own death and resurrection. The appearance of these themes is brought about by the freedom the evangelists used in handling their sources. Gilbert offers an extended analysis, as it was proclaimed by the earliest gatherings.

lieved it could not be achieved in the world, it became salvation from the world. Redeeming the individual grew into a Hellenistic industry.[12]

A particularized theological language emerged from out of this cultural dimension of mythological and spiritual diversity. It indicated the relational ties of the 'spirit world' *above* to the 'earthly domain' *below* in the mystic scenarios of salvation. Platonism, a dominate philosophy of the times, provided a systemic and philosophical structure for the religious adaptations among the various faith-groups. Thus, symbolic interpretations of these relational concepts were metaphorical ways of socio-religious understanding by these groups. The cultic rituals[13] were quite compatible conceptually with the early christological cult's basic religiosity (as a revelatory understanding) in the proclamation of the Jesus myth to the Hellenistic world.

Linguistically, this was not a problem; since in the ancient world of mythological religiosity, these kinds of ideas (symbolic, mystic, and metaphorical) could be shared without much difficulty. But what about our own present world of modernity? "Bultmann is right in maintaining that if modern man is to talk of God at all, it must be done in some other language than that of myth."[14] Paul Tillich, in his *Systematic Theology* concludes a similar linguistic posture. Yet, it seems that, at least in

---

12. Doherty, "Main Article -- Part Two" 2. Dillon, *Middle Platonists*, 396 notes that the apostle Paul fitted quite nicely into this diverse, cultural milieu and as a historian states: It was a culture of "a seething mass of sects and salvation cults." Segal, *Paul,* 198 adds an explanation that even with a diversity of salvation cults it is well to recognize the cautious notation that "... proselytization could be considered a capital offense in Roman law."

13. A historical note suggests the explanation of a liturgical form in the use of a 'cross' as imprinted on the forehead with an anointing of oil, which provides a link, the forgiveness of sins with the theological perception of a sacrifice (cf., Ezekiel 9:1f.) with its communal significance, was a salvific event. Nordet and Taylor, *Origins*, 430-435.

14. John Macquarrie, *God Talk: An Examination of the Language and Logic of Theology* (New York: Harper & Row, Publishers, 1967), 36.

the modern world of biblical theology and church dogma, that it is primarily the conservatives, fundamentalists, and evangelicals within the Christian faith that will not even admit to the fact that an essential volume of mythology is contained within the biblical textual tradition.

This is not to say that the concept of resurrection, as it was spiritually (metaphorically) understood (Col. 3:1-4) and the later promise of a belief in immortality, lacked any real religious and moral value when it appeared in the reformulated biblical tradition (Mark's Gospel) in its historicized form. This may be the case where immortality is embraced merely as a way of escape from the contemporary problems of life. That form of escapism (a belief in order to escape from going to a literal hell) is a poor spiritual, social and religious, faith-substitute for moral living according to the psychodynamic strength of human rationality. Traditional Jewry, for the most part at this time, retained a conservative posture and was not religiously open to new faith ventures.

Yet, Hellenistic Jewry in the diaspora, and even various groups of the Essenes mostly in Palestine, give indication that religious change among the Jews was possible. The Qumran community's social and religious circumstances[15] reveal the influence and somewhat adaptation to Judaic-Hellenistic, mystic reformulations. They had not been the only ones that blended philosophical, theological, and mythological concepts with traditional Jewish eschatological, apocalyptic views,[16] and a legacy of

---

15. Even the canonical Gospels maintained the earlier christological moral formulations concerning the love requirement (Lv. 19: 16-18) that was radically different in the Dead Sea Scrolls (1QS 1:9-10; 2:1-9) where the Qumran community was explicitly commanded to 'hate' their enemies, which is also found in the *Book of Jubilees* (31:29). The Jewish christological gatherings extended this love of neighbor to one's enemies beyond the communal relationships. Cf. Albert Nolan, *Jesus before Christianity* (New York: Orbis Books, 2001), Chapter 9, "The 'Kingdom' and Solidarity," 73-88.

16. Israel Knohl, *The Messiah before Jesus: The Suffering Servant of the Dead Sea Scrolls,* Trans. David Maisel (Berkley: University of California Press, 2000), 27 states that, "in an apocalyptic work the

a messianic idea. As Boccaccini notes, it was the current philosophical methodology that was based on an ancient philosophical and historical tradition.

> The multiplicity of philosophical systems is as ancient as philosophy. Since in every moment of the [historical] process the actual present is diverse and polycentric, the ideas that express the aspirations [of the present], and the system that give structure to the cultural articulations [of the present], cannot help being diverse, in conflict with one another or in peaceful coexistence. There is not in any one epoch only one idea, but many ideas and systems.[17]

This assessment reveals the cultural, religious, and philosophical dynamics of the ancient Hellenistic world during which time the Christian faith emerged.

Life, lived under the social and religious dictates of traditional Jewry and Hellenistic mythology, was perceived by the christological Jews, as being 'dead.' Thus, in Ezekielian fashion, new life by the Spirit of God's presence could only come by way of a mystic (spiritual) resurrection. For these christological Jews, they were born (resurrected, transported) out of death, metaphorically, and the new life (spiritual and eternal), which previously existed under the Satanic rule in the present age, was now transformed into the end-time, fellowship's mystical and communal existence.[18] This theological understanding (*gnosis*) was 're-

---

author usually describes the events of his tine as a prophecy of the future. This is why apocalyptic works should be interpreted against the background of the historical events of the time they were composed."

17. Boccaccini, *Rabbinic Judaism,* 24-5. Brackets are his. He quotes Eugenio Garin, "Osservazioni preliminari a una storia della filosofia," *GCFI* 38 (1959): 21-23.

18. This new understanding was based on a revelatory experience born out of sacred scripture (Romans 16:25-27, Colossians 2:2, Ephesians 3:4-5 and cf., Jeremiah 29:18. Cf., 1 John 1:1-4). In the proclamations of Paul, it was the Spirit of God who provided the 'new understanding,' the revelation, its manifestation, and was based on Paul's exegetical study of the sacred text. See Segal's sociological approach and his views concerning Paul's and others' new understanding

vealed' to them by the new spiritual 'call' of the heavenly Son, YHWH's Spiritual presence. This occurred when they entered into new life 'in Christ.' The older traditional faith categories, within the context of the Greco-Roman world, did not bridge this new metaphorical significance. Therefore, this new christological interpretation saw the world as living in 'death,' which had suffered the loss of 'resurrection' life. Significantly in the Gospels when Jesus is raised from the dead, the Greek text has that he was raised (literally) *from out of the dead ones*. This reflects the above mythological and symbolic conceptualities that were based on an ancient religious world-view.

The early christological authors (especially Paul) referred to the Christ as a divine force who operated within the (cosmic) eternal spiritual world 'above.' This understanding was disclosed through the ancient sacred text, the original covenantal scriptures. Thus, their study of the Mosaic tradition enabled them to understand that God's ancient mystery (a revelatory act by divine *anointing*), had now been revealed in the last days by the apostles, Paul and other Hellenistic Jews. The sacred text became a window into the spiritual events '*above*' in the heavenlies as they related soteriologically in Platonic fashion to humanity's earthly existence '*below.*' This was accomplished without any reference to a real flesh-and-blood historical Jesus. Consequently, this is why midrashim became the foundational hermeneutical tool and methodology in the fabrication of the canonical Gospel of Mark.

In contrast, Paul conveys an ethical, metaphysical, religious, philosophic, and theosophical paradigm in the proclamation of his gospel. The import of this symbolic, mystical, and mythological interpretation for the historical development of later orthodox Christianity is clearly stated by Smith:

It is this ethical, metaphysical, religious, philosophic, theosophical Idea that meets us in endlessly diverse forms throughout the earliest Christian literature, whether apostolic or post-apostolic, whether in the New Testament or in the Fathers, whether in Apocalypse or Apocrypha, whether in Evangelist or Epistolist or Apologist: an

---

as a conversion/call experience derived from a change to a different religious community, in *Paul the Convert*.

idea quite as conspicuous by its presence in all this literature as the human personality of the Jesus is conspicuous by its absence. It is this Idea that conquered the circummediterranean world for Christianity.[19]

The redemptive Spirit in the kerygma (understood as the presence of YHWH within the cult as his Spirit sent from the eternal, seventh Heaven) manifested itself within the context of cultural, philosophical, and religious categories. Thus, eternal life, perceived within the Jesus sect's fellowship, was perceived as a mystical life experience with the divine presence (God's *anointing*) and with one another (1st John). This was understood symbolically as the quality of a spiritually resurrected life by the power of the divine presence. This kind of understanding was made possible by the divine *Logos* (YHWH's presence, cf. Rom. 8:11, II Cor. 4:16). Their communal existence was perceived as resurrected life, both in their religious experience[20] (Col. 3:1-4), similarly in the Hellenistic myths,[21] and in the liturgical forms of the early gatherings (baptism and the Eucharist).

The theological tension between the 'already fulfilled present' and the 'not yet consummated future' belongs essentially to and a result of the historicized tradition (the Gospels) in the New Testament of formative Christianity. This theological ten-

---

19. Smith, *Ecce Deus*, 141. This statement -- the necessity of the resurrection to the events of salvation -- is a philosophical one with religious dimensions, and the reader is asked to consider the whole breath of Israel's vast experiences which brought about her deliverance (i.e., perceived as salvation within the context of religious history), historically and at other times as depicted in her religious literature.

20. Hence, the spread of Christianity became a historical reality. Compare the religious ritual controversy that faced the spread of the Christian religion, between the Jews and the Gentiles, on the issue of Jewish law, e.g., circumcision (John 12:2).

21. Harpur notes that "Horus, like Jesus at his resurrection [in the narrative text], rose in a new body of light on the third day." Also relates the symbolic significance of the 'third day' expression in the mythic tales of Greek deities by myth making, religious minded peoples in the ancient Mediterranean world cultures. Harpur, *Pagan Christ*, 106.

sion was a later intrusion, a secondary solution that conceived the Gospels as actual historical accounts of Jesus' life and ministry, as Bultmann had suggested.[22]

The name *Yeshua* (the Spirit of God's anointing power and presence in the gatherings' salvation) became thematically identified with another former spiritual leader like Joshua in the Mosaic tradition. His name was translated as Jesus (Joshua in Greek is *Iēsous* and is *Yeshua* in Aramaic). Thus, the Jewish christological gatherings, like the Joshua of the biblical Israel, would enter the 'promised land' and would lead the new spiritual Israel (i.e., the christological communities of the end-times) into the mystical Promised Land, YHWH's Kingdom. These end-time gatherings were socio-religious brotherhoods that represented a widespread phenomenon in the diaspora, which became a very influential part of the emerging Roman world. At least, the earlier christological communities were transformed and survived. They were more persistent and survived through cultural competitiveness and adaptation.

This interpretation, of cultural mythologies and its use of symbolism, is seen as the basis for their mystic religiosity.[23] For

---

22. Contrary to popular opinion, Bultmann does not deny the spiritual and existential reality of Jesus' resurrection as such, when is he denies the historicity of the resurrection. Many scholars today readily admit that "we cannot be sure of a single biographical detail about Jesus if we follow the ordinary historical principles, so it is not a matter of great importance whether there was such a person or not." McCabe, *How Christianity Grew Out of Paganism – The Real Origin of the Christian Religion* (Girard, Kansas: Little Blue Book No. 1775), 13 as cite in Historicus, *Did Jesus Ever Live? Or Is Christianity Founded Upon a Myth?* 7. I disagree. Historically, it really does make a difference. Delusion is always a detriment to rationality and humanity's well-being.

23. In formative Christianity, the cultic title (i.e., the Christ, along with the forgotten symbolism and its spiritual significance) became a term that was equated with and synonymous for the historicized Jesus figure. This term, the Christ, is used as a last name with current usage (e.g., John Smith, Jesus Christ, etc.). See Vincent Taylor, *Names of Jesus*. Also, William Manson, *Jesus the Messiah* (London: dodder & Stoughton, Ltd., 1943). Note: In I Cor. 15, the title Christ or

example: We are aware that the birth of the Persian sun-god, Mithras, was celebrated on the 25th of December. Furthermore, "Mithraism, a contemporary and keen rival of early Christianity, had a Eucharist-type meal, observed Sunday as its sacred day, had its major festival at Easter (when Mithras' resurrection was celebrated), and featured miracles, twelve disciples, and a virgin birth."[24] These types of mythothemes were foremost in the so-cial-religious consciousness of the various Jewish fellowships of the Jesus cult. This leads us to suggest that the religious stories within the biblical tradition (cf. Luke 17:11-19) are not historical; they are symbolic in essence, mythological with their own histor-ic and spiritual meaning for the christological communities.[25] Even given these cultural and diverse proclivities, some scholars, such as E. P. Sanders maintains that "underneath the diversity of Second Temple Judaism, he recovers the profound unity of 'common Judaism' as the conceptualization of the essence of ..." Judaism's 'covenantal nomism.'"[26]

Nevertheless, many of the metaphorical themes, cultural religiosities, and mythological language comprised a large por-

---

the Christ is represented 13 times throughout; only in verses 31 and 57 does it appear Christ Jesus our Lord and our Lord Jesus Christ, but never only Jesus.

24. Harpur, *Pagan Christ*, 82.

25. Most of the insight, with reference to the biblical text and its explanations in their symbolic form, has been based on the excellent work of William B. Smith. By now we know that several forms of Gnosticism predated the Christian faith throughout the diaspora. Christianity (more correctly, Christianities) was derived from many inde-pendent areas from out of the broad fertile soil of Hellenistic Judaisms. Its original theological base was as diversified as its cultural moorings within a mythological world of the first century.

26. Boccaccini, *Rabbinic Judaism,* 10. For more views, see E. P. Sanders, *Jesus and Judaism* (Philadelphia: Fortress Press, 1985). Boc-caccini also summarizes a few other scholars' views: Lawrence H. Schiffman, *From Text to Tradition* (Hoboken: Ktav, 1998), Shaye J. D. Cohen, *From the Maccabees to The Mishnah* (Philadelphia: Westmin-ster, 1987), Martin S. Jaffee, *Early Judaism* (Upper Saddle River, N.J.: Prentice-Hall, 1997), and Jacob Neusner, *The Four Stages of Rabbinic Judaism* (London: Routledge, 1998). Ibid., 8-14.

tion of the ancient world view as Doherty describes the cultural milieu:

> For the average pagan and Jew, the bulk of the workings of the universe went on in the vast unseen spiritual realm (the "genuine" part of the universe) which began at the lowest level of the "air" and extended ever upward through the various layers of heaven. Here a savior god like Mithras could slay a bull, Attis could be castrated, and Christ could be hung on a tree by "the god of that world," meaning Satan.[27]

Symbolism formed the basis of the cult's theologizing when they expressed, by midrashim, the mystical significance of YHWH's activities in their community of faith, which was perceived as 'resurrected' life in the Kingdom of God.

Paul's concept of 'the Christ,' perceived within the Jewish christological gatherings, as the divine anointing given by YHWH, was also perceived as the living Word (the *Logos*, the divine cosmic force) giving life to the resurrected people of God (1 John 1:1-4). The Jewish fellowship became the christological proclaimers of God's revelatory understanding in history in order to bring about reconciliation to the pagan world of Hellenistic polytheism. The Jewish gatherings, as the anointed, christological body of YHWH's divine Spirit, had accommodated a theological and mythological basis as they proclaimed the 'gospel' (i.e., the Spirit's divine instruction, the *anointing*) within the ancient world of Hellenism. Paul was an apostle, sent by God to proclaim this 'revealed gospel' (hermeneutically derived from the sacred Mosaic tradition) along with its required moral faith-commitment (observance of Torah?).

It had been the content of the apostolic kerygma from which the later Gospel of Mark took form. Jesus (*Yeshua*) was the name for the self-identity of these apocalyptic Jewish communities' new christological end-time and anointed existence. As previously noted, their socio-religious, communal existence was

---

27. Doherty, "Main Article -- Part Two," 7.

understood as the body[28] (a new community, a new Temple) and the presence of YHWH's anointing Spirit. Only later, due to the appearance of the Gospel Jesus in Mark, did the fictional character, Jesus, became interpreted as an actual historical person in the historicized biblical tradition. This literary fabrication became the central, dogmatic content of the formative, Christian proclamation. It also was the Roman church's focus and the theological basis that, due to Imperial authoritative and religious hierarchical structures, required and maintained a literal and historicized interpretation.

This scenario occurred not only in Christianity, but also in Islam. It seems that "religions begin with a group of radical gnostic mystics and end up as authoritarian institutions dominated by Literalists."[29] Thus, the literary transformation of *Yeshua*, in the newly emerging biblical tradition, made it possible for the historicized (fabricated life of) Jesus to become the object of faith (a process already begun in the Gospels) for formative Christianity's faith. This had already occurred by the mid-second century. The decisive fact in the experiences of the early gatherings was the understanding of their resurrection (originally understood symbolically)[30] as a socio-religious empowerment of the community.

It was God's power to gather them into a new end-time community, resurrected (metaphorically) as in Ezekiel (37:1-14).

---

28. Paul's imagery of the 'body of Christ' is reflected in the Gospel narrative in connection with Jesus' resurrection in three days (Mk. 14:58) symbolic of a new community. This mythotheme was also found in the Sea Scrolls where the community of Qumran also saw itself as a new temple, a new house of God where the Spirit of the Lord dwells (Q Flor 1:1-13; 1QS 5:5-7; 8:1-10; and 9:3-6).

29. Freke and Gandy, *Jesus and Lost Goddess,* 205. Remember that all history is revisionist and the winning historiographers enjoy their literary structural foundations.

30. In the following biblical passages symbolism determines the spiritual meaning: Colossians 2:9-13; John 3:3-6, and Romans 5:8-15. Cf., Kahler, *Meaning of History*, and Karl Lowith, *Meaning in History* (Chicago: The University Press, Phoenix books, 1949). See Romans 1:16, 17; 3:26; 4:5 and 5:1.

Hence, the various Jewish renewal groups were depicted as being called by God and apocalyptically were being gathered together as God's faithful servant, the son of man in the last days. These apocalyptic mythothemes and various mythological dichotomies that developed in Paul's christological thought are seen, by some scholars, as originating in his conversion (more particularly, a prophetically 'called' religious) experience. Thus:

> The dualism – of flesh and spirit, life and death, darkness and light, life apart from the law and under it – derives from the perspective of a person who is trying to look at his previous values within Pharisaic Judaism after having adopted a new basis for salvation in Gentile, God-fearing [christological] communities of faith. He is also using older, apocalyptic imagery to express something new.[31]

These original meanings, while mythologically similar to the spiritual and religious values of the mystery religion's historical and mystical significance, became the literal interpretation of Jesus' narrative life and ministry with the appearance of Mark's Gospel. This hermeneutical development continued as a new historicized faith-understanding so that by the Fourth Century, Christianity's political and religious systemic power structure ('the' Church under the Roman Emperor, Constantine) had consolidated its vast theological, hermeneutical, and systemic authority.

The earliest literary tradition of the mythological resurrection, as a mystical event and its symbolic interpretation, had been part and parcel to Paul's kerygmatic proclamation. For the Apostle Paul, there was no historical Jesus, only the divine Cosmic *Christos* event, which reflected the mystical union of God's presence with his resurrected people in a mystic communal fellowship. The distortion of a clear and unambiguous, historical picture by later Christianity is not one of just tampering with the religious hermeneutic and historical fabrication; but, it also became a matter of significant historical incompleteness. The early fragmentary sources "... do not give a complete account of their historical course, and thus, they do not enable us to see the caus-

---

31. Segal, *Paul,* 126. Bracket is mine.

es and effects, the inner connections and developments."[32] These omissions are natural, and the biblical tradition that purports to be of a historical life of Jesus (in the Gospels) reflects a historical process of fabrication and reformulation of its own scriptural foundation. By the second century, many different genre of literature had come into existence[33] to 'fill in the gap' due to a lack of real historical evidence about the fabricated life of the so-called historical Jesus. Archeological finds are bringing to light many texts and artifacts that are indicative of these 'gaps' that provide additional understanding of early Christianity's origin.

The early proclamation of the Jesus myth was an interpretive response to their biblical, hermeneutical methodology by the christological cult as the 'revelatory' experience (i.e., the activity of YHWH's Spirit). It was the symbolic interpretation of the community's life as it related to their religious experiences and the primitive, christological faith-understanding within the community. Hence, it was theological in origin, mythological in imagery, mystic in its experiential content, and was anthropologically dynamic in its social and religious intent. Freyne, commenting on Ogden's use of philosophical categories and their blending into a religious system in his historical research, suggests that "what he

---

32. Bultmann, *Form Criticism*, 64. Any historical analysis of Christian origins should also consider those aspirants to fame and fortune as renewal prophets, as socio-religious and political messianic pretenders, and as militant threats to Roman presence in Palestine. Nolan, *Jesus before Christianity,* 156 lists a few: a prophet called Theudas, a Jewish prophet from Egypt, the Zealots and Sicarii, the Galilean, and many more could be mentioned that appeared during the turbulent days of Roman oppression and economic instability among the Jewish people from 100 BCE to 100 CE.

33. Many non-canonical materials of varying genre have become popular in modern times and produced some interesting scholarship, which includes such literary works about non-canonical Gospels, Acts, Letters, and Apocalypses. These include critical studies of these materials: for a moderate view, see Bart D. Ehrman, *Lost Christianities: The Battle for Scripture and the Faiths We Never Knew* (Oxford: University Press, 2003), and for a more conservative view, see Craig A. Evans, *Fabricating Jesus: How Modern Scholars Distort the Gospels* (Downers Grove, Ill.: IVP Books, 2006).

is calling for is an approach to Christian faith that examines the way in which the Jesus movement has interpreted the central symbols of Judaism and the consequent new way of life that emerged."[34] Freyne concludes: "That is not to suggest that one can uncritically adopt the social world of the text as the real social world of the historical characters that are portrayed within the narratives. To do so would be naïve historicism in the light of our modern historical consciousness and our awareness of the nature of the sources."[35] This hermeneutical fact is significant when the historical sources of the kerygma of the formative Christian church reveal various historical stages of alteration that finally led the later church to accept several[36] 'Gospels' as historical accounts of a historicized Jesus.

This religiously and theologically formulated Jesus myth was later seen through the eyes of a new apocalyptic faith-understanding after 73 C.E., as the later formative church lived out its own theology and religious existence. Most biblical scholars agree that this historical event for Jewish/Christian history, the Jewish war with Rome 66-73 CE, was probably one of the major reasons that the Gospel of Mark came to be written. His literary narrative was not to create a 'historical Jesus;' but, it was to present the early christological communities' world detractors (Rome) with a mythological 'hero' that would anchor the new gatherings' social and religious developments (as Spiritual Israel) within the ancient, Mosaic tradition. This kind of mythological evidence Rome could understand and accept. In the estimation of Rome, this new Gospel could be perceived as an ancient tradition of Jewish religious history.

Myth is understood as a narrative story that explains or describes natural phenomena by the use of images, metaphors,

---

34. Sean Freyne, *Galilee, Jesus and the Gospels: Literary Approaches and Historical Investigations* (Philadelphia: Fortress press, 1988), 14.

35. Ibid., 11.

36. A concise and scholarly consideration is presented in Oscar Cullmann, *The Early Church: Studies in Early Christian History and Theology*, abridged ed., ed. A. J. B. Higgins (Philadelphia: Westminster Press, 1956).

symbols, and other mental constructs to demonstrate the intervention of deities into the affairs of humanity usually as mystic and ritualized communal experiences. The great mythologist Joseph Campbell wrote: "Whenever the poetry of myth is interpreted as biography, history, or science, it is killed."[37] Even some biblical scholars of the historical position recognize the mythological elements that are embedded within the canonical, biblical tradition. As Archibald Robinson acknowledges:

> The idea that a great religion must have a personal founder is a relic of the 'great man' theory of history. [And while maintaining a historic posture of enquiry, he further concludes:] If we had to choose between the mysticist interpretation and the view which tries to explain Christianity by the genius of a personal founder, we should have to pronounce for the myth theory as more scientific.[38]

Thus, these symbolic understandings in Mark's Gospel were instrumental in the formation of the Jewish christological cult's self-identity. The name, *Yeshua*, (Jesus) was conceived theologically as the enfleshed divine presence in the narrative story, and was used to enable the Jewish members to engage in the christological interpretation of the traditional Hebrew Scriptures.

This method of midrashim was used in order to understand the spiritual (metaphorical) meaning of the resurrection as new life (God's power to gather a new faithful people into a viable community with sins forgiven) and this provided additional meanings for other significant texts "according to the scriptures."[39] One can plainly see the conceptual relationships of the

---

37. Freke and Gandy, *Jesus and Lost Goddess,* 189 as quoted from Joseph Campbell, *The Hero with a Thousand Faces* (New York: Paladin, 1949), 249. Freke's and Gandy's major thesis for historical study that is called "the Jesus mysteries" maintains that "Christianity was originally a Jewish adaptation to the Pagan Mysteries." Ibid.

38. Archibald Robinson's comments appear in *the Monthly Record* (London: The South Place Ethical Society, March, 1945) 10 as cited by Historicus in "Did Jesus Ever Live" (1972), 12. Bracket is mine.

39. I Cor. 5:1-4. For other symbolic significances and attitudes concerning the death/life dichotomy as they pertain to the afterlife in Diaspora Judaism, see P. vander Horst, *Ancient Jewish Epitaphs*

Hebrew expression 'the savior of his people' in the idea of Israel's kingship in the Old Testament tradition. This was also the work of divine salvation in and through the new Jewish faith-understanding of the christological communities.

The religiosity of this new universal monotheism as seen in the cult's mystic theology saw its social/religious existence in terms of YHWH's work of grace and faith response. The divine presence within their communal existence was their king (*Yeshua*, a presence that was the basis for spiritual authority and spiritual rule) over the religious cult. This meant: to enter into the community of faith (by the rituals, baptism and Eucharist) was to enter into YHWH's kingdom, a mystic union. The conceptual basis of kingship, within the literary phrases 'kingdom of God' and 'kingdom of Heaven,' appears in the Gospel tradition and still reflects the symbolic and essential aspect of myth and religious salvation within Christ's kingdom, the renewed Spiritual Israel.

The acceptance of the gospel message as the initiation into the christological community, the Jesus cult's adoption of the revelation of God's mystery, and the new faith-understanding that was perceived by the initiates as eternal salvation formed their essential core, a communal hermeneutic. It was 'eternal' because God is the eternal one, the highest God in the eternal heavenlies. This salvation was offered by YHWH; thus, they were born from above. Thereby, the believer received the 'Christ' and entered into the resurrection life as an 'anointed' member of the religious community, and in their physical bodies (cf. II Cor. 4:7-17), a divine work was accomplished by God's grace. The initiates of the christological gatherings, similar to the Greek mystery religions, were taught the inner, symbolic meanings of the cult's mysteries. The symbolic interpretations, the oral sources, and the written tradition were mystically meant for the inner believers not for outsiders, the unbelieving world. The traditionalist Jews

---

(Kampen: Kokpharos, 1991), 114-26. The religious and poetic language of Hellenistic religiosity was highly symbolic, mystic, and metaphorical, and Judaism and Christianity availed themselves to these rich linguistic modes for their spiritual expressions in their literary texts.

who were not observant and the Gentiles were perceived by the christological communal members as being lost.

As a theological necessity, the mythical drama of redemption had been maintained in the earliest christological fellowships; but, it became reformulated in the process of historization. The original spiritual experiences that were based on a new faith-understanding of the resurrection now became a literal historical occurrence in the narrative of the Gospels. This interpretation from the Gospels led to other hermeneutical discrepancies to which a sense of futurity was added. When interpreting the gospels as literal history, the fact that the gospel narrative was written many years after the historicized life of Jesus needs to be a constant reminder within our enquiry in order to analyze the Gospels for historical accuracy. Those so-called future eschatological events referring to the end-times (that in the liturgical life of the community, which had received the Gospel) had already occurred in historic, narrative actuality.

Boccaccini explains that the introduction of the 'end of days' concept by Enochic Judaism suggested to the christological gatherings that it was "the time of final judgment and vindication beyond death and history." And he further states that,

> What in the prophetic tradition was the announcement of some indeterminate future event of God's intervention became the expectation of a final cataclysmic event that will mark the end of God's first creation and the beginning of a second creation – a new world qualitatively different from, and discontinuous with, what was before. Such an idea has become so closely associated to Judaism (and Christianity) that it is difficult for us even to imagine a time when it was not.[40]

---

40. Boccaccini, *Rabbinic Judaism,* 91-2. This historical scenario was adapted by Paul who infused it with a metaphorical and mystic significance to describe the faith experience of a new initiate as having died, been buried, and was raised into a new life, as a new creation. It was an original Pauline myth behind the historical understanding associated with God's judgment. Thus, for Paul, anyone who experienced this rebirth was no longer under the judgment of God.

What the early christological gatherings heard from the Gospel was a socio-religious commentary on their existence in the grips of Roman domination. The narrative text required a symbolic interpretation in order to understand the metaphorical significance of the narrative, its message, and its mystic relationship for the fellowship.

This historical posture had depended on their inward spiritual susceptibility that they possessed (the will to believe). Forrest speaks of this as the paradox of the resurrection.[41] Paradox seems to be the only result when Christian thought presses for a historically real entity, namely, Jesus. This paradox simply disappears when the rational logic of reality and the symbolic nature of mythical religiosity are used to describe the historic literary event as a socio-religious resurrection experience depicting religious life within the symbolic context of communal life. This is how the resurrection concept was metaphorically understood by the early christological gatherings and proclaimed by their missionary, the Apostle Paul to the Gentiles. But, historically, that all changed when historization provided a hermeneutical posture and theological 'literalism' to postulate the divine son of God, Jesus, as a historical person.

The term *Yeshua* (Joshua, Jesus), as applied to YHWH, the Lord of Heaven, was the responsive and mystic understanding of the formative period of an expanded covenantal literature.[42] The earlier religious categories of Middle Platonism had aided this development of theological formations in the christological gatherings by later conservative generations of literalists. By now, it is plain to see that mysticism had a special appeal to the Jewish consciousness by the Hellenistic members of the christological cult. Just as Moses gave the people the land promised by the LORD for their worship of YHWH, the new land (i.e.,

---

41. Cf., Forrest, *Christ of History and Experience,* 137-168 where he offers an interesting appraisal of the early church's resurrection experience *with* their 'risen' Lord. The entire Kerr Lectures for 1897, contained in this volume, are relevant to the whole theme of the Christians' experience *with* the resurrected Christ of faith.

42. Dodd, *Parables of the Kingdom,* 167-8. Also, cf. Dodd, *The Authority of the Bible,* 61-2.

the new faith, monotheistic universalism of Christ's Kingdom) would in the end-times be given by Joshua (i.e., Jesus, the Savior) for the salvation of the New Israel (cf., Matt. 1:21). *Yeshua* is understood by most to mean, as a religious concept, Jah-helps (YHWH's deliverance). Similar linguistic forms also had a religious significance meaning deliverance or healing and carried with them the understanding of a divine Savior.

The name, *Yeshua*, Jesus, would have easily been identified,[43] religiously, with reference to spiritual healing by them (the Hellenistic Jews) as well as by the general Greco-Roman mind. The name implying healing was closely related, at least on a conceptual basis, in form and sound with the divine name, *IAO* in Greek (cf. Rev. 1:8). This literary form of the name was found in early gnostic circles. Similarly, the early Christian prayers were, in a mystic experiential sense, to be in Jesus' name, *Iēsous*. The cult of the Jesus myth found spiritual healing within the communal context of YHWH's fellowship (cf. "where two or three are gathered in my name, there am I in their midst" Matt. 18:20). It would seem quite natural for the formative Christian churches therefore to consider the name, Jesus, as a mythological designation of deity along the lines of similar usage of names in the Hellenistic theosophical circles.

It is necessary to keep in mind a hermeneutical posture that recognizes the religious language that is being used and its phenomenological connection to the faith-communities that understood their own religious convictions. Given that premise, it is also necessary for a historical analysis to provide a scientific focus in an interpretation of the canonical texts. Macquarrie is of the opinion that,

One has to first establish, by textual criticism, what the actual text is. Then one can bring the whole battery of philological science to bear upon it. Questions of grammar, of accidence and syntax, of usage and idiom, of the meanings of words and of variations of meaning in the course of time or from one area to another – these matters all call for close consideration. Philological questions merge into historical ones, for the language and its usages has to be

---

43. Wright, *God Who Acts*, 110ff.

understood in the context of the culture where the language was used and where the allusions of the text had their home. Most of these questions can be settled in a more or less scientific way, so there are provided certain objective criteria that rule out wildly subjective interpretations.[44]

The historical categories that were placed into some texts' narrative style did not always summit to the above criteria for their mythic formulations.

The Book of Acts is a case in point. The speeches in Acts do not reflect historical actualities; they summarize the primitive kerygma[45] and omit the 'Son of Man' designation as a cultic title for Jesus. Paul also does not use this phrase with reference to his cosmic Christ figure, the heavenly Son[46] and certainly has no claim to a historical Jesus in reference to it. It does appear in the later Gospel tradition that reflects the cult's mystic integrity with the other divine cultic titles. We see that Luke retains this designation in his Gospel, but shows a considerable decrease in its use in Acts (1:9-11; 17:31). As the early church began to expand and take on its missionary concerns, the eschatological term 'Son of

---

44. Macquarrie, *God-Talk,* 152.

45. The kerygma is to be found in Acts 2:22ff; 3:13ff; and 13:23ff. Also, 5:30ff. For similar references, see Matt. 28:18-20, and for the tradition which records the transformation of Jesus, also cf. 8:38 and 9:1-2.

46. Earl Doherty has pointed out the degree to which biblical scholars (literalists) have tried to connect a historical Jesus to the very noticeable Platonic schema of theological and mythological categories found in the Book of Hebrews. In his review of Mack's *Who Wrote the New Testament,* Doherty states that "the writer presents the Son as speaking in scripture, in the present ("he says"). ... Again, as in 1:6, we have a timeless or ever-present mythological scene embodied in scripture. (To style these two present tense verbs as a use of the 'historic present' would be somewhat begging the question, especially considering that neither context is dealing with history but rather with heavenly or spiritual dialogues.)" E. Doherty, Book Review of Burton L. Mack, *Who Wrote the New Testament: Making of the Christian Myth in THE JESUS PUZZLE: Was There No Historical Jesus?* 22, at http://www.jesuspuzzle.com/html (accessed July 07, 2006).

Man,' that was an original cultic title based on apocalyptic themes and used by the Essenes as well, was replaced by other titles.

Even though this occurred, the Son of Man designation was still proclaimed in its historicized form in the Gospels. By then, it had lost its original socio-religious sense as one who was a faithful servant of the Lord (Ezekiel 37:1-14). It no longer designated the spiritual anointed servant of YHWH, the eschatological community, a people of God's calling and anointing with his Spirit. The Son of Man now became linked to a historicized Jesus by way of Mark's Gospel; but, this application to the literary Jesus met with some religious opposition from the Essene-like communities. Boccaccini notes: "The presence of an ancient, first-century CE interpolation in *Similitudes*, claiming that Enoch is the Son of Man (1 Enoch 71:14), shows that mainstream Essenism reacted vigorously against the Christian identification of Jesus as the Son of Man."[47] The Essene communities remained active through the Jewish War (66-73 CE) up until the final encounter with Rome in the Bar-kokhba revolt (135 CE).

Although the summaries of the early Christian kerygma indicate the noticeable absence of 'Son of Man' as a title for the historicized Jesus, it does not mean that this was not a consideration as such by the early Aramaic, speaking christological communities in Palestine. This term, which was destined to take on a significant eschatological meaning, became synonymous for the Jewish 'Messiah.'[48] The terms, Son of Man and Messiah as theo-

---

47. Gabriele Boccaccini, *Beyond the Essene Hypothesis* (Grand Rapids, Mich.: Wm. B. Eerdmans Pub., Co., 1998), 189. He points out that "Neither the destruction of the Qumran community in 68 CE nor the growth of Christianity as an autonomous movement meant the sudden death of Essenism." Ibid. On the parallel origins of Christianity and Rabbinic Judaism, see H. Shanks, ed., *Christianity and Rabbinic Judaism: A Parallel History of Their Origins and Early Development* (Washington, D.C.: Biblical Archaeology Society, 1992).

48. Horsley, *Bandits*, 90 mentions that "there was no uniform expectation of 'the Messiah' until well after the destruction of Jerusalem in 70 CE, when it became standardized as a result of scholarly rabbinic reflection." Interestingly, J. Collins states that in "the *Simili-*

logical aspects of Jewish religiosity, both reflect the early Jewish understanding of YHWH's anointing of the cultic activities via his Spirit. The concept of Messianism was late to develop, slow in its geopolitical locations, and diverse in its religious and political acceptance without maintaining a unified structure. Thus, several biblical scholars (Martin Hengel, S.G.F. Brandon, Morton Smith, and Richard Horsley, just to mention a few) in their historical analysis of Christian origins have noted several individuals as likely candidates for messianic consideration.

Some of these characters are: Theudas the Judean, Jesus, son of Hananiah, Judas the Galilean, Judas, son of Hezekiah, the Samaritan prophet, Hanina ben Dosa, John of Gischala, the returned Egyptian prophet, as well as several *sicarii* and zealot sympathizers and followers. Strangely though, not even Josephus had mentioned the biblical Jesus as a historical person (barring the late Christian interpolations) that could be numbered among these motley characters just mentioned. Josephus had mentioned in his multi-volume, historical works some twenty-two various persons named Jesus; but, not one of those was identified as the biblical, historical Jesus.

The absence of a single system of theological thought, in the early community of the christological gathering, is not a negative idea.[49] It reinforces the statement that Christianity's earliest development was a dynamic and developing spiritual response to the historic Jesus myth (i.e., it was an interactive, communal and mythothematic response). Macquarrie has clarified this when he states that a mythothematic category such as: "A myth properly

---

tudes *'that Son of Man'* is identified as Enoch, the seer who is given knowledge of what is above the heaven, what is and is to come in the course of his visions." John J. Collins, *Between Athens and Jerusalem: Jewish Identity in the Hellenistic Diaspora,* second ed. (Livonia, Mich.: Dove Booksellers, 2000), 226. Cf., what is stated similarly in the Gospels of Jesus as the Son of Man: He was, he is, and he is to come.

49. A survey which presents historical attempts to explain the resurrection of Jesus on the basis of imported conceptions -- indeed the whole New Testament Christology -- can be found in Orr, *Resurrection of Jesus,* 235-261.

so-called has its social or communal dimension. It serves not only as a cohesive force in the community, perhaps by telling the story of its origin such as will give its standing and significance, but also as a kind of basic ideology in relation to which the various events that happen in the community's history can be referred and explained."[50] The early Jewish gatherings throughout the diaspora and in the Galilee understood the early symbolism of resurrection as descriptive of their spiritual and mystic existence in the christological faith-fellowships.[51]

Hence, they perceived, as a revelatory experience, their lives as being quickened by God's Spirit (to be made alive, raised up, by the power of YHWH) to a new life by the divine anointing of the Lord. The earliest apologists referred to themselves, philosophically, as Christians primarily because they believed that they had an 'anointing' from the Lord. The salvation experiences (a divine union with God, mystic transformations, and conversions) were based philosophically, similar to the Greek mysteries on a system of spiritual rationality (wisdom, spirit, gnosis, and the *Logos*). The concept of the *Logos* during Hellenistic times was much broader in its philosophical and religious adaptations. With regard to mysteries and mythology in general, the *Logos* concept's historical development was on three levels: that of myth, nature allegory, and its fullest expression in Platonism as metaphysics. Burkert summarily measures out that particularized historical development:

---

50. Macquarrie, *God-Talk,* 178.

51. Within the religious context of the Hellenistic world, there was no necessity to formulate a concept having a singular nuance. Resurrection did not have to maintain one standard interpretation. Especially among the Greeks, it would have been a repugnant idea if it was restricted to life in the flesh after death. There was no real confinement of this concept in its application to the gods to be of a similar nature as found in the Gospels to Jesus' resurrection. In fact the earliest testimony of this religious concept by the diaspora Jews (and Paul as a representative of this kind of salvific thinking) depicts Jesus as 'raised in the spirit,' exalted to heaven immediately after death on the cross, a cosmic and mythological event. Cf., Philippians 2:9, 1 Peter 3:18, and Hebrews 10:12.

These levels emerged in a historical sequence, without the later stages destroying the earlier ones; they may be seen as an evolution from the Homeric through the Pre-Socratic to the Platonic stage. If this sequence is seen as one of increasing intellectual elaboration [which is only one way based on non-religious adaptation], the contact with the practice of mysteries declines simultaneously, until in later Platonism one could find just *logos* without any corresponding rituals [which only seems plausible since the mysteries maintained a strict silence to mystic rituals and cultic practices].[52]

The prologue to the fourth Gospel clearly represents a philosophical base that found a ready body of hermeneutical posturing by Gnostics, Stoics, Platonists, dualist ideas, and early christological faith-communities that recognized the *Logos* concept in a religious setting. The divine *Logos* (like Spirit and Wisdom, as sacred intermediaries), once anchored into the religious community's theology, has remained into modern times. God had sent his Spirit, his divine presence, his heavenly Son. Jesus like the Spirit was a divine intercessor. God in the eternal heavens above could thusly be present among his people in a mystical sense. Paul acknowledged this spiritual unity as the *Logos* of God being embodied in Christ Jesus, the communal, corporate gathering. Like divine Wisdom and the *Logos*, Jesus was the spiritual intermediator providing salvation to the new faith-community.

Under Hellenistic influences, this theologically based communal scenario was also part of the Essenes' social understanding, although it was not uniformly maintained. Boccaccini's historical analysis indicated that "while some joined the community of the teacher of righteousness, the majority of the Essenes did not accept the call, and even fewer followed the sectarians when they decided to move in a voluntary exile to the desert and

---

52. Burkert, *Ancient Mystery Cults,* 72-3. Brackets are mine. Burkert frequently seems to down play any connection between Christianity's origin and development with the Hellenistic mystery religions even when the historical evidence, considering all probabilities, could be interpreted either way.

cut off all relations with the religious and political institutions of Israel."[53] This same type of theological interpretation, among the earliest Jewish christological members concerning their socio-religious understanding, continued to expand when formative Christianity, with the appearance of Mark's Gospel, had established Jesus' so-called historical existence. Most modern biblical scholars today are beginning to identify the 'Jewishness' not only of Jesus in the Gospels, but also the idiomatic and linguistic influence of the Second Temple period of Middle Judaism on the canonical texts of the New Testament. Segal's comment is well attested by historical evidence that "Jewish Christianity probably continued to be the dominant form of Christianity for at least two generations and maybe for several generations after Paul."[54]

The original symbolic significance, understood by the use of the divine personal name (*Yeshua*) was given a historic, literary personality and was designated as the God-Savior (the Jesus myth in the kerygma). It continued to be reformulated by formative Christianity through the prism (midrashim) of the original covenantal literary tradition. It is on this basis that a theological and a historic significance to the divine name was used and developed by later generations within formative Christianity. With the demise of the Hellenistic, mythological religious influences (i.e., the fading power of polytheism) and the use of the cult's commonly accepted divine persona in the Greco-Roman world, the so-called historical Jesus quite naturally filled the religious gap, conceptually, in a world whose religious syncretism was well underway. It was the historical direction of spirituality and mythology that was seemingly being directed intentionally, conceptually, and methodologically[55] toward a monotheistic faith.

---

53. Boccaccini, *Essene Hypothesis,* 187.

54. Segal, *Paul,* 275.

55. Philo of Alexandria is a good example of fusing philosophy with symbolic vitality into a synthesis that incorporated the current religious mythology with an acceptance of and an appreciation for the larger world of humanity. Cf., P. Borgen, "Philo of Alexandria," in *Jewish Writings of the Second Temple Period,* Ed., M. E. Stone (Philadelphia: Fortress Press, 1984), and his *Early Christianity and Hellenistic Judaism* (Edinburgh: Clark & Clark, 1996).

As indicated earlier, both the Greek and the Hebrew linguistic terms, used for a name and its conceptual significance, were perfectly adapted to serve as the divine persona and indicative of the divine presence for the cult's deity (YHWH as the healing, saving deity). Literary personification was used extensively in the Wisdom literature of this period (cf., for example Matthew's Gospel descriptions of Jesus' life, as the embodiment of God's divine Wisdom, personified). It is a central theme, the divine mystical and heavenly Christ as Savior that runs throughout the expanded covenantal corpora as evidence[56] for the development of a new universal monotheistic religion.

Hence, much of Jewish Wisdom literature and knowledge was accumulated during this time and enjoyed a sense of cultural authority outside the control of the priesthood as 'Sapiential Judaism.' Boccaccini notes that,

> The debt of wisdom literature to foreign cultures and secular education is massive, and is marked by an impressive series of literary and conceptual borrowings from foreign wisdom (Egyptian, Mesopotamian, and later, Greek). Sapiential Judaism passes over any particularity of Jewish history and tradition and views human beings simply as creatures of one God regardless of their ethnic origin, cultural identity, or cultic affiliation.[57]

It is not difficult to understand how this philosophical dimension of wisdom became incorporated into the several diaspora gatherings' mental frame of religious reference. From earliest primitive Christianity, the resurrection of a mythical Jesus (and for some, wisdom personified), symbolically understood and proclaimed in the kerygma, had a significantly real historic and moral meaning for their social, religious, and communal existence.

Yet, modern Christianity accepts the resurrection concept as a pure fact of history and as the under girding basis for faith

---

56. Vincent, *History of Textual Criticism* (1899) provides relevant information.

57. Boccaccini, *Rabbinic Judaism,* 104. Also see Salo Wittmayer Baron, *A Social and Religious History of the Jews*, 2nd ed., 18 vols. (New York: Columbia University Press, 1952-1993).

and "... not a mythical idea arising out of the creative imagination of believers,"[58] which it originally had been. Well, so much for rationality within the ranks of biblical scholarship, who so quickly jettison reason along with the scientific world-view that is maintained by secular modernity.

58. Braaten, *History & Hermeneutics*, 78. Cf., Thomas William Doane, *Bible Myths and Their Parallels in Other Religions* (Kila, MT: Kessinger Publishing, 1997).

8

*The traditional history of Christianity cannot convincingly
explain why the Jesus story is so similar
to ancient Pagan myths.
Freke and Gandy*

The meaning of Spirit, which in the Jesus cult was an essential aspect of the resurrection understanding, was attached to the meaning of 'being anointed' by God's Spirit giving new life and spiritual instruction. It was attested by the symbolism of the spiritual reality of their socio-religious, physical existence, as a new end-time community. This understanding also preserves the religious integrity of the biblical tradition and is submitted for the reader's understanding for a symbolic interpretation. When reference is made to the human spirit, the spirit of the age, the Spirit of God, or the Holy Spirit; there exist a conceptual unity of meaning.[1] Its several aspects may be elaborated to show a particular historic significance; but, if that unity of meaning is kept basically in mind, we will be able to comprehend the historical dimensions and the development of its primary usage (both through myth and its symbolism) for the religious minds of the

---

1. Karl Barth, *Church Dogmatics*, 4 Vols., trans. G. W. Bromiley and others (Edinburgh: T. & T. Clark, 1957). A judicial appraisal concerning Barth's total spectrum is in Herbert Hartwell's *The Theology of Karl Barth: An Introduction* (Philadelphia: Westminster Press, 1964). Note chapter II, and especially sec. 6, "The Word of God," 59-67. In Hartwell's appraisal, the last analysis for "the Word of God with Barth, is the living Lord Jesus Christ Himself," he is "speaking to man ... through the witness" of the "Holy Scripture and the church's proclamation ..." by "the revealed Word of God." Ibid., 60 and 63. This is a non-mystic way of a modern scholar who puts forth a theological posture that is dissimilar to the apostle Paul's mystical understanding of a 'revelatory' experience of God's word from the sacred texts.

first century, which is also depicted in the religiosity and development of western civilization. Hanson notes: that the "Myth has provided a means of envisioning the restoration on a plane insulated against the frustrations of a historical order, which had demonstrated itself to the visionaries to be completely hostile." And further adds, thus "... the historical context heralds the death of prophecy and the birth of apocalyptic eschatology."[2]

With this insight, the meaning of '*spirit*' refers to the inner psychodynamic '*understanding*,' which comes to us (within our minds) as thought perceptions. These perceptions with regard to religiosity are the basic 'understandings,' the spiritual insights that we derive out of the religious symbols, metaphors, and mythological functions. These provide us with the religious meanings for our socio-historical existence. To receive the spirit is to receive ('to become aware of') a new internalized perception and understanding, which we did not have previously. In this hermeneutical context, spirit is a 'revelatory' experience that involves an inner religious understanding of who we are and our relationship to the world around us. Thus, in the canonical Gospel of John where we have to be born from 'above' (to be born 'again') is to receive the spirit by entering into a new faith-understanding of our personal existence.

Part of this methodological process for this study is to elucidate an unknown (the biblical textual narrative) with another unknown (the geopolitical social situation) by historical analysis. Holmberg suggests: "The only legitimate procedure is to reverse this procedure and work inductively, i.e., to start from sociologically relevant data that exists independent of the theological text, and investigate whether they 'fit' structures in the symbolic world."[3] In this way we see that the metaphorical relationship of the spirit descending from 'above' for one to receive it becomes an intellectualized systemic category, and as myth this concept was internalized philosophically. Any religious metaphor that

---

2. Paul D. Hanson, *The Dawn of Apocalyptic: The Historical and Sociological Roots of Jewish Apocalyptic Eschatology,* Revised Edition (Philadelphia: Fortress Press, 1979), 161.

3. Bengt Holmberg, *Sociology and the New Testament: An Appraisal* (Minneapolis: Fortress Press, 1990), 128.

incorporates an ascent, gnostic, Platonic, or theological posture, starts with our minds (*nous*), then upward into the heavens (*hoi houronoi*), whether three, five, or seven) until we reach the highest heaven, that of 'Pure Spirit,' the domain of the highest God (eternality), the highest 'moral essence' or virtue. All this was done in Platonic fashion according to the interplay of cultural, religious, and philosophical categories within the Hellenistic world.

The biblical proclamation that had emerged from the symbolic interpretation of those experiences (first as initiates, then sustained by the communal rituals and their social and religious involvement within the fellowship) arose from the new faith-understanding of the resurrection as symbolically perceived. Thereby, a fresh mentational way was found for comprehending the mythical symbolism of the cross that had been a curse according to Jewish theological opinion.[4] This interpretation was not only significant for a historicized understanding of Jesus' narrative life in the Gospels for later formative Christianity; but, it was also necessary for this new faith-understanding of the resurrection concept (a reflection of their new existence), which was perceived only as a historic event (the formation of the end-time, eschatological community). Early on, the '*Christos* faith-community' in Rome was perceived, by those outside the community, as a separate group and was victimized along with the Jews by the political and military measures taken by the Roman Senate.[5]

---

4. See Gal. 3:13; also cf. Luke 24:26f. An understanding of symbolism allowed the early believers to acknowledge an international mythology that existed in the world of diverse religiosity in the first century. For instance, in chapter twelve of Revelation one finds a rich mixture of several myths used to tell the story. These come from Greek myth, Babylonian creation myth, and are fused with features from Persian and Egyptian elements, so that biblical scholars recognize that the literary style of the story represents myth and not historical reality.

5. Karl P. Donfried and Peter Richardson, Eds., *Judaism and Christianity in First-Century Rome* (Grand Rapids, Mich.: William. B. Eerdmans Pub., Co., 1998), 117. They point out that "the term, 'Christians' (*Christianoi*; Lat. *Chrestiani* or *Christiani*) only became tangible

In Paul's correspondence (and other apostles' epistles) the cosmic, salvific event takes place either in a primordial past or before the creation of the world, but always as a spiritual/cosmic event; and for Paul, it occurs as a salvific event in the heavens above. Then immediately after the cross event, Christ ascends to the right hand of God. Paul did not perceive this comic event as a historical actuality (as depicted later in the Gospels); but as a 'revelatory' experience (as a 'mystery' that was made known and made understandable). It was hermeneutically based on his reading of the sacred, original covenantal tradition. Primitive Christianity, also used these Old Testament scriptures (formulated by midrashim) and based on their eschatological interpretations, adopted, synthesized, and maintained the new forms of Hellenistic religiosity as part of their new found communal identification. How one writes history as an interactive hermeneutic is always a revision. Aristotle and Dio Chrysostom in the ancient world recognized that,

> Authors carefully selected and crafted their material in order to convey a coherent message. The interplay between fidelity to tradition and the freedom to shape or even create new material varied among authors. Aristotle, for example, took the general truths conveyed by dramatists more seriously than the particular facts recounted by historians and even counseled authors to shape a cogent plot outline before inserting the names of particular characters.[6]

Similar literary dynamics were most probably used in the creation and formulation of the canonical Gospels. I would agree with Schnackenburg, who says that the evangelist of Johns' Gospel created characters and historic scenes to convey a symbolic

---

in documents after the year 70 (Acts 11:26; Tacitus, *Ann.* 15.44; Suetonius, *Nero* 16.2)," Ibid.

6. Craig R. Koester, *Symbolism in the Fourth Gospel: Meaning, Mystery, Community* (Minneapolis: Fortress Press, 1995), 38. Even the *United States Congressional Record* employs this literary device: many Congressional speeches that appear in this governmental journal were worked up sometimes by committee and the final form is printed in the journal as though it was given on the floor of Congress.

meaning.[7] The new faith-based hermeneutical standards, especially in Mark's Gospel provided a new socio-religious expression of their 'resurrected' existence as an end-time community of 'the way.'[8] *Yeshua*, as the cult's self-identity (i.e., purely as a mental construct, an understanding of YHWH's divine presence), had appeared in the activity of the cult's religious instruction, as their anointing (cf., baptism and the Eucharist).

The cultic presence, of YHWH's Spirit as the divine Wisdom of God, was personified as Jesus by most of the christological gatherings. It helps to understand the various cults' religious beginnings that were based upon a mythological foundation. In historical analysis of early Christianity a certain amount of speculation must naturally occur wherever empirical data is sketchy. Ramachandran, with great sagacity, notes that,

> Every virgin area of scientific inquiry must first be explored in this way. It is a fundamental element of the scientific process that when data are scarce or sketchy and existing theories are anemic, scientist must brainstorm. We need to roll out our best hypotheses, hunches, and hare-brained, half-baked intuitions, and then rack our brains for ways to test them. You see this all the time in the history of science.[9]

This same methodological process is also applicable to good historical analysis of the biblical text and the religious and theological conceptions that appear therein. Given the cultural and contextual constraints, we can obtain a better appreciation of the hermeneutical data involved. It is with this understanding that the meaning for 'spirit,' that was the essential formulation of and basis for the early theology of the Jesus cult with regard to an 'understanding' of resurrection (as their gathering into communal

---

7. Rudolf Schnackenburg, *The Gospel According to St. John* (New York: Herder/Seabury/Crossroads, 1968-82), 244.

8. Reddish, *Apocalyptic Literature*, 135. A core teaching of this new fellowship had some connection with an earlier tradition: cf., 2 Baruch 75:6-77:9 that says, "… go now and spend these days teaching the people as best you can, so that they may understand what will lead to death and what to life in the last times."

9. Ramachandran, *Brain*, xvii.

life and fellowship with God), can be understood. The gathering of the faithful, as a body of God's Son, represented God's glory, the *Kavod*, since it reflected the divine *presence* and the transformative 'power' of the *Logos*, their new creation. Hence: Jesus was the healing empowerment sent from God among them, for he (as God's Son, as God's Spirit) brought salvation (healing, deliverance, emotional and mental well-being, and wholeness).[10] The cult's understanding of spirit as an anointing empowerment continued throughout the biblical tradition in primitive Christianity; but, the moral and intrapersonal significance (the symbolic and metaphorical understanding) became pushed aside by the manifest theological concern for the afterlife.

The dialectical tendencies and developments in the conceptualization of early religious thought are reflected in the early gatherings' theology[11] as essentially a vital, mythical *christology*. There was no pretense at this time, historically, that suggests that *christology* refers in any way to a messianic consideration.[12] A

---

10. The symbolic application of 'spirit' was only one aspect of its significance. Other ways of its use as a duality (spirit - flesh) is seen in its corresponding gnostic type of dualism of darkness – light in which light not only empowers, but also illuminates (makes one wise), such as in John 1:9. Koester, *Symbolism*, 131 where he notes that enlightenment comes with understanding (2 Bar. 38.1; Sir. 45:17; 1QS iv 2; 1QH iv 5-6) and the Greeks spoke (in Platonic philosophy) of a "process of illumination corresponding to the movement from darkness to 'the true light.'" Cf., Paul's idea that to receive God's Spirit is to receive God's wisdom (1 Cor. 1:18 – 2:16) as a moral defense and a transformed life based on faith in his gospel of the cross.

11. See Grant, *The Earliest Gospel*, where he provides a readable and invaluable aid to the studies of the early evangelic tradition, from its point of crystallization in literary form. Note especially, in reference to early theological concepts of the church's faith, Chap. VII, "The Theology of Mark," 148-174. Further development in historical Jesus studies, by some, suggests that the early Gospel narratives were compositions that originally were intended as largely allegorical for spiritual instruction and were mainly symbolic of the christological, faith communities that produced them.

12. In modern orthodox Christianity there is too much non-historical bias such as Jesus as 'the Messiah,' which from a historical

theological 'Christology' (capitalized) developed later by primitive Christianity when the Gospel Jesus had appeared in narrative form and was literarily represented as the 'Messiah.' This might have been a polemical device to separate the early Jewish christological members who were progressives with some possible gnostic feelings, from the 'Gentile' members of primitive Christianity who constituted the dominant conservative element and came to have leadership roles and authority in the emerging primitive church.

The theological formulations were also eschatological in character and were assimilated into the religiosity of formative Christianity together with an apocalyptic significance. Hanson suggests that it was Israel's prophets that were responsible for historicizing Judaism:

> [They were responsible] for integrating the cosmic vision into history, for causing myth to retreat before a more "secularized," "humanistic' worldview. ... The prophets were the ones who forged the visionary and realistic aspects of the religious experience into one tension-filled whole, allowing Yahwism to develop into an ethical religion in many ways unique in the ancient world. In this process they forced the translation of the pure cosmic vision into the terms of plain history; the result was prophetic eschatology.[13]

---

analysis just does not wash. This is formative Christianity's emphasis based on the canonical Gospels. The Messiah as a politico-religious figure is a later adaptation in biblical history. Jacob Neusner, William S. Green, and Ernest Frerichs, Eds., *Judaisms and Their Messiahs at the Turn of the Christian Era* (Cambridge: Cambridge University Press, 1987), 2 states that "the [Hebrew] noun *mashiah* ('anointed' or 'anointed one') occurs 38 times in the Hebrew Bible, where it applies twice to the patriarchs, six times to the high priest, once to Cyrus, and 29 times to the Israelite king. In these contexts the term denotes one invested, usually by God, with power and leadership, but never an eschatological figure. In citing Joachim Becker, they mention that "in fact, there was not even such a thing as a messianic expectation until the last two centuries B.C. Ibid., 8.

13. Hanson, *Apocalyptic,* 17. Note that this basic 'moralistic' aspect of eschatology was part and parcel to Paul's kerygmatic focus both in his gospel and his pastoral communications to the christologi-

The earlier kerygma (the apostolic preaching) was proclaimed at first, historically within the original christological gatherings, secretively (a first level mystery?), and then, later in missionary activities expanded to the Gentile world, of which Paul is our best example. The new faith-understanding was a reaffirmation of YHWH's 'presence' (as the Christ of God), which was symbolic and conceptually based in the social and religious activities of the community. This mystic relationship (the fellowship's encounter with the divine presence) was interpreted as a spiritual encounter, a mystical union with their deity. It was an eschatological encounter similar to the Greek mystery religions.

This mystical and revelatory dynamic was lost when it became historicized with the objectification of the divinity, of Jesus into a historical person, the object of faith for formative Christianity. The earlier interpretation by Paul of this faith-event was purely a revelatory experience, a hermeneutic of spirit, God's heavenly Son as the Christ. Wood's interpretation of Buber's ontological views relates to this understanding of spirit for the purpose and meaning of revelation.

> The act of revelation is complete in this way by being sent into the world as the source of new meaning in a set of new ways to give a sense of Presence to the whole of man's life. Original faith (Hebrew *emunah*), which moves from the forms to the Presence, is gradually forgotten in favor of the acceptance of a faith object: faith is transformed into belief (Greek *pistis*) in a dogma. Greek visual thinking supersedes Hebrew aural thinking, and for Buber the dogmas that result are "the most exalted form of invulnerability against revelation."[14]

---

cal gatherings. A transformed life was basic to several philosophical sects whose ideas were well known for over six or seven hundred years throughout the Hellenistic world. John E. Stambaugh and Davis L. Balch, *The New Testament in Its Social Environment,* Wayne A. Meeks, Gen. Ed. (Philadelphia: Westminster Press, 1986), 45 references the Orphic preachers, Pythagorean communities, and the Cynics, Stoics, and Epicureans as examples. Bracket is mine.

14. Wood, on *Buber's Ontology,* 107. Embedded within the context of the original covenantal scriptures, the prophets' voice was "thus

The cult of the Jesus myth was the authentication of YHWH's presence by the very fact of the cult's socio-religious existence. This mystic and revelatory understanding was that YHWH's Spirit was actively and redemptively, commissioning the members of the christological gathering for the Lord's service (note: where Jesus would be with his followers even unto the ends of the age, Matt. 28: 16-20 and its corollary, the Son of Man concept of Ezekiel 37:1-14). Kee and Young point this out when they state the historicized view of traditional Christianity. "The work of revealing God that [the literary] Jesus had begun was now being carried on by the illuminating work of the Spirit which the Risen Lord [as the later community of formative Christianity called him] had sent in their midst."[15] This was the religious culmination (symbolically and metaphorically) of their eschatological interpretation of the kerygma; but now, it was viewed literally as a historical occurrence.

The historical reality that allowed this change in religious perception of Second Temple Judaism was a reactive posture by many in Israel and in the diaspora. It was expressed as distrust in the Temple priesthood's improper Hasmonean performance of

---

says the LORD" and was understood as 'God's word' spoken in and through the holy text. In Hebrews and literary text excluding the Gospels, everything that the Son said emerged out of the scriptural context as midrashim and continued the tradition of "thus says the Lord" for early Christianity. Nothing is indicative of real history since a mythological vantage point employs abstractions, visions, religious understandings, psychological elements, and mystical revelations. Sayings and activities are validated through the narrative context of scripture.

15. H. C. Kee and F. W. Young, *Understanding the New Testament*, (Englewood Cliffs, New Jersey: Prentice Hall, Inc., 1957), 56. Brackets are mine. The earliest Gospels seemed to serve several purposes. Besides being polemical in essence, reflective of the communal witness to the Hellenistic world, the Gospels finally functioned from a sociological perspective as the 'foundation document' which served the needs of a developing hierarchal Church. Much of the transformation of renewed Jewish religiosity in the diaspora of the Hellenistic period began much earlier in the dynamic historical events of the first century BCE.

their priestly offices. They were considered to have lacked the traditional and authoritative requirements as ordained in the Levitical law by God. One can by historical analysis detect that the psalmists were attempting to provide an alternative social conception for Israel in the form of a new socio-religious identity (the actual and the ideal) because of this conceptual distrust. To think of Israel in a new way, one had to image (a new) Jerusalem,[16] one that was independent of the Second Temple model.

In Christian mythological formulations, similar to other ancient religiosities, Jesus was perceived symbolically as the ruling authority (*Kyrios*), the King of Kings, as the power over the living (i.e., the living spirits of the cult, the believers) and the dead (those not yet quickened by YHWH's Spirit into a new resurrected life within the cult). In accordance with ancient symbolism within Second Temple Judaism, any separation from Torah in the Jewish community was considered as spiritual death. And according to Paul, in theological terms, this symbolic death could be assimilated via salvific theological categories into the idea of being crucified with Christ. And, with a mystic initiation by baptism; one became a new creation (resurrected, transported into) the new faith-community in fulfillment of the new covenant.

The *Christos* event was the divine power and the Spirit of YHWH's presence[17] that enabled this to take place. This was a logical conclusion based on their perception of the mythical role that Jesus was assigned by virtue of a faith-understanding of the cross/resurrection aspect for the forgiveness of sins proclaimed in Paul's gospel among the gatherings of YHWH's people. This salvific role had been based on the covenantal commandments from an earlier tradition.[18] Thus, the application of the divine

---

16. Neusner, *Judaisms*, 33-41. In the diaspora, it was Paul with other apostles as missionary representatives of the Jewish christological gatherings who reconfigured the priestly dynamics for forgiveness as a new faith posture. Paul considered the cross/resurrection as a christological event (the new faith commitment) to be a stumbling block to the (traditionalist) Jews.

17. Cf., Luke 1:31-35, 80; cf. 2:52; 3:21 and 4:16-22.

18. Cf., Crossan, *The Birth of Christianity*, 314 with the covenantal commandments found in Deut. 30:11-14 and the Gospel of

name in the Jesus myth was not a late phenomenon in the experiences of the early gatherings.

There had been in the earlier tradition and patterns of eschatological thought the idea of a prophetic figure returning from the dead so that the fulfillment of his eschatological mission[19] could be accomplished. This was not uniformly accepted by several of the early gatherings; although that changed, and it later became a messianic standard by the later formative church. The theological formulation of this concept by its symbolic use has been evidenced in the literary tradition and its kerygmatic intentiality as set forth in Mark's Gospel[20] Since the early gatherings of the Jesus myth perceived themselves, symbolically, as the body of the anointed gathering of YHWH, this symbolism was also reflected in the fellowship's identity, as a religious 'brotherhood.'[21] Efforts to modernize this aspect of the earlier gatherings'

Thomas, 18, 51. Also see Mark 13 paralleling the Gospel of Thomas, 3:1-5. Modern biblical scholars have concluded that a primary source Q was assembled over time and in distinct stages. The earliest stratum Q1 had a set of sayings on ethics and discipleship often similar to Cynic philosopher-preachers and represents a formative stage that collected wisdom sayings. Q2 the next stratum has been styled prophetic and apocalyptic that reflects the communities' hostility and rejection from the wider world and may have been written before the Jewish War with Rome. It was the final stratum Q3 which introduced a historical figure who is perceived as the founder of the established community. Cf., Mack, *Myth of Innocence*, (1988) and John Kloppenborg, *The Formation of Q: Trajectories in Ancient Wisdom Collections* (Philadelphia: Fortress Press, 1987).

19. Bultmann, *History and Eschatology*, (1963) where he offers contrasting opinions to explicate a wide range of eschatological themes.

20. See Mark 6:14; 9:11, 12.

21. Where the Greek has brothers in the text, often the word sisters is added. Modern translations of the Bible then are not true to the Greek text by their translations in order to adjust to modern times, gender acceptance, and diversity. Yet within the context of the first century, Hellenistic world individual women and children were understood as having membership in a 'brotherhood' devoted to the deity; mystery cults and pagan religious associations were also brotherhoods

societal make-up can be historically misleading. The brotherhood, strictly speaking, was a male dominated enterprise whose male leadership roles determined the patriarchal atmosphere of the group's societal identity. When Paul wrote his letters to any christological group, he wrote to the leaders of the brotherhood (even though the letter would be shared with the whole community that included women and children).

There was a common element of secrecy within the early gatherings that was also a similarity of the Hellenistic mystery religions. Thus, the christological communities had no problem with a religious and cultural accommodation of the mythologies of the Hellenistic world. God had chosen, anointed, and empowered them with his Spirit for their own deliverance (salvation, healing) from a world of Satanic influences. The christological communities perceived that their traditional Jewry had become static, unresponsive, and ineffectual in the diaspora (especially in regard to the 'authentic' role of the priesthood and their officiating function of the sacrificial, Levitical requirements) and was in need of revitalization in order to include Gentiles into God's family. This religious transformation would be accomplished by the apostolic preaching of missionary individuals like Paul and other apostles of the christological communities. They had become the 'New Israel' during the end-times, and its dynamic faith-understanding was proclaimed as the Jesus myth, which was anchored theologically in its cultic kerygma.[22]

One should not deny that the manifold expressions of religious, theological, and social identification were efforts that provided a creative attempt of legitimization of a diversified Israel during the Second Temple period. Burton Mack's contribution to Neusner's discussion of the Second Temple Era and its

---

as well. Reading Paul in the Greek gives a different sense to communal involvement and may reflect a similar understanding to "the brother of the Lord" (Galatians 1:19).

22. Scholars today are beginning to acknowledge that much material in the Gospels reflect a Jewish longstanding concern for the myth of divine Wisdom entering into this world with salvific significance. Cf., Jesus as a child of Wisdom (Luke 7:35) along with Matthew's presentation of Jesus as an incarnation of Wisdom herself.

diversity within Judaism is most interesting. Mack's thematic consideration is the 'anointing' concept as it relates to the many idealized figures appearing in Jewish literature of the time. He states that "these figures functioned as symbols to center essentially social anthropologies. They were not put forth as heroes of achievement, mimetic ideals, or saviors." And, "they were not invested with ontological significance as objects of faith or veneration." In fact, "these figures collected characteristics that in effect were functions and qualities essential for the social formation of Israel … given the political and social realities." He then concluded his analysis with this; "all were issues needing resolution in the struggles to conceptualize, actualize, and defend the notion in the many forms of Judaism attempted during this time."[23] It might have been, in all probability, the dynamic process; but, on a different trajectory, it began and developed into the first Gospel that we know as Mark's literary achievement. As seen in Mark, it was given an ontological quality and presents the historical Jesus as a hero in Greek fashion. Yet, this also goes to show the range and depth of literary mythothemes that could be employed to symbolize a *christological* and *communal* identification for the creation of a new Spiritual Israel for Jews in the Hellenistic Diaspora.

The symbolic significance of the resurrection concept that had been employed structurally in the early christological theology[24] continued to convey the concept in the early gatherings'

---

23. Neusner, *Judaisms,* 19. Richard D. Hecht also contributed to Neusner's assessment of the messianic theme found in works of the Jewish Philo of Alexandria (ca. 15 BCE – ca. 45 CE) who adopted, adapted, and appropriated Greek philosophical categories in his discussion. Although Philo used Greek extensively in his literary corpus, "nowhere in the corpus does Philo mention the term *christos* ('messiah')" and understood one meaning of "the messianic figure to be an allegorical or symbolic designator for the *Logos.*" Ibid., 140.

24. Grant, *Earliest Gospel*, 153-154. Most scholars generally agree that the earliest reference to Gospel materials came with the writings of Justin Marty around the 150's CE where he refers only to 'memoirs of the Apostles' without identifying any particular one. Since the reference text does not agree with the canonical text we have, it is

expanded covenantal literature, but without its symbolic significance. Hanson cites J. L. Adams' historical analysis remarking that symbols can be used differently so that,

> The 'use' made of a symbol may vary according to the social status or frustration or demands of particular social groups: the 'use' made of a symbol by a ruling group will be different from the 'use' made by a deprived group. In the case of Zechariah, the forms and symbols utilized on behalf of the ruling group bear a *prima facie* resemblance to the forms and symbols of deprived apocalyptic groups.[25]

The historical development within the early christological communities needs to be studied together with the cultural, environmental, and historical situations (*Sitz im Leben*) in which the resurrection concept developed and through which it was transmitted. The mystic and mythological religiosity that was found in the imaginative narratives of the later Gospels (as the later orthodox, biblical tradition) accounts for nothing in terms of any real historical verification. They have provided the historic vehicle by which the Jesus myth was historicized and developed among formative Christianity. This process and its symbolic interpretation, based on an early christological tradition, were formulated, transmitted, and accepted within the later orthodox, Christian tradition. Myth was well on its way to becoming history.

The primitive christological fellowships had sought a symbolic interpretation within the context of the original covenantal tradition (based on Paul's 'revelatory' methodology of scriptural analyses by his hermeneutical posture), which also had

---

indicative of the 'floating traditions' (H. Koester's term) that were still being revised. E. Doherty, "Main Articles -- Part Three: The Evolution of Jesus of Nazareth," *THE JESUS PUZZLE: Was There No Historical Jesus?* http://jesuspuzzle.com/html 3, (accessed 22 June 2005).

25. Hanson, *Apocalyptic*, 253. It is not difficult to see how Paul with all of his symbolic religiosity, and as an in-group member among the earliest Jewish christological gatherings' leadership, could be among "the most influential members, especially the missionaries and principal patrons, [who] came from the upper social levels of Hellenistic Judaism." Stambaugh, *Social Environment*, 54. Bracket is mine.

included various dimensions of paradigmatic parallelism.[26] The early christological gatherings formulated their proclamation of the gospel on the previous biblical meanings and placed them into contemporary religious categories. It was Paul's and other apostles' 'gospel;' it was not the narrative mythology of a historical Jesus encountered in the canonical 'Gospel' literature. This process called midrashim worked quite well for the most part. An interesting issue, which existed within the diaspora, had to be dealt with from a socio-religious and cultural context.

How does faith function when the regular (acceptable) religiosity within Judaism (the Second Temple system; its priesthood and sacrificial requirements) is no longer accepted by many faithful Jews even in the pre-70 era both in the diaspora and in Palestine? The answer became an attitudinal perception that was politicized. The city of Jamnia had been and continued to be a historically important influence even after the destruction of the Temple and the Jews' traditional way of religious life. Leaney presents a short overview of Jamnia's influence:

It had been captured by Vespasian early in his campaigns and from 67 had been used as a refuge for Jews who remained loyal to the Romans during all the succeeding hostilities. ... In fact, [Rabbi] Johanan [ben Zakkai] taught and legislated in such a fashion as to

---

26. In ancient mythology, paradigmatic parallelism provides a mystic religious experience within the early fellowships (cf., 1 Thess. 1:10). The spiritual activities of the Christ recorded in Hebrews and based entirely on scriptural tradition (midrashim) is an excellent example of this paradigmatic parallelism. The author of Hebrews when referring to Jesus as an 'apostle' provides a mystic connection in the Christ's activities of being sent by God. Part of that mystic drama was the 'preaching to those souls' in Sheol while descending into Sheol and ascending back again to heaven as savior. When the author of Hebrews mentions Joseph and Moses, he/she does not necessarily consider them as real people having been on earth. They were religious persona embedded in the text of accepted sacred scripture. They were icons of cultural religiosity -- not necessarily examples of historical personages.

make the way of life enjoyed at Jamnia a supersession of the practices centered upon the Temple.[27]

The author of Hebrews discloses the salvific activity of the Christ in mythic fashion as the great heavenly priest. If Jesus had an actual physical life on earth as a historical reality, then the author's statement in the book of Hebrews would be superfluous, given his linguistic conditionality when he states that "If he were on earth, he would not be a priest at all." Heb. 8:4-5a.[28] This type of mythical expression was parallel to the Platonic style and with the mystic mythologies of Hellenistic religiosity. Even the Jews, especially in the diaspora, had their sacred scriptures translated (the Septuagint) into the Greek of the Hellenistic world culture. Scholars have noted that "Papyri found in Egypt and the Jewish inscriptions found throughout the empire also make it clear that the diaspora Jews used Greek for nearly all communications, personal and official."[29] A similar phenomenon has been used "... by continental theologians like Bultmann, Bornkamn, Fuchs, and Ebling to describe the interpretation of biblical meanings in modern categories."[30]

The primary mythological significance of this process is the confrontation of God and humanity within a context of faith-understanding. Religiosity today, as a human spiritual dynamic by its physical and psychological nature, is just as viable for a modern understanding as it was for the original, Jesus cult mythology. Yet, the difficulty of understanding the biblical myth has

---

27. A. R. C. Leaney, *The Jewish and Christian World 200 BC to AD 200* (New York: Cambridge University Press, 1984), 120. Brackets are mine.

28. See E. Doherty's excellent biblical analysis of this passage in Hebrews in his *Jesus.*

29. Stambaugh, *Social Environment,* 50. Cf., Leaney, *Jewish and Christian World,* 147, where he notes that the social and cultural institution of the Jewish synagogues have an abundance of evidence for their existence throughout the diaspora dating back to 100 BC.

30. Hunter, *Gospel According to Paul*, 109. This type of theological thought follows along existential lines and has presupposed an existential intent in the revelation of God's word.

emerged on several levels due to the historization of the Jesus myth within the tradition. We see this difficulty now as it confronts modern humanity in secularism, atheism, humanism, and the scientific understanding of humanity's bio-evolutionary existence. This socio-religious difficulty with modernity is directly expressed by present-day Christians who have transported a first century mythological world-view that is found in the biblical literature into a twenty-first century scientific understanding of the modern world.

Modernity is scientific, rational, and bio-evolutionary in its anthropology; and the first century world-view is totally unnecessary for our existential understanding or for living in the twenty-first century. That ancient world-view is no longer necessary.

There is no more concrete evidence today for the existence of heaven than the ancients had for their own view of a layered world of the spirit above the earth. In both cases, it has been entirely the product of the mind. ... Today, we ought to know better. [According to ancient Middle Platonism and Jewish writers] this world was subject to change, decay, chaos, and seemed to cause all manner of evil; God is good and created everything; therefore there must be a superior, perfect world not subject to change, decay, chaos, and evil; and that must be the heavens (the only thing left, and the only thing that seems not subject to change, decay, chaos, or evil— besides elevation, is a universal human notion of superiority; no culture has ever imagined a "better" world below the earth, all have imagined it *above*).[31]

---

31. Doherty's response to Bernard Muller, "Responses to Critiques of the Mystical Case," Part Three, THE JESUS PUZZLE: Was There No Historical Jesus? 4 at http://jesuspuzzle.com/htm (accessed 14 April 2004). Bracket is his. In further response to R. Carrier, Doherty provides his impression of the philosophical and religious atmosphere of the time. He states: "The deaths of the Hellenistic savior gods took place not on earth or in history; they inhabited mythical settings. Philosophers had already created the upper dimension where divine intermediaries revealed and rescued." Ibid. Cf., 1 Corinthians 15:35-54 to appreciate these two worlds as a religious/theological construct.

These two world-views, the ancient and the modern, are not compatible. They are in tension; modernity's world-view cancels out the earlier mythological one. All modern religiosities must deal with this rational and structural reality, which remains in diametrically opposed tension.

The symbolic and mythological character of Christian religiosity does not essentially differ from the ancient Hellenistic world religiosities[32] out of which it sprang, even though its inner religious structure was based on Jewish (YHWH as Spirit) religious categories. Among the Greeks and Romans, the Platonic school at any rate, regarded the traditional mythic conceptions of an anthropomorphic deity as symbolic of a reality that could be apprehended only by the higher mind, the *nous*, and had no characteristics perceivable by the natural senses.[33] This *nous* is reminiscent of Paul who said, "... have this mind (*nous*) in you, which was in Christ Jesus our Lord" (Phil. 2:5; cf. I Cor. 2:16). Also, the Jesus cult's instruction by the Spirit of YHWH was to render to each initiate a new spirituality (a new creative identity) so that they would understand the cultic secrets (inner mysteries?), the "deep things of God" (I Car. 2:10) as initiates (*mystae*) in union with the eternal God.

This symbolic interpretation of new faith-understanding, which they had been allowed to behold (a revelatory insight that witnessed YHWH's power via a metaphorical understanding of

---

32. R. M. Wilson, *The Gnostic Problem: A Study of the Relations between Hellenistic Judaism and the Gnostic Heresy* (London: Mowbray, 1958), and Burnett Hillmann Streeter, *The Primitive Church* (New York: The Macmillan Co., 1965).

33. Bevan, *Symbolism and Belief*, 253. Kennedy states that "... even the language of Paul uses in defining the relations of the created universe to Christ, more especially the prepositional phrases, 'by him,' 'through him,' 'for him,' 'in him,' find remarkable parallels alike in the literature of Stoicism, and [through Stoic influence] in the regular vocabulary of the popularized philosophy of the day." Kennedy, *Theology of Epistles*, 155. This style of interpretation fits into the understanding of historization of the biblical tradition that is being considered in this study.

the resurrection, as divine forgiveness and as a historical act of God in their personal experience), also became for them a spiritual and historic 'revelation.' The christological communities perceived their Jewish spirituality as a continued renewal by the Spirit of the Lord, (God's Son). It also maintained a dynamic and mystical encounter between YHWH and an offer of salvation by Paul's gospel to the Greek world of humanity. In the later historicized biblical tradition, Jesus had been raised from the dead and was proclaimed as the risen Christ, the Lord, by the formative Christian church. Consequently, given this understanding Barth states: "Because He is and in that he is, the Church is."[34] In this way, the historical Jesus serves as a paradigm for the church's historical development, which is an untenable position to maintain given that a standard of physical and historical evidence is required for historical validation.

The early christological believers were depicted as being possessed by an 'empowerment' because of Jesus' resurrection (Rom. 1:4, 6:9). This spiritual power was interpreted as the living religious reality of YHWH's Spirit in their midst,[35] the cult's new found self-identity. It was the communal existence of the gatherings that had been anointed (as the body of the Christ) so that they, collectively, perceived themselves as the Son of God, God's faithful end-time servant. This idea of a faithful end-time servant

---

34. Barth, *Dogmatics*, IV, 661, as cited by Hartwell, *Theology of Karl Barth*, n. 3, 41. For the early christological communities, the psychodynamic 'understanding' of their personal relationship to God's presence within a communal context was referred to as a 'revelation.' And, this revelation reflected God's anointing of the community by his power to affect his Christ in them.

35. Martin Buber offers some penetrating comments in which he makes a comparison of Christianity, Judaism, and paganism. He focuses the neo-paganism in the world as a severance of spirit from modern life. Wood interprets his (Buber's) criticism of traditional Christianity (i.e., wherein the core of criticism is focused on the historicized tradition) and indicates Buber's perception: The spirit of humanity as "... elevated in holy detachment and life negated" in Wood's, *Buber's Ontology*, 24.

appears in the canonical Gospels as the Son of Man designation from the lips of the historicized Jesus.

This symbolic and mythological perception was the motivation for the process, formulation, and fabrication of the Gospel tradition regardless of the multiplicity of the oral and literary sources.[36] The literary mythothemes from the ancient religiosities were prevalent in a syncretic socio-religious culture when the Christian faith had emerged from several divergent mythological strains in order to formulate their own particularized religious form. The 'cultural atmosphere' was conceptually full with a multitude of religious and mythological scenarios from which anyone was free to pick and choose. Here are just a few examples. Hellenistic philosophical thought abounded on a conceptual and symbolic level with the idea of the good person, the just individual, as being a righteous person. The idea of righteousness, as one who would suffer for others, permeated the philosophic writings and also the astral faiths of the Hellenistic world of religiosity. The second book of the *Republic* conveys this profound magnanimity.

The mystery religions speak of the death and rising of deities. The Greek philosophers speak of the impalement of the righteous and the suffering of the Just. The faith of Israel, in the Psalms, speaks of the suffering of the Righteous (Psalm 5:17). It is not difficult to make mythological and conceptual connections in order to form a faith-community's religiosity at this time. Thus, it is easy to accept that the resurrection was understood symbolically and referred to the new life of spiritual monotheism (the Jesus myth) in the early gatherings. As Diaspora Jews (now as the new Spiritual Israel), these members of the Jesus cult were raised out of spiritual death (the Hellenistic mythological world of Satanic influences on the one hand and on the other hand, as Spiritual Israel, the diaspora gatherings were delivered out of the

---

36. Brandon, *Jesus and Zealots*, 179 ff. Many things within the developing tradition were similar patterns of Hellenistic philosophical, religious, and mystical sensibilities. The religious and cultural idea of 'taking up ones cross' had its counterpart in the larger first century world. It didn't need a historical Jesus to utter this popular idea. See Doherty, "Main Articles -- Part Three," 7. Cf., Luke 14:27.

old Judaism) into a new resurrected communal, life relationship with YHWH (via Jesus, the cultic persona).

There were still traditional Jews that embraced a christo-logical point of view, as a renewed people of God. This new symbolic perspective became the bed rock for future generation's education and religious development within the several gatherings. We should note, at this point, Pinker's discussion of Harris' 'Group Socialization Theory' in order to understand the communal and social dynamics of this religious educational process. Pinker states that,

> Socialization—acquiring the norms and skills necessary to function in society—takes place in the peer group. Children have cultures, too, which absorb parts of the adult culture and also develop values and norms of their own. Children do not spend their waking hours trying to become better and better approximations of adults. They strive to be better and better children, ones that function well in their *own* society. It is in this crucible that our personalities are formed.[37]

Given this group socialization theory, it is reasonable to expect that social mutational dynamics are always present to change, alter, redirect, and modify the handed-down symbolic and mythological categories in this process that can make theological adjustments within the children's peer group. Children have a propensity for literalism. Eventually, myth will have a tendency to become historical as part of the younger generation's in-group socialization. The symbolic nature of the resurrection concept, as a 'historic' experience within the religious reflections of the early christological fellowships, revealed to the apostolic witnesses, a decisive spiritual and mystic aspect of the proclamation, which was the primitive kerygma.

The emerging faith of formative Christianity[38] was historically based on this kerygma with its intentional theological con-

---

37. Steven Pinker, *The Blank Slate: The Modern Denial of Human Nature* (New York: Viking, Penguin Books, 2002), 390.

38. The early Christian community's faith gave public expression (i.e., the cult's propaganda which was later historicized in the

tents that became historicized with Jesus as the objectification of that faith. This was made significantly possible through an early historicized understanding of the resurrection that differed from its traditional, original christological formulation. This process can be seen in the early speeches of Acts, which depict the so-called historical events of Jesus' life according to the means of an eschatological interpretation, in which the Spirit of God permeates the entire historical trajectory as its primary aspect for its literary motivation. The christological communities came to reflect on their religious existence as the New Israel, while the Old Testament Jewish literature became for them the vehicle for finding the 'hand of God' via his Spirit in their cultic lives (where both Pesharim and Midrashim were amply used).

As an example from the Gospels, they literally made the story *'fit.'* In the process of historization, "the evangelist showed that Jesus' death [as a historical narrative event] was consistent with the scriptural requirements for a perfect Passover sacrifice." Keeping in mind that "unlike other sacrifices, [it] was not ordinarily considered to be an offering for sin but a sign of *deliverance from death.*"[39] They accepted this as a natural and religious methodology of symbolism for their interpretations on which their spiritual understanding of the original covenantal literature was based. For Paul, these sacred texts became the 'revelatory' means by which God spoke to his people in the end-days by him (Paul) and other apostles. Paul's conceptual uniqueness, which the christological gatherings theologized for their religiosity from the Mosaic tradition, became the new universal monotheism of

---

proclamation) by speeches that constitute primary source material for historical study of the kerygma. Cf., Acts 2:14-40; 3:12-26; 4:8-12; and 10:34-43 attributed to Peter and 13:16-41, which is Paul's first recorded sermon in Acts. Cf. Filson, *Risen Lord*, 31ff.; and C. F. Evans, "The Kerygma" in the *Journal of Theological Studies*, Vol. VIII, Pt. 1, (April 1956), 25 ff.

39. Koester, *Symbolism*, 197. Brackets and italics for emphasis are mine. Paul's gospel tied the 'cross' sacrifice to the forgiveness of sin together with resurrection (deliverance from death -- the mythical and devastating, negative effects of the flesh by Satanic forces over a person's life, expressed symbolically).

YHWH as the mystic experience in the *Christos* event (a new faith-understanding of sins forgiven). This included the Gentiles, who by a moral faith-commitment to the gospel that Paul proclaimed could be reconciled to God and enter into the Kingdom of his Son.

It was also the moral integrity of their faith that related to divine salvation and an existential life in response to YHWH's Spirit (II Cor. 3:1-18). The traditionalist Jews had boasted of their monotheism and religious knowledge of the one true God, YHWH. But, the Jewish Jesus cult opposed this religious stance as being inadequate as an understanding of the real essence of monotheism, Judaism, and spiritual religiosity in a spiritually enslaved world of polytheism.[40] This had been the christological community's religious understanding as evidenced by the letters of Paul and the others, which used a symbolic, methodological hermeneutic. Deacon reminds us that "as in so many scientific [historical, biblical, and theological] enterprises, we must always keep in mind the caveat that 'absence of proof is not proof of absence.'" He also reminds us of the function of the symbol, in that

> Most of the symbol use in a society, even excluding language, is not even embodied in any material, but only in ceremonies, habits, and rules that govern everyday life. And what we know about most artifacts is that the vast majority are made of perishable materials. This is particularly for aging peoples, who move continuously from place to place. Like the words that prehistoric people spoke, the vast majority of their creative efforts would have produced results that vanished with them, or shortly afterwards.[41]

---

40. Cf. Matt. 3:9 and Luke 3:8 and John 8:32-41. The historical revolts of the second century BCE (cf., the Maccabean era, ca. 165 BCE) prepared the way for the socio-religious reactions so that the stage was set for social, political, and religious revivals of new faith understandings and new interpretations of their older sacred texts. Especially eschatological categories and apocalyptic features were introduced into their creative literary works from this period on to include the final revolts against Rome in 66-73 CE, 114-115 CE, and 134-135 CE.

41. Deacon, *Symbolic Species*, 367.

Christ, the heavenly Son, was their Lord (i.e., the cult's entrusted power and authority via the religious instruction of YHWH Spirit, the cult's mystic rites and ceremonies). Originally, the cult's propaganda was for the Diaspora Jews first (e.g., as the living, and past chosen people of YHWH) and then to the Gentiles (the spiritually dead whose spiritual death was perceived as their polytheism). It then became the theological perception by these sectarian gatherings, which was revealed to them by Paul, that the end of the age had dawned experientially on those who had accepted his gospel (by their faith-acceptance through baptism into the community of the Jesus myth, the body of the *Christos* event). The christological communities, of which Paul was one of their apostles and missionary, "stood within the great tradition of Judaism, as did the Essenes, the Pharisees, and the Therapeutae; but unlike them, he drew the boundaries of the sacred community differently and more narrowly than [or more progressively] than the established leaders in Jerusalem"[42] had done.

In modern times, some have made a feeble attempt to explain the mythological process of the deification of Jesus by its later developed Christology of orthodoxy. These attempts state that the narratives, that depict a truly human Jesus in Mark's Gospel, have undergone a reformulation that makes Jesus into a divine being in John's Gospel. This is precisely the historically reverse of the religious scenario that is now accepted in the Church's tradition. It is the authentication of the symbolic and mythological data that reflects the emerging christological faith-understanding, which is based on the actual historical evidence. In Paul and the other epistles, and in the early christological community's midrashic understanding, this supernal Jesus is consistently portrayed as a 'divine' being,[43] while his earthly

---

42. Holmberg, *Sociology*, 96-7. Bracket is mine.

43. In the personification of a literary figure, one can detect how the heavenly Son of Man can equate with the people of Israel reformulated by the resurrection of the sacred community; Ezek. 37:1-14. Hengel, *The Zealots*, 239 states that "... the Son of Man is a heavenly being or was interpreted as the people of Israel and neither can be simply identified with the Messiah."

mythological existence (presented symbolically and as metaphor in this study) is seen in the Gospels as a faint imitation of any real human person. Midrashim, as fabricated in the biblical story (*mythos*) in Mark's Gospel, does account for the new literary genre.

Yet, all of these stories with the attending general categories of 'the suffering and vindication of the innocent' have been in the original covenantal literature of the Mosaic tradition for a very long time. Others factors, such as Platonism, Greek religion, the several mystery cults, Gnosticism, and various philosophic schools during the Hellenistic age, have a far greater historical share in the theological and socio-religious, literary fabrications that made it possible to transform myth into historical reality (at least in its literary form). The Gospel accounts, true to their middle Platonic focus and to various degrees, historicized the early christological tradition. As an example: the Jesus myth in the biblical narrative, Jesus claims to be "the light of the world." As biblical historians, we admit that

> The intricate arguments about Jesus' status as rabbi, Messiah, and prophet, as well as the connection between light and the feasts of Booths, presuppose a certain familiarity with the Old Testament and Jewish traditions, but the divine character of light was recognized by people throughout the ancient world. In Greco-Roman sources, the god Serapis was lauded as the "light of all men," and the goddess Isis was "light of all mortals." Zeus could be called "the light of men," and it was said of Jupiter that "the whole world was filled with the light of his glory."[44]

This is no indication that one literary source is dependent upon another because of religious and linguistic similarities. It simply is an example of metaphoric language that indicates, within the Hellenistic world, how in general, various peoples used the available symbolic language to talk about the deities

---

44. Koester, *Symbolism*, 142. Koester cites BAGD *phōs* 2; on Serapis and Isis, also Cicero, *De Divinitatione* 17; on Zeus, Lucian, *Alexander* 18; on Jupiter, Cicero, *De Divinitatione* 1.10 §17 for his evidence about the ancient deities in his quote.

that captivated their spiritual interests. It is now recognized by modern, critical scholars (especially of the mystic posture) that the Gospels were originally intended to be allegorical for their communities; as for their spiritual instruction, they functioned symbolically on behalf of the faith-communities that produced them.

This difference, found in the literary and historicized tradition of the canonical literature, indicates the kerygmatic intention (to convey the divinity of *Yeshua*, Jesus) that not only was in the apostolic preaching (the speeches in Acts), but was also an indispensable symbolic part of the confessional proclamation within the Jesus cult as Paul proclaimed it. Together, these two basic types of proclamation provide us with an authentic picture of the early symbolic understanding of the mythic resurrection experience that was theologized by the early christological gathering. Even though this was perceived originally as the spiritual 'anointing' by YHWH, according to the primitive christological community's faith-posture,[45] it was preserved, adapted, and reformulated in the later church's Christology. We realize that sometimes theological changes run parallel with socio-cultural changes.[46] It was the early Jesus gatherings that understood that they were the Israel of God who had received his Spirit (knowledge from religious mystical union and divine revelation from YHWH).

---

45. Kahler has a lengthy note in which he discusses these aspects of a 'double proclamation' that are found in the New Testament portrayal of Jesus, *Historical Jesus -- Biblical Christ*, n. 19, 84. Also see John E. McFadyen, *Old Testament and the Christian Church* (New York: Charles Scribner's Sons, 1903), and Goldstein, *Jewish Tradition* (1950).

46. For at least two decades, 30s and the 40s, a sizable community of Jews lived in Rome. By the end of the 40s decade, Gentile members of the faith who lived in Rome became predominant so that theological perspectives shared within the Roman community shifted away from a hermeneutic based on Traditional Jewish categories into the Hellenistic mythos as a differential social religiosity. Cf., Donfried, *Judaism and Christianity*, 248-264.

This symbolic understanding had delivered them from this present, evil age (the world of polytheism, the Devil, evil spirits, and daemons) and their present influences of the evil one, Satan. They had been raised from 'out of' the dead 'ones' (their acceptance into a new resurrected [i.e., spiritual] life within the Jesus cult, born out of the death of polytheism). The perception, by formative Christianity, that a historical Jesus, having been literally resurrected and would come back as the Lord Jesus from heaven as Judge and Savior, was not an early christological formulation. It certainly was not part of Paul's preaching or his christological formulations. It was this theological point of view (the second coming of Christ expectation) that became a later Christian historicized interpolation[47] as several biblical passages provide evidence of textual editing show.

In the earlier theological formulations (the *Christos* event for Paul), it was spiritual power, moral integrity, and religious blessings that were made available to the communal initiates. The mythological *Christos* event, for Paul and others apostles, was a cosmic revelation embracing Platonic categories that still reflect a Hellenistic Jewish connection. The Christ event (a death and resurrection hermeneutic that stands for divine forgiveness) enabled the salvific mythological experience to be relied upon as being derived out of the heavens[48] where the resurrected Christ figure came to be seated at God's right hand. Yet, Jesus is depicted only in the later canonical Gospels as a man, born of the flesh, grew with all semblance of human attributes, suffered death, was buried and then, literally raised again to earthly life.

This mythology still is the very core of the God-Man Christology in the orthodox theology of Christianity that is also

---

47. Cf. Romans 1:1-4; Gal. 4:4; Romans 8:34; Col. 3:1; Romans 14:9; Gal. 6:16; 3:2; 1:4; and I Thess. 1:10; 5:2, 9.

48. One can gather the commonly understood meaning and similarity from the Psalms where a believer awaits the eternal 'help' or spiritual assistance from 'on high' from the LORD, YHWH. Then note in Paul's Thessalonian letter, 1 Thess. 1:10, where this same idea is reflected in his pastoral ministry, together with its moral and ethical characteristics, rather than a theological interpretation of Jesus' second coming.

unequivocal in its religious dogma. Regardless, as a historical narrative in the Gospels, it cannot ignore nor deny its mythological base. It is simply the religious fabrication of the formative, literalist Christian mind-set. Mainstream scholars seem to forget that,

> A more sensible solution would be that all these expressions of the idea of "Jesus" and "Christ" were separate distillations out of the concepts that were flowing in the religious currents of the day. ... Scholars now admit that "the beginnings of Christianity were exceptionally diverse, varied dramatically from region to region, and were dominated by individuals and groups whose practice and theology would be denounced as 'heretical.' " It is no longer possible to maintain that such diversity -- so much of it uncoordinated and competitive -- exploded overnight out of one humble Jewish preacher [Jesus] and a single missionary movement.[49]

There is really no debate; divinity, in all ancient mythic traditions with all its essential conceptualizations, is a purely religious fabrication historically and culturally based. It is certainly refreshing to see a good scholar like Richard Carrier supporting Doherty (a mythicist biblical scholar) based solely on rational and scientific arguments when dealing with symbolism. Bernard Muller had made the statement that Doherty had 'ignored' some references in explicating a Book of Romans passage, which dealt with the historical Jesus concerns. It is clear from this example from Doherty's analysis: Carrier remarked that Muller's remarks were based on several misunderstandings and misinterpretations. "If the first reference to Jesus being of David's stock (in Romans 1) can be shown to be symbolic, then all subsequent references to it are similarly symbolic." In reading Doherty's remarks, it was plainly seen that he had not ignored any of those references. Carrier's conclusion needs to be noted. "All Bernard does here is use an emotional appeal to invite the reader to fall back on the biases built in by 2000 years of historicist exegesis. He does not make

---

49. E. Doherty, "Main Articles -- Part Three" 10, where he quotes Ron Cameron summarizing Walter Bauer, *The Future of Early Christianity*, 381. Bracket is mine.

an argument based on logic, content, linguistic, or history anywhere in these matters."[50] Ancient myth and symbolism was the historical means for humanity to deal with the interactive psychology of human existence and its spiritual meaning (or a lack thereof) for a religious Weltanschauung.

As seen previously, the demonic, as symbolic in understanding, is the imagery that disclosed the false religiosity, the idolatry, and the false faith of polytheism in the Hellenistic world perceived by the christological gatherings in the diaspora. The 'casting out' these demons, as depicted in the ministry of Jesus in the Gospels, was a metaphor and refers to the overthrowing of the false religiosity of the Gentiles by the supplanting of the Jesus myth, the new monotheistic universalism (the new faith and the symbolic understanding of the early Jewish christological cult). This type of interpretation is fundamental for a proper understanding of the historic origin of the Jesus myth in its original formation and later development by formative Christianity. It is essential to a proper historical understanding and analysis of the Gospels' account of the so-called historical Jesus as originally intended; that is, symbolically as myth. It is for all practical purposes, that the conceptual realities of the demonic accounts in the Synoptic Gospels are all seen as references that belong to the Galilean ministry of Jesus. We note that the importance of this particular geographic location has more to do with the theological formulations of primitive Christianity than with topographical or geopolitical considerations.

The area of the Galilee was far more Hellenized than the rest of Palestine and therefore was perceived by the early gatherings as having far more demonic activities. Historically, this area boasted of being a hot-bed for rebellion against the Imperial Roman interlopers that oppressed and exploited Judea, the Jews, and Temple politics at this time. The apocalyptic, theological formulations by primitive Christianity were not etched in stone. Their function by the use of a dynamic symbolism could also be applied as a polemical device in different historical times. Hanson rightly pointed out that,

---

50. E. Doherty, "Responses to Critiques," Pt. three, 11.

Apocalyptic modes of thought are thus not the property of one religious party in Israel. In the sixth century the opponents of the Zadokite priests expressed their faith with the use of apocalyptic forms and were oppressed by the Zadokites; in the second century the Zadokite priests expressed their faith with apocalyptic forms and were oppressed by the Hasmoneans. What did the visionaries of the sixth century and the Zadokites of the second century have in common? Not party affiliation, but a common status in the community.[51]

That status, as a social dynamic, can work for or against the community's own socio-religious institution. This religious tension is demonstrated in the Gospel narrative when it depicts Jesus' ministry in socio-religious conflict with the religiosity of the Gentile world. As cited before, there can only be one natural and historical explanation of this evangelic distinction between the two geographic areas, the Galilee and Judea in the Gospel narratives. The casting out of demons (i.e., the false deities that was understood as Hellenistic polytheism) seems to be, at least from the Gospel narratives, the main activity in the ministry of Jesus as the son of man while in the Galilee of the Gentiles. The power over those beings (e.g., spirits, powers, etc., and other supernatural entities), has been extrapolated from its conceptual mythological basis and has been reformulated into a later New Testament Christology.[52]

In Acts 2, the message of the apostles is to proclaim the beginning of the Messianic age with the experience of the resurrection of Jesus. It is not the theology of the biblical tradition that emerged and facilitated the transformative and historic power of early Christianity. It was probably the actual historical events (positive or negative) of the social and economic forces by the

---

51. Hanson, *Apocalyptic,* 408-9.

52. An example of scriptural midrash that formed a new intratextuality of symbolism is when the evangelists, Matthew and Luke, give the birth place of Jesus in Bethlehem as stated by the prophet Micah (5:2). This is not an example of historical rationality; just a religious 'rationale' in symbolic form. Cf., John 10:21; Acts 5:16; 8:7.

political domination of Rome in the land of Palestine[53] and in the area of Judea that did more to transform the primitive churches' experiences and theological understanding. For example: "in Rome the Jewish community was divided into a number of district synagogues. In all probability the decree of expulsion was directed against the members of one or two specific synagogues, who would have been forced to leave the city until there was a guarantee of no further disturbances."[54] Many of the political and social ideas within the religiously creative circles of the times provided the reactive and creative spirit to bring about the underlying reconfigured interpretations for early Christianity (cf., the Qumran community also in its struggle with Rome and its corresponding religious interpretations).[55] It was during the period of Second Temple Judaism that the Greco-Roman world was seen as a period of historical syncretism of many deities; and as such, the idea of divinity and a savior transformed the Jesus myth into a practical experience of monotheistic universalism. This had

---

53. Edwin Ewart Aubrey, *Secularism: A Myth*, (New York: Harper & Brothers Pub., 1954), gives his astute comments and insight into the relationship of Christianity with the secular world, which seems to be very reasonable. Much of the transformation of renewed Jewish religiosity in the diaspora of the Hellenistic period began much earlier in the dynamic historical events of the first century BCE.

54. Donfried, *Judaism and Christianity,* 204.

55. Helmer Ringgren, *The Faith of Qumran: Theology of the Dead Sea Scrolls*, trans. E. T. Sanders (Philadelphia: Fortress Press, 1963), and D. S. Russell, *The Method and Message of Jewish Apocalyptic, 200 B.C -- A.D. 100, The Old Testament Library* (Philadelphia The Westminster Press, 1964). It should be noted that in the Hellenistic world most of the deities were accorded an ethnic identity of sorts. In general, the people knew that Osiris, Isis and Horus were divinities of Egypt. Dionysos, Attis, and Mithras were understood as having cultural associations with the peoples from which they were derived. And Jesus is associated in the Gospels with Israel. "It would not be unusual for Paul to regard his savior figure, growing to some extent out of the Jewish tradition, as identifiable with that racial group," especially, since Paul's revelatory understanding came from Israel's sacred Scriptures. E. Doherty, "Main Articles -- Part Three" 12 (accessed 22 June 2005).

occurred within the social, political, and symbolic speculations that developed within the cultural tensions of the early christological gatherings.

According to the biblical tradition, primitive Christianity arose essentially as a revolt against the gods (cf. Acts 17) and whose missionary thrust was to overthrow polytheism. The new monotheistic faith-understanding of the christological gatherings came into open conflict with the idolatry of polytheism. An intense religious struggle occurred when the kerygma was made public by missionary activities. The early proclamation of the primitive community of believers understood the kerygma, symbolically and eschatologically. They interpreted the Kingdom of YHWH as the hope of many generations of 'Spiritual Israel' not merely as an imminent event in history, but as having finally come within the actual spiritual experience of the new covenantal community.[56] The primary preaching of Jesus, seen in the Synoptic Gospels, was that God's Kingdom was about to break into history; this historical thrust had been accomplished by the early efforts of the christological communities through their mystic religiosity. Unfortunately, today for the most part, the Christian 'gospel' tends to be literalized and is primarily about escaping physical death with the promise of living forever beyond the grave in a mythological heaven above, beyond, or somewhere. In most of the Greek philosophies, mystery cults, and Roman religions any idea of an afterlife, although present, was an afterthought. The real moral concern for a members' behavior, social values, and transformed life style, prior to death, was of primary importance. The benefits of living a good life in this world was the guarantee of a good life in the hereafter. Much of the essence of this kind of moral concern is lost in modern Christianity.

The eschatological idea of the kingdom (the presence of YHWH's Spirit within the Jesus cult) is presented in the Synoptics in a different sense than presented in the rest of the earlier biblical tradition. It was the concept of the resurrection in the

---

56. Cf., Mark 10:15; and Matt. 13:44-46. By the time the Gospel of Mark had been penned, the early Jewish christological communities had been around for a long time. They had begun to be established in the first half of the first century BCE.

kerygma that ushered in the kingdom reign as perceived by the early Jesus cult as noted by Pauls' preaching. It was understood via its symbolic interpretation that God's Kingdom was the in-gathering of YHWH's holy people, which would include Jew and Gentile. Deacon speaks directly to the issue of this symbolic flexibility when he states that "As languages evolve and meanings and patterns of use drift away from older patterns, reference is maintained by continuity but not fidelity to the past." And he concludes:

> Symbolic reference is at once a function of the whole web referential relationships and of the whole network of users extended in space and time. It is as though the symbolic power of words is only on a loan to its users. If symbols ultimately derive their representational power, not from the individual, but from a particular society at a particular time, then a person's symbolic experience of consciousness is to some extent society dependent -- it is borrowed. Its origin is not within the head. It is not implicit in the sum of our concrete experiences.[57]

The essence of these, that is the historic cultus as the Kingdom of God and the Jesus myth as the propaganda[58] of the kingdom's mystic gatherings, are easily understood historically, when the hermeneutic of symbolism is applied to the concept of the kingdom and tied to the concept of resurrection even in the biblical tradition. The Kingdom of Heaven, the Kingdom of Christ, the Kingdom of *Yeshua*, or the Kingdom of God was the christological gatherings' spiritual totality with their mythological religiosity. It was the vehicle of YHWH's redemptive power (the instruction by the Spirit, the fellowship in the communal life, and the mystic ceremonies) by which salvation had come to humanity. It began by faith exercised in the acceptance of Paul's gospel that proclaimed the forgiveness of sin through the cross of the *Christos* event (1 Cor. 15:1-4). God's redemption had come, and it was realized by the christological gatherings. Thus, universal monotheism (faith in YHWH) was established through the

---

57. Deacon, *Symbolic Species,* 452.
58. Propaganda is a symbolic expression, a linguistic enterprise.

271

sociological and religious structures of the divinely anointed community. The details of this idea and its relationship to the Jesus cult have been worked out in superb fashion by Smith[59] and need not detain us any further.

The principle hermeneutic of symbolism, as applicable to the resurrection concept in the kerygma, has been adequately demonstrated to show how plausible it was for the historic origin of the Jesus myth (Rom. 1:18-32) to develop as the bases for later Christianity without a real historical person, namely Jesus. Thus, the members of the early Jewish christological-community would not agree with Dodd's modern interpretation; that "the Gospel is not a statement of general truths of religion, but is an interpretation of that which once happened."[60] This kind of so-called interpretive happening in the Gospel narratives (i.e., the religious experience that supposedly encountered an actual person) was really and essentially historic. But, its non-historical basis, including the spiritual interpretation of the mythological concept and the metaphorical realities, provided a rich and diverse 'ritualization' for their communal religiosity. Koester does admit that "symbols are a major way in which the Gospel brings potentially discordant elements into agreement with each other." And further indicates that "it has often been noted that the root meaning of the word *symbol* is 'to put together.'"[61] Hence, we can see how

The entire concept of descending redeemers (recurring in gnostic texts) is dependent on them receiving 'bodies' and performing and suffering things that are human-like but not specifically physical

---

59. See Smith, *Ecce Deus*, 267ff. regarding salvation in Jesus' name, and its significance from the older tradition, that can be seen in these biblical texts; Deut. 33:10; Num. 6:22 ff., and compare with Acts 2:21; Rom. 5:10; and Eph. 2:5-8.

60. Dodd, *Parables of the Kingdom*, 163-4. That which occurred in symbolic fashion in their religious experience, not as literal physical reality; but, a spiritual revelation (i.e., their understanding) brought about salvation in their experiences with the divine presence, Yahweh's Spirit, his presence.

61. Koester, *Symbolism*, 27.

and historical. The Savior god mythology casts them … (according to Plutarch) to the mythical and spiritual realm, not the earthly historical sphere.[62]

This ultimately does not detract from the symbolic, mystical, and religious value. Consequently, symbolism gave to the early christological gatherings a spiritual significance for the cults' own socio-religious history and theological formulations. It is quite possible that those who oppose the mysticists' posture and their interpretation of early Christian origins will claim that there is too much speculation within the historical analysis by the methodology used. In the acquisition of new ideas and seeking to provide evidentiary findings that support the main thesis undertaken, sometimes speculation provides an avenue for enlightenment.

Some great world thinkers who have used it in their own discoveries have found it to be fun. With regard to speculation, Charles Darwin said in his *Descent of Man:* "False facts are highly injurious to the progress of science, for they often endure long; but false views, if supported by some evidence, do little harm, for everyone takes a salutary pleasure in proving their falseness; and when this is done, one path toward errors is closed and the road to truth is often at the same time opened."[63] We may all benefit from historical analysis that considers all avenues in which we can gather evidence for the early Christian origin of the 'faith.'

---

62. E. Doherty, "Main Articles -- Part Three," 23. A consideration of theology for a hermeneutical posture can be seen in the category of God 'sending' his son. It is also noted that God has sent the *spirit* of his son into our hearts. These are not ontological categories of historical reality, these statements are epistemological (part of religious mythology), and they provide understanding by symbolically anchoring the religious significance of the 'sending' in a communal context. The concept of 'sending' means 'providing an understanding' for a new way of religious thinking about one's relationship to God through the context of scripture as revelation.

63. Ramachandran, *Brain,* 244 where he quotes from Charles Darwin's *Descent of Man*.

9

*Memory is as much or more a reconstruction
than accurate recollection.*
J. D. Crossan

The early Jewish gatherings, while developing their mystic theological position, maintained the *christological* perspective as the basis for their reflections, worship, doctrines, and ethical[1] response. This perception of their *anointing* provided the basis for the kerygmatic intention and represented the central christological conviction that became uniformly presupposed by the later community's historiographer (Acts 10:38-43). The distinction that *Yeshua* is Lord (*ho kyrios*) and Savior (*ho Iēsous,* Jesus) also developed in the nascent church's kerygma. This resulted from the thematic shift from a historic and symbolic understanding to the historical, literalistic interpretation by later formative Christianity. Such is the later testimony of Christian dogma, which is based on the historization of the eschatological and apocalyptic concepts.

These were based on the earlier mythological features. It seems that the religious titles in all their theological variety reflected a very early usage by the christological cult in its hermeneutical development. Paul's use of them was purely within a mystical and mythological context as symbols and metaphor, which had become embedded in the community's religious rituals (baptism and the Eucharist). As a result, Pamela Eisenbaum offers her assessment of Paul's role within these mystical com-

---

1. For a study of the so-called Messianic consciousness of Jesus, the theory of interim ethics, the relation of eschatology, and ethics in Jesus' teachings, see Amos N. Wilder's book on the subject, *Eschatology and Ethics in the Teachings of Jesus*, rev. ed. (New York: Harper & Row, Pub., 1950).

munities' hermeneutical posture. With reference to Isaiah 25:22-23: She states that,

> Paul's [revelatory] experience of the risen Jesus leads him to move up the apocalyptic clock. Jewish literature of Paul's day clearly indicates that the resurrection of the dead is something that is associated with the final judgment and the end of history. Resurrection was not something that was supposed to happen to one individual at a time; it was envisioned as a collective experience that marked the end of time and the final reckoning of the wicked and the righteous. ... Once he believed [metaphorically] the end of time was much closer than he had previously thought, he necessarily had to revise his understanding about some other things, most importantly, the Gentiles.[2]

Eliade also recognizes the religious style in the earliest symbolic significance of baptism for the cultic experience. Thus, baptism for the christological cult is seen as being "... from the first equivalent to an initiation. Baptism introduced the convert to a new religious community (the Jesus mystic cult) and made the initiate worthy of eternal life."[3] Baptism, like the other mythic and objectified formulations (similar to Hellenistic mystery religions) had also become woven into the fabric of the Christian tradition (e.g., I Cor. 10). Yet, in the Gospels that had later become perceived as historical records of a human Jesus; baptism reflects the later church's sacramental meaning and was well on its way to becoming dogma. And since it was based on an earlier

---

2. Eisenbaum, *Paul*, 149. Brackets are mine.

3. Eliade Mircea, *Rites and Symbols of Initiation: The Mysteries of Birth and Rebirth*, trans. by Willard R. Trask, the Academy Library (New York: Harper & Row, Pub., Torchbooks, 1958), 116. Parenthesis is mine. The Hellenistic mystery cults were extremely popular and diversified. The word 'mystery' (*mystērion*), which referred to a sacred rite, was attached to a particular deity that allowed the initiates to become united with that deity in a personal relationship. This new relationship granted to them certain mystic insights and guaranteed them certain benefits in this life and in the next. The term was usually used in the plural (mysteries, *mystēria*) to refer collectively to a whole range of religiosities that was received by the initiates.

hermeneutical posture, the biblical text also preserved the original symbolic idea as a reflection of the christological communities' mystic, socio-religious experiences of faith. It is now clear that Hellenistic, religious philosophies (e.g., Platonism) had influenced Jewish thought, the mystery religions, and especially Paul; yet it was diversified, spontaneous, and adaptational to the literary needs of those who relied on these categories to formulate their religious views during the previous century and in the first century CE. Logan noted that,

> It would seem that it was the gnostics ... who were the first Christians to develop a thoroughgoing Platonic understanding of the world in terms of a hierarchy of being on two levels, the transcendent, spiritual level emanating from God the Unknown Father, and the terrestrial, material level, a poor travesty or imitation of it, the work of the Demiurge of the *Timaeus* and his archons, with Sophia as the mediating World Soul. ... However, Pétrement is surely correct to see behind this unique combination and perspective the Pauline and Johannine theology of the cross as the revelation of the hitherto unknown Father, and hence of the ignorance and folly of the Creator/Demiurge of this world and his rulers/archons.[4]

YHWH's presence, as deliverance (salvation),[5] was a free gift that also signified a new birth by water (i.e., the cleansing and healing from the false religious categories of the Hellenistic world of polytheism). It also signified a new birth by the Spirit as the acceptance into the cult of Jesus together with its religious instruction and brotherhood authority. This was similar to the

---

4. Alastair H. B. Logan, *Gnostic Truth and Christian Heresy: A Study in the History of Gnosticism* (Peabody, Mass.: Henderson Publishers, 1996), 12.

5. Note G. A. Well's "Earliest Christianity" article in which he identifies the concept of salvation that could relate to the literary personality of *Yeshua*, Jesus, (Matt. 1:21) and cites R. Eisenman and M. Wise (in their *The Dead Sea Scrolls Uncovered*, Shaftsbury, Dorset, 1992) who point to a use in the Qumran community as it relates to "the personification of this concept in the Gospel presentation of Messianic events in Palestine in the first century," 10, electronic version, 2000.

Logos of gnostic religious sensibilities. In Logan's view: "In the end the particular sect names do not matter; it is the myth and the ritual which are decisive."[6] It was the spiritual and interactive presence of YHWH that was maintained in the biblical tradition: for "the Spirit when it comes shall teach you all things" (John 14:26)[7]. Within the social context of biblical theology, the resurrection (the formation of the faith-community's empowerment) can be historically identified with its essential symbolic meaning.

This christological concept reflects the existential and mystic significance of the social, religious, and theological life that was communally maintained in the diaspora. The communal life was ritualized by the fellowship's mystical experience of the divine presence, the *parousia* of the *Christos* event. Even Hoeller mentions that "It is no doubt psychologically significant that Sophia's first awakening from the unconsciousness occurs through the archetypal symbol of the cross."[8] This was a symbol of trans-

---

6. Logan, *Gnostic Truth,* 10. The symbolic nature of these early identified personas and personifications that provided a metaphorical identification of the communal activities (especially their preaching significance) blurs the lines of the historical and religious so-called leaders, which appear in ancient literature. For example: the Teacher of Righteousness of the Dead Sea Scrolls. "According to T. H. Gaster, *The Scriptures of the Dead Sea Sect,* 1957, p. 6, it does not indicate a historical person at all, but an office (*mebaqqēr*)." as cited by Oscar Cullmann, *The Christology of the New Testament,* Rev. Ed., Trans. Shirley C. Guthrie and Charles A. M. Hall (Philadelphia: Westminster Press, 1963), 21.

7. Compare the idea of divine instruction in the faith community in 1 John 2:27 where the divine instruction is by the 'anointing' (*chrisma*) that they had received from God. This anointing is a metaphor, a symbolic reference, and is parallel with the same idea of the 'spirit' that God sent also for their instruction.

8. Stephan A. Hoeller, *GNOSTICISM: New Light on the Ancient Tradition of Inner Knowing* (Wheaton, Ill.: Quest Books, Theosophical Publishing House, 2002), 43. The signing of the cross, also a non-Christian symbol was used by some early Jews. Hoeller adds that "Perhaps the conjunction of the horizontal and vertical bars of the cross even reminds the psyche/Sophia of the needed conjunction of the opposites." Ibid.

formation. And within Pauline influence, it was perceived as an ongoing resurrection experience. It was a new life born of the Spirit (that was transformed out of death, a mystical metaphor) and developed theologically out of the spiritual and religious instruction of the christological sect. This was understood as the participation (divine inheritance) by each member in the gathering of YHWH's Kingdom on earth.[9] It was a mystical fellowship within a cultic religiosity that faithfully proclaimed the mythological gospel (the sacrificial forgiveness of sins) by Paul and other apostles representing the christological gatherings.

The Eucharist of the later Christian tradition was firmly embedded in the historical structure of the original, eschatological, and cultic ritual by the christological fellowships' symbolic hermeneutic. Even though their ritualistic style of a banquet seems to have religious and conceptual commonality with the frequent ritual banquets found in the mystery religions; it has in all probability a closer connection and a Jewish flavor when comparing this ritual with the similar one of the Jewish Essenes.[10] Hershel Shanks has identified the Essenes with the Dead Sea Scrolls community members and states:

---

9. Cf., the Kingdom of Jesus, Eph. 5:5, and Matt. 16:28. There was a mystical perception that was applied to the 'new creation' of the believer in God's Kingdom whose opposite was seen by the term 'flesh.' While in the flesh one was under the satanic influences of the Prince of this evil age. Although the term is found in Jewish and Pagan thought that can refer to non-human flesh, the flesh of supernatural beings; its primary ethical nature, especially in Paul, refers to something mystical and metaphorical that is transformed by the power of Christ's resurrection, which by a faith commitment brings one into God's Kingdom.

10. J. Danielou, *The Dead Sea Scrolls and Primitive Christianity*, trans. S. Attanasio (New York: New American Library, 1962). Also, A. Dupont-Sommer, *The Essene Writings from Qumran*, trans. G. Vermes (Cleveland: Meridian Books, 1962). The sacred mythical meal between Mithras and Helios the sun god is depicted on several Mithraic monuments and meeting places. These are highly symbolic, yet we lack historical writings that would help us to understand their full meaning to the initiates in the mystery cults.

The second fundamental argument for the claim that the residents of Qumran were Essenes is the contents *of the specifically sectarian texts* among the scrolls are in remarkably close agreement with what the ancient writers—Pliny, Philo, and especially Josephus—tell us about Essene beliefs and practices. What the sectarian text have to say coincides much more closely with Essene thought and actions than with what the sources say about the Pharisaic and Sadducean views.[11]

Communal meals were part of the Essene community and the Hellenistic religious world where they were deemed with a mystical function, a union of the cultic initiate with the cultic deity who provided deliverance. These were culturally shared religious understandings in which initiates and the whole membership could experience its full spiritual significance for and within the community. It was not a necessity for any group to intentionally borrow this type of ritual from others. It was part of an overall cultural phenomenon that was shared since it had a commonality of religious form, mythic significance, and symbolic and metaphorical meaning. Particular groups, depending on their theological and mystic basis, could reshape and refashion their own ritual to accommodate their own community's spiritual needs. For example: The Qumran community regarded their meals, taken in common, as symbolic and anticipatory of the expected Messianic Banquet.

The resurrection of Jesus, in the later historicized, Gospel tradition, differentiated the conceptual similarities of this ritual banquet of the Jesus cult from the one by the Essenes. They (the Essenes) looked forward to the resurrection of the Teacher of Righteousness. But in the Jesus christological gatherings, the resurrection was perceived as the divine ingathering of the initiates by YHWH into the new resurrected life of the eschatological

---

11. Hershel Shanks, *Understanding the Dead Sea Scrolls: A Reader from the Biblical Archaeology Review* (New York: Random House, 1992), 54. The community of Qumran, just like the early christological faith communities, was organized precisely as a 'new Israel,' and both had repudiated the priesthood of Jerusalem. While the fellowships of Paul were more progressive, the Essenes at Qumran were radical separatists. Ibid., 24.

cult, via the Spirit of YHWH through baptism into their end-time community. When you consider the progressive nature and influence of the Wisdom Tradition in the diversity of early literary expressions, Hoeller's comments provide an additional insight.

> All archetypal myths possess a timeless quality that makes them applicable to the concerns of any place and time. The story of Sophia, in particular, fixes in comprehensible forms the universal elements that join psychic and transcendental experiences. Insights into the development (individuation) of the individual psyche, into sociological issues (including the elevation and emancipation of women in society), and into theological and metaphorical ideas can all be derived from the Sophianic myth.[12]

Many modern biblical scholars now realize the extensive use of the Wisdom Tradition that influenced so much of Matthew's canonical Gospel literary form. This influence of Wisdom is much broader than first expected as part of a much larger cultural and religious context.

Much of the narrative opposition by the Pharisees and the Herodian factions to Jesus found in the Gospels is in reality a socio-religious tension that reflects the actual historical experiences of the progressive, Jewish christological groups that broke away from the traditional, conservative members (Essenes) of the Qumran community's thinking.[13] Reflected in this point of view, is Eliade's interesting observation that closely resembles the original symbolic interpretation by these Jewish christological cults. He states that "we do not find in the Qumran texts any redemptory significance according to a historical person."[14] In the

---

12. Hoeller, *Gnosticism,* 45.

13. Although Marvin Vining refers to a historical Jesus in his *Jesus the Wicked Priest: How Christianity Was Born of An Essene Schism,* (Rochester, Vermont: Bear & Company, 2008), he outlines this tension, 28-37. This criticism is still valid even when a non-historical Jesus is considered from within the biblical text.

14. Eliade, *Rites and Symbols of Initiation,* 117. In this study, we shall affirm that the cultic worship of a Jewish eschatological, religious sect of the One God, YHWH perceived him apocalyptically as Spirit (i.e., as a teacher-healer and conceptualized him as the divine persona,

Jewish fellowships, the redemptive christological significance of the resurrection, symbolically understood and taught to its initiates for the cult's levels of initiation into the community, was the essential mystical and metaphorical meaning for the existence of the community itself.

Some progressive members (who were originally within the Essenes), who had rejected the Qumran community's rigid formalism, may have perceived themselves as a resurrected,[15] Spiritual Israel. They based their mystical, (gnostic?) communal experience on their understanding that YHWH's Spiritual presence had anointed them (as the *christological* Jesus *parousia,* a religious phenomenon). The socio-religious empowerment (their salvation, a healing in which one is made whole) was perceived by them as a divine command to evangelize the Hellenistic world of polytheism and bring into Christ's Kingdom (the christological gatherings), both Jews and Gentiles, men and women, slave and free. The apostle Paul was one of the most effective in this regard, at least in the historical development of the Christian faith tradition.

The common fantasies and creative imaginations of our childhood must not divert us from the realities of rational adulthood. With honest moral integrity for scientific understanding of physical reality, one cannot stretch the human imagination by accepting the mythic foundational stories, such as, that Peter or others in actual history could have eaten and drunk with the so-

---

namely *Yeshua,* Jesus). *Yeshua* (Joshua, Jesus), means that Yahweh saves, redeems, and delivers. And, by this holy name, *Yeshua* (Jesus), universal and spiritual redemption would come to the world of humanity.

15. Meyer suggests a scholarly view gathered from the Valentinian Treatise on Resurrection, the fourth tractate of the Nag Hammadi Codex I (a similar view was also maintained by the earlier christological gatherings). He refers to the true meaning of resurrection found in the tractate that "the author insists that the true resurrection is a spiritual resurrection and the spiritual resurrection has already taken place within the lives of people." Marvin Meyer, *The Gnostic Discoveries: The Impact of the Nag Hammadi Library* (New York: HarperSanFrancisco, 2005), 136.

called Jesus after his physical, literal bodily resurrection. Note especially the details of the biblical reference that gives to the mythical story the essential, spiritual (symbolic) meaning of this historic and metaphorical occurrence (John 20:24-31). The modern liberal critic suggesting that the actual spiritual experiences of the early Christian witnesses to this historical (and literary narrative) event were given, by faith, a revelatory 'vision' by God only exasperates the rational sensibilities of a scientific modernity. Clearly, this type of biblical 'evidence' (a literary story of essential religious mythology), illustrates for us the significant historic and symbolic fact that the earliest documents contain no real historical references to an earthly, human Jesus; but, what appears here (a literary text) is the historicized religiosity, the later historical faith of the formative church's dogmatic Christology,[16] the Gospel Jesus.

It is in this sociological sense, that the early christological communities used symbolism so that they could grasp the mystical reality of their Lord's presence, YHWH. This psychodynamic and historic process allowed them to expand their cultic vision to an interpretive, functional level, albeit still reflecting the mythological significance. Thus, they were able to perceive themselves, metaphorically, with a revitalized faith as having a different religious spirituality (as a new Spiritual Israel) that was not 'confined' to the ancient Jewish tradition. These kinds of literary transformations were part of the ancient worlds' cultural adaptations for religious development. An example is provided by Meyer: "Before the Secret Book of John was Christianized, how-

---

16. There exists an irrational and dysfunctional attitude among most religious conservatives who reject certain theological propositions because of their non-scientific understanding (or more importantly, their rejection of an anthropological posture that is based on a lot of scientific evidence of human evolutionary development). They continue to think that human beings are special creations by God; and thus are distanced from the rest of the animal world of nature. Science's best evidence today indicates that "humans diverged from chimpanzee between 3.6 and 4 million years ago, and that the gorilla line may have split from the common ancestral line just a little bit earlier than that." Gribbin and Cherfas, *The First Chimpanzee*, 131-2.

ever, the text seems to have been a Jewish gnostic text that combined innovative and revisionist interpretations of the Jewish scriptures with Greco-Roman philosophical and mythological themes in order to proclaim a gnostic view of the world and to place God and humankind in the world."[17] They were led by the Spirit's presence (the theological instruction and socio-religious ritualizations of the christological community). Thus, the initiates were taught and understood the symbolic interpretations of the mystical experiences within the communal assemblies. Faith was required as an essential commitment for spiritual and theological sight,[18] and they progressed accordingly.

The biblical tradition expressed it thusly; "blessed is he who has not seen, yet believes" (John 20:29). This reflects a hermeneutical progression of the resurrection and exaltation as a later theological posture having a creedal and dogmatic Christology. "The belief in Christ's resurrection, that is, his exaltation, is based, not upon any report of the open tomb -- which came later -- but upon the visions of the earliest witnesses [such as Paul]." Grant continues: "The earliest view ... is either that Jesus ascended at once, or that his resurrection was his ascension and exaltation."[19] Regardless of the historicized context in Mark, the original symbolism based upon these revelatory 'visions' was deleted from the kerygmatic intention by the later Gospel writers due to its symbolic substance as myth. And much of the original

---

17. Meyer, *Gnostic Discoveries,* 91.

18. Cf. Paul S. Minear, *Eyes of Faith: A Study in the Biblical Point of View* (Philadelphia: The Westminster Press, 1946). Paul Tillich has outlined concisely the functional aspects of faith in the experience of an individual in his, *Dynamics of Faith* (New York: Harper & Row, Pub., 1957).

19. Grant, *Earliest Gospel,* 169-70. Bracket is mine. Paul maintained his vision to be similar to others (Peter, the twelve, and the other apostles, 1 Cor. 15). Grant further states that "the technical term for their [visionary, revelatory] experience is the vary one (*ōphthē*) used in the Old Testament and elsewhere to tell of heavenly appearances, 'epiphanies,' and visions." And, "the idea of the Ascension after a long interval, say forty days, is a very late conception, not anywhere in the earliest tradition." Ibid.

metaphorical dynamic of the Jesus cult's religiosity then became transformed as a result. Myth was becoming a form of historical memory. Faith no longer was the spiritual and mystical encounter of physical existence with God's presence by the believer. It no longer was the mystic meaning out of which that spiritual (symbolic) reality spoke. It became the simple acceptance of a literal and 'historical fact' (the Gospel Jesus), which fostered a literalist tradition by later orthodox Christianity. It ceased to be a moral imperative and ethical basis for an ongoing salvific communal process; and, it became the means to identify those who were the official, acceptable members of the orthodox, church community. This literary construct, which emerged out of the old Roman world, became the official, doctrinal understanding that the hierarchy of the Church dogmatized, as Christian orthodoxy. It soon became the official and the only acceptable Christology.

This symbolic interpretation is inescapable even as recorded in its historicized form in the New Testament tradition. Jesus' resurrection, even though it is fabricated history in Mark's Gospel, should still be tested by the same critical, analytical, and literary assessment procedures that are brought to bear on all mythological themes in literature. The original symbolic idea, that the cult's members were 'raised' into a new communal life experience and a loftier moral status, and given the earnest of the Spirit's presence (their *anointing*), and that they were his body (i.e., from its earliest formulation, the body of the cultic Lord) was essentially lost. Consequently, the later formative Christian community's 'mission' was seen as a historical extension of Jesus' earthly ministry to a lost humanity, which is the dominant theological and evangelistic understanding of modern Christianity today. One must accept the dogma of faith in the doctrines of the Christian church to find salvation.

As a result, much of the moral and ethical nature of Paul's preaching is lost. The one essential posture that he wanted was to know the "power of Christ's resurrection" and his "suffering" that results from fighting against the evil forces that destroy our humanity (our new creation, our moral/ethical development in Christ). With this view in mind, Rita Brock's comments take on a truly ethical imperative:

Evil … can be managed in such a way as to make life more humane if we struggle to minimize pain, to keep connections to life-giving relationships, and to work against what makes us helpless. … I would argue that *the loss of innocence* and the acceptance of our responsibility for struggling to minimize evil, the knowledge that we have some power, even if only minimal, to contribute to life-giving forces is a knowledge [faith] that gives hope. Hence, we must *lose our innocence* in order to gain hope.[20]

The earliest christological gatherings perceived that the anointed one of YHWH (by the power of his Spirit, the Christ) lived among them as an anointing 'moral' empowerment. It was the later generations (beginning with the Gospel evangelists) that fashioned their Gospel stories to demonstrate Jesus' shadowy historical character as a prophet in Israel. It was now this Gospel Jesus that had the divine power over the physical and evil forces during Satan's age.[21] Elaborate additions, interpolations, and the rewritings of older texts were continued by later formative Christian scribes. They also maintained the mythological world-view of a layered universe inhabited by all kinds of spiritual forces and

---

20. Maryanne Stevens, Ed., *Reconstructing the Christ Symbol: Essays in Feminist Christology* (New York: Paulist Press, 1993), 46-7. She has an interesting take of the idea of the coming Christ. For her, it "is not the historical Jesus returned, but rather the fullness of all this human diversity gathered together in redemptive community." Ibid., 24. She could have very well quoted Paul (Col. 1:28). Bracket and emphasis are mine.

21. Some of the major influences that entered into the arena of myth-to-history development were the ancient Greek, religious world-view, mystery cults, Gnosticism, mystical dualism, Apocalypticism, and Middle Platonism. The Jewish eschatological elements that concerned 'this age' and the 'next age' were reconfigured to absorb and amend Hellenistic religious thought that could also express, in elaborated ways, these same concepts. The cosmic dualism of middle Platonism redirected the Jewish linear format to a more Greek vertical mythic and spiritual dualism where Satan was seen as the demonic power that plagued humanity (mortals) on earth. See the *Ascension of Isaiah* and cf., with the Book of Hebrews in the canonical text.

beings; beliefs that were held in Judaism and the Hellenistic re-ligiosities. One example is seen in *"The Ascension of Isaiah,"* which is a composite of earlier Jewish parts and reworked with Christian emendations. It also follows the basic decent/ascent mythology of Hellenistic, middle Platonism.[22] Carrier compares Jesus descent into Sheol in a parallel account of Inanna's descent into *Hades* (hell). Thus, "Inanna descends from heaven to the underworld, skipping earth right by. She is incarnated in hell, killed, crucified, raised from the dead (in hell) with the water and food of life after three days, then ascends back to heaven, again skipping earth. This is pretty standard stuff in ancient cosmology and theology."[23]

The fabrication of a new literary genre (the Gospels) may have occurred in order to historically set before the Roman world that, this new faith (the primitive christological gatherings), had emerged out of, and thus had, an ancient socio-religious "connec-tion" with the older Jewish tradition, which the powers of Rome had accepted as a legitimate religion. In this way it would find its socio-political acceptance by Rome and thereby would be more in keeping with Rome's social, religious, and political stand-

---

22. Cf., Logan, *Gnostic Truth,* 22-3. He perceives Platonism as a functional and determinate tool of earliest Christianity as it "reflects Christian ideas and ways of interpreting the Old Testament in the light of the message of Paul and John ... on the basis of Christian speculation on Christ and Wisdom." This "reflects the experience of salvation through a Christian Gnostic initiation ritual based on baptism in the name of the Gnostic triad, and unction (or sealing) patterned on the primal chrismation and perfection of the heavenly Son and promising the eschatological descent of the Spirit." Ibid.

23. Bernard Muller, "Responses to Critiques of the Mythicist Case," Part Two, *THE JESUS PUZZLE: Was There No Historical Je-sus?* 6 at http://jesuspuzzle.com/htm (accessed 14 April 2004). In the descent, the divine being took on the form of the beings (rulers) of that sphere. Each heaven had distinct beings who ruled that heavenly sphere and the divine descending being, for self-preservation, by tak-ing each heavenly form maintained a disguise and safely descended further in Greek mythological fashion.

ards.[24] And eventually, when Rome did accept the socio-religious and cultural existence of the Christian Church, Rome also enabled 'orthodoxy' and 'heresy' to become factional considerations that facilitated and furthered the discontinuities within the developing church. Karen King states: "Orthodoxy and heresy may be understood as rhetorical constructs ... fashioned in the arena of political debate. Understood in this light, orthodoxy and heresy have little to do with truth and falsehood and everything to do with power and position. In a vote, the majority defines what is orthodox, and the minority is charged with being heretical."[25]

The diversity of spiritual concepts was linked to the various divine names and was applied to Jesus, as the identity of Yahweh's presence in the christological gatherings. It was a natural outgrowth of the same diversity of various religious mindsets, together with the interaction of historical and intellectual forces. The christological Jews in the diaspora had experientially absorbed, adopted, and accommodated some of the Hellenistic traditions, culture, philosophy, religion, and mythic concepts.[26]

---

24. Tacitus, *The Histories*, 5, 5 where he admits that "whatever their origin, [the Jews] observances are sanctioned by their antiquity," and as Elaine Pagels also notes: "the Romans respected tradition." in *ADAM, EVE, and the SERPENT*, New York: Vintage Books, 1988, 50. n. 64.

25. Karen L. King, *What is Gnosticism?* (Cambridge: MA: Harvard University Press, 2003), 15 as cited by Meyer, *Gnostic Discoveries*, 55.

26. The apologists of Platonic Christianity who traveled throughout the Roman Empire in the early second century wrote largely in keeping with the *Logos* religion in mind and defined themselves in a manner that had nothing to do with a historical Jesus as a founder-teacher. Cf., Tatian's *Apology to the Greeks* written around 160 CE and a Latin apologist around 155 CE, Minucius Felix' *Octavius,* and Theophilus of Antioch's work, *To Autolycus* around 180. They referred to themselves as Christians because they had been 'anointed' with the Spirit of God, and were converted to the 'faith' because of the Jewish scriptures: not a belief in a historical Jesus. Doherty's latest book deals with these and other apologists' writings in scholarly detail in *Jesus: Neither God nor Man: The Case for a Mythical Jesus,* Age of Reason Publications, 2009.

The assimilation of names (e.g., the cultic titles, Christ, Son of Man, Savior, etc.) with the metaphorical, midrashic interpretations, and mystical theology was because they had been based on religious devotion to the older Jewish biblical tradition. This fabricated, literary development also lent itself to the vagueness of a uniform theology[27] and lacked an organizational structure of religious and conceptual unity. The literary form (the canonical Gospels) that embraced this earlier mystical tradition reflected the earlier christological, mythological, and symbolic interpretation, which is still embedded within the sacred text. Only later, once it became historicized, has it become difficult to detect the original symbolic and metaphorical content in the literary form of the Christian biblical tradition.

Hoeller notes that "Christendom was split from the beginning; it was a gathering of many kinds of belief and interpretation and many kinds of gnosis as well."[28] Applying the law of probabilities, we could predict a natural and inevitable outcome for the mythological development within the context of ancient non-scientific views of the universe. Thus in Platonic fashion:

We would expect … the Christian version of this widespread type of mythology would begin precisely as a reflection of all others, namely as the descent of a spiritual figure working in the spiritual parts of the world with beneficial effects on humans in the material (fleshly") realm. And lo and behold, that is exactly the focus we find in the early Christian epistles and the pre-interpolation *Ascension of Isaiah,* while the concept of actual incarnation into a human, earthly man is missing.[29]

---

27. Redaction, interpolation, and hermeneutical and theological conformity were the intended methodologies used in the formative church to bring the sacred text into uniformity. The efforts of the author, who constructed the non-historical preaching in Acts, are indicative of this effort for uniformity.

28. Hoeller, *Gnosticism,* 203.

29. Bernard Muller, "Responses to Critiques of the Mythicist Case," Part Two, 19. In destroying the works of Satan, the intermediatoral Son was conquering 'this present evil age' on behalf of God; thus, this is how the myth develops in the scriptures: "God was reconciling the world unto himself -- through his son, the Christ." 2 Cor. 5:19.

It is also possible to detect some phrases of later Christian interpolation embedded within the contextual scheme of the apostolic literature (an example: 1 Thess. 2:15). It was the symbolic interpretation that defined the mystic significance of the resurrection event for the religious and historic experiences within the christological gatherings. It was the mythothematic history that actually represented the historical experiences, which gave them a sense of religious involvement in their communal salvation. Shanks points out: "Scripture was interpreted to refer to their own time, [and to] … their understanding of themselves as people of the new covenant and their messianic outlook."[30] When considering also the whole of their religiosity, the Qumran covenanters as well as the early christological gatherings all shared some essential viewpoints.

The mystic categories that reflected the socio-religious essence of the divine presence in their midst, metaphorically based, were the historic and essential symbolic terms culturally available to them at the time. They expressed the mystical realities of the new faith (the christological myth of Jesus' presence, his *parousia*) as a symbolic understanding that also expressed its mythological foundations, which are found in the later Gospels. This symbolism was demanded by the communal hermeneutic of the primitive christological sect. The language of the gatherings expressed their spiritual existence (life in the Christ, the anointed one) in relation to the divine presence, (*Yeshua*, Jesus who was God's revelatory Spirit). All of this religiosity, mythology, and its developmental hermeneutics became reformulated on a different basis, which is historical factuality.

What we have is an image confusion by our modern minds, which seeks definition, distinction, and discontinuity of religious categories. Evidently, it needs repeating: "Christianity, for the first 150 years was a mosaic of uncoordinated expres-

---

30. Shanks, *Dead Sea Scrolls,* 184. Although any suggestion of Christians borrowing from the Essenes is perceived as an 'unacceptable' idea by some and a better evidential view is that both groups developed out of a common tradition available to all in the time of the diversified Judaisms. Bracket is mine. Ibid., 185.

sions. It was a variegated organism that took root and flowered across the landscape of the empire, a widely divergent mix of Jewish and Greek features."[31] Within the cultural and religious context of this faith-expression, a divine persona took pre-eminence. We might ask: who is the one they had in mind? Is it God, Christ, the Holy Spirit, Jesus or a Hellenistic deity?

The earliest gatherings' perceptions within the diaspora were based on a fluidity of mythical experiences that could be answered in the positive, yes; all the above. Their religious experiences, collectively shared in communal life, were defined as a mystical relationship, as a fellowship with the divine presence, the eternal one, the heavenly father. This perception of a heavenly father held true also for gnostics, mystery religions, Stoics, Pythagorean, the Cynics' philosopher-prophets, and many others in Hellenistic times. In Semitic thinking, the idea of collective identification is quite common. The use of symbolic language, as a midrashic description for the deity as the Son of Man, was also a cultic expression, eschatologically derived, that can also be seen in the original covenantal texts.[32] There is a christological development that is characteristic of this in the *ebed Yahweh* hymns "that a plurality is progressively reduced as an always decreasing minority takes over the task, which was originally that of the totality."[33] It was a pervasive and universal human desire

---

31. Doherty, "Main Articles -- The Second Century Apologists," *THE JESUS PUZZLE: Was There No Historical Jesus?* 6, http://jesus puzzle.com/htm (accessed 22 June 2005).

32. Cf., Daniel 7:13-14 with Ezekiel 37:1-14 where the formation of communal life (as a resurrection event) is based on the Spirit of YHWH. Ezekiel's son of man designation is reflective and contains the religious idea of being a 'faithful servant of God.' Cullmann notes that "the 'servant of God' is one of the oldest titles used by the first Christians." Cullmann, *Christology,* 51.

33. Ibid., 55 to which could be added: The Book of Enoch, The Apocalypse of Ezra, The Apocalypse of Baruch, and the biblical book of Ezekiel when considering the *ebed Yahweh*, the servant of God (*pais*), and the son of man themes. Cf., H. Wheeler Robinson, "The Hebrew Conception of Corporate Personality" *BZAW* 66 (1936), and A. R. Johnson, *The One and the Many in the Israelite Conception of God* (1942).

for mortality that had developed within the tradition of Israel's past historical experience, which also had been influenced by Zoroastrianism.[34] Hence: it also had been an expression of Israel's national hope that was proclaimed in her prophetic literature as well.

This dimension of Israel's hope found additional expression in a variety of literary forms, especially the apocalyptic and eschatological literature[35] of late Second Temple Judaism. It appeared at a time when Israel was under foreign domination and being compelled to cast off her traditional ways of religiosity by the dominant political power. It was under Antiochus that "the reason for the decrees against the Jews was that they showed no inclination to live 'according to the customs of the Greek.' ... The forcible Hellenization of the Jews was the reason for the persecution."[36] Thus, this does not mean that the resurrection, within the context of Judaism, is only a development of thought used to comfort Israel[37] in time of distress. Their perceptions meant, religiously internalized, that YHWH (God) was still using Israel to bring about the 'formation of a community' through religious

---

34. The Zoroastrian and later Iranian religious preaching of ethical and eschatological dualism found acceptance with late, sectarian Palestinian Judaism (cf. the life and literature of the community at Qumran).

35. See Barrett, *The New Testament Background: Selected Documents*, for selected materials that present a good coverage of this period. 11. On apocalyptic literature, see H. H. Rowley, *The Relevance of Apocalyptic*, rev. ed. (New York: n. d.). Also, cf. Maurice Goguel's argument that Jesus' thought was eschatological not apocalyptic, *The Life of Jesus*, trans. Olive Wyon (New York: The Macmillan Co., 1933), 569-72. For a denial that Jesus thought in apocalyptic terms, cf. Bowman, *Prophetic Realism and the Gospel*.

36. Victor Tcherikover, *Hellenistic Civilization and the Jews* (Peabody, Mass.: Hendrickson Pub., 1999), 179-80.

37. Also see Ernest Ludwig Ehrlich, *A Concise History of Israel*, trans. James Barr (New York: Harper & Row, Pub., Harper Torchbooks, 1963), chaps. 13-19, 3-140. "The Sleeked sing, Antiochus Epiphanes IV (175-164 B.C.) forced Hellenization upon the Jews and made their worship and ceremonies illegal to practice. The death penalty was given for anyone found practicing Judaism."

concepts and spiritual expectations according to his ancient plan and purpose,[38] which had been established with the Abrahamic Covenant to include all of humanity. Somewhere along the way, Paul acquired this historic perception and it formed the core of his theological perspective as an apostle to the Gentiles. God, the Lord of Heaven, could "in the fullness of time," by the person of his (the 'father's') heavenly Son,[39] bring immortality to light (II Tim. 1:10). For the Apostle Paul, that expected time of fulfillment had finally come during and with his ministry. And, in the kerygma, God's salvation as the forgiveness of sins was proclaimed "to the Jews first then to the Gentiles."

The primitive christological tradition incorporated many gnostic modes of mystical expressions that reflect primitive Christianity's early socio-religious diversity. Logan notes that: "If there is one point of agreement in the fantastic plethora of gnostic systems, it would appear to be that human beings are composite, a mixture of heterogeneous elements, light and darkness, good and evil, spirit and matter, corporeal and incorporeal. Salvation is a matter of unscrambling this mixture."[40] Hellenistic philosophies, Mystery Religions, Platonism, Judaisms, and Paul extracted by theological modification different ways within this matrix of thought a route for salvation. The revelation of the cross and faith-response was Paul's gospel, an act by God that brought about forgiveness of sin (redemption) to humanity.

From the second century on, the developing christological communities were influenced by the Gospel tradition. Then the later Imperial Roman authorities within the systemic organization holding political and theological sway over the Christian churches of the Mediterranean world found themselves in a

---

38. Cf. James L. Price, *Interpreting the New Testament*, (New York: Holt, Rinehart, and Winston, Pub., 1961), where he presents the general atmosphere, political stage, sects, and movements of this period, 31-84. Also, most general introductions to New Testament studies will also provide a concise report of this historical period.

39. This mythical type of language that expresses a religious relationality (the father and the son) has "its parallels in the Hellenistic mystery cults." Cullmann, *Christology,* 278.

40. Logan, *Gnostic Truth,* 167.

struggle against Gnosticism.[41] This had occurred when the Roman Church began to formulate, apologetically, its historicized theological perspective[42] of a historical Jesus that emerged within the canonical Gospels. Hence, we can hear such apologetic statements that the "... Christian proclamation does not know the idea of the heavenly journey of the self-made possible by Gnosis and sacraments; but, it does teach the resurrection of the dead and the last judgment."[43] These last two concepts were commonly accepted in traditional Jewish circles among the common folk within the area of Judea and among many in the diaspora during the Second Temple period.

The earlier apostolic kerygma, which had been preached by Paul, had maintained a symbolic, mythothematic, and metaphorical understanding. This is especially true in his ministry and his proclamation of these eschatological focal points (the cosmic *Christos* event): the declaration of Jesus' death as a salvific sacri-

---

41. The Church's orthodoxy, under Roman authority, had battled against Jewish sectarians, christological mystics, and pagan Gnostics who had predated official Christianity by several generations. The early Diaspora Jews were christological in the same religious vain as the apologists of the mid-second century. The Christ (the anointed one) was a philosophical concept in keeping with the *Logos* type, a divine entity who revealed 'Wisdom,' as part of the act of salvation (cf., 1 John).

42. These attempts were made to spiritualize the resurrection doctrine by formative Christianity (II Tim. 2:18; but, Cf. also John 5:24f. and Eph. 5:14). Cf. I Tim. 6:4; II Tim. 2:23; and Titus 3:9; with I Tim. 1:4; 4:7; II Tim. 4:4; and Titus 1:14.

43. Bultmann, *Theology*, I, 168. Also see Schweitzer, *The Mysticism of Paul the Apostle*; and Gershom G. Scholem, *Jewish Gnosticism, Merkabah Mysticism, and Talmudic Tradition* (New York: The Jewish Theological Seminary of America, 1960). In the 'Star Wars' trilogy, "may the *force* be with you" is as close of a parallel meaning to the ancient Platonic concept of the *Logos* (the sacred Word) that you can find. Those who found salvation experienced the 'force,' the *Logos* which was rooted in Greek mysticism and was embraced by Diaspora Jews who maintained a christological hermeneutic based on Jewish moral and ethical imperatives. Paul's 1st letter to the Thessalonians is an ideal example of moral directives to a christological brotherhood.

fice and the resurrection of Jesus as a mystical union through communal life. Eisenbaum and I would be in agreement "that those passages in which Paul speaks of the experience typically called his 'conversion' are really about Paul's 'call' to a new vocation, namely, as Apostle to the Gentiles."[44] A mystic semblance remains of a symbolic kernel in the overall structure of the later historicized biblical tradition, even though the earlier apostolic epistles have now been influenced by the later Gospel narratives.

It seems odd that so many biblical literalists have such a problem[45] with understanding that the canonical texts have a long socio-religious history with a gnostic pedigree that undergirds much of its theological contents, religious categories, philosophical concerns, and literary structure. The christological gatherings' socio-religious perceptions, during this time, were concerned with their existence in a hostile polytheistic world.[46] Their desire was to bring into their community the lost (non-conforming) traditional Jews along with the Gentiles. This would necessitate a different hermeneutical basis and an expanded understanding of socio-religious themes that were essentially provided by Paul's gospel message.

There was a mythological matrix of mysticism that formed the world-view within the christological cult. Perhaps there were various levels within the various communities where initiates could advance according to their acquired skills and knowledge similar to those levels of initiation in the Greek mystery religions (cf., 1 John 3). All of these communal concerns found expression in a quasi-political form, linguistically. In the later development of the kerygma, the title 'Son of God' with its

---

44. Eisenbaum, *Paul,* 133. Also cf., Jeremiah 1:4-5, with Galatians 1:15-16.

45. The reasons are in all probability the same when it comes to their rejection of modern science (its bio-evolutionary thought with its anthropological considerations). These kinds of issues always come into conflict with a literal, ancient, and mythological world view.

46. See Elias Bickerman, *From Ezra to the Last of the Maccabees: Foundations of Post-Biblical Judaism* (New York: Schocken Books, 19-62), and Guignebert, *The Jewish world in the Times of Jesus,* 1939.

political derivation was retained while 'Son of Man' with its eschatological significance was seemingly used "... only as a self-designation of Jesus in the gospel tradition"[47] which also reflects the process of mystical and communal reflection. In this way, the kerygma, using the title Son of God, allowed the proclamation of Jesus' resurrection to take on the additional socio-religious and gnostic meanings gathered within Hellenistic pagan religiosity. This may have occurred in the earlier period[48] of the historically based Jewish christological cult. The formative church of a later period determined its historicized Christology on the basis of the (literary) witnesses of the resurrection myth in the Gospel narratives, which now were perceived as historical events in their hermeneutical posture.

---

47. Price, *Interpreting the New Testament*, 117. A significant work which deals with the centrality for the New Testament of the primitive Christian message is C. H. Dodd, *The Apostolic Preaching and Its Developments* (New York: Harper & Row, Pub., 1951). Bultmann provides a concise outline of this development relative to the Synoptic tradition and suggests a brief bibliography of works which deal with special problems relating to the general growth and literary formulations of the early Gospel tradition, *Form Criticism*, 81-85.

48. There is some evidence in the earliest tradition that would indicate that Jesus was considered by the early Jewish Christian community (Gnostic) as 'pre-existent,' 'begotten by God,' or 'begotten by the Spirit of God,' which is expressed in John's Gospel. This was also the trust of Pauls' proclamation. Gentile Christianity took the proclamation and interpretation of Jesus' life and ministry beyond the limited eschatology, when in defense of Hellenistic thought, it developed a definitive Christology. See M. Burrows, *More Light on the Dead Sea Scrolls* (New York: The Viking Press, 1958), especially in the section where he establishes the uniqueness of Christ, Chapter VI, "The Person and Saving Work of Jesus Christ," 64-73; and his comparison of Jesus with the Teacher of Righteousness in Chapter VII, "The Life and Character of Jesus," 74-86. For 'eye-witnesses,' see Acts 2:32; 3:15; and 10:40ff. And for "fulfilled prophecy" cf. Luke 24:27, 44 f., with Acts 2:30ff., 13:34ff., also Matt. 1:22; 2:15; 4:14; and 13:14. Note H. G. Wood's arguments in *Did Christ Really Live?* (New York: Harper & Row, Pub., 1955). See the tradition in John 12:38; Matt. 8:17 and cf. with I Peter 2:24-25.

When the Son of Man theme is considered in Daniel 7:13, Cullmann mentions that "where the expression occurs ... it had no messianic character; the term simply distinguished between a human being and the beasts which appeared in the vision." He goes on to further mention the results of a dynamic historical process of mythic adaptation within the Hellenistic world by formative Christianity. He declares that "the early Church invented this self-designation of Jesus by giving 'man' a messianic significance and making it a title."[49] This entire historical process as presented by traditional biblical historians seems like begging the question, a tautological masterpiece. In the social and religious development of the faith gatherings, it was the primitive community's kerygma that provided the raw materials for their later Christological confessions. These theological ideas could only have taken place in the Hellenistic world in view of the linguistic considerations together with an interactive religious engagement with Platonic categories. This occurred at a time when the formative Christian fellowships took on missionary activities to evangelize the world according to Gospel directives.

With this in mind, Kummel states that "... the reports of the resurrection present no uniform tradition."[50] In the Gospels, Matthew locates the resurrection appearances in Jerusalem and he goes to the Galilee (chapter 28). Luke states that Jesus' resurrection appearances are to be found in Emmaus and Jerusalem (chapter 24), while Mark gives no appearances. John, on the other hand, who belongs to the same literary category of 'Gospel' is

---

49. Cullmann, *Christology,* 139. It must be remembered that this theme (son of man) especially in Daniel is maintained by several scholars to have a collective meaning. In Ezekiel, the son of man is a 'faithful servant of God' who, in a salvific sense, represents 'the whole house of Israel' and they collectively represent the whole of humanity so that 'the knowledge of Yahweh would fill the entire earth.'

50. W. G. Kummel Ed., *Introduction to the New Testament,* Trans. A. J. Mattil, Jr. (Nashville: Abingdon Press, 1966), 36. Also see Ernst Lohmeyer's main thesis is that there were two main centers of primitive Christianity in Palestine, one in Jerusalem, the other in Galilee in his, "Galilaa Und Jerusalem," *Journal of Biblical Literature,* LVI (1937), 217-252.

usually differentiated from the synoptic Gospels by its purely external aspects,[51] refers to Jesus' appearance in the 'upper room' and later 'by the Sea of Tiberius' (chapter 20-1). All of the Gospels' narratives develop their interpretive views of the early tradition with definite theological intentionality. These definitely are not documents that present actual history. They concentrate their historic material (the historicized life of Jesus in the Gospels) into christological and soteriological constructions that fit theologically into the kerygmatic motif by the conservative, literalists of a later period.

These were a generation of folks who were far removed from the times of the events narrated in the Gospels. By this time faith was the acceptable means to adopt the authoritative doctrines of the established, church's systemic authority and gain access into its membership. By the fourth century, much of the earliest theological understanding based on symbolism and metaphor had now been replaced with a sense of historicity that, for the orthodox, Christian Church was now a reflection of the historical Jesus as dogma. Myth had finally become history (but in the minds of literalist believers only).

Finally, within the faith-understanding of the early community's resurrected experience (the original symbolic interpretation) and the 'gift' of the Spirit (the symbolic hermeneutic that raised this understanding to the level of the cult's spiritual instruction and propaganda), formative Christianity interpreted the resurrection experience so that it would culminate with Christ's historicized so-called 'return.' Thus, the resurrection of the Christ, which was proclaimed in the later church's historicized kerygma in the Gospels, was extended on a futuristic basis (i.e., Christ's return as part of the same redemptive act of YHWH). The earlier symbolic understanding of Paul in I Thess. 4: 13-18 was now perceived as the final spiritual redemption when all the literally dead would physically rise from the grave. Or, this same text, when gnostic religious categories are overlaid, might divulge a ritualistic scene similar to the mystery religion initiation ceremony. Then a full spiritual disclosure could be made that re-

---

51. Kummel, *Introduction,* 142-154.

counts, in cultic experiential form, the communal involvement of all initiates into a mystic call and joining together the mystical relationship of the initiates with the divine 'presence' (the *parousia*) of the deity, as a resurrection into a new communal life experience.

Since the discoveries of the Dead Sea Scrolls, scholars have been able to compare the many similarities between the Qumran community and the early christological gatherings. Scholarly opinion has determined that both have emerged within the complex world of Hellenism while at the same time developing their own style of Judaism. There are some similarities of text, theological themes, and interpretation. While looking at the following examples, keep in mind the text of 1st John as a comparative literary document. The eschatological features that were their self-identification markers, within these two communities, are also reflected in some of the major socio-religious hermeneutics they embraced. Also notice the interplay between the ethical considerations depicted in the 'two ways' of rabbinic teachings.

Shanks indicated that: "Both employ dualistic language to describe the options in the universe: There are just two positions, with no mediating ground between. Since both communities are still Jewish at this time, the dualism is ethical [Paul's emphasis]; the two opposing camps (or principles) are light and darkness."[52] He provides a couple of examples from the Qumran text, the Manual of Discipline 3 and 4 that, from a thematic posture, parallel 1st John. Thus:

He [God] has created man to govern the world, and has appointed for him two spirits in which to walk until the time of his visitation: the spirits of truth and falsehood. Those born of truth, spring from a fountain of light; but, those born of falsehood, spring from a source of darkness. All the children of righteousness are ruled by the Prince of Light and walk in the ways of light, but all the children of falsehood are ruled by the Angel of Darkness and walk in the ways of darkness (Manual of Discipline 3:18-21).[53]

---

52. Shanks, *Dead Sea Scrolls,* 199.
53. Ibid.

Within the socio-religious matrix of the times, there seemed to be a continuous conflict. He also provides another text that indicates this aspect of their relationship. Again, keep the text of 1st John in view. "For God has established the spirits in equal measure until the final age, and has set everlasting hatred between their divisions. Truth abhors the works of falsehood, and falsehood hates all the ways of truth. And their struggle is fierce in all their arguments for they do not walk together (Manual of Discipline 4:16-18)."[54] This was the practical, ethical, and spiritual purpose of the communal instruction as perceived by both camps, (*gnosis*, to gain spiritual understanding for living), and was used for their moral development and ethical behavior.

The concept of the resurrection was part of this divine drama (of moral development and salvation) by YHWH's wisdom (the cultic instruction and proclamation by apostles and prophets) through its symbolic interpretation. In 1 Cor. 2:6-7 the text reflects the idea that the instruction by the cult via the Spirit leads to the initiates' perfection, spiritual maturity (Greek, *teleios*). When the Jesus myth was made into an evangelistic effort, as the cult began its missionary endeavors, this spiritual/ethical perfection became the theological understanding of the cult's redemptive energies (note especially Col. 1: 28b, which still had spiritual maturity as its proclamation goal).

The Gospels do not present a convincingly clear or precise portrait of the character of a human Jesus. Each evangelist formed his own ideas of the historic Jesus as they felt he ought to be, based on their theological and christological hermeneutic. Most modern scholars agree that the Gospels' account of Jesus' life maintained in the Gospel narratives have been the literary

---

54. Ibid. Symbolism and religious metaphor abound in ancient literature, which find similar expressions in the canonical writings. For example: In the second tractate in Hag Hammadi codex VI, Thunder (Perfect Mind), in an aretalogical text, the Egyptian goddess Isis offers disclosures of herself and her activities in 'I am' statements (cf., Johannine categories) and another goddess female figure is the revealer who identifies herself as wisdom, or Sophia, as life, or Zoe, (cf., 1st John) and also identifies herself with knowledge, which is related by Meyer, *Gnostic Discoveries*, 155-66.

constructions of a human characterization, a divine persona, which is based on a reflection of the evangelists' own ideas and philosophic ideals.[55] These philosophical concepts can be seen in contrasting socio-religious categories with other cultural mindsets existing at that time. Hence:

> Scholars specializing in the second century have characterized the Christianity of the apologists as essentially a philosophical movement. Whereas the premier expression of Christian development in the first century, the one centered on Paul and his circles, was an apocalyptically oriented phenomenon with a strong Jewish flavor. … The apologists, who were all located in cosmopolitan centers across much of the empire, were grounded in Platonic philosophy and Hellenistic Judaism.[56]

These philosophical categories and spiritual concepts were formulated from the earlier and original symbolism of the kerygma.

The development that occurred, theologically, is based on the kerygmatic intentionality[57] that grounded the so-called historical Jesus of the Gospels firmly into the tradition of formative Christianity; then it later became a hermeneutical dogma. The evangelists did not write history, nor did they intend to write it. They wrote the Gospels with their mythical basis as the historic, passion drama for the Christian religion (the incarnate God in the

---

55. Moral integrity should always be followed in historical analysis. This is not always the case among biblical investigators due to their own personal theological demands. As a skeptic and rationalist I realize that this can also be true in the arena of science. Even for some scientists, their personal "hopes, beliefs and desires, and fears too, get in the way of the dispassionate alternation of hypothesis and tests. So the actual progress of science is not so much a smooth climb to even higher states of knowledge as a series of conversions as [personal] beliefs are overthrown." Gribbin and Cherfas, *First Chimpanzee,* 148. Bracket is mine.

56. See E. Doherty, "Main Articles – The Second Century Apologists," 2.

57. Also, cf., Reginald H. Fuller, *Kerygma and Myth*, Ed. Hans-Werner Bartsch, Trans. R. G. Fuller (London: S.P.C.K. Press, 1954), xi-xii.

salvation of humanity; purely mythological). These gospels, as a new literary genre, are nuanced by their style, form, and content, which are similar to many Greco-Roman 'hero' stories (*mythoi*) and are comparable to our modern historical novels and the many pulp fictions. Even though the characters are fictional and the story line purely the artistic imagination of the author, the story's setting can find its social and historical environment in an identifiable historical period. This in no way makes the fictionalized characters real in a historical sense.

Religious beliefs have always been taught to the younger generation as a communal and pedagogic function of religiosity. Thus, the children's perceptions of religious reality and spiritual understanding vary enormously. What seemingly had been an easy and natural understanding of the symbolic interpretation of the Jesus myth, by the early christological cult's adults, was just as naturally taught to the younger generation by the cult's parental membership and community leaders. Jesus' life and all his spiritual ministries were presented as acts of divine power over the evil 'Satanic' powers around them. God had provided them with spiritual/ethical empowerment for living in a hostile world. There is no real humanity depicted in these mythological stories of Jesus. There is no real suggestion of verifiable human compassion, ethical kindness, or familial affection. These were only a kind of 'show and tell' myths, exemplified in the narrative events of the Gospel. Yet, the youth heard and constructed mental images of a historical reality that would remain with them into adulthood.

The consciousness of the modern Christian reader of these Gospels, and the Christology of the modern Church, is confronted with a deity (albeit, historicized 'in the flesh'). There is no real humanity, only divinity in mythical garb. All the spiritual deeds of Jesus are based upon his divinity and his cosmic power over the satanic forces within the mythical sphere of Platonic thought.[58] In time and by the natural inclination of the mind, the

---

58. These ideas are all various parts of a diversified religious and philosophical "descent/ascent mythology" within the cultural context of Hellenistic thought. Even in Egyptian mythology, Pharonic religious sensibilities conceived of a royal 'ascent' into the next world by the

new generation of traditionalist 'grown-ups' interpreted their historical experiences non-symbolically and began to accept reality within the context of physical existence by a literal, historical understanding. This conceptual transformation for the theological and historic religiosity within formative Christianity became reformulated as historical fact (physical actuality). This process continued within formative Christianity in order to make sense of the religious existence for the second and third generation of children who became mature adults within the Christian Church.

The mystics of the early christological fellowships did not withdraw from worldly life; but, they understood the totality of life and one's own spiritual involvement in it. They had been spiritual partners with God, having been resurrected with their risen Lord, and were involved in an evangelistic ministry of reconciliation, especially in Paul's case to the Gentiles. This type of christological mysticism reflects the original symbolism of the Jesus cult and its metaphorical understanding of religious existence. The early christological cult and later formative Christianity as well perceived the salvific community as the body of YHWH's anointing Spirit (as the *Christos* event using the former cultic term). And as such, through the kerygma, the fellowship perceived itself as the necessary spiritual ingredient in YHWH's divine plan for the Gentile's salvation.

Unfortunately, the Apostle Paul's absorption into these early believers' faith structure has caused a distortion by most modern scholars concerning his Jewish socio-religious faith endeavors. Eisenbaum's contention is that the apostle's main trust in his missionary endeavors was "a thoroughgoing commitment to Jewish monotheism and how to bring the nations of the world to that realization as history draws to a close."[59] For Paul, sym-

---

Pharaoh who was a Son of God on earth. In Greek concepts the descending 'son,' the divine intermediator disguised himself by taking on the 'forms' of the spheres' inhabitants he traveled through in order not to be recognized. These ideas were significant for Gnosticism and several Greek mystery cults.

59. Eisenbaum, *Paul*, 173. Other biblical scholars and I would be in full agreement with her historical analysis concerning Paul's attitudinal role. Cf., Mark Nanos, *The Mystery of Romans: The Jewish*

bolism had been the earlier spiritual expression of the earliest gatherings' communal religiosity.

The resurrection in the propaganda of the christological fellowship had maintained this symbolic understanding as a mystical application to the experiences of the initiates in relation to fellowship with their God, as the divine presence, the *parousia*. But the historicized literary tradition maintains a definite Christological distinction for the historical Jesus. This is a modern, theological interpretation. The traditional theological understanding of this ancient mythological world-view has been accepted as 'historical reality' by the research of most modern, biblical scholars. They maintain the ancient mythological world-view as a historical reality in their own minds, while hedging around a modern secular world-view that is based on a bio-evolutionary and anthropological understanding of scientific modernity.

Therefore, in this analysis "history" (objective history, actuality, outer history, written history as physical occurrence) is set in contrast to *'geschichte'* (existential meaning, inner history [i.e., spirituality], and we understand this history then as 'historic' religiosity). We thereby sense a difference between a historical fact and a historic event that has been perceived as having significance in religious experience. This difference is explained thusly: "A historic event has great significance for the future and is remembered by posterity as the determinative in the continuous life of people. A historical fact may be completely insignificant to anyone and registered as a mere disconnected jot in an ancient chronicle."[60] The reformulated and historicized sources, the whole of the expanded covenantal literary corpora, indicate that the kerygma is a historical proclamation.

We have seen that the literary Jesus of the Gospel (the historicized reality) was originally the divine presence, as Spirit (the presence and power of YHWH), within the earliest christo-

---

Context of Paul's Letter (Minneapolis: Fortress Press, 1996), 166-238 and my earlier introductory remarks in this study.

60. Martin Kahler, *Historical Jesus-Biblical Christ*, 21-22. For an expanded and detailed analysis of these distinctions, see Macquarrie, *An Existentialist Theology* and H. Richard Niebuhr, *The Meaning of Revelation* (New York: The Macmillan Co., 1941).

logical fellowships and was not a historical entity. The historic Jesus was the theologized understanding (a personification of Wisdom, cf., Matthew's Gospel) by some of the developing christological communities. It was the natural and historical basis for the Jesus cult's social and religious existence that can still be detected within the later Christian, biblical tradition.

The primitive Christians had expressed this myth as their cultic spirituality and cultic life (perceived symbolically) as resurrection, mystically experienced as a faith-community. The cult's religious leadership was responsible for the initiate's theological instruction together with its metaphorical and symbolic understandings. The members perceived and interpreted their communal existence in symbolic and religious terms as the new Spiritual Israel of the times. Thus, there was a moral and ethical component to eschatological thought rather than a historical significance. Logan notes that in a gnostic sense:

> 'Eschatology' means chiefly the release of the spirit from matter. The gnostic thus experiences a kind of 'instant' or 'realized' eschatology: with his or her response to the 'call' he/she experiences awakening, resurrection, and rebirth. This kind of realized eschatology is expressed in ... the *Gospel of Truth*: 'Since the deficiency came into being because the father was not known, therefore when the father is known, from that moment on the deficiency will no longer exist.'[61]

These types of moral/ethical categories were the essential aspects of the earliest christological formulations by Paul and other apostles and the communities that supported them. All these ethical concerns bear testimony in his and their canonical literary forms. This is clearly understood once the Gospel story of Jesus (the myth) is not used as a hermeneutical marker to read these earliest texts of Paul and other apostles.

The earliest Jewish gatherings maintained a symbolic and christological understanding that established the theological parameters for their mystical and communal existence. This was a theological posture that was taken from the Jewish scriptures,

---

61. Logan, *Gnostic Truth*, 301.

from interpretations (midrashim, theophanies, and personifications) that perceived the gatherings' self-identity as the suffering servant, the faithful Son of YHWH.[62] The Ezekielian expression "the son of man" became most apropos within Judean christological gatherings for their own self-identities as faithful servants of YHWH in the last days. These fellowships together with their diaspora brotherhoods perceived that they were the anointed and redemptive forces that were bringing about salvation to the entire Hellenistic world. The socio-religious process, which they perceived as vital to their eschatological survival, gradually was changing its mystical form and mythological shape.

This occurred when the christological groups among the Hellenistic Jews in the diaspora interacted with relatives and friends as they continued their economic trade in the various areas of Judea. Thus, much of the apparently historical narrative seems like a transparent invention to dramatize the Jesus myth as historical in its theological development. The Gospel evangelists' kerygmatic intentions still reflect the process of historization. These Gospels, which now proclaimed the new monotheistic universal salvation, by faith in the divine, historical Jesus and in his physical resurrection, had become an institutionalized Christology (the later dogma of the orthodox, Christian church).

Hence, the transformation of the early Jesus myth, into the current dogma of the Christian church, demands a revival of the symbolic, hermeneutical understanding in modern, biblical scholarship. One that can cut to the essence of Christianity's mythical irrationality and provide at the same time an honest

---

62. Cf., Isaiah 53; Psalm 2; and Ezekiel 37:1-14. Most modern biologists agree that a common feature of evolutionary development is the notion of exaptation (an old structure gets borrowed to perform a new function). An example is when legs on a fish are used to walk on land. Zimmer, *Evolution: The Triumph of an Idea* (New York: Harper Perennial, 2001), 377. Cultural integration of religious and theological categories that once performed social needs in one community were adapted and infused with new meanings in other communities over various historical times. This historical process of religious borrowing is similar to biological exaptation. And in literary form is expressed as midrashim.

humanistic rationality; one that understands, engages, and works to change the political oppression, systemic immorality, and the economic exploitation in the global life of modern, secular humanity.[63] It will become necessary to jettison the ancient biblical and mythological world-view and to passionately use modern language to describe and formulate strategies to bring about reasonable and ethical solutions.

---

63. See, Spong, *Why Christianity Must Change or Die* (1998). Also, for traditional arguments for religious negativity caused by historical events, compare Jenkins, *Jesus Wars* (2010) and Carroll, *Sword* (2001).

PART FOUR

Canonical Era: *Confirmation* 116 CE to 325 CE
The Orthodox Christian Church affirms its official Christology.

10

*The conventions of ancient historiography called on historians
to invent speeches appropriate for their characters.*
Alan E. Segal

The critical problem in this study is to formulate a historical understanding and to explain how and why the metaphysical religious sensibilities and the mythological cultural basis (the historic social sensitivity in the religiosity of the Jewish christological gatherings) became historicized as an objectification of faith. This is the result of a theological and hermeneutical posturing in the development of the earliest communities of faith. Religiosity can be considered as the all-encompassing of the whole context of human experiences, the ontological (ritualization, institutional organization, and religious customs), and the epistemological (the beliefs, theology, and religious expressions and conceptualizations) in which the focus is on the interactive and systemic relationships for cultural and religious existence.

The thread of the mystical, mythological, and religious elements of the ancient christological religiosity still survives in the biblical tradition due to the various historical forces at play within the Hellenistic world out of which they emerged. The destruction of Jerusalem in 66-73 C.E. and the discontinuity of the Jewish christological cult (the primitive church) at that time coincided with the adaptation of the Hellenistic version of Paul's writings,[1] the gospel kerygma, and the emergence of a new systemic faith that became to some extent historicized (Mark's Gospel) prior to the emergence of a later Romanized Christianity.

---

1. Mead, *Echoes,* 101, offers some insight as to name changes. He indicates that "change of name is found in almost all initiatory rites, and corresponds to an inner change of [em]power[ment]." Brackets are mine.

When the kerygma became solidified in literary form, as the Gospel of Mark, it emphasized (maybe unintentionally) the process of historization of Jesus' life by the evangelists. This theological perspective, metaphorically based, is referred to by biblical scholars as the 'kerygmatic intention.' His Gospel, which depicts a mythical and historical Jesus, is not biographic and its literary form and was never intended to be. It presents the central and historic aspect of Jesus' life, in an original symbolic fashion, as the life and religious experiences of the Jewish christological gatherings.[2] For Paul the cross/resurrection was a revelatory *Christos* event to which Bultmann adds that they formed "a single, indivisible comic event which brings judgement to the world and opens up for men the possibility of authentic life."[3] If Paul had lived in a more recent age and known of existential terms and categories, he would have agreed with Bultmann. Thus, it is necessary to consider the Hellenistic, religious atmosphere when dealing with the communal aspects of early Christian origins.

Modern biblical scholars, who realize this historical connection, indicate that a paradigmatic relationship exists within the early text. It is a relationship that depicts these activities in communal earthly existence with a cosmic, heavenly counterpart (cf., Platonism?). This can be seen in the *Similitudes of Enoch* with the 'Son of Man' figure in heaven that reflects a counterpart in the earthly, community of believers. This would suggest a concept similar to the Hebrew idea of 'corporate personality.' Doherty has argued that "the one like a son of man" in Daniel 7 should be understood in this sense, "as the heavenly counterpart of the faithful Jews."[4] Both testaments merged in their historical

---

2. Burton Scott Easton, *The Gospel before the Gospels* (New York: Charles Scribner's Sons, 1928); and compare it with Hunt, *Primitive Gospel Sources*. Cf., with Marcel Simon's, *Jewish Sects at the Time of Jesus* (Philadelphia: Fortress Press, 1967).

3. H. W. Bartsch, Ed., *Kerygma and Myth: A Theological Debate* (London: S.P.C.K, 1953), 39.

4. Doherty, "Responses to Critiques of the Mysticist Case: Part One," *THE JESUS PUZZLE: Was There No Historical Jesus?* 14 at http://jesuspuzzle.com/htm (accessed 16 July 2005). He is quick to point out that the Son of Man follows a mythological pattern in that the

development so that Mead asserts that, "As the Old Covenant books were considered to be replete with types and figures, images and shadows of the Gospel-teaching, so were the books of the New Testament, in their turn, held to be figurative and symbolical of the inner teachings of the Gnosis. The former were intended for those of Faith, the latter for those in Gnosis."[5] A mythological connection can also be made by these ideas to the characterization of Jesus in the Gospel narration by Mark.

Yet, it is significantly true, that the meaning of his passion (the cultural expression of crucifixion) once historicized could only be understood because of the resurrection that followed as a literary event in the narrative. This vital connection was a religious dynamic mentioned much earlier by Paul. For him, it was a revelatory expression of divine forgiveness[6] that was always intended by God since the beginning of time. Yet, it has now been accepted as a historical event for humanity's redemption. It was given a religious value (i.e., his passion-death-resurrection) together with a historic and spiritual significance by the formative church in the Greco-Roman world. Its historicized

---

concept does not equate with the faithful community as its personification. It is a heavenly 'doppelgänger' (a double), Ibid. Cf., the Egyptian's religious idea of the *KA* and *BA* in their religious meanings (a psychodynamic spiritual double of personality). In Greek mythology, this double was thought of as being more real than its earthly counterpart. Cf. M. Eliade, *The Myth of the Eternal Return*, 3-6.

5. Mead, *Echoes*, 131. Hence: Christianity maintained both traditions as their canonical Scriptures. Mead also maintained that "the christological and soteriological theories of the gnostic philosophers were not ... invented altogether *a; priori;* they rested, I hold, on the basis of a verifiable historical fact." He believed that this historical fact was obscured by "historicizing narratives of the origin." Ibid., 133.

6. Cf., I Cor. 15:1-4 where Paul indicates that his revelatory experience, based on his hermeneutical posture, was understood as "the forgiveness of sins," and was unencumbered by the Mosaic legalities "according to the Scriptures," which had required the priesthood in Jerusalem to officiate the sacrifices. This may be why he felt it was a scandalous point of view for the Jewish Judeans for whom the Temple sacrifices were a religious identity issue.

form that developed later won the hearts of orthodox, literalist believers.

In this way, it cast off the Jewish exclusiveness and took on the characteristic features of a universal mission of ethical monotheism. This can be seen in the tension between the christological fellowships with traditional Judaism and with the Hellenistic religiosity of polytheism that is recorded in the expanded covenantal writings.[7] This spiritual break with traditional biblical Judaism provided the christological gatherings (as a renewal Judaistic movement) with a renewed ethical dialectic. Out of the earlier symbolism came the later significant theological elements that are embedded within the formative Christian scriptures. Along with the process of midrashim, the early christological Jews found the sacred text to be a revelatory blessing. The ancient texts taught them to view the world (earthly, their fleshly experiences) through the prism of faith as a different world (heavenly, by their spiritually anointed experiences). This Platonic conceptualization was an expression of religiosity that was familiar in the Hellenistic environment. Faith truly created, by their revitalized perceptions, "a new heaven and a new earth."

The ancient myths also had their own historical developments. Wells suggests that the mythological process which developed the stories (*mythos*) were "originally vague stories" that "are later given an exact setting in time and place – just as personages originally nameless are later supplied with names."[8] This whole scenario also developed in the christological gatherings and depicted a salvific process that incorporated myth and a mystic relationship with God, the divine father. There is also an indication that there was a dwindling emphasis on the eschatological

---

7. Almost any critical introduction to the New Testament writings will provide a general view of the tension that existed during the early church's development. On the speeches in Acts (i.e., the proclamations), see H. J. Cadbury, *The Making of Luke-Acts* (New York: The Macmillan Co., 1927), Ch. XIV; and his, *The Beginnings of Christianity, Part I*, "The Acts of the Apostles," Vol. V (London: SCM Press, 1933), 402-427. Also, cf. F. F. Bruce, *The Acts of the Apostles* (London: Tyndale Press, 1951), 18-21.

8. Wells, *Can We Trust*, 135.

significance of the earlier kerygma. Formative Christianity developed these mythothemes along Hellenistic lines rather than continuing its primitive Jewish influence.

Beginning with an eschatological view that was embellished with pungent apocalyptic language, the christological assemblies, through their cultic worship and through their own christological proclamation in their missionary endeavors, now entered into a religious and cultural conflict. This cultural process of conflict was reminiscent of an earlier historical and political time in which conflict was a determining factor of social perception. Tcherikover remarks that,

> The Maccabean revolt was from a broader point of view only one link in a long series of uprisings on the part of the oriental countries against their western rulers. These uprisings manifested a deep social antagonism between the towns, which supported the central power and compromised with Hellenism, and the countryside, which upheld ancestral tradition and fought the foreign power and the local aristocracy simultaneously.[9]

The christological gatherings, from their homes in the diaspora to their familial roots in Palestine, were under the dominance of Roman authority, economic exploitation, and political oppression. And thus, their social perceptions were reformulated accordingly. A consideration of cultural attitudes is necessary to understand the level of distrust, conflict, and confrontation by Jews living in a Gentile world. In the eyes of the Greeks as a whole, the Jew's refusal to worship the gods had definite attitudinal repercussions. "'If the Jews are really of our community,' claimed the Ionians, 'let them also honor the gods whom we honor.' 'If the Jews belong to the citizenry,' asked Apion, 'why do they not respect the gods whom the Alexandrians respect?'"[10] Paul also found that physical suffering and emotional anguish became an expected circumstance among those to whom he ministered (1 Thess. 1:9-2:2) for which Jewish and Greek cultural difference was a matter of religious concern.

---

9. Tcherikover, *Civilization*, 207.
10. Ibid., 375.

The reformulation of the ancient Mosaic tradition by midrashim was the spiritual impetus of the new faith and the communities' hermeneutical posture. The new biblical tradition in its expanded covenantal literature has preserved this new dynamic perspective. The earlier symbolic interpretation, within the kerygma of the primitive church, found its metaphorical basis in the narrative of the Gospels' literary form. Being grounded in this hermeneutic, it became a radical religious difference, theologically, when the Jesus of the Gospel narrative is depicted as a historical person.[11] This may account for the various episodes of conflict that Paul experienced in his missionary endeavors with the Jerusalem congregation under James conservative leadership. This whole process of historization was based on the persona, the historical divine presence of *Yeshua* (Jesus, as the *Christos* event) within the communal, religious dynamics and social interactions.

It makes better sense to speak of and to understand the ideas of the death and resurrection of Jesus in the Gospel narratives as a historic, spiritual, and hermeneutical event (see Rom. 5:8-15). Jesus' resurrection was symbolic as well as a theological and revelatory statement. This kind of process was common to the religiosity of the Hellenistic world.[12] Jesus' death was understood as occurring "from the foundation of the world" (Matt. 25:34; John cf. 13:8 with 17:24). This kind of mythological religiosity makes it preposterous to make any claim of historicity for an earthly life of a man, the so-called Jesus of Nazareth. In fact,

---

11. Brandon, *Jesus and the Zealots*, 182f. See Matthew 16:18; I Corinthians 10:4, and cf. II Samuel 23:3. The conceptual similarities may be more than co-incidental when considering the cultural religiosity and other factors of intrusion on earlier Judaism.

12. Note Bart Ehrman, *The Orthodox Corruption of Scripture: The Effect of Early Christological Controversies on the Text of the New Testament* (Oxford: Oxford University Press, 2011), 208, note #164 where he cites evidence of a Valentinian notion that "Jesus' apparent sufferings on earth were allegorical reflections of the catastrophic passions of Sophia within the Pleroma (Irenaeus, *Adv. Haer.* I, 8, 2)." This type of mythotheme was referenced to the death of Jesus in the biblical tradition by Ehrman. Ibid., 182.

Scholars have long asked questions like that of Elizabeth Schlü-sser-Fiorenza ... "Why do the hymns use the language of myth to speak of Jesus of Nazareth who was not a mythic figure but a concrete historical person?" [Doherty has pointed out] that the very earliest expression about Jesus we find in the Christian record presents him solely as a cosmic figure, pre-existent creator and sustainer of the universe (Paul and his school), a heavenly High Priest and Platonic *Logos*-type entity (Epistle to the Hebrews), a descending redeemer in the spiritual realm (the pre-Pauline hymns), and so on.[13]

Yet, to emphasize the symbolism of this religious formulation and its theological significance (Heb. 7:3; cf. Rev. 1:4) does justice to the social, analytical, and religious assessment of the historical Jewish gatherings and their self-identity as the New Israel. This same identification as a New Israel was maintained by the Essenes. The Essene Library of Qumran "stands for a social group that conceives of itself as 'Israel,'" and spelled out "what that 'Israel' is and must do."[14] Seen from this perspective, the christological 'New Israel' also retained the historical and spiritual integrity of the cult's propagandized myth (Rev. 13:8). In fact, the earlier gnostic aspects of various passages, which underlies so much of the biblical text as orthodox Christology, are only understandable when the earlier symbolic hermeneutic is used to establish the symbolic formulations and their theological significance as they relate to the overall religious structures of mythology.

---

13. Doherty quotes Elizabeth Schlüsser-Fiorenza's question from "Wisdom Mythology and the Christological Hymns of the New Testament" in *Aspects of Wisdom in Judaism and Early Christianity*, 34, in "Main Article -- Postscript," *THE JESUS PUZZLE: Was There No Historical Jesus?* 6 at http://jesuspuzzle.com/htm (accessed 22 June 2005).

14. Bruce Chilton and Jacob Neusner, *Judaism in the New Testament: Practices and Beliefs* (New York: Routledge Press, 1995), 88. In the Essene community, "the system as a whole forms an exercise in the definition of 'Israel' as against that 'non-Israel' composed not of Gentiles but of erring (former, lost) Israelites. The saving remnant is all that is left: 'Israel.'" Ibid.

The kerygmatic intention, within the structure of the later Gospels, was an interpretive reflection of the meaning for the historicized life and ministry of the historicized Jesus. The believers' cultic base was geographically differentiated throughout the diaspora. The effect of this is that the kerygmatic intention did not emerge with a uniform theological 'system' of thought. The expanded covenantal text presents a variety of theological concepts, which suggests that a variety of similar christological thoughts (e.g., the interpretive basis, which reflects the differences within the concepts of the Jewish gatherings) were also contained in the earliest non-canonical sources. This conceptual diversity influenced and contributed to the expanded covenantal (fabricated) Gospels' narrative formation.[15] Ehrman provides an example of this development within the canonical tradition:

> As I have already stated, most of the later adoptionists that we can actually identify—the Ebionites, Theodotus, Artemon—located the time of Jesus' adoption not at his resurrection but at his baptism. One would naturally expect that unless they had invented this notion themselves, traces of it should be found in earlier traditions. Such traces do in fact exist, and most of them ... were changed in one way or another by various scribes during the history of their transmission.[16]

With this in mind, it must be realized that the Gospel accounts are not the total picture of the historicized Jesus' life and ministry, as understood by formative Christianity. It seems that a multitude of literary forms have been uncovered in modern times

---

15. A concise introduction to the traditions which emerged in the literary 'Gospel' forms and suggests references to further literature, more recent on this subject, can be found in Appendix I, "Introduction to the History and Sources of the Synoptic Gospels" of Gunther Bornkamm, *Jesus of Nazareth* (New York: Harper & Row, Pub., 1960), 215-220. Cf., also his "Faith and History in the Gospels," chap. I. Ibid., 13-26.

16. Ehrman, *Orthodox Corruption,* 57. Keep in mind that these changes were made based on theological grounds (spiritual perceptions), the expansion of mythothemes, not on actual historical observations.

that provide a wealth of varying portraits of the historicized Jesus. Much of them are very controversial to say the least. It was the kerygmatic intention of the evangelists that was responsible for the Gospel form, its structure, and the historicized narrative content. Furthermore, the proclamation of the primitive, christological gatherings had been directed by an eschatological outlook.[17] Later, when the Gospel of Mark appeared, a historicized scenario took effect, and an apocalyptic interpretation of the life and ministry of the biblical Jesus emerged. In literary form, Jesus was a Hellenistic/Jewish hero. The historical situation and religious experiences of the Jewish gatherings are still embedded in this newly formed biblical tradition. They can still be found (for those who have eyes to see) also in the later theological conceptualizations of the formative church's Christology.

The Christian biblical tradition confirms the symbolic interpretation when the bulk of modern scholarship has concluded that the sources in that tradition do not contain pure, reliable history.[18] Even a critical, biblical scholar such as Bart Ehrman has noted that the biblical data provided by Paul, concerning the so-called historical Jesus, is sorely lacking as verifiable history. "It has struck some people as odd that Paul, our earliest author to discuss Jesus' resurrection [as a mythic and cosmic event], does not mention the circumstances that Jesus' tomb was empty nor name any women among those who first believed in Jesus' resurrection."[19] This type of historic reflection, even within the bibli-

---

17. For significantly detailed views of these eschatological positions which relate to the coming Kingdom, see Dodd, *The Parables of the Kingdom*; and compare his ideas with Albert Schweitzer in his *The Mystery of the Kingdom of God: The Secret of Jesus' Messiahship and Passion*, trans. Walter Lowrie (New York: Macmillan Co., Schocken Books, 1964); and Jeremias' *The Parables of Jesus*.

18. See Herbert Butterfield, *Christianity and History* (New York: Charles Scribner's Sons, 1950). Also, cf., Braaten, *History & Hermeneutics*, 84; and cf., Macquarrie's *An Existentialist Theology*.

19. Bart Ehrman, *Jesus: Apocalyptic Prophet of the New Millennium* (Oxford: Oxford University Press, 1999), 232. Note 1 Cor. 15:3-8. In his *Jesus Did Exist?* Ehrman writes as a man of faith rather than as a scholar seeking historical verification for a historical Jesus. The

cal tradition and its mythological basis that developed, although it later was historicized, still shines through the biblical text (the expanded covenantal literature). It verifies the historical analysis and provides authentication of the hermeneutical process of turning myth into historical reality.

The symbolism, mysticism, and hermeneutical basis, which reflect its social and religious significance, can be detected plainly from the canonical Gospels and other New Testament writings. Dodd's comments are very instructive when relating symbolism to the Gospels as mythological, apostolic creativity:

> Thus the very nature of the symbolism employed by the evangelist reflects his fundamental Weltanschauung. He writes in terms of a world in which phenomena -- things and events -- are a living and moving image of the eternal, and not a veil of illusion to hide it, a world in which the word is made flesh. In the light of this, [we have] ... the leading ideas of the gospel ... bound together by an intricate network of symbolism.[20]

The literal and historical anointing of both a person and things in the ancient eastern forms of religiosity were used with sweet smelling oil poured or smeared over them. It was in this fashion that the divine presence within the early gathering was understood. The divine Spirit resided within the community as its *anointing* so that the initiates (collectively, as one divine body, 1

---

historical 'oddity' by some, that he mentioned, certainly did not enter into or phase his own historical methodology.

20. Dodd, *The Fourth Gospel*, 143. Brackets are mine. In Galatians 4:24, we find the stamp of approval for this symbolism in the story of Sarah, Hagar, and Ishmael, which Christian theologians have for centuries deemed as historical (i.e., from its older Jewish tradition). Nevertheless, the biblical text states, by textual commentary, the religious significance of the story; thusly, we read: these "... things [i.e., stories] are allegorical" (Galatians 4:24). This familiar religiosity in early Christian thought and the symbolism of the Jesus myth, evidenced in this study, is not limited to the explicated biblical text itself. Its mythical expressions are found throughout the entire scope of Christian literature. These represent the most natural and a sense of historical, spiritual integrity for primitive Christianity.

John 2:20-25) became God's 'faithful servant,' his mythic Son. In fact, "the 'servant of God' is one of the oldest titles used by the first Christians to define their faith in the person and work of Christ."[21] This mythological perception denotes the symbolic and cultic ritualization (baptism) that empowered them in a mystic union with God. The anointing of the cultic stone was regarded as the power-conferring act, and it transferred the divine spiritual power in order to make the stone holy. In this same way, the anointed fellowship by the Spirit made 'the gatherings' holy and they became 'the body of Christ' (the anointed one). Even though the results of the historicized religious theology are somewhat similar to the spiritual meanings of the original primitive gatherings, they do not maintain the same historical integrity that the original symbolic interpretation provided. Furthermore, it tends to polarize faith and fact for modern humanity when the meanings of 'historic' and 'historical' are not hermeneutically considered as discussed above.

This hermeneutical polarization continues to exist today for many as a distortion of ancient history for modern religiosity in relation to a rational, scientific understanding of human existence within a unitary, physical universe. The symbol of oil used in the Gospels was indicative of the spiritual indwelling power of YHWH to bring together into an end-time community, a resurrected people, for this is how the early Jewish community understood its christological anointing.[22] One might speculate and wonder if the play on terms, used by the evangelists where Peter is called a *rock* and is seen as the basis for religiosity residing in its confessional form (i.e., faith as was provided in the cultic stone), might reflect in a conceptual way, a much earlier cultic

---

21. Cullmann, *Christology,* 51. Also see H. H. Rowley, "The Servant of the Lord in the light of Three Decades of Criticism," *The Servant of the Lord and Other Essays on the Old Testament* (1954), 1-58. Note especially Mark's Gospel idea of Jesus as "the servant of the Lord" in 10:45 with its cultic sense of mysticism.

22. Cf., 1 John's theme of anointing as a communal experience that had a revelatory and wisdom significance for the mystically based fellowship in its understanding of their ethical conflicts and social responsibilities.

practice of anointing the stone, which represents the presence of the deity's Spirit for the cult.

The criticism that this new faith-understanding of the primitive church was projected back upon the lips of the historical Jesus, by the process of historization of the biblical tradition (understood as the spiritual revelatory encounter with their risen Lord), has been a major concern in biblical and theological research. This criticism, as Beare has stated, is a distinction that must be considered most seriously. He states that the early church "had no motive for making a distinction between sayings of the historical Jesus and sayings of the risen Lord."[23] Following this traditional logic, Christians might maintain that there was no reason to limit the appearances of the risen Lord to one place or even to one time.

In general, the whole of the expanded covenantal literature can stand firmly on the stated religiosity and mystical purpose of John's Gospel, which states that "these are written that you may believe that Jesus (the end-time resurrected fellowship) is the Christ (anointed by the divine Spirit) the Son of God (a faithful servant [community] for bringing in the Gentiles into YHWH's Abrahamic Covenant)."[24] Paul made a cultural adaptation, as a diaspora, Hellenistic Greek speaking/thinking christological Jew, to embrace and gather into the Yahwistic faith the rest of the Greek world. Tcherikover explains that,

---

23. Frank W. Beare, "Concerning Jesus of Nazareth," *Journal of Biblical Literature*, LXXXVII, Part II (June 1968), 127. Also see, Cf. Grant, *Gnosticism and Early Christianity*. Cf. the significance and use of the divine name in Gnosticism as it also relates to salvation; also note Rev. 1:8.

24. John 20:31 by using parentheses and brackets, the application of a symbolic hermeneutic allows the text to come alive with its historical, social, religious, and original understanding. Perpetuation of a literalist, historical posture does not negate a well-recognized principle in mythological studies in which deities can die within mythic settings (the spiritual, cosmic narratives) and do not occupy real events upon the earth. Most college students having read Homer's *Iliad* and *Odyssey* are familiar with these types of issues.

Greek sources do not always distinguish between racial Greek and Hellenized Oriental; and there was a reason for this, since sometimes they themselves did not even notice the difference. In the Hellenistic period the term "Greek" ceased to be a purely ethnic, and became also a cultural, concept. The Greeks did not always make a distinction between a Greek who had come from Greece to settle in oriental lands, and an Oriental who had learned Greek and acquired Greek culture.[25]

Platonism, within Greek culture, was one of many rich sources of mythological categories that also provided the early communities with metaphoric language and symbolism. Even the form-critical study of the earliest christological tradition has established this purpose of religious symbolism beyond reasonable doubt.[26] Remember that symbolism in the apocalyptic literature abounds in abundance as part of the intellectual atmosphere of this historical and eschatological age.

I am reminded of the ideas by E. L. Doctorow who stated that, "... when ideas go unexamined and unchallenged for a long time, certain things happen. They become mythological and they become very, very, powerful."[27] The transformation of the Jesus myth into a literary, historical modality and its historical acceptance by formative Christianity needs to be examined and challenged because of the present, mythological church dogma

---

25. Tcherikover, *Civilization,* 30.

26. "But by far the most pleasing picture of the Gentile and the Jew in their relations to the new Jesus cult was given by Luke (10:38-42)." Cf., Smith, *Ecce Deus*, 104. Matt. 26:6-13, Luke 7:36-50, and 10:38-42. And, Emil Schurer, *A History of the Jewish People in the Time of Jesus*, ed. and intro. Nahum N. Glatzer (New York: Schocken Books, 1961); and G. F. Moore, *Judaism in the First Centuries of the Christian Era*, 3 Vols. (Cambridge, Mass.: Harvard University Press, 1927-30).

27. B. L. Doctorow as quoted in *Signals*, spring issue (St. Paul, Minn.: WGBH Educational Foundation, 1991), 17. In terms of mysticism and myth as a hermeneutical posture, "speaking historically, the Apostle Paul leads just as certainly to Marcion and Valentinus as he does to Irenaeus and Origen." Ehrman, *Orthodox Corruption*, 43, n. 40.

concerning the so-called historical Jesus. This social, theological, and historical analysis seeks to redefine the religious, categorical foundation of Orthodox Christianity. It does this by establishing a historical overview, which provides historical evidence that the originator of the Christian faith was not a historical person (Jesus). The dogmatic portrait of a historical Jesus is ill fitted for the modern secular mind. Historical reality, as it has come to be understood in modern times, needs to be encountered by that experiential interpretation, which allows humanity to exist with moral and ethical integrity on its own terms.

It should be based solely on humanity's own existence; not the mythological and fabricated existence of a non-reality or a historic religiosity of subjectivism. Believers in the formative years of communal, faith-development were not critical in their hermeneutical reflections when accepting the new Gospel tradition. Bultmann states that,

> Every exegete is dependent upon terminology which has come down to him by tradition, though it is accepted uncritically and without reflection, and every traditional terminology is in one way or another dependent upon a particular philosophy. But it is vital that we should continue neither uncritically nor without reflection.[28]

It has often been cited that in a description of the cosmic significance of Christ's religious achievement (as Savior) that an intimate affinity with certain tendencies of the mystery religions and gnostic, religious thought had existed. These mythothemes were current in contemporary Hellenistic religious circles and were used in the language of the New Testament.[29] Given this philosophical bent even the Alexandrian Jewish-Greek Philo was able

---

28. Bartsch, *Kerygma*, 193.

29. Smith, *Ecce Deus*, 23f. In Middle Platonic thought, the upper or 'Platonic heaven' was a most significantly real domain, comprised of a reality more real than earthly materiality. Note the views of Origen, Xenocrates, Plutarch, and Philo on the subject of the heavens as a layered universe. Some held to three, others to five, seven, or even eight heavens; in ancient myth, this imprecision was not a problem.

to designate the cosmic physicality, the divine creation of God, as 'His only begotten Son.' For Philo the cosmos was brought about as the recipient of Wisdom's divine procreative power.[30] This same type of philosophical undercurrent of ideas was embraced by Paul and is even indicative of some passages in Mark's Gospel.

The result for the formative gatherings is an interpretation of the biblical tradition that, from the beginning, indicates a singular historical trajectory to enlighten the Gentiles by the introduction of the mystical, Jesus-myth through the kerygma. It would seem that the biblical tradition, especially the Gospel accounts of the purely human Jesus, is nothing but shifting sand on a theological beach. In this respect, the historical development of the Christian religion, the biblical tradition, by way of a literalist interpretation, agrees with a preconceived theological conception of Jesus as the 'divine' Christ. In order to alter this theological posture, we need to consider the implications of the symbolic interpretation that was fostered among the early, christological communities.

The divine *Christos* event was originally perceived as YHWH's redemption (via the cultic resurrection experience, an aspect of salvation glory) and manifested itself through a socio-religious community's commitment of faith. This was precisely Paul's position. His gospel was presented so that one would exercise faith in the symbolic and mythical substance of his proclamation, and as a response to the '*parousia*,' the *presence* of the anointed one, the Christ, *resurrected* was now available for moral assistance among believers.[31] Christ's mystic presence was the

---

30. Mead, *Echoes*, 471.
31. 1 Thess. 1: 9-10. Paul indicates that their newly found religious devotion to God would be met with difficulties; but, the presence of Christ in heaven was a present power and was continuously available for them for their assistance and aid in their soon to be times of troubles. This was a theological formulation by Paul and does not refer to a 'second coming' idea of a later generation's historicized consideration. That would not be a part of Paul's theological construct nor his moral, religious, and mystical formulation.

325

divine and spiritual force made available through the preaching of Paul in order to empower them.

The symbolism, which is foundational to a historical, christological understanding of the Jewish community's development, is still detectable in the canonical Gospels. Statements having mystic connotations are found in the biblical, canonical Gospel (Matt. 11:27) in which the significant relationship between the Father and the Son has "its parallels in the Hellenistic mystery cults."[32] Yet, biblical exegetes have laid aside the mystical understanding of symbolism; and thus, the expanded covenantal corpora are read through the lens of the historicized life and ministry of a so-called historical Jesus. Later literary interpolations, Christological reformulations, and historical reflections led the Roman Church authorities to legitimize the formative Christian gospel as historical fact, as Christian pedagogical dogma. They used a more literal and non-metaphorical language to break away from the imagery of the earlier symbolic and mythological forms and responses.

If the Jesus of the New Testament Gospels had been in actual history, a truly human personality, we would certainly expect a distinctive and imaginative picture of such a personality. This definitely would shine through the evidence of historical research. It doesn't. The conclusion of most Christian and non-Christian scholars of historical analysis in recent times has been that an actual historical life of Jesus cannot be adequately uncovered even when based on the biblical tradition, apart from the religious and mythological significance of his divinity (which is also based on faith). Doherty has suggested that the Apostle Paul,

Specifies ... his object of worship in terms of a spiritual, transcendent figure, without equating it with a historical man; he believes in a Son of God, not that anyone was the Son of God. He

---

32. Cullmann, *Christology,* 278. He also makes reference to W. Bousset, *Kyrios Christos,* 48 where he (Bousset) "cites among other examples a prayer to Hermes in the Magical papyrus, Lond. 122.50: 'I know you, Hermes, and you know me; I am you, and you are I.'" Ibid., n. 2. Cf., the Gospel of John 14:8-24 where this symbolic relationship is extended to the followers of Jesus in the narrative story (*mythos*).

and others describe this Son in terms of *Logos* and Wisdom philosophy; the "interpretation" of Jesus of Nazareth which scholars have insisted on reading into these descriptions is never hinted at. Paul and others state in no uncertain terms that their Christ is a "mystery," a secret long-hidden by God and revealed in the present time [by Paul's proclamations] through scripture and the Holy Spirit [a revelatory understanding].[33]

Our only conclusion, based on the socio-religious and historical development of the Jesus myth that is embedded in the tradition, is that the symbolic significance of the divine Spirit (*Yeshua*) having been sent by God to them was a revelatory perception. He was the divine *presence* that was manifested in the 'flesh' (i.e., entered into their communal existence). His divine *presence* is the *parousia*. Unfortunately, the mystic element expressed in the Eucharist as a symbol of his *presence*, has become a theological adaptation to suggest Jesus' future second coming. Although Cullmann has done just this when he says that in "the Eucharistic celebration ... there takes place an impressive anticipation of Christ's 'coming'—or more accurately, his 'return'—which he promised."[34] He is postulating a hermeneutic through Gospel lens, which is not history by quoting tradition (Matt. 18:20. "Where two or more are gathered together in my name, there I am [his *presence*, the *parousia*] in the midst of them.") to justify this anticipatory stance.

The text does not say 'I will be at some future time with them;' but, 'I am *presently* there with them.' Jesus was the divine *presence* in the communal gatherings, which made them a Holy nation, a peculiar people[35] because he was YHWH's Spirit, which anointed and empowered their fellowship. In this type of emerg-

---

33. Doherty, "Responses to Critiques of the Mysticist Case: Part One," 28. Brackets are mine.

34. Cullmann, *Christology*, 211.

35. See 1 Peter 2:9 and James in its entirety. From a sociological perspective, B. Ramsey's assessment *Beginning to Read the Fathers* (London: SCM, 1993) is probably correct in his moral assessment of the early gatherings in that "the problem of poverty and wealth was the most important specific social issue that the early church faced" (195), as cited by Wells, *Can We Trust*, 150.

ing religious dynamic, the transformation of the Jesus myth into the biblical tradition of formative Christianity makes historical sense and validates to a large degree our historical methodology and analysis.

If a historical person such as Jesus is taken literally to have really existed we are faced with a rational distortion of the modern understanding of science and physical reality. Also the integrity of monotheism is jeopardized, theologically, when you transform the deity, YHWH, who was perceived as Spirit and cannot be seen, into a being of physical reality that had form, substance, and was actually seen (namely Jesus in history). Even for the modern religious mindset, the many religious and rational contradictions for monotheism still remain.[36] The scientific and secular mind cannot, with rational integrity, accept the mythological basis of the biblical tradition as currently historicized. Yet, if the original symbolism of the historic socio-religious Jesus myth is understood; then, the kerygma of the primitive, christological end-time communities, as a historical understanding, will speak to the current, essential, and natural understanding of the modern mind. This would restore a sense of human integrity to biblical scholarship and would provide a greater historical understanding for modern, secular humanity.

As we have noted previously, it was the original symbolic interpretation that was based on the mystical faith-understanding of the Jesus cult's apocalyptic religiosity; and as such, "... each interpretation presupposed a particular pattern of eschatological outlook."[37] Contemporaneous salvation, as proclaimed by Paul, was always a moral and eschatological work in progress, in which he was bringing others into the fold of a renewed Jewish faith by extending the boundaries of Judaism. According to Chilton and Neusner[38] these "boundaries were precisely among those things which were melting away in his [Jesus'] eschatological imagination." This would describe Paul's social and religious imagination as well. This does not negate the symbolic nature

---

36. Theophile James Meek, *Hebrew Origins* (New York: Harper & Row, Pub., Harper Torchbooks, The Cloister Library, 1960).

37. Grant, *The Earliest Gospel*, 147.

38. Chilton, Neusner, *Judaism*, 126.

used to describe the eschatological outlook in the presentation of his gospel. The initiates' 'resurrection' experience (was their entrance into the end-time communal fellowship) and it began with baptism. And, as beings of a new creation, it continued their spiritual development that was to reach maturity (*teleios*).

The idea of resurrection, symbolically understood, was a psychodynamic pattern for growth and development, and this was worked through its eschatological and salvific dimensions. Others have noticed this kind of hermeneutical application to a wider socio-philosophical structure. Hence, Cullmann finds some agreement with Bultmann when he remarks that,

> In Gnosticism the *Logos* is a mythological intermediary being between God and man. He is not only creator of the world, but above all revealer, and as revealer also redeemer. Gnosticism also believed that the *Logos* temporarily became man, but only in a mythical and docetic sense, it was never in the historical sense of a real incarnation. Bultmann finds here the myth of the descent and ascent of the redeemer who saves the world in saving himself. This Logos is the same figure we find in non-Christian speculations about the 'original man.'[39]

We are reminded that even in the heartland of Jewish religious activities, Jerusalem, had become a Greek *polis* and could easily express religious ideas within a Hellenistic frame of reference without losing its religious identity.[40] It was the Essenes of the Qumran community that did exactly this in their eschatological and apocalyptic literature when considering themselves as the New Israel of God.

As this study proposes, it was the apocalyptic and eschatological interpretations (the historic words) that the primitive, Jewish gatherings proclaimed. These were not the actual, literal

---

39. Cullmann, *Christology*, 252. It might be more intellectually honest to admit that all theology is also just religious speculation. What is good for the goose is good for the gander, metaphorically speaking. One does not have to look far in one's imagination to find symbolic patterns or a relationship of these mythic categories and what appears in the biblical tradition, especially the Gospels.

40. Tcherikover, *Hellenistic Civilization*, 180.

spoken words of a historical resurrected person called Jesus. We can validate the historical evidence that they were believers; but, we cannot validate that substance, that essence, the 'in what' they believed as historical evidence. Also, as historians, we need to keep in mind the process of historical verification. What we have uncovered by a socio-religious analysis of history, was the content, the mythological and symbolic basis within the christological fellowships.[41] We have historical evidence established by the theological parameters (the symbolic hermeneutics) of universal monotheism. We note that a mystical posture of redemption was lived out among the communities of the Jesus myth, which had some religious affinities with gnostic and mystery, religious cults. From this socio-religious analysis, the early christological gatherings' historicity is clearly identified.

Thus, faced with the evidence of this symbolic and methodological interpretation: "We are then logically, and even morally, bound to exploit the symbolic method to the utmost, as far as possible, and to reject it -- not when we have actually failed to succeed with it -- but only when it becomes clear that in the nature of the case 'no one' can ever succeed with it: in other words, that the historic explanation is positively demanded."[42] This historic hermeneutic contains a religious, social, and theological matrix and is also embedded in the historical biblical tradition. Regardless of other historical forces, this interpretation has preserved the actual symbolic essence for a modern understanding of the earliest, christological and historic spirituality, which, regardless of its theological focus, is still basically mythological in form, structure, and with its mystical context.

---

41. The Hellenistic synagogues were available to many Greek worshipers as 'God-fearers.' "*Arndt and Gingrich's Lexicon,* art. Sebō, describes them as 'pagans' who accepted the ethical monotheism of Judaism and attended the synagogue, but who did not obligate themselves to keep the whole Jewish law," as quoted by Wells, *Can We Trust,* 46. These were the folks to whom Paul ministered with his gospel to assure that they would continue to fully embrace Judaism as a renewal movement.

42. Smith, *Ecce Deus,* 110.

The idea of resurrection, while it gave metaphorical significance and theological meaning to Jesus' death (proclaimed as the *Christos* event by Paul), was also understood as a necessity in the soteriological scheme of the early Jewish christological community. This mythic understanding, perceived as the coming of the Spirit (the mystic relationship of YHWH with his people), began the new age, the 'Age of the Spirit' (Pentecost: cf., the statements by the prophet Joel with regard to the outpouring of God's Spirit). Within the wider world of Hellenism, there was also an imaginative spirit of religious syncretism. Mead rightly notes that, "The Alexandrian religious philosophy proper was a blend of Orphic, Pythagorean, Platonic, and Stoic elements, and constituted the theology of the learned in the great city, which had gradually, from the third century B.C., made herself the center of Hellenic culture."[43] These overall theological elements, as personified, were originally understood metaphorically by a symbolic interpretation in the christological gatherings both in Palestine and throughout the diaspora.

Although similar conceptual realities remain to foster an expanded theological religiosity for formative and modern Christianity, much of the original spiritual dynamic as myth is lost with the demise of its original symbolic understanding. YHWH's eternal Word (the *Logos*, divine wisdom, Spirit), according to the earliest Jewish gatherings' understanding, had finally entered the context of communal and religious experience by conceptual personifications. This religious methodology had a wide appeal among most religious and philosophical communities. Cullmann notes[44] that the "concepts of a personified revealer and redeemer *Logos* are foreshadowed in ancient religions. Hermes and the Egyptian God Thoth, for instance, were both called '*Logos*.'" One could as easily add Mark and John's literary character, the

---

43. Mead, *Echoes*, 299.
44. Cullmann, *Christology*, 253. He further noted these sources for the methodology as well: (for Hermes) Plato, *Cratylus*, 407 E ff.; Hippolytus, *Refut.* V, 7.29; R. Reitzenstein, *Poimandres*, 1904, 88; (for Thoth) Plutarch, *De Iside et Osiride*, 54 f.; and for the voluminous Hermetic literature, A. D. Nock and A. J. Festugière (Paris, 4 vol. 1945-1954). Ibid.

Gospel Jesus. This was primarily a symbolic aspect of christological existence on a purely metaphorical basis for the early
gatherings. Historically, this was perceived as a social, religious,
and rational experience, and not as an irrational event.[45] The decisive factor of that historic event, which possesses the rational
power of truth and its religiosity, is the language of symbolism.
Language, as an event in our experience, must communicate
meaning of our physical existence if it is to be viable and to function rationally.

In order to recapture the mythical and theological essence
of the early christological communities' world-view and its faith-
understanding from a linguistic basis, modern biblical scholars
must realize that it is necessary to accept the modern, scientific
world-view. We are not to superimpose their ancient world-view
and its cosmological underpinnings to secular modernity. Our
modern and scientific world-view has demonstrated the bio-
evolutionary and anthropological basis for the understanding of
the nature of physical reality. This is a secularly based, scientific
world-view, which is a non-mythological construct of rationality
for modernity. Christianity must reformulate its theological basis
and religious symbols with non-mythical language in order to
philosophically (i.e., on rational grounds only) define the social
experiences of human existence as being natural, basic, and totally within the bounds of physicality (by using a demythologized
anthropological foundation).

In other words, Christianity must go beyond Feuerbach,
Bonhoeffer, Bultmann, Tillich, Hamilton, and Altizer: even beyond these radical biblical theologians and their religious
thoughts to a pure secular humanism. Humanism with its moral

---

45. Mackintosh, *Modern Theology*, 291. Also, Paul Tillich offers
a comprehensive understanding of the media of revelation within the
context of human experience when he cites these examples: nature,
history, groups, individuals, and the word, in *Systematic Theology*, 3
Vols. (Chicago: The University of Chicago Press, 1951), Vol. 1, 118-
126. A penetrating analysis of this theme is presented in concise form
in Wolfhart Pannenberg, "Redemptive Event and History," *Essays on
Old Testament Hermeneutics*, ed. by Claus Westermann, trans. James
Luther Mays (Richmond: John Knox Press, 1964), 314-315.

integrity would be the acknowledgement that the consciousness of humanity is the real essence of divinity, which Christianity throughout the ages has sought to explicate.[46] Modern science can provide an explanation for this methodology of symbolism. Deacon[47] has suggested that, "brains have elaborated this causal realism to an extreme, and minds capable of symbolic references can literally bring even the most Platonic of conceptions of abstract forms into the realm of causal particulars."

No better commentary could be more appropriate to popularize Bultmann's argument of his theological polarity than the astute insight afforded by the words of Braaten when he says:

> The meaning of the Easter proclamation has its center of gravity not in the faith that receives, but in the [revelatory] event which makes the faith of Easter a possibility in the first place. The resurrection event is God's act of exalting Jesus beyond the nihility of death. Without this [revelatory] event having really occurred, there is no existential core of meaning in the resurrection stories worth talking about. The basis of the Church's proclamation would thereby be removed and the content of its faith evacuated of all meaning.[48]

---

46. Marx and Engels, *On Religion*, 15. Religion's true basis is humanism and the human condition. Bartsch quotes Bultmann's idea that "the only truth behind myth is therefore … the understanding of human existence which its imagery enshrines [by symbolism and metaphorical language]." Bartsch, *Kerygma*, 125. Bracket is mine.

47. Terrence W. Deacon, *Incomplete Nature* (New York: Norton & Company, 2013), 483. We can better assess the hermeneutical process that was involved when Mark's Gospel became the source for a transformative and theological understanding. As a symbolic species, Deacon further states that we "can literally transform arbitrarily created abstract general features into causally efficacious specific physical events." Ibid. This may be how myth became historical reality for some.

48. Braaten, *History & Hermeneutics*, 84. Brackets are mine. Most ancient is the resurrection concept in its religious and political form found in Egyptian texts with regard to Pharonic authority. As an abstract conception that had religious power, it was adopted, adapted, and transformed by various cultures from Egypt to the ancient Per-

If one was not able to maintain the possibility of non-physical reality and its corresponding possibility of non-physical human experiences, and could no longer objectify these religious abstractions as a spiritual (a supernatural) reality, conceptually based, as though they were in essence and actually a real physical and historical fact (e.g., God, Jesus, resurrection, life after death, etc.), then we would be forced to agree with his conclusion, that there is no existential or significant spiritual meaning in the mythical stories of Jesus' resurrection at least for Christian religiosity.

But, that is precisely the main point of this study. These theological formulations are religious 'stories,' mythologically based as religious fabrications used for spiritual truth (with moral and ethical dynamics). These conceptual, core markers are not historical, factual reality even though they hold religious and spiritual values precisely because of their original symbolic interpretation. They expressed the essence of existential meaning in the 'historic' experiences of the early Jewish christological communities, which cannot be seriously denied. This hermeneutic of symbolism, in the consideration of the text, is necessary in order to reveal the real historical situation. At the same time, a socio-religious historical analysis retains the historic spiritual understanding (symbolism) and the religious basis (mythology) for the historical origins of the early Christian religion.

The result is that it lends credence to a symbolic focus and provides modern biblical scholars with a definite mythological and historical understanding. The mystery religions and the earliest faith-communities that were the supporters of the apostle Paul shared a similar mythological atmosphere of religious categories and cultural symbols. Mead points out that if the mystery, "Be the 'way down,' equally it is the 'way up.'" It was "the way by which Dionysus ascended to the Gods." Here again I think, Plutarch refers to a mystery-myth into which he was initiated. Generally, it may be said to refer to the 'greater mysteries' --

sians. See Mead, *Echoes,* 163-205 on the history and development of the mysteries of Mithra.

those of 'regeneration,' the 'way up,' while the 'lesser mysteries,' those of 'generation,' pertain to the 'way down.'"[49] These cultural mythologies were accepted quite broadly among the ancient world within their diverse religiosities.

In fact, Gnosticism, a composite of mythological ideas, was not really considered heretical prior to about 150 C.E.[50] It is modern scholars who have hoped that Paul would have been more precise in his theological adaptations when developing a revelatory faith by putting new wine into old skins. Midrashim did not always provide a clear and distinct transition of thought, at least from our modern perspective. Nevertheless, as some have pointed out, the paradigmatic parallel system of mystic union with a deity was part and parcel in the Hellenistic mystery cults. This idea of mystic union was a pattern that Paul used in the formulation of his faith and proclamations about the *Christos* event. The myths of the savior Gods were part of the thought world in Paul's time, and he applied these categories where he could for his own religious and theological development as a missionary representative of the several christological gatherings.

Yet, we see that previous scholarship has perpetuated the non-historical elements of the traditional biblical text, and thereby, this has created a litany of problematic interpretations. If we ignore or minimally reject the mythological aspects of the early Christian apostles, in our hermeneutical interaction with the Hellenistic culture,

> We risk missing the entire meaning if we don't take into account the cosmological ideas of the culture within which these writers moved, if we choose to reject any interpretation based on those concepts, simply because we don't like them or find them alien:

---

49. Mead, *Echoes*, 110. Jesus ascended to the father after his cosmic, cross/resurrection event (a revelatory experience for Paul) that held redemptive power for those who exercised faith (the acceptance of the myth) in the kerygma and acted upon it as an spiritual and moral empowerment for their lives.

50. Ibid., 127.

partly from ignorance of the subject, partly from standing at the very different cosmological vantage point of our modern era.[51]

Much that has passed as history within the context of the Gospel narratives seems to be based precisely on the above stated concern. Myth has become history, and biblical scholars, a few for polemic reasons and others for apologetic reasons tend to denigrate the mysticists position rather than to seriously deal with the mythology that is at the roots of the Gospel texts and all religious literature.

Thus far, we have seen that the actual, literary Jesus in the story, who is perceived as historical within the context of the Gospels for Christian orthodoxy, is truly a wondrous and divine being. But, this type of hermeneutic is non-historical, and it is unwarranted as history in the analysis of the biblical tradition. It has been the result of a distortion to the original symbolism, to its metaphorical focus, and the theological language of the early Jewish, christological fellowships.

The religious acceptance of this non-historical position (Jesus as a real person in history) has led for centuries to greater mythological and fanciful exegesis of the biblical text not to mention the evil that has plagued humanity with religious wars, global human atrocities, and modern terrorism. Political oppression and injustice, economic exploitation and hording of wealth by the few, and human social discrimination based on racism, sexism, gender identification, and ethnicity can be dealt with by a humanity that realistically sees things as they are and joins forces to protect themselves by correcting these issues, by and for themselves, without thinking that a supernatural force will intervene in order to correct them or just wait until death and be transported to a supernatural realm were all of these problematic human issues no longer exist.

Thus, an understanding of a 'historical Jesus' tradition grew out of this historical process and was articulated by the Second Century as a midrashic, literary construct that became reformulated in the Gospel of Mark. By the end of the third Cen-

---

51. Doherty, "Critiques of the Mysticist Case: Part One," 6 (accessed 16 July 2005).

tury, it became a socio-religious, literalist construct that had been historicized and theologically accepted as the official hermeneutic (dogma?) of the Roman Catholic Church. It was embodied theologically in the early community's reflective experiences and mind-set concerning their self-identity within the Greco-Roman world. This study confirms this hermeneutic: to hear Mark's Gospel is to understand and experience the inner Jewish life of the historical, christological community as it was dramatized in a literary form, regardless of its later historization.

After investigating by a historical analysis the origins of the Christian faith, in relation to a historical Jesus and concluding that no such person existed in actual history, even though the mythological, mystic, and symbolic dynamics of an ancient culture and diverse religiosities allowed for Christianity's development; how should we feel? Exhausted, yes; but relieved, for we have a scientific, bio-evolutionary, and a new creative, human spirit (understanding?) to explore and experience our world of modernity. Waal has offered an excellent perspective for life without confusing myth as factual history.

> No, the big difference for scientists [and the rest of us atheists] is that the thirst for knowledge itself, the life blood of our profession [and any person with honest moral integrity for factual truth], fills a spiritual void taken up by religion in most other people. Like treasure hunters for whom the hunt is about as important as the treasure itself, we feel great purpose in trying to pierce the veil of ignorance. We feel united in this effort, being part of a worldwide network. This means that we also enjoy this other aspect of religion: a community of like-minded people.[52]

---

[52]. De Waal, *Bonobo and Atheists,* 106.

11

Beware of finding a Jesus entirely congenial to you.
Robert Funk

The quality of human existence should be an extremely important focus for modern religiosity. So we find that "... the authentic person of the spirit receives a summons from above, not for the purpose of being preoccupied with the above [ancient religiosity] but for the purpose of returning creatively to the community, contributing to the formation of the human cosmos [modern spirituality]."[1] Therein lays the possible danger for what Christianity can culturally[2] and religiously become (or might we say has become?). Paul had a creative perception in which the outside Hellenistic world would be drawn into the religious faith-community of Judaism. This aspect of his faith ministry was just as applicable to his lost, fellow Jewish believers when he sought to bring them as well (who had hardened hearts, Rom. 2:28-9) into the new revelatory experience of his gospel. "He predicts that they will finally be converted and join the community, much as the Qumran community imagined that the congregation of Is-

---

1. Wood, Martin, *Buber's Ontology: An Analysis of I and Thou,* 107. Rabbinic Judaism historically took opposing positions. Levine notes: "the school of Hillel adopted a moderate position and that of Shammai a much stricter one, advocating a maximal degree of isolation of the Jew from the non-Jewish world," in *Judaism and Hellenism in Antiquity: Conflict or Confluence?* (Peabody, Mass.: Hendrickson Publishers, 1998), 105. See M. Hengel, *The Zealots,* 200-6.

2. Robert N. Bellah, *Beyond Belief: Essays on Religion in a Post-Traditionalist World* (Berkeley: University of California Press, 1970), 114. His definition of culture is "a collection of symbol systems ... as cultural patterns ... in themselves," which are "interrelated with a social system ... to a certain degree independent, detachable elements that ... can be transmitted to other social systems." Ibid.

rael would join them in the last days (1Q Sa I. 1ff; cf., 4QpNah III, 1-8)."[3]

Historically, for the most part, the Christian faith has become a static religion, totally preoccupied with mythology and focused upon its own historicized creation, the biblical Jesus. Bultmann has recognized that "a biographical apophthegm from its very nature is not a historical report -- and that applies to Jesus as much as to any other historical personality." He has also indicated that there are numerous parallels in rabbinic stories, the nature of which was "not intended to be actual historical reports, but rather metaphorical presentations of a life."[4] This would seem to be evident even when that literary 'life' within a story's characterization was a mythic person or a personification of a moral abstraction. Symbolism and metaphorical themes found in literature abound in these types of situations.

Christianity has lost touch with its own spirit of symbolic understanding and moral imperative; and thus, has lost its modern theological creativity to form a rational respect for living with global, human mutuality. Most religious-minded people have attempted to live in the modern world based on the terms of modern reality (i.e., to authenticate existence on the basis of its facticity in history). The modern world of secularism and science triumphs because it has that human integrity that is lacking in Christianity's historical objectification of faith. Most of today's biblical religiosity lacks an understanding of the essence of the modern, unitary physical universe and humanity's developmental existence within it.

All the diverse miracles in the overall canonical, biblical tradition are obviously religious and purely literary devises intended as metaphors, which are symbolic in their theologically intended forms. Thus, the modern mind, due to the acceptance of secularism and the scientific views of physical reality, should

---

3. P. M. Casey, *From Jewish Prophet to Gentile God: The Origins and Development of New Testament Christology* (Louisville, Ky.: Westminster, 1991), 121. See Romans 9-11.

4. Rudolf Bultmann, *History of the Synoptic Tradition*, Trans. John Marsh, rev ed. (Peabody, Mass.: Hendrickson Publishers, 1960), 57.

reject them (all miracles) as utterly impossible to have happened in historical reality; but, they can still be easily accepted as the occurrences within literature as symbolic events to make a point for religious or moral purposes. At this point we need to remember Deacon's perception, which is "a necessary assumption of scientific materialism that the essence of life does not arise from a realm outside of physical substrates of its constitution." And "only life begets life."[5] This is genuinely true not only for bio-physicality, but also for historic religious spirituality, which is depicted by metaphor and symbolic language.

Thus, Jesus, as a historical person (in the Gospel literature) and his resurrection (as a historic event as symbolism), not only was understood to have identified the early gatherings' communal experience as a spiritual salvation event (mythothematically) for the socio-religious meaning of history for them; it also marked, as a theological interpretation, the christological beginning and their involvement in the "age of the Spirit" (Acts 2:15). For the early Jewish fellowships, the Spirit's presence was the validation of that mystic reflection of the cult's own socio-religious experiences, and it was the dynamic theological direction that the cult took in the diaspora -- the bringing about of universal monotheism (via the Jesus myth) to the whole world. Paul had declared that God, based on a revelatory basis, was in the *Christos* event "reconciling the world unto himself." In the later Gospels this becomes the activity and ministry of the mythic Jesus as the Son of God. Vermes points out that the phrase 'Son of God' would

To a Greek speaker in Alexandria, Antioch or Athens at the turn of the eras, the concept *huiou theou*, son of God, would have brought to mind either one of the many offspring of the Olympian deities, or possibly a deified Egyptian Ptolemaic king, or the divine Emperor of Rome, descendant of the apotheosized Julius Caesar. But to a Jew, the corresponding Hebrew or Aramaic phrase would have applied to none of these. For him, the son of God could refer, in an ascending order, to any of the children of Israel, or to a good Jew; or to a charismatic holy Jew; or to the king of Israel; or in particu-

---

5. Deacon, *Nature*, 431.

lar to the royal Messiah; and finally, in a different sense, to an angelic or heavenly being. In other words, 'son of God' was always understood metaphorically in Jewish circles.[6]

It is not difficult to realize that for Diaspora Jews not only would a metaphorical connection be made; but, in Platonic fashion, many symbolic categories as well as gnostic mythothemes could fit easily into the developing structure of the christological faith-communities that Paul represented. In terms of religious morality, it was always the 'inner persona' of one's being that was of vital concern. Hence; Vermes continues by stating that, "he [the mythological Jesus of the Gospel] was not the only Jewish teacher to insist on symbolism, inwardness and sincerity. Philo and Josephus did the same. So did many of the rabbis, and the Qumran sectaries."[7]

All theology that has been practiced from ancient times to the present is essentially a reflected, phenomenological anthropology. Therefore; if we consider dogmatic Christian theologies, it is necessary that we redefine and reaffirm human existence in the rational light of modern scientific understanding. This new reformulation on a modern anthropological basis should develop into a full expression of human social interaction, in which we encounter our own human existence (existential humanism).[8] The ancient idea of a 'divinity' that was encapsulated within the historical experiences of humanity and could suffer and die was

---

6. Geza Vermes, *Jesus in His Jewish Context* (Minneapolis: Fortress Press, 2003), 66.

7. Ibid., 43. For Philo, see. R. Goodenough, *An Introduction to Philo Judaeus* (1962). For the rabbis and sages, see G. F. Moore, *Judaism: In the First Centuries of the Christian Era: The Age of Tannaim*, vol. II and III (Peabody, Mass.: Hendrickson Publishers, 1927-30). And for Qumran, see 1QS ii, 25-iii, 5; 1QS v, 13-14.

8. Cf., Marx and Engels, *On Religion*. Also see John A. T. Robinson, *Honest to God* (Philadelphia: The Westminster Press, 1963); and Thomas J. J. Altizer and William Hamilton, *Radical Theology and the Death of God* (New York: The Bobbs-Merrill Co., Inc., 1966). And Ludwig Feuerbach, *The Essence of Christianity,* Trans. George Eliot (New York: Harper & Row, Publishers, Torchbooks, Cloister Lib., 1957).

commonly understood by the early primitive fellowships as well as other ancient religious cultures. Within the historic lines of Christianity's development, this idea had emerged through the influence of ancient Hellenistic mythology. Levine also provides an overview of these ancient times:

Indeed, the Hellenistic world was a scene of a veritable potpourri of cultural forces, a market place of ideas and fashions from which one could choose. In this light, therefore, Hellenism is not merely the impact of Greek culture on a non-Greek world, but rather the interplay of a wide range of cultural forces on an *oikoumene* (the civilized world as then known) defined in large part -- but not exclusively -- by the Greek conquest of the fourth and third centuries B.C.E.[9]

This was an aspect of acculturation that provided certain socio-religious success. "Only when cults acquired a communal organization and borrowed sufficient traits from the cults of the dominant Greek culture" is when they had really "felt a sense of social involvement."[10] The incorporation of Greek religious ideas was also a common exchange with others' culture, their religions, and their philosophic thought.[11] This social aspect of religious, cultural interaction was accomplished in the several commercial, trading cities in the ancient world. Berquist has pointed out some significant linguistic and hermeneutical occurrences that come from a previous historical period. Thus,

Greek influences would have been rampant in *Yehud* long before Alexander's conquest of the Persian imperial core. During the middle of the fifth century B.C.E., the growth of trade between Je-

---

9. Levine, *Hellenism,* 19. Cf., S. J. Lieberman, "A Mesopotamian Background for the So-called '*Aggadic* Measures' of biblical Hermeneutics," *HUCA* 58 (1987): 157-225.

10. Thompson, *Book of Revelation,* 159-60, where he quotes Price, S. R. F., *Rituals and Power: The Roman Imperial Cult in Asia Minor,* (Cambridge: Cambridge University Press, 1984), 98.

11. Aubrey, *Secularism: A Myth,* 80-88. His excellent work represents an attitude that needs current attention by the various denominations of modern Christianity.

rusalem and Athens (as well as other Greek city-states) would have allowed a significant interchange of ideas, and these ideas would have been most clearly felt within the wisdom traditions of scribes who needed to know about other languages and cultures.[12]

Let us again direct our attention to the previous statement that the kerygma, having lost its symbolic basis, had to become intimately bound and grounded in the historicized Jesus. Even a modern assessment of bio-anthropological dynamics based on a neurological understanding recognizes this scientific process to formulate new conceptual categories. It is useful to repeat Deacon's observation: "Brains ... and minds capable of symbolic references can literally bring even the most Platonic of conceptions of abstract forms into the realm of causal particulars."[13] As an example, Bultmann's previous conclusion, on the nature of a non-historical event of the resurrection of Jesus is correct, and a hermeneutical need for the restoration of this kind of symbolic interpretation of these historicized events is further vindicated. Any historical insight that we might gain is always "reflected in the famous dictum of experimental psychology that 'absence of evidence is not evidence of absence.'"[14] Therefore; this study submits this perspective of the historic origin of the Jesus myth as a correct validation for a historical understanding. It represents the Jewish christological cults' historical development as the origin of the Christian religion without a historical Jesus.

The early proclamation was that Jesus (*Yeshua*), YHWH's Spiritual presence had been revealed as a historic revelation to those who were previously considered as spiritually dead. Jesus, personified in the later narrative Gospel of John, had been a mythological person, the divine Savior (the Heavenly Christ, and the Jesus of Paul's ministry). The deity's appearance in human form (a literary devise of symbolic significance) also included

12. Jon L. Berquist, *Judaism in Persia's Shadow: A Social Historical Approach* (Minneapolis: Fortress Press, 1995), 206.

13. Deacon, *Nature*, 483.

14. Frans De Waal, *The Bonobo and the Atheist: In Search of Humanism Among the Primates* (New York: W. W. Norton & Company, 2013), 116.

some popular ideas that were also accepted in Gnosticism, in Jewish Wisdom literature, in the various mystery cults, and among the literature of the Essenes at Qumran. Casey mentions that the "Wisdom content and terminology in this work [the Similitudes' 'vision of Wisdom' in 1 Enoch 37.1] form significant background to the myth of 1 Enoch 42, where Wisdom's dwelling is in heaven. She came down to earth to live among the sons of men, but found nowhere to stay, so she returned to heaven and took her seat among the angels (1 Enoch 42.2; cf., Bar 3.29, 38)."[15] Mysticists are quick to point out, and rightly so, that this same mythotheme is found in Matthew's Gospel; but, there it is mythologically reworked into the narrative and applied to Jesus (Matt. 8:20). The gender change is insignificant when mythology and symbolism are the primary concerns.

Nevertheless, the historic origin of the Jewish, christological community became transformed over the years by its later historicized theology and developed its literal understanding[16] of Jesus' life as historical reality. This was the commonly accepted mythological and mystical basis, when it is said that God had entered into history in order to encounter humanity (which is a basic theistic, religious idea). It is the same type of mythological statement that is part and parcel to the fabricated basis of the communal, mystic religiosity (expressed in the biblical literature) and was used to depict Christianity's theological and historical development.

The transformation from disciples of Jesus, which is a purely historicized fantasy, into the evangelists of the kerygma (the historicized understanding of formative Christianity) was in actuality a new literary depiction of the transformation of faith-understanding within the christological fellowships (John 14:12-14). Thus, the resurrection as a mystic communal experience, via its christological reflection, allowed the various assemblies to perceive God's Spirit as the divine Savior. Hence; Paul uses these

---

15. Casey, *Jewish Prophet,* 89.

16. Rudolf Bultmann, *Jesus Christ and Mythology* (New York: Charles Scribner's Son, 1958). Compare Fuller, *Kerygma and Myth,* with Schubert M. Ogden, *Christ Without Myth* (New York: Harper & Row, Pub., 1961), 21.

expressions: God *sent* his son, God *sent* his Spirit, and God *sent* the spirit of his son, which symbolically signified that he (Paul) had received a *revelatory* experience. He (the Spirit/Jesus) had been manifested as the divine revelation from above (as God's communal *presence*, seen in the Eucharist as Christ's presence, his *parousia*).[17] The evangelists also expressed this theological understanding (cf., Gnosticism) by means of their faith and theological categories (both in proclamation and in literary form)[18] as a social, religious, and historical reality. The anticipation of final redemption was significantly not an intricate part of the earlier christological kerygma that the primitive Jewish gatherings had proclaimed.

The *parousia* of the Lord (YHWH), a necessity in the mythical drama[19] of the cult's redemption, was reformulated and historicized, but not as the former activity of YHWH. It became part of the redemptive function of the mythic Jesus in the Gospel narrative, and thus, was not disconnected from the total kerygmatic intention. The original understanding of the anointed Lord Jesus' presence became identified as his return on a historicized basis (the *parousia,* as the so-called second coming) and became perceived as the Spiritual consummation of the Christians' resurrected experience for Orthodox Christianity. This was not the

---

17. The holy Eucharist "was the most significant meal [and metaphoric ritual in worship] of all, because it became the symbolic meal of the community [the body of the Christ and his presence]." Casey, *Jewish Prophet,* 132. Brackets are mine.

18. Grant, *The Earliest Gospel,* 38. Note Chap. vii, "'The Theology of Mark," also n. 28, p. 156. Spong has noticed that "Paul seemed to think resurrection and ascension were two parts of the same divine action and used various forms of the word 'exaltation' to communicate that conviction." John Shelby Spong, *Liberating the Gospels: Reading the Bible with Jewish Eyes* (New York: HarperSanFrancisco, 1996), 282. Cf., Phil. 2:5-11.

19. See W. G. Kummel, *Promise and Fulfillment.* Also, Rudolf Bultmann, "Prophecy and Fulfillment," *Essays on Old Testament Hermeneutics,* ed. by Claus Westerman (New York: John Knox Press, 1964), 55-58 where he offers a criticism against Johann Christian Konrad von Hofmann's (1810-1877) theology of '*Heilsgeschicte*' as being theologically irrelevant.

original mystical significance of the *parousia* by any means, since it lacked the moral imperatives that were utilized in Paul's preaching and letters. Conceptually, for Paul and the early gatherings, it had conveyed these moral imperatives that embraced a believer (mystically) with divine assistance in a Platonic sense (1 Thess. 1:8-9).

The later orthodox position became a drastic alteration of its previous basic mystical and theological formulation that had been proclaimed originally by Paul.[20] Even though it (the *parousia*) had become separated, on a conceptual and religious level from Jesus' own literary resurrection experience, it had been the existential manifestation of YHWH's Spiritual *presence* and his power in the early communities. It had been maintained by the earlier Jewish gatherings' socio-religious interpretation of their communal identity. They were a resurrected people living in a new communal life, anointed by God's presence. The new age of the Spirit, the time of God's Kingdom, had come through the preaching of apostles like Paul. It had been the christological power of the Spirit in formative Christianity by granting eternal life 'in the Christ,' by God's Spirit (his eternal presence) within the community that lived within the 'present evil age.'

With this in mind, we can understand the religious development of the earlier myth by its historical evolution into later Christian thought (theology and dogma). The earlier myth now depicted this literary and historicized understanding of a historical Jesus. The *parousia* was now seen as Jesus' return and related that theological fabrication, soteriologically, to the believers' ex-

---

20. Paul developed his theological posture over time and often reacted toward earlier traditions. Sid Green states that "Paul certainly entered the community in 'Damascus' as a novice, serving three years [Galatians 1:17-18] before 'graduating' prior to becoming apostate over the issue of the law." in "Sons of Zadok," 8, http://www .christianorigins.com/zadok.html (accessed 19 July 2004). He expands the Essene type community to embrace "the early Nazorean believers, as well as the somewhat later Christian followers of the gospel Jesus, [and] were gnostics of the adoptionist variety." Ibid.

perience known as *"Christusmystik."*[21] When we hold to a real historical restoration of this earlier christological mysticism and the miracles that that entails, we would move our present understanding of mythology closer to the actual and historical Jewish community's socio-religious interpretation. Bultmann has suggested that the Hellenistic miracle stories, both in motif and in form, offer at least a cultural parallelism. They also offer "a wealth of parallels to the Synoptic, particularly in style, as to create a prejudice in favor of supposing that the Synoptic miracle stories grew up on Hellenistic ground."[22] No one should argue that religious tradition undergoes changes in a natural way, given enough time by its common usage within the social dynamics of cultural development.

The merging of conceptual terms, such as the resurrection for instance[23] as a miracle in its own right, into a new unified frame of theological reference (seen from an eschatological basis within the range of apocalyptic literature) is also one of those natural, christological changes that can be seen in the Christian, biblical tradition. What clouds the issue is that new theological ideas were added into a former mythological schema often without jettisoning some older concepts that just would not gel as part of a newly composed composite work. The tenuous confusion of theologically, schematic categories is what resulted, and these were simply maintained in the literary forms that have come down to us. The early primitive Jewish assemblies understood the kerygma as the symbolic expression of their communal and *christological* faith experience. It was the primitive cult that was given socio-religious life by the divine power of YHWH's Spirit.

---

21. See Arthur Darby Nock, *Early Gentile Christianity and its Hellenistic Background* (New York: Harper & Row, Pub., Harper Torchbooks, 1964). Also cf., his "The Theology of Christianity a Mission-Religion," Sec. 7, "Mystic life," 52-56.

22. Bultmann, *Synoptic Tradition,* 240.

23. See Crossan, *The Birth of Christianity,* 548 where he mentions the concept of resurrection as a 'communal resurrection,' like Ezekiel 37:1-14. These are revelatory expressions; thus, the third day is about communal resurrection "according to the scriptures" reminiscent of II Cor. 15:20 and its parallel in the Gospel of Peter, 10:42.

The primitive kerygma expressed this internal metaphorical understanding depicted in Mark's Gospel, narrative account. This mystical experience symbolized in the narrative was also expressed through the rites and ceremonies of the early christological communities. Scholars have long been aware of the fact that religious literature had been produced as a result of social and political pressures upon a community under foreign domination. Roman oppression helped to produce its share of Wisdom and apocalyptic literature in the diaspora and in Judea well before the first century B.C.E. Scholars have known that creation stories, mythological understandings, symbolic references, and wisdom literature in their tradition had been based on perceptions of reality that reflected their oppressive social conditions, with some theological points of view, going back to ancient Persia's administrative rule of *Yehud* (539-333 B.C.E.) as a Persian colony.[24]

A rich array of literary works utilized mystic and mythical categories, metaphor, symbolism, Platonic perspectives, and gnostic themes and continued into the Hellenistic era to narrate stories and events that reflected significant aspects of religious life. This is when Paul and other apostles wrote, and later, the Gospels were written. It was the religious and social tensions that also account for the attitudinal support or lack thereof by many Jews in the diaspora and by many of the Judeans in Palestine with regard to the Temple, the priesthood, and the acceptability of the sacred sacrifices. This was also a very significant Jewish distinction among the Essenes at Qumran. Vermes tells us that an "important feature differentiating the members of the sect from mainstream Judaism was their withdrawal from the Temple. ... They disagreed with the conduct of ceremonies by the Jerusalem

---

24. Berquist, *Judaism,* 177-240. The very nature of social and religious conflict has been transformed in modern times by our formation of secular, constitutional governments and a scientific modernity. "From the nineteenth century on it became possible to assert that there is no God, no after life, and no eternal reward and punishment, without, as in previous centuries, going to jail or the stake, and social order has not collapsed." Bellah, *Beyond Belief,* 218.

priests."[25] The Jerusalem priesthood, because of the political and religious implications within Judaism's religious regulations, had become a partisan appointment fiasco (being bought repeatedly by the highest purchaser) under the patronage of Roman authority.

What we need now is a more critical examination of the biblical texts in order to illuminate the historicized significance of the early Jewish witnesses and to set the bounds of historical verification, as it relates to those christological origins and their eschatological existence. Wobbermin offers a kind of relative facticity of this view for traditional Christianity: "The Christian religion begins ... historically viewed (i.e., apart from faith and so far as documents carry us) it begins, not with the religious self-consciousness of Jesus but with that of the first disciples. We carry back the line of Christian faith straight to them, but not beyond them to Jesus himself. Beyond the whole chain he stands as the person who first made this form of faith and life possible."[26] Such a view as this is made possible only because of the Gospel evangelists' writings, which impregnate the literary stories with a historicized concept of Jesus. In this sense, it was the original and symbolic understanding in the early kerygma that continued the first call for the christological faith within the early Jewish assemblies.

In mythological terms, the Jewish gatherings, collectively, were the anointed christological Servant of YHWH, the body of the divine Spirit of Truth. This spiritual 'collectivity' did have a historical basis in which even in the biblical tradition, it (Israel, the king, etc.) was occasionally referred to as God's son. This mythological terminology that was used to represent conceptual, mythological categories did not depict actual history; although the actual communal experience of spiritual 'collectivity' had occurred in history. These mythological categories became the historic religiosity of formative Christianity that was based on the reformulated, historicized, and conceptual sources of the

---

25. Vermes, *Jesus,* 122.

26. This is Wobbermin's statement as cited by P. T. Forsyth, *The Person and Place of Jesus Christ,* The Congregational Union Lecture for 1909 (New York: The Pilgrim Press, 1909), 59.

primitive, christological gatherings' faith-understanding. These kinds of ideas were amply available within the vast culture of the Hellenistic world. "Thus Christianity, when it came into the world, had not to insist that God had no human form and was an omnipresent Spirit: it found this idea already established among Jews and philosophic pagans."[27] The eschatological scenario in the divine drama, which also used the cultic expressions, Lord, Messiah, Redeemer, Savior, etc., is best understood by the symbolic hermeneutic as the spiritual discernment and methodology of the Jewish christological brotherhood (communal leadership) who can be depicted as being in search of wisdom[28] (Sophia, cf., Bar. 3:14-37 and John 14:1-14). Therein lays just one of many strands that yield the historical basis for the historic origin and religiosity of the Jesus myth for the early Jewish christological understanding.

The various uses of these mythological terms provided the christological cult with its historic and mystic understanding of its eschatological relation to the divine *presence* (*tēs parousias* of Jesus). It is vastly important to keep in mind that,

> Religious symbolism, too, is part of the religious experience itself, and the experience would not be complete without its symbolization. Only when the symbol has been torn from its experiential

---

27. Bevan, *Symbolism and Belief*, 254. From a social science historical analysis perspective the symbolic world functioned differently within various social contexts. Many Jews in Judea and in the diaspora felt disillusioned by the political and religious practices by the Temple priesthood. The exiled Zadokites, Essenes, and Qumran covenanters held to similar views. The Dead Sea, Cave 4 document (4Q MMT) has been cited as pointing out these many points of practice that were blasphemous to their religious sensibilities.

28. One scholar of Wisdom literature suggests that "a stronger case for a relationship can be made between Wisdom and the Egyptian *ma'at* (recall the abstract 'justice' or *ma'at* was also personified as a goddess). The description of *ma'at* seems to have influenced the presentation of wisdom in Proverbs 1-9." Roland E. Murphy, *The Tree of Life: An Exploration of Biblical Wisdom Literature* (Grand Rapids, Mich.: William. B. Eerdmans Publishing Company, 2nd ed., 1990), 137.

context and taken literally, as a belief "about" something, must we assert its fictional nature. As part of the experience itself, it is perfectly and supremely real [the experience that is, not the myth upon which the symbolism is formed]. ... But in principle, no particular symbolization is itself above criticism.[29]

Consequently, the interpretation of the resurrection experience as a historic (mystical) event became, for the evangelists, historicized into a written literary form and indicated to them, clearly with firm religious conviction that Jesus, who died, now lives in a new spiritual realm of (mythological) existence. This was the new theological basis for those conservative (traditionalists) members. For them, this now became the only acceptable social and religious hermeneutic.

This historicized interpretation became the literalists' mind-set for many in the later fellowships. This point of view was consolidated as historical theology in the emerging period of formative Christianity. The later historicized, biblical statements were a religious dynamic and the interpretive force of apocalyptic myth for their religiosity. Also, mythology and its mystic components became the social, religious, and cultural factors for determining the redemptive changes within the later theology (as Church dogma?).[30] Robinson concedes, in contradistinction to the modern fundamentalist formulation of the biblical statements (i.e., regarding them as predictions, prophecies, etc.), that recent writers "... have argued that the true character of the biblical statements about the end of the world, as about its beginning, is not that of literal history but of myth."[31]

---

29. Bellah, *Beyond Belief*, 204. Bracket is mine.

30. Paul Tillich, *The Protestant Era*, Abridged ed., Trans. James Luther Adams (Chicago: The University of Chicago Press, Phoenix Books, 1957) where he relates the need for a shaping of a new philosophy of history and culture in order to face secularism. He offers a positive view in that Christianity, he believes, can find new forms of expression to serve humanity. This is also his basic idea, *Systematic Theology*, Part V, "History and the Kingdom of God," 297-423.

31. Robinson, *Jesus and His Coming*, 10. Early Christianity, in the Gospel narratives at the baptism of Jesus (i.e., the religious rite that accepted the initiate into the Jesus cult), connects the righteousness of

In general, the expanded covenantal literature's use of the kerygma "refers primarily to the message proclaimed by the apostles, not to the act of preaching."[32] This message, in essence, was historicized by some traditionalists within the christological fellowships when it entered into the Gospel's literary tradition. It is recorded in the biblical tradition that Paul experienced (in mystical fashion) the resurrected Lord (a mythological statement) through a personal and spiritual revelation.[33] It was his own theological basis in his proclamation that was part of the Hellenistic cultural atmosphere of religious thought (that is, his gospel of the cosmic *Christos* event). This was most likely similar in understanding to the Jewish christological cult's symbolic religiosity and their mystical and hermeneutical basis. Hellenistic influence on Jewish culture, religion, and philosophical ideas has had a longstanding and turbulent tradition in history. Levine's position is that,

> The pièce de résistance of Judean Hellenization, and the most dramatic of all these developments, occurred in 175 B.C.E. when the high priest Jason converted Jerusalem into a Greek *polis* replete with *gymnasium* and *ephebeion* (2 Maccabees 4). Whether this step represents the culmination of a 150-year process of Hellenization within Jerusalem in general, or whether it was only the initiative of a small coterie of Jerusalem priests with no wider ramifications, has been debated for decades.[34]

In Hellenistic times, Greek culture was full of traveling holy men, religious and philosophical sages, and an assortment

---

the historicized Jesus with the descending Holy Spirit (i.e., in the Jesus cult, once accepted, the initiate received divine spiritual anointing as instruction into the mysteries of the cult and perceived this instruction as YHWH's Spirit in their lives). Compare the Essenes at Qumran who were taught by the Teacher of Righteousness (cf. the Christian cult's divine instruction of the Jesus myth) for spiritual edification. These ideas were in the air of a culture whose peoples reached out for religious significance to their historical existence.

32. James L. Price, *Interpreting the New Testament*. 108.
33. Cf. Acts 9; 22; and 26; see Gal. 1: 13-17.
34. Levine, *Hellenism*, 39.

of mystery proponents all delivering their intellectual wares to anyone who would listen. Paul was most likely a missionary representative of an Essene-like community (Hellenistically influenced) that expressed his kind of *christological* understanding of the heavenly Christ. It is precisely a three-fold distinction in the spiritual process of Paul's christological experience that Barth found a religious description of the mutual relationship between the three forms of God's 'word' that is proclaimed to humanity. Thus, in Barth, we find the relationship expressed:

> The revealed Word of God we know only from the Scripture adopted by the church proclamation or from church proclamation based on Scripture. The written word of God we know only through the revelation that makes proclamation possible or through the proclamation made possible by revelation. The proclaimed Word of God we know only by knowing the revelation attested through Scripture or by knowing the Scripture that attests revelation.[35]

The difficulty, which has arisen from this indiscriminate usage, is that, in biblical exegesis it is often confusing to identify whether the reference is to the Lord God, YHWH of the original covenantal literature (O.T.), or to the Lord Jesus, YHWH's Spirit of the expanded covenantal writings (N.T.). In the historic origin of the christological gatherings among the diaspora communities and according to their Jewish consciousness this definitely was not a difficulty, since God as Savior was called by a new name, *Yeshua* (Jesus). This name was symbolically understood as God's divine healing, spiritual salvation, and social deliverance based on the *Christos* event (Jesus crucified 1 Cor. 15:1-5) stated in midrash fashion, for 'the forgiveness of sin.' Much of the expanded covenantal literature contains evidence of midrashim that is alleged as actual history.[36] This theological position[37] of Jew-

---

35. Karl Barth, *Church Dogmatics*, I, 1, p. 124, as cited by Hartwell, *The Theology of Karl Barth: An Introduction,* 63.

36. A good historic example of midrashim that was included in the biblical tradition is mentioned by Berquist, *Judaism,* 86 in his remarks that "Many scholars understand the Branch in Zechariah 3:8 to

ish religiosity in the diaspora was maintained in the social and religious perceptions of the christological cult. The original conceptual nature and mythology of this redemptive drama had been perceived as part of YHWH's salvation experience (mysticism, Gnosticism, and Essene eschatology) and had incorporated the mythic figure of the Heavenly Son, the Son of God, and the Son of Man into the later Gospels. These titles were a blend from different traditions that were brought together when the Gospel of Mark was written. The mystic stories that fleshed out Jesus' life and ministry are carbon copies of the earlier Mosaic tradition's prophetic hero stories, which were recast into a new Hellenistic, narrative 'gospel' genre.

Consequently, the sources themselves are not historical documents that scientifically validate past events. They are the 'historic' documents of the earliest church's eschatological and apocalyptic faith that were mythologically based and viewed from a socio-religious and political perspective. These Gospels represented an interpretation of the social and religious, historic experiences of their communal existence. And now, as then, this literature calls for a decision based on a commitment of faith as a moral requirement for Christian salvation and acceptance into a communal religiosity.

According to the major thesis of Wm. B. Smith, the Jewish communities arose within the Hellenistic culture essentially as a christological revolt against the gods (cf. Acts 17). Their primary theological perception (being called by God's Spirit) was the unitary thrust to overthrow polytheism in the Hellenistic

---

refer to Zerubbabel. However, the verse begins with a redirection of the voice, which now addresses not only Joshua but also those colleagues called to witness Joshua's anointing. These colleagues are an 'omen of things to come,' and Joshua, God's servant, the Branch, is the thing that is to come, the event to which the omen colleagues point and testify."

37. On the subject of unity, perceived as unity in diversity, see H. H. Rowley, *The Unity of the Bible* (London: Carey Kingsgate Press, 1953).

age.[38] This new monotheistic faith-understanding of the Jewish cult often came into open conflict with the established idolatry of polytheism. They had interpreted the Kingdom of YHWH as the hope of many generations for a New Israel[39] (the Essenes had expressed similar kingdom ideas) not merely as an imminent event in history, but as having come within the actual spiritual experience of the christological cults. This faith-understanding also used the dynamic, Platonic categories of a heavenly/earthly ontological and epistemological schema.[40]

Thus, the historic symbolism began to be crystallized in the biblical tradition over a period of at least three generations and at various cultic locals. Finally, it took on an interpretation that regarded the events as actual historical reality, which was naturally taken literally by many traditionalists within the developing communities. Once this had emerged into the church's thinking, it remained anchored together with the loyalty of the new generation of formative, Christian believers in the diaspora

---

38. Just as today, the dominant culture and its systemic control would affect various groups differently. Conservatism and liberalism are psychodynamic methodologies internally functioning as value indicators which determine perceptive outcomes within a cultural context. In an arena that is determinative, conflict or confluence, historical evidence is always a good guess based on the historian's analytical focus. Thus, "there were individuals and groups within rabbinic society [and the christological gatherings in all probability] whose use of Greek and knowledge of 'Greek wisdom' were well known." And, "... in the studies conducted by Rabban Gamaliel's academy; students studied Greek language and wisdom no less than the Torah." Levine, *Hellenism*, 128. Bracket is mine.

39. The Essene community's ideas were expressed in various forms of mythology; both from past historical traditions that were born in their Persian experience and from the sectarian perceptions within the Hellenistic culture. Levine's statements about Greek influence, above, could be just as applicable here.

40. Cf., Mark 10:15 with Matt. 13:44-46. On the historicity of Jesus, see M. Goguel, *Jesus the Nazarene: Myth or History?* (New York: Charles Scribner's Sons, 1926). Compare Wood, *Did Christ Really Live?* Also see C. C. McCown, *The Search for the Real Jesus* (New York: Charles Scribner's Sons, 1940), Chap. V.

who by now were predominantly Gentiles.[41] They fostered a non-symbolic religious hermeneutic in written form that found its way into the newly emerging biblical tradition, the Gospel of Mark. The historic representation of the incarnation of the divine God-man, Jesus, relied on a third and newly conservative fourth generation of Christian believers. It was these later generations who were to be the champions of this spiritual materialism (i.e., a religious, literalist historicity).

The new communities of monotheistic faith (based on the Jesus myth) had not been planned, but had grown out of an awareness of their own unique mystic existences and spiritual relationship.[42] Formative Christianity, along with its newly trans-formed and historicized understanding, proclaimed its revised Christological understanding.[43] The gospel of YHWH's grace (a call to faith in response to this new revelation of the resurrection) was viewed as a necessary component to faith that was required now for the spiritual salvation of humanity. This was a social and religious process similar to the mystery religions within the mythological, contextual, and systemic nature of the Hellenistic religiosities. In this respect, the mythical proclamation, which

---

41. Cf., the effect of Bishop Usher's dating of creation, 4004 BCE and its retention by fundamentalist Christianity and its later addition, which it occurred at 9 a.m. on October the 23rd.

42. Brandon, *Jesus and the Zealots*, 150 ff. Their relationship to God within the community was perceived as his *presence,* the *presence* of his Spirit, the *presence* of his Son, the *parousia* (meaning *presence*).

43. See Douglas Groothuis, *Revealing the New Age Jesus: Challenges to Orthodox Views of Christ* (Downers Grove, Ill: Intervarsity Press, 1990), where he states that the resurrection was not historical. He views the rapid spread of Christianity (e.g., its origins and development) as an enigma that cannot be explained in non-supernatural terms. I would also suggest that he read Wm. B. Smith, Drews, and Peter Jensen for an alternative view in which to gleam the symbolic interpretation for Christianity's historicity. And for a recent historical attempt to answer the Mysticists position, see Bart Ehrman, *Did Jesus Exist? The Historical Argument for Jesus of Nazareth* (New York: Harper One, 2012). This, in my judgement, is more faith based biblical hermeneutics and an apologetic work rather than a real historical analysis to resolve the issue.

357

was contained in the expanded covenantal literature, still reflected the earlier spiritual and biblical tradition's mythology and symbolism. Most biblical and classical scholars maintain that there has been an affinity of understanding in the ancient world that is reflected through cultural, conceptual, and mythological contents as religious commonalities within most literary forms.

Some Christian theologians have attempted to redefine Christian mythology and explain the nature of humanity in modern terms, which also takes into consideration the nature of our physical existence. Thus, Paul Tillich notes that,

> The words which are most used in religion are also those whose genuine meaning is almost completely lost and whose import on the human mind is nearly negligible. Such words must be reborn, if possible; and thrown away if this is not possible, even if they are protected by a long tradition. But there is only one way to re-establish their original meaning and power, namely, to ask ourselves what these words mean for our lives; to ask whether or not they are able to communicate something infinitely important to us. This is true of all important terms of our religious language.[44]

It is time for modern Christian believers to acknowledge the original mystical and mythological basis in Christianity's historical origin. Much of the New Testament (its biblical theology from Paul, or the kind of thinking that Paul represents, and from Gospel narrative accounts) draws upon various mythical points from a common historical stock of established eschatological and apocalyptic symbolism. "Paul ... specifically [had a] Gentile mission ... following the model of proselytization in Judaism (flourishing in those days). Paul's pronouncement that the Christian communities now formed the 'Israel of God' (Gal. 6.16) will have neutralized the sting of the insults preserved in the gospel text."[45] As Tillich has suggested, the explanations and interpreta-

---

44. Paul Tillich, *The Eternal Now* (New York: Charles Scribner's Sons, 1963), 112-13.

45. Vermes, *Jesus*, 50. This statement is more acceptable once we realize that Paul was not a Christian in the modern orthodox meaning of the dogmatized designation.

tions of the biblical tradition must reflect a closer proximity to the original Jewish, christological cult's dynamic religiosity.

This should be the historical methodology used in scholarship and not the goal of modern spirituality. The language of theology also needs clarification, and has given a new thrust and linguistic development to the present use of 'language theology' in America.[46] A polarization has occurred theologically that has resulted in several different modern day tensions. For example: note the continuous efforts to interject religious views in the midst of a secular and scientific culture, such as creationism into the science curriculum of public school systems, even though these attempts have been rejected by District courts and the U.S. Supreme Court since 1985.

Rational minds have been forced by the inevitable growth of modern scientific and historical knowledge to seek out a new spiritual and non-mythological understanding to the old theological controversies within the modern Church. This is done even while traditional Christianity continues to maintain its current interpretation of a historical Jesus. In the biblical tradition, from the original covenantal literature (the Old Testament) to the expanded covenantal literature (the New Testament), there have been a wide range of symbolic interpretations that have developed within the Christian faith. As an example, consider *to pneuma sophias*, the spirit of wisdom.

---

46. Robert W. Funk offers a presentation of this new language theology in his, *Language, Hermeneutics, and Word of God* (New York: Harper & Row, Pub., 1966); note especially Part One, "Language as Event and Theology," 20-122. Also, see section 2, "The Problem of Language -- Man and His History" in the article by Manfred Metzger, "Preparation for Preaching -- The Route from Exegesis to Proclamation," trans. by Robert A. Kraft in his, *Translating Theology into the Modern Age*, Vol. II of the *Journal for Theology and the Church,* ed. Robert W. Funk (New York: Harper & Row, Pub., Harper Torchbooks, 1965), 170-175. An analysis of German thought, as related to the above subject, can be found in "The Hermeneutic," Vol. II of *New Frontiers in Theology: Discussions among German and American Theologians*, ed., James M. Robinson and John B. Cobb, Jr., 2 Vols. (New York: Harper & Row, Pub., 1964).

In its most general meaning, *pneuma sophias* designates the action of wisdom ..., But the Greek *pneuma* had acquired specific meanings in Hellenistic thought. It stood for the Platonic "soul" of the world, and in Stoicism it took on a particular nuance: "a universal divine principle which animated and penetrated the entire universe, giving it substance and unity." This idea is always hinted at in Wis. 1:7, "The Spirit of the Lord fills the world, is all embracing. ..." The cosmic function is specified further in 12:1, "Your imperishable spirit is in all things." This is the real presence of the divine spirit. [In the Pauline sense it was the *parousia*, the _presence_ of God's spirit, his Son.][47]

Hence; we see that the theological concepts of religion, which have been philosophically explored, have also enter into dialogue with the secular world at the precise juncture of human commonality, our personal and social experiences. It could be imagined, that to some extent, the exegetical motivation (to communicate the christological gospel) was part of the original impetus that caused those of a conservative posture to reformulate the fabricated tradition of the Jesus myth into a historicized 'form.' They were the ones who, by a literalized understanding in the later assemblies, depicted the mythical Jesus, as a historical person. This metaphorical understanding, which was utilized by the early Jewish community of the *Christos* event (Paul's mystical conceptualization, the dawning of the 'new age'), its perception as divine 'revelation,' and its theological interpretation, are all considered by Martin Kahler to be acts of God.[48] And, only as such do they give any historical and spiritual meaning to the Church's life and spiritual understandings, which are based on the kerygma's historicized events.

Yet, they do not give any historical dignity nor do they reflect the original religious and moral integrity of the historical, Jewish christological communities, which have been glossed over by modern, biblical exegetical studies. This new age experi-

---

47. Murphy, *Tree of Life*, 42. Bracket is mine.

48. Martin Kahler, *Dogmatische Zeitfragen: Fur Bibelfrage* 2d ed., (Leipzig: A. Deichert, 1909), 188 as quoted by Carl E. Braaten in Kahler's, *Historical Jesus -- Biblical Christ,* n. 33, p. 32.

enced by the early christological communities was a living-out of the end-times as viewed by the out pouring of God's spirit (Joel 2:28-9). The Jews in the diaspora, being at a distance from the Temple precinct could and did explore other spiritual avenues of development as communities of the end-times. This made it a lot easier to develop greater theological and dynamic mental constructs that involved Hellenistic mythothemes, symbolic nuances, and metaphorical language.[49]

The original Jewish cult's methodology was dynamic in that it also determined their historic christological existence as having a spiritual life with a vital, mystic relationship with their deity's presence, YHWH (the Lord). This primitive christological cult of the new age objectified its communal faith from the early kerygma into a faith of resurrection hope. They "... began to live even then in the assurance of the reality of the resurrection."[50] The fellowship was also perceived as existing in the power of the Spirit,[51] since it was a mystic fellowship '*with*' the risen Lord.[52] This gave to them the assurance of eternal life, which evoked an awareness of the 'quality' of communal existence and not its temporal duration. They only had eternal life because it was

---

49. Berquist, *Judaism*, 7.

50. Jack Finegan, *Jesus, History, and You* (Richmond, Virginia: John Knox Press, 1964), 139.

51. For a more recent argument based on the presupposition of God and immortality which are considered vital parts of religion, see Friedrich Schleiermacher, *On Religion: Speeches to its Cultured Despisers*, trans. by John Oman, with an introduction by Rudolf Otto (New York: Harper & Row, Pub., Harper Torchbooks, 1958), 92-101, and 114-118.

52. See I John 1:1-3; 3:24. Even though in Jewish thought 'wisdom' was identified with Torah and Paul identified the Christ with God's 'wisdom,' both are in both cultural and religious expressions, the Jewish and Hellenistic, one could find agreement in wisdom as the divine *presence* that empowers and transforms individual behavior. See E. E. Urbach, *The Sages: Their Concepts and Beliefs* (Jerusalem: Magnes, 1975), 198 ff., 286 ff. Also see E. Johnson, "Jesus, the Wisdom of God: A Biblical Basis for Non-Androcentric Theology," *ETL* 61 (1985), 261-94.

permeated and encapsulated by the 'Eternal One,' the divine *presence* of the Heavenly Father.

We see that this type of assurance was also manifested in the waters of baptism (a cultic practice which originally reflected the symbolic understanding of the Jesus myth and the cult's religiosity).[53] "This baptism symbolized return to God (Mk. 1:4-5). Ritual washing was therefore a natural symbol for the earliest Christians to use to symbolize the return of Jews to God (the upward ascent for gnostics) when they joined the Christian community."[54] The cultic practice of baptism was continued to be preserved in the later forms of religious worship for orthodoxy.

In all of this, the biblical tradition still maintains some of its original symbolic character. When modern historians seek to explain how Jesus became accepted as God, we are dealing with an apologetic methodology that is only necessitated by the appearance of the Gospels in order to explicate a historical, literary development. They have altered for all time, the actual historical sequence of historic development (based on Paul's and the early christological gatherings' perceptions) of the cosmic, heavenly Christ, who was sent by God, crucified and exalted (raised) for the 'forgiveness of sins.' This entire projected scenario and its mythological, component Platonic categories was not actual history; but as part of religious conceptualities, these were symbolic and cosmic events that were metaphorical, mythological, and of 'historic' religious significance for the development of the faith of the formative, Christian orthodox believers.

Some biblical scholars, like Robertson and Jeremias, have acknowledged the fact that symbolic and metaphorical interpreta-

---

53. Baptism within the community (brotherhood) was perceived as a public confession that signifies their existence within the body of the Christ as separate from the outside culture; Rensberger, *Johannine Community*, 69 and 148. Also, see Col. 2:12-13. It was part and parcel to the Hellenistic culture to safeguard the inner secret symbolism of the group, community, or brotherhood. In fact, the initiates of the Greek mystery cults (on a threat of death) and even the Jewish Nazoreans took an oath never to reveal the inner secrets of the sectarian brotherhood.

54. Casey, Jewish Prophet, 108.

tions can be found within the literary style[55] of the expanded covenantal parables. The parables also have used a literary form whose historic significance was based on the kerygmatic intentiality of their authors. As allegories, for the teachings about the Christ (i.e., the propaganda of the anointed Jewish christological fellowship), they are unmistakable. It is this faith, which is the reflective mind-set of human religiosity that perceives the divine power for spiritual purposes.[56] This faith was depicted in terms of humanity's religious redemption as immanent within physical experience and spiritual understanding. It was all part of the common fabric of ideas (cf., Gnosticism, Middle Platonism, Greek religion and philosophy, the Hellenistic mystery religions, various Judaisms, and formative Christianity) just to mention a few. These were readily available for the cultural and religious understanding of religious-minded peoples during this age.

---

55. Robinson, *Jesus and His Coming*, 60. Cf. Mark 13:35 and Luke 12:40 with Matt.24:44. Also cf. Jeremias, *The Parables of Jesus*, for his detailed comments.

56. Seen in this way, we understand Spong's expression when he declares that the resurrected Jesus was not an actual physical body, but as Paul had stated: he was a "life giving spirit" (1 Cor. 15:45). In modern terms we can understand that a 'spirit' (the intellectual and moral understanding) can give a person 'life' (a new dimension of authentic existence) that will deliver them from living in a world of constant immoral, emotional, and psychological turmoil.

12

All war is based on deception.
Sun Tzu

The theological proposal for a spiritual realm of existence, communicated eschatologically and embellished by the language of symbolism, is religious rationalism, a significant form of a modern genre, fantasy. This is maintained for the most part by a modern, literalist Christian mind-set. This mythological and ancient religious foundation, for modern, Christian religiosity has continued to be its essential objectified form. It seeks to validate past biblical events as having historical and factual existence.[1] The absence or at least a greatly diminished sense of an existential value in modern Christian religiosity, by this relative method of historical verification, which equates biblical mythology with a sense of historical facticity, is undeniable. Physical reality, as we now scientifically understand it, would become a mere rational contradiction if one accepts the given 'God-Man' dichotomy as conceptualized in modern Christianity's dogma. This ancient mythic dichotomy is non-historical at least as it relates to physical actuality. And when it relates to the historical Jesus myth, it cannot be reconciled with a modern scientific understanding of physical reality.

Even Paula Fredriksen, as a biblical scholar, notes that Paul's hermeneutical posture when unpacking his theological language is metaphor, symbolism, moral, and ethically based. As

---

1. This would be like taking any historical 'novel,' *Gone with the Wind* for example and then seeking to uncover the actual history of the lives the 'characters' that appear in the story as though these characters were real historical figures. It isn't going to happen no matter how hard we try (historicism) or how sincere we might be in our efforts (confessionalism).

religious language, it is not a physical description of reality. She states that "Those who were apostles before Paul, who had followed the [so-called] earthly Jesus and witnessed the risen Christ, presumably against evangelical tradition, did not see a physical body either."[2] This study's conclusion is singular: The essence of religious mythology finds its common ground in human experiences[3], which express religious concepts as metaphor and as the symbolic understanding of human existence. Meeks suggests that even though "a large and growing number of social scientists construe ritual as a form of communication" and say that "ritual communicates the fundamental beliefs and values of a society or of a group: this definition does not distinguish ritual from other social behavior." This is similar to Goody's conclusion: "Indeed such an approach simply involves the reification of an organizing abstraction into a causal factor."[4] Thus, the earliest

---

2. Paula Fredriksen, *From Jesus to Christ: The Origins of New Testament Images of Jesus* (New Haven: Yale University Press, 1988), 175. For historical accuracy, her title should have been "From Christ to Jesus" as this study proposes. Bracket is mine. Based on Paul's sense of moral imperatives, Paula and mysticist, biblical scholars would agree that "Christ could not have been raised physically; else, where would his body have gone?" And, she notes that "flesh and blood cannot ascend to the right hand of God." She further explains that Paul's eschatological perception was "Paul's choice of an al enemy: not Rome, nor indeed any earthly power, but the astral archons [Platonism?] of the Hellenistic cosmos." Ibid. Bracket is mine.

3. Even the social dynamics of Paul's gospel was expressed in mystical language that reflected the symbolic nature of the mystery religions. They used Greek terms that signified the reception of 'revelations' within the fellowship as did Paul. Being a diaspora Jew, he certainly traveled in Hellenistic circles and was educated in Greek philosophical thought, so that it is not strange to find vast similarities of mystic, mythic, and linguistic, religious connections. Note also Schweitzer, *Mysticism of Paul,* who negates any influence of Hellenistic religiosity.

4. Wayne A. Meeks, *The First Urban Christians: The Social World of the Apostle Paul* (New Haven: Yale University Press, 1983), 141. He has quoted Jack Goody, "Religion and Ritual: The Definitional Problem," *British Journal of Sociology* (1961), 12:157.

christological gathering, by making a decisive point of entry into their exclusive community of faith through the rite of baptism, whose function was an initiatory experience, had created a ritual something akin to the Hellenistic mystery religions.

Tillich, Bultmann, Bonhoeffer and others have failed to advance their theological critiques completely in the direction that their understanding has taken them -- to an authentic humanity that seeks self-understanding and expresses its anthropological existence in honest terms for a true and realistic historicity of socio-religious development. Take secularism, as expressed in a humanistic world-view, it would seem be the only option for a modern, moral integrity to replace the traditional mythological religiosity. Humanity's real 'spiritual' value is itself. We are the basis for human values. We determine the real issues that rational people have and are able to provide solutions in order to bring about a just (fair-minded) world redeemed from myth, which can be restructured with moral integrity.[5] This would allow us to maintain a rational understanding of physical reality. Even in a traditional biblical sense, to cast out the demons of today would be to cast out the myth of divinity as a supernal reality. It would be to release humanity from the supernatural and mythological bonds in order to establish an honest, rational understanding of humanity on a modern secular, scientific, and humanistic basis (a spiritual redemption?).

Communal religiosity is not dependent on nor are human experiences meaningful because of historical facts (i.e., all the mundane actualities of physical reality). The real meaning of human existence is not the eternal and divine goal to become spiritual or religious; it is what we in our humanity make it to be. We create the meaning of life through human existence. It has always been the creative and imaginative spirit of humanity[6] that

---

5. Moral integrity is defined as a commitment to a life style that seeks to bring about mutual respect, an acceptance of human dignity that accepts others as they are. It is a basic integrity based on love that supports, sustains, and nurtures others for the goodness of all.

6. Braaten, *History and Hermeneutic*, 84ff. Cf., 1 Corinthians 15:3 with Galatians 1:11-12. See Fredriksen, *Jesus to Christ,* 82 where she indicates that "literature flourished in this troubled period between

provides its own meaning for existence. What we seem to have in the early first century CE is not a Jesus movement, but a *christological* movement; an apostolic, missionary encounter (the revitalization of the Jewish faith), which was representing the 'good news' of freedom from the demonic forces preached by Paul and other apostles. It was a philosophical movement to bring into human experience the power of moral transformation in our ethical relationships. In order to uncover this historical development, we must also understand the alteration of the historical, biblical texts that contains basic data for analysis. Most scholars today would agree, in general terms at least, that what we have as textual evidence has had its own tradition, which also reflects editorial changes. Watson quotes Fox's position[7] that is well accepted today, since it is based on papyrological evidence, "the Christian scriptures were a battlefield for textual alteration and rewriting in the first hundred years of their life."

These theological changes were more of a philosophical enterprise that was based on later scribes' perception of divine inspiration, a revelatory understanding, and mystical unification with the supreme deity and the lord, the *Logos* (Divine Wisdom).[8] Modern Christianity needs to rediscover this metaphorical

---

the Maccabees and Bar Kochba, a literature whose esoteric symbolism could cloak a political critique. The final enemy was always the 'Babylon' be it incarnated as the Seleucid Empire or Rome."

7. Alan Watson, *Jesus and the Jews: The Pharisaic Tradition in John* (Athens: University of Georgia Press, 1995), 3 where he quotes Robin Lane Fox, *The Unauthorized Version: Truth and Fiction in the Bible* (New York: 1992), 139. One should consult the biblical and textual scholar Bart Ehrman and his tomes that represent the best in modern textual examination and hermeneutical references for modern scholars today.

8. Cf., 1 Corinthians 15:3 with Galatians 1:11-12. It was the 'scriptural' revelations Paul received by inspiration from the heavenly Christ that enabled him to redirect a new theological basis for the older Jewish traditions. "Once this is acknowledged, the way is open to regarding the scene Paul creates as a myth attached to the spiritual Christ, a myth designed to explain (as many myths do) the origin of a practice within the community, or at least, the origin of the significance that has now been attached to an older practice." See Doherty.

dynamic that was employed earlier by the symbolic and anthropological understanding of the primitive, Jewish christological gatherings in their history. Derrett offers a critical review of Neusner that indicates the nature of faith-based historiography:

> First faith-history is not history, and therefore pseudo-orthodoxy must be recognized for what it is. Secondly, since rabbinical material, e.g., the Mekilta, Midrash Rabbah, the Talmuds, and so forth, are compilations by compilers each with his/their own agenda(s), and since individual passages, especially biographical and haggadic, are often pseudonymous inventions -- and some are forgeries -- no reliance ought to be placed on them except to show that such a view was expressed by the compilers always centuries after Christ, and therefore probably irrelevant to [the historical analysis of the] Jesus' situation.[9]

It was the mythological basis out of which the static, literalist, and later dogma of the Roman Church's Christology was born. The process of historization, from its theological, socioreligious basis and by systemic authorization of Roman power, became the Church's authoritative dogma. It doesn't do historical analysis any good simply to suggest that, if the "resurrection did not actually occur; how can we account for the origin and rapid growth of Christianity across the face of the ancient world?"[10] Their answer: simply ignore the wealth of historical, sociologi-

---

"Supplementary Articles -- No. 6: The Source of Paul's Gospel," *THE JESUS PUZZLE: Was There No Historical Jesus?* 12 at http://jesus puzzle.com/htm (accessed 10 May 2005). Baptism and the Eucharist are not examples of Paul's own invention, but are adaptations and applications of his mystic speculation from the sacred scriptures.

9. J. Duncan M. Derrett in his review of Jacob Neusner's *Rabbinic Literature and the New Testament: What We Cannot Show We Do Not Know* (Valley Forge, PA: Trinity Press, 1994) in *JHC* 4/2 (Fall, 1997), 151-154. Bracket is mine.

10. Douglas Groothuis, *Revealing the New Age Jesus: Challenges to Orthodox Views of Christ* (Downers Grove, Ill.: InterVarsity Press, 1990), 235-6, and he quotes C. D. F. Moule's views, *Phenomenon,* 13. See also 1-20 for Moule's entire argument on the issue (Moule's position: it's *an unsolved enigma*).

cal, and countless scholarly treatises that have been undertaken, which provide a rational evidential explanation; and then, you can explain it all in supernatural terms that does not demand historical evidence. Even the saving activity of YHWH, which was recorded in the original covenantal writings, was not a narrowly and precisely defined concept of spiritual deliverance. Yet, even this understanding also became reformulated, theologically, by orthodox Christianity.

For Smith, salvation in the ancient tradition "… means not only deliverance from earthly, cosmic, and demonic enemies, and from distress and misfortune, but good conditions, well-being, outward and inward prosperity, fertility in field, flock, and nation, quietness and order in the state, peace, and the like."[11] It truly encompassed the totality of cultural and historical existence. It was this same breath of conceptual interpretation that the primitive Jewish cult understood by its christological relationship concerning their anointed election. Jesus (*Yeshua*, the spiritual presence of YHWH), the mediator of salvation, brought about spiritual healing and deliverance as well as encapsulated for the initiates a 'communal self-identity.'[12] They and Jesus' anointing

---

11. Smith, *Ecce Deus,* 47. These conceptualizations fit neatly into the religious dynamics of Paul's preaching of the heavenly 'Christ' as the anointed one of God's choosing without any messianic significance at all. "The most obvious conclusion therefore is that *there was no conception of a pre-existent Messiah current in pre-Christian Judaism prior to the Similitudes of Enoch.*" James D. G. Dunn, *Christology in the Making: A New Testament Inquiry into the Origins of the Doctrine of the Incarnation,* 2nd Ed. (Grand Rapids: William B. Eerdmans Pub., Co., 1989), 72 where he references J. Drummond, *The Jewish Messiah* (1877), Chap. XI.

12. This is the mystical and theological understanding of being born (a new life derived by God's presence) from above in John 3 (a merging of the heavenly and the earthly). "Moreover, the denser or more esoteric the symbolism, the more flexible [is] the text. For symbolism invites interpretation; and reinterpretation preserves the relevance of the text for the future readers: its symbolic code can always be made to fit a new context." Fredriksen, *Jesus to Christ,* 83. Bracket is mine.

presence (the *parousia*) were united as one.[13] The apostle Paul maintained his dynamic affiliation with his Jewish roots while as a member in these christological communities.

Paul's mention of the thirty-nine stripes he received is a sociological dynamic that indicates that he was perceived by the Jewish believers as still part of their community of faith. Setzer[14] points out that: "There would be no reason or possibility to discipline an apostate or outsider with this particular punishment. From the Jewish point of view, then, the punishment was a gesture toward a fellow Jew that implied an expectation (or hope) for his reform and continued participation in the community." Paul always, as far as we can tell, historically, remained faithful to his Jewish tradition within the christological communities.

The religiosity of the early fellowships was a responsive spiritual dynamic -- a faith-commitment and spiritual revitalization of human existence that was recast with moral responsibility. It was ritualized by sacraments within the fellowships; and thus, they provided a new mythothematic understanding in symbolic terms.[15] When applied to the resurrection concept by the christological groups, the Jesus gatherings proclaimed the same mystic understanding of communal regeneration as proclaimed by Paul and the Hellenistic mystery cults.[16] The initiate overcame 'death'

---

13. This is the essential thought in John's Gospel were it is recorded that Jesus says to his disciples that they should be one with him as he is one with the father. This reflects the mystical relationship of communal existence in and by the divine presence.

14. Claudia J. Setzer, *Jewish Responses to Early Christians: History and Polemics, 30-150 C.E.* (Minneapolis: Fortress Press, 1994), 14.

15. Mark's Gospel was a piece of midrashim that developed its symbolism with a narrative character, Jesus, who served as an allegory for the experiences of the community to whom his gospel was written.

16. For instance, Paul's institution of a sacred meal is sacramental in Greek, Hellenistic religious terms. His institution of the Lord's Supper is an adaptation: it is a reflection of the sacred meals of the Greek mystery celebration. Maybe the reason we have little to no literary evidence of the first century mystery cults, is because Paul's brand of early Christianity was a form of the mystery cult that won out when Rome cleared away the ancient debris of mythological traditions and

(a symbol of being under satanic power and influence in the current evil age); and then, by a faith-commitment (upon entrance into the cult's fellowship) they were 'resurrected' (cf., 1 John 4 'transported') from darkness (symbolic death) into the christological gathering, the light, new life in a community through a mystic union with the divine presence (the spirit of God's Son).

This religious activity (as a ritualized celebration) actually occurred in the historical existence of the initiates; but, the 'new understanding' (the revelation) by the study of scripture was considered as derived by the Spirit of God through a ceremonially conditioned act (baptism), which then continued by an experience of the inner mystery (a deeper ritualization) of the christological cults' communal meal (the Eucharist). It is to be remembered that historical verification can authenticate, in these cases, the evidence of theses existing rituals; but, it cannot in any possible way verify the conceptual categories of religious faith nor its inner perceptions.

Therefore, we must be cautious of historical verification and apply it to actual physical evidence and not to the symbolic or metaphorical aspects of the 'spiritual realities' to which they signify. For example:

> Scholars agree that Paul died by about A. D. 65, so all his letters predate this. F. F. Bruce estimates that all of Paul's letters were written between A. D. 48 and 60. The very early dating of these letters witness their veracity, as does their very character as letters. Historians relish personal letters as primary source material, especially if they contain trivia and lists of details, are written in an unpolished style and were originally for a small audience. Thus, Paul's letters fulfill most, if not all, of these requirements and thus evidence historical reliability."[17]

---

cults, except for what became orthodox Christianity. The significance of these meals expressed the mystic union of the initiate with the cultic deity and provided a salvific experience by its symbolism.

17. Groothuis, *New Age Jesus*, 139. Along with the evidence of historical reliability, supernaturalists tend to use this admission as evidence for the reliability of theological concepts giving them the same 'reliability' for the religious 'truth' as supernal 'reality' that they pro-

The resurrection experience within the Jewish fellowship necessitated the readjustment of its christological hermeneutic, metaphorical language, and its new faith-understanding. The later historicized tradition also emerged as a revision of the earlier kerygmatic proclamation concerning the historic role of the Jesus that appears in the narrative Gospel literature. The orthodox, Christian church has maintained its traditional historicized proclamation through the ages; but, it has lost its mystical sensibility of symbolism and metaphor by becoming 'the' revelation of God through his 'word.'[18] One can just as easily claim that most Christians today quote the Bible to justify what they believe what God has said; rather than by expressing their own inner moral valuation as an outcome of a personal relationship with the divine presence, which they also claim to have. Their faith (by quoting the Bible) seems to have replaced God with the written word. This could be stated as a form of modern spiritual idolatry.

The whole process, which was part of a cultural and religious dynamic of an expanding religiosity, made the preaching of reconciliation (the Jesus cult's spiritual and symbolic understanding of its own existence and its mystical relation to YHWH) an extension of Jesus' literal ministry (the anointed power by the Spirit of Wisdom to reach out) to the world.[19] Thus, it was the kerygma, reformulated in its non-symbolic modality that was the medium as well as the message of the later, official 'church.' It was historically the Jewish cult that had its self-identity as the christological people of 'the way.' This identification became

---

fess. This is traditional begging the question about mythological ideologies.

18. This foundational theme ("thus said the Lord," "the word of the Lord said") is often referred in the Old Testament as God's 'word' to his faithful community -- Israel by the prophets. Yet, today's Christians use the phrase, 'God's Word' with a literal meaning as primarily referring to the Bible.

19. On the historicized tradition, see II Cor. 5:14-21 and Rom. 5:9-11. 1 John represents a community that realized the mystical working of Wisdom to guide their communal understanding by way of the Spirit's anointing.

known as Christian (Acts 11:26, cf. I Peter 4:16) as a result of the reformulated and historicized basis. This also became a later communal identification, which had resulted from earlier socio-religious antagonisms and hermeneutical conflicts. It is noted that "eventually, the leaders of the Jews' [communal authority] had the Christians expelled from the Synagogue. The above events occurred between the fifties and the late eighties ... in a Greek-speaking part of the Diaspora."[20]

All existence in the universe is unitary in its foundational and physical essence. All religious conceptualizations and their historic objectifications are the psychodynamic abstractions from human experience within this world of physical reality.[21] An honest understanding of the meaning of divinity (past or present) is the ethical commitment to the basic rational essence and moral honesty for human existence. In order to maintain this honesty, theology must become anthropological and humanistic. Any historical analysis that hopes to verify the factuality of the origins of Christianity and its historical development must use a modern methodology that considers these socio-religious, political, and philosophical dimensions as well. In order for us to understand the historical era with all of its religious and literary compositions, it may be necessary to disassemble these anthropological phenomena within their historical context.

A process that is offered for science may fit equally well for historical analysis.

So, instead of trying to eliminate intentional properties from science, [or historical analysis of religious categories] I propose we try to understand how they could have come into existence where

---

20. Watson, *Jesus,* 105. Bracket is mine, added for clarification.

21. This reflects the essential core and understanding in Ludwig Feuerbach, *The Essence of Christianity,* Trans. George Eliot, intro. Karl Barth, foreword H. Richard Niebuhr (New York: Harper & Row, Pub., 1957), especially 1-32. "Myths present ideas that guide perception, conditioning us to think and even perceive in a particular way, especially when we are young and impressionable." Suggested by Merlin Stone, *When God was a Woman* (New York: Harcourt Brace & Company, 1976), 4.

none existed before. In other words, we need to start without any hint of *telos* and end up with it, not the other way around. In some ways, this is a far more difficult enterprise because we are not availing ourselves of the intentional phenomena [theological categories] most familiar to us; living bodies and conscious minds [mythological scenarios]. Even worse, it forces us to explore domains in which there may be little science to support our efforts. It has the advantage, however, of protecting us from our own familiarity with teleology [i.e., faith], and from the appeal of allowing homuncular assumptions [supernaturalism] to do the work that explanation should be doing.[22]

This necessitates more than a redefinition of terms and socio-religious applications of Christian truth.[23] It is essential for moral integrity to the current scientific categories of physicality, to bio-evolutionary anthropology, and for the mutual social and political survival of global humanity.

Modern Christianity has lost its symbolic basis, its metaphorical understanding, and its mystic relationality; finally, its religious innocence should have died. The dinosaurs died out and were replaced by other forms of life; why not mythological faith so that mutual, moral humanism might become a reality. Many today would agree with the idea that "there are no such things as facts ... only interpretations exist."[24] Such an interpretive posture as this would allow us to penetrate the historical basis that can be verified as history, and would give us greater meaning to the real historic mode of human experiences in traditional religiosity (*Geschichte*). That is why Braaten's remarks, concerning this

---

22. Deacon, *Nature,* 138. Brackets are mine, which are added to show that a scientific methodology could have serious application as well when applied to historical analysis for the origin of Christianity.

23. Gustaf Dalman, *Jesus-Jeshua*. Also, Cf. R. M. Grant, *Gnosticism and Early Christianity*. Cf. the significance and use of the divine name in Gnosticism as it also relates to salvation; also see Rev. 1:8.

24. Rudolph Otto, *The Idea of the Holy* (London: Oxford University Press, 1957), 388. Also see Heinrich Ott, "The Historical Jesus and the Ontology of History," *The Historical Jesus and the Kerygmatic Christ*, Ed. and Trans. by Carl E. Braaten and Roy A. Harrisville (Nashville: Abingdon Press, 1964), 166.

problematic area for modern theologizing within the historical and critical methodology, are well taken: "History consists of two layers, one of historical facts that can be objectively established, the other of existential meanings that one can perceive only through participation and involvement, through dialogue and personal encounter with history."[25] Hence, this study regards the biblical tradition, concerning the historical Jesus in the Gospels, as a fabricated literary myth comparable to other mythic heroes within the ancient Hellenistic culture and other religious traditions. It is understandable that the historicized narratives, which were within the eschatological framework and supernal categories, are fabricated religious stories similar in nature to other mythological literary categories. For an example: "The Essenes saw themselves as living on the edge of time, in the very last days; and they dedicated every moment and aspect of life to preparing, after their fashion, for the coming Kingdom of God."[26] This was similarly a perception of these christological communities' mind-set.

The later members of the christological cult used these literary fabrications to continue its social and religious mission (to provide YHWH's salvation). This was perceived as the fulfillment of the Abrahamic Covenant, which for Paul included bringing all peoples of the world into God's end-time Kingdom. The original, metaphorical symbols were later dropped (as a theological understanding) and were reformulated, elaborated, and dramatized with a didactic, ritual, and ceremonial purpose by the

---

25. Braaten, *History and Hermeneutics*, 38. This existential participation is what gives historic epistemological and linguistic elements their mythic expressions. Thus, Paul considered the revelatory experiences of 'seeing' the lord, which was given as a list of appearances in 1 Corinthians 15, were appearances that were of the same existential type. They were all 'understandings' within each person's mind. They were not actual physical encounters with a bodily, 'risen' Jesus of Nazareth. Cf., 1 Cor. 15 with Gal. 1:11-12.

26. Fredriksen, *Jesus to Christ*, 89. Cf., Marvin Vining, *Jesus the Wicked Priest: How Christianity Was Born of An Essene Schism* (Rochester: Bear and Company, 2008), 69 also agrees that "the Essenes believed themselves to be the true Israel."

formative church. The efforts of Christian scholars to explain the origin and development of Christianity, based on a historical personality, have failed -- and will always fail because of the physical nature of ontological reality. Their conclusions that maintain a historical Jesus as a real person (or as God who takes on human existence) in the ancient world do not and cannot convince the rational, scientific, and critical mind of modern secular humanity.

To conclude that this rejection is simply due to a lack of faith on an individual's part confuses the issue and usually represents begging the question. This is also true even for those who quote I Cor. 2:10 as though spiritual truth were of a totally separate, supernatural[27] realm beyond the parameters of our physical reality. That argument just doesn't wash. All of these spiritual conceptualizations are just part of the natural, dynamic and the psychological possibilities of a common, neurologically based, thought process for humanity.[28] The rational willingness to accept or reject any particular religiosity (the choice of believing and the commitment to a faith) is the real basic difference. It is a human choice that anyone can make and is not a divine mythological intervention into the inner recesses of our neurological consciousness,[29] the human mind.

The most significant result relative to our understanding of the kerygma within primitive Christianity is the distinction

---

27. Even the attempt of some to suggest that supernatural only means that a sense of an extraordinary understanding (something above and beyond the ordinary, the mundane) is what the term really signifies is a feeble attempt to make the message of the scriptures palatable with modern rationality while maintaining a traditional and ancient religious world view.

28. It seems that some scholars go to such lengths to denigrate believers' religious identity as being different from (the historical) Jesus. Rensberger cites Marinus de Jonge (n. 21) that Johannine Christians were God's children but not God's 'sons.' Only Jesus was 'the son.' Rensberger, *Johannine Community*, 120.

29. Hofsteder in his *Strange Loop* has done a masterful job in explicating the significance of our consciousness to physicality and the emergence of 'I' ness and 'We' ness of personality. See 281-300 where he converses with his psychodynamic and rational argumentation, as an example.

between '*der historische Jesus*' and '*der geschichtliche Christus.*' This theological distinction has its problems to be sure,[30] especially in rendering it into acceptable English. It is designated in many ways: the historical Jesus/the historic Christ; the Jesus of history/the Christ of the proclamation, or faith, etc. This entire discussion has presented the theoretical foundation for an understanding that is based upon the underlying symbolic interpretation of the historical, Christian tradition.

It has laid hold of an understanding of the historic origin of the Jewish, christological fellowships as a distinctive religious movement and cultural phenomenon. The earliest primitive sect, to a large socio-religious measure, was similar to eschatological mystery religions in the Hellenistic period. VanderKam reminds us that, "by 175 there had been a long history of Greek influence, in one form or another, on Jewish people."[31] The same religious issues, mystic and mythological concepts, and ritualistic practices were part and parcel to a common, cultural religiosity of the Hellenistic world. Many, including high ranking Roman officials, families of wealth and social position, and other religiously minded peoples, could freely move into and out of a various number of mystery religions as participants of the first century's cultural diversity.

Our best historical example of Hellenistic influence is the Alexandrian Jew, Philo, who merged Platonic cosmology with Jewish, faith-categories in his biblical exegetical and philosophical writings. Philo states: "From *Stoicism* comes talk of divine reason (*logos*) immanent in the world, permeating all things, and

---

30. Bultmann, "History and Eschatology in the New Testament," *New Testament Studies*, I. 5ff. See John 12:50; and cf. Luke 18:30. Also, see Matthew 19:29 and John 3, 15, and 16.

31. James C. VanderKam, *Enoch: A Man for All Generations* (Columbia: University of South Carolina Press, 1995), 61. "It is apparent that with the campaigns of Alexander and the rise of Hellenistic monarchies, Jewish residents of Palestine came into even closer and more constant contact with Greek political structures, education, language, and religion. The Ptolemies in Egypt controlled Palestine for approximately one hundred years (roughly 300-200 B.C.E.), and the Seleucids, centered in Syria, ruled them thereafter." Ibid.

present also in man, the seminal *logos* (*logos spermatikos*), so that man's highest good is to live in accordance with and by assent to this divine reason."[32] God (YHWH) was the heavenly power who had sent the anointing Spirit as an end-time marker (1 John 2) for social behavior. This was perceived in the Jewish, christological community as a moral imperative for communal life. Thus, the members perceived themselves as the body of the cultic deity, they were his Son, and as his faithful servant, they were reconciling the world.[33] This dynamic and mythological statement of theology, by the early christological believers, was the christological interpretation and the new faith-understanding (eschatology), and it was based on symbolism.

The first appearance of Jewish, apocalyptic literature occurred around the time of the Maccabean revolt. A widely used definition of the genre *apocalypse* was formulated by J. Collins.

A genre of revelatory literature with a narrative framework, in which a revelation is mediated by another worldly being to a human recipient, disclosing a transcendental reality which is both temporal, insofar as it envisages eschatological salvation, and spatial insofar as it involves another, supernatural world. [And thus has made an amendment to clarify its purpose: an apocalypse] is intended to interpret present earthly circumstances in the light of the supernatural world and of the future, and to influence both the understanding and behavior of the audience by means of divine authority.[34]

---

32. Dunn, *Christology*, 222. And similarly, like the early christological community (1John), Philo also "counsels his readers to live in accordance with 'right reason' (*orthos logos*) – *Opif.* 143, *Leg. All.* I.46, 93, III.1, 80, 106, 148, 150. etc." Ibid. See H. Kleinknecht, *TDNT* IV, 84ff.; and Armstrong, *Introduction*, 119-29 as cited by Dunn. Ibid.

33. Cf. "For God was in Christ" II Corinthians 5:17-20 with Romans 5:10-11.

34. VanderKam, *Enoch*, 62. Collins modification is in his "Genre, Ideology and Social Movements in Jewish ism," *Mysteries and Revelations: Studies since the Uppsala Colloquium*, Ed. J. J. Collins and J. H. Charlesworth, *JSP* Supplemental Series 9 (Sheffield: Sheffield Academic Press, 1991), 19 as cited by VanderKam. Ibid.

It also embraced metaphor as it proclaimed YHWH's *presence* in the communal gathering as the presence of his Spirit and his Son.[35] The early, Jewish gatherings accepted the resurrection (symbolically, as a transformative power) as the newness of their spiritual and communal life, as an anointed fellowship with their cultic Lord.

The gathering's efforts to establish a ministry of reconciliation (a spirit of cultural accommodation to the Greco-Roman world) was perceived as the deity's power through the indwelling Spirit and the abiding christological presence of 'the anointed Savior' (Christ Jesus).[36] In reference to an early "Q" saying, Dunn suggests that

> It comes from a very early stage of the Palestinian Christian community's self-understanding when prophetic inspiration was in some cases at least attributed to divine Wisdom and not yet to the exalted Christ, or from a particular community which greatly valued the Jewish Wisdom tradition and saw Jesus as the climax of Wisdom's 'stretching out her hand' to Israel and rejection by Israel (cf., Prov. 1:20-31).[37]

---

35. That is why the Jesus of the Gospel narrative is able to say, "where two or more are gathered in my name, there am I in their midst."

36. Unfortunately, too much literalism has been used in the church's formulation of theology. Since it has occurred, it has robbed out of an eschatological context, the term 'presence' (*parousia*) and has emphasized an significance, totally foreign to Paul's gospel declarations, so that now, theologically, the *parousia* has been restructured to represent a non-historical reality of Jesus' 'second coming.' In reality, as this study has shown, there was no actual, historical real flesh and blood person, as the Jesus of the Gospels. How then can he come a second time? *parousia* is not a verb. Its primary and significant nuance is a consideration of the actual '*presence*' of someone who had been expected and arrived and whose very '*presence*' is celebrated.

37. Dunn, *Christology*, 201-2. As Wisdom Christology, cf., where Jesus in the biblical tradition is identified as Wisdom: Matt. 23:34-6; Matt.23:37-9/Luke 13:34f; with Ps. 118:26; and cf., Paul's references in 1 Cor. 1-3.

And as such, the narrative Jesus in Mark's Gospel, which also reflects the actual historic experiences of the gatherings' socio-religious encounter, is seen casting out demons. Much of the ancient world was preoccupied with demonic forces as the powers behind earthly phenomena.

One scholar has put it this way: "Earth is full of demons. Humanity is plagued by them. Almost all misfortunes are because of demons: sickness, drought, death and especially humanity's weaknesses about remaining faithful to the covenant (with God). The region between heaven and earth seems to be almost cluttered by demons and angels; humanity is often seen as a pawn, helpless in the face of such cosmic forces."[38] This was the religious task of the end-time communities, to cast out the false demons (polytheism) of the Hellenistic world by their gospel proclamation of universal monotheism. Hence, God's Kingdom had now actually taken place in the historical reality of their new end-time communal existence. This was seen as a vindication of God's power and his presence in the christological community's spiritual activities to eradicate a satanically infested world.

Consequently, the Christian tradition, which had deeply rooted itself within Jewish religious history as the symbolic expression of the Jesus myth, emerged with a historical spirituality (the mythological level of historic meaning) intact. This historical process has come to be the accepted historicized religiosity of

---

38. J. H. Charlesworth, *Old Testament Pseudepigrapha,* 66. Cf., 1Cor. 2:6-8. Even though many scholars identify the "rulers of this age" as comic powers that crucified the Christ, they hold on to a literalist historical position relative to the historicity of Jesus and fail to question how Paul could speak in these other worldly terms. S. G. F. Brandon, *History, Time and Deity,* 167, states that Paul's statement "may seem on cursory reading to refer to the Crucifixion as an historical event ... the expression 'rulers of this age' does not mean the Romans and Jewish authorities. Instead, it denotes the daemonic powers who ... were believed to inhabit the planets (the celestial sphere) and control the destinies of men ... Paul attributes the Crucifixion not to Pontius Pilate and the Jewish leaders, but to these planetary powers." These are cited by Doherty in "Supplementary Articles -- No. 3: Who Crucified Jesus?" *THE JESUS PUZZLE: Was There No Historical Jesus?* 7, at http://jesuspuzzle.com/htm (accessed 23 May 2005).

the Christian Faith. Unfortunately, it has also become part of a distorted, conceptual understanding of physical existence, which along with the ancient world-view that they have appropriated also embraces the supernatural (Spirit) realm. Ancient literature tended to merge some similar titular concepts into a theological structure that served the symbolic nature of the various titles for their similar function in the eschatological community. Some examples of these earlier linguistic categories readily available for adaptation are: "the son of man" in Ezekiel and in 1 Enoch; "the chosen one" in 2 Isaiah; and "the anointed one" prevalent in the Mosaic tradition. In the *Similitudes,* Enoch[39] is identified as "the son of man" and "therefore as the righteous one, the chosen one, and the anointed one, since all four titles refer similarly to the same person" as an eschatological functionary in the literature.

It is not very difficult to understand that the original symbolism was used by the Jewish, christological gatherings in an eschatological sense. This was proclaimed in the early kerygma, and was later proclaimed with the literal understanding of Jesus' historicized and mythological resurrection. This later, literal understanding also developed, in Christian theology, into the fixed dogma of orthodoxy. This was a historicized Christology that maintained a historical Jesus and became, in the formative church's understanding, 'the man from Galilee.' This was the accepted narrative for the historicity, and it became the official Christian dogma of the Roman Catholic Church. This became the 'historical significance,' which used a literal interpretation of the Gospel Jesus, the 'Jesus of Nazareth' in the later proclamation of the formative church.

It was midrashic symbolism by the evangelists that had been the interpretive fact and spiritual perception for this new understanding of the resurrection of Jesus as an act God.[40] It was their faith-understanding, that by the divine presence of his Spir-

---

39. VanderKam, *Enoch,* 140-1.

40. Hence, in the Gospel narratives we encounter symbolic expressions as "three days and three nights" that have been derived from scripture (the mythic story of Jonah). This expression does not represent a literal history nor was it intended to accomplish such a feat as that. Myth always speaks to the existential experience of our humanity.

it, God gave birth to his primitive community's social and religious existence, their spiritual life, and religious hope. When we apply historical analysis to the mythical resurrection of Jesus' appearances in the biblical tradition, it will become clear just what is meant symbolically by the metaphorical nature of the resurrection statements.

For Paul, these 'resurrection appearances' were revelatory, mystical, and an expanded visionary adaptation of Jewish, biblical hermeneutics. Dunn expresses that the revelatory belief was a fundamental embodiment of an ancient Jewish, hermeneutical posture. He says that: "Clearly then basic to the Hebraic concept of the word of God was the conviction that Yahweh revealed his will immediately and directly to his people through prophetic inspiration and vision."[41] Paul simply adopted this perception and adapted it to Hellenistic and Platonic categories for his own personal end-time hermeneutical posture. His posture was based on a hermeneutic that embraced mythology in terms of symbolism, metaphor, and Platonic, philosophical categories in order to express salvific concerns for moral behavior. Thus, the appearances of the risen Lord and the testimonies that concern themselves with the resurrection of Jesus are not the supernatural validations that traditional Christianity has made them out to be. Resurrection served as a symbol of transformation of human behavior, a metaphor, which was made known to Paul, eschatologically. The appearances of a risen Jesus do not now, nor did they then, exist in actual historical reality. These are an epistemological example of myth being accepted as real, actual history.

Those narrative appearances (as a literary device) will be reflected in the natural psychodynamics of human religiosity, the historic theological posture of faith-understanding, and the mythical and mystical relationality of a particular religious group. The biblical 'narrative' witnesses and the experiences of those who 'saw' the risen Lord Jesus Christ are all part of the same mythical religiosity that conveys human existence in the language of 'spiritual truths' by the use of myth, symbolism, and metaphori-

---

41. Dunn, *Christology*, 217.

cal language. These were the social and religious intentions, the meaningful mystic expressions, which functioned as historicized theological statements. They also expressed the fundamental nature, essence, and perception of YHWH's divine activity within the religious consciousness of the believers,[42] which is also mythologically based from an older religious tradition. Thus, the spiritual instruction, used to develop these newly formulated religious categories within the Jewish, christological communities, was equated with God's Spirit of Wisdom, his anointing within the fellowship for their discernment.

The power of YHWH to teach, which was perceived by the original Jewish cultic religiosity (through the communal 'anointing' cf., 1 John 2), was the intellectual illumination on the consciousness of the narrative witnesses to the narrative resurrection event. The original symbolic understanding of these communities demonstrated for the christological gatherings their mystical relationship with God's presence, as a socio-religious experience, which they called 'eternal life.' It was perceived as a metaphor, as a resurrection experience (new birth by the Spirit). Wright has captured the inner essence of Paul's religious convictions when he states:

As far as Paul was concerned, the most important eschatological event, through which the living God had unveiled (or, if you like, 'apocalypsed') his plan to save the whole cosmos, *had occurred when Jesus rose form the dead* [Paul's revelatory vision]. He wasn't just living in the last days. He was living in the *first* days – of a whole new world order. ... 'Resurrection' was, in Ezekiel 37, a metaphor for the return of Israel from exile [to new communal *living*]. When Paul was faced with the fact of Jesus' resurrection [his vision], he concluded that the return from exile had in fact happened. Death ... the ultimate exile ... meant that the Age to Come, the Eschaton of Jewish expectation, had already arrived. ... It meant that Israel had in principle been redeemed; it meant that

---

42. Cf. II Cor. 4:6 also, cf. the Greek idea of '*nous*.'

the Gentiles were now to be summoned to join Israel in celebrating the new day, the day, of deliverance.[43]

It was this faith-understanding of Paul's proclamations that announced the new life possibility in the heavenly Christ experience. YHWH's revelatory power to teach via his Spirit (the communal 'anointing') was an experience that validated their salvation. An initiate was reborn into eternal life, which was fellowship with the Father and his son (according to the Jesus myth). As faithful participants, they were transported into God's Kingdom (Platonic relationality?). It was a resurrected life within the christological cult, born out of the death of traditional biblical Judaism (as Hellenized, Diaspora believers) as the cult perceived Jewry's demands of the Law (Torah) and its demands of religious rituals. It became for them a cultural adaptation on a symbolic level of the diverse mythologies within the religious categories of a Hellenistic world that provided a sense of social and religious assimilation.

The christological understanding of the Jewish groups gave some of them the excuse to attack the false worship of Hellenistic polytheism. It was the cult's perception of its religious role. The 'lost' Jews[44] and the Gentiles were offered salvation by the new dynamic faith of the christological, cultic movement. This new faith-movement of universal monotheism, expressed by the revitalized Jewish mythology, was transformative in its socio-religious dynamic. It transformed a number of devout Jewish gatherings in the Diaspora into the new christological communities, as Spiritual Israel. These christological assemblies understood that they were YHWH's gift of salvation to the world of Hellenism. It was offered as God's divine spiritual healing. Their perceived resurrected communal life was to be humanity's en-

---

43. N. T. Wright, *What Saint Paul Really Said: Was Paul of Tarsus the Real Founder of Christianity?* (Grand Rapids: William B. Eerdmans Pub., Co., 1997), 50-1. Brackets are mine.

44. Like many Christians today, in ancient times not everyone who identified themselves as a Jew was faithful in obeying Torah. These were considered lost. The gospel was extended to them first than to the Gentiles.

trance into YHWH's Kingdom of Heaven (the acceptance by faith into the inner secrets of the Jewish christological community), the kingdom as God's son, *Yeshua*, Jesus.

The resurrection appearances of Jesus, as recorded in the biblical tradition and maintained by Christian faith as divine revelation, were religious descriptions of the conversion of initiate members into the new christological relationship with YHWH in the Jewish, eschatological gatherings. These are mythological stories that symbolize the religious impact of their communal lives, metaphorically reflected within the gospels, which later became the historicized life of Jesus. These appearances were not intended to be proofs of Jesus' humanity or to depict the actual physical existence of an earthly Jesus who abandoned this world for some lofty spiritual existence elsewhere. They are not being offered as proofs of an eternal realm transcendent from this earthly physical reality (cf., Middle Platonism). They are social, religious, and mythological in their total narrative scope.

They were understood in their symbolic fashion as metaphorical testimonials to YHWH's divine grace (his revelatory *presence*). This created a new identity in the lives of those who committed themselves to live a resurrected life of faith in fellowship together as followers of 'the way.' They had become the true, faithful Israel in and of the end-times. They described, in kerygmatic fashion, the believer's spiritual requirement to accept by faith the evangelist's report (the proclamation of the gospel) that was given by apostles like Paul.[45] Thus, when seeing Jesus in the gospels' narrative, what we really understand is that we are seeing a reflection of the early communities' experiences of faith that were expressions of their mission and ministry in the Hellenistic world.

Within the Jewish gatherings, these faith-fellowships of christological believers via cultic rituals, prayers, and religious ceremonies gave testimony to a 'new born' diaspora religiosity. These new socio-religious interpretations concerned their resurrected lives in relation to YHWH's *presence*, (his wisdom, his Spirit, *Yeshua*, his Son, his 'anointing') and his grace (the chris-

---

45. Cf. the biblical tradition in Romans 10:14-17.

tological understanding, as revelation). Dunn has captured the Platonic and philosophical essence of this hermeneutic while suggesting caution when he states that:

> The language of philosophy, Stoicism in particular, agreed at this point with the language of Jewish prophecy in providing the most useful term for talking of this experience of revelation and 'right reason' -- *logos* -- and by means of allegorical interpretation this divine Logos could be shown to have a wide-ranging symbolic expression within the Torah. But in the end of the day the Logos seems to be nothing more for Philo than God himself in his approach to man, God himself insofar as he may be known by man. ... In both cases indeed (Word and Wisdom), it is highly doubtful whether the thought ever goes beyond a literary personification of the immanent power and revelation of God.[46]

The symbolism used by the early Jewish gathering provides our historical analysis with the socio-religious answers for the 'historic' origin of the Jesus myth. Symbolism also reveals how and why the various eschatological communities expanded mystical monotheism and a universal religiosity into a later form of non-Jewish Christianity. In some of the Jewish communities of the Diaspora, *Yeshua* was the name of YHWH's deliverance from the false divinities under Hellenism. He, as the divine anointing, had raised them to the new christological faith-understanding (the universal monotheistic belief). This could be understood as the divine drama of salvation on the historic scene of human redemption. It was a theistic mythology, an encounter of YHWH with his people, (as in the mystery religions they became encapsulated in union with their deity) and became a new creation.[47] They were the new, Spiritual Israel. Wright correctly assessed this mystical dynamic. He concludes that, "The Jewish framework of interpretation within which Paul understands and

---

46. Dunn, *Christology*, 228.

47. See Paul's conceptualization of salvation in terms of being "new creations" in Christ Jesus. This finds a close parallel in the Greek mystery religions. This is not to say that he has barrowed this metaphor; these are simply the kinds of concepts readily available within their culture to the ancient religiously minded person.

expounds the death and resurrection of Jesus [in Platonic fashion] is, of course, that is, these events carry cosmic [mythological] significance."[48]

To speak of a religiosity is only to communicate the nature and essence of the rational and experiential elements that make up the unlimited range of human reason and experience. It is that mentational power of psychodynamic expansion that finds the common basis of humanity as the moral justification for our existence and life. The supreme function of reason for our common humanity is to reduce, by interpretation of our experiences, the observation of this universe to a logical order, which provides a personal understanding (a Weltanschauung) for mutual, human survival. The christological Jesus myth of the early Jewish communities had also been formulated along these psychodynamic lines of religiosity. The historical biblical tradition, within the expanded covenantal literature, expresses the concept of the divine *presence*. It took on a mythological form[49] with reference to the encounter of the divine presence within a religious group's internal, socio-historical dynamic. This was perfectly natural for the ancient's systemic consciousness, for the use of metaphorical language, and for the mythothemes that developed their diverse religiosities.

The spiritual idea of a divinity taking on the form and nature of humanity is a familiar literary style that is recorded in the Hebrew Scriptures (theophanies, apparitions of deity, divination, and angels in human disguise). In the Christian Scriptures, the mythological basis that constitutes the idea of a suffering and dying deity, which underlies these literary expressions, is also found in some diverse Hellenistic religions. Thus, it is not strange to see how these ideas found similar expressions in the emerging Christian, biblical tradition.[50] This reflects a text where

---

48. Wright, *Saint Paul*, 90. Brackets are mine.

49. Cf. the literary instances in both the original covenant texts and expanded covenantal literature that depict the symbolic nature of 'putting on a garment.'

50. See Philippians 2:5-11. It is apparent that even the genuine letters of the apostle Paul have gone through a long process of editing, with emendations being added, additions from his other writings or

the mythothemes are cast into a historicized form as a historical event reminiscent of faith concerns in Gnosticism. One such gnostic element known was attached to the Gospel of John. The christological incarnation of the anointed one, *Yeshua* (Jesus), was theologically foundational to the early Jewish gatherings' mysticism in the Diaspora. Nevertheless, regardless of its theological basis, Sheila Collins, with astute insight, indicates that: "Theology is ultimately political. The way human communities deify the transcendent and determine the categories of good and evil have more to do with the power dynamics of the social systems which create the theologies than with the spontaneous revelation of truth from another quarter."[51] The 'victory over death' was a theological and a political expression by the communal brotherhood (those in leadership roles), symbolically understood, and used metaphorically to instruct the initiates into the community's religiosity and its cultic existence.

This also included the spiritual activities of YHWH's Spirit of Wisdom via the cult's propaganda to the idolatrous world of polytheism. The gnostics found Paul's writings to be an easy read especially since his theological formulations parallel close to gnostic religious ideas. In his proclamations within the Hellenistic world, his concept of the heavenly Christ had more to do with gnostic mysticism than with any Hebraic concept of a Messiah (an anointed one). Much of our current understanding of messianic focus comes from the Gospel materials and does not reflect the real historical attitudes about Jewish messianic expectations in the middle Temple period. Horsley realized, upon "closer examination of Judean texts from late second-temple times, that they indicated that there is virtually no evidence for the supposedly standardized Jewish expectation of 'the Messi-

---

other non-Pauline texts and a piecing together of materials considered to be worthy of Pauline ideas or relevant material based on the church's theology. Notice 1 Thess. 2:15-17 as an example of later Christian interpolation, which most biblical scholars would agree has been added to Paul's original text.

51. See Stone, *When God was a Woman*, 66. She quotes Sheila Collins, "A Feminist Reading of History," *Radical Religion Journal* (Berkeley: University of California, 1974), 12-17.

ah'…" and this appears "to be yet another modern Christian theological construction without historical basis."[52]

In all of these early cultic formulations, there is no pretense or even a remote suggestion that conveys a human birth, a human history, or any semblance of genuine humanity with reference to the historical Jesus. It is the divine being, the Jewish christological cultic Christ, the deity, *Yeshua* in human guise that suffers the momentary humiliation and its corollary, religious exaltation.[53] Without an understanding of middle Platonism, we would certainly miss the philosophic and mythological connections and would not appreciate the historic religious experiences and theology of these early, Jewish gatherings in the Diaspora. It was their symbolic interpretation of these Jewish, christological gatherings that was the historical basis for the reformulation of the historicized theology of the later orthodox Christology that became church dogma.[54] It was this theology within the tradition that became historicized so that human existence became evaluated differently.

Some feminist scholars today have brought to our attention the sexual and religious biases that were part and parcel to the transmission of the biblical text themselves. Stone brings to our attention that, "We absorb attitudes as well as subject matter in the learning process. Moreover, the attitudes tend to determine what we see, and what we fail to see, in the subject matter. This is why attitude is just as important as subject matter in the educational process."[55] This pedagogical dynamic in all probability played into the historization of the Jesus myth in formative

---

52. Horsley, *Bandits*, xii-xiii.

53. Cf., the historic resurrection and ascension into heaven, back to Glory (*Kavod*); Rom. 15:3; II Cor. 8:9; cf. Mark 14:51, 52.

54. Most historians would agree that the formation of church dogma was an expression of the demise of paganism when "the conversion of Constantine was the killing blow …" that resulted in "cutting off the flow of funds to the pagan temples," Stark, *The Rise of Christianity*, 196-7.

55. Stone, *When God*, xxiii where she cites the ideas of Cyrus Gordon, former Chair of the Department of Near Eastern Studies at Brandeis University in Massachusetts.

Christianity. Human experiences and social existence has remained essentially the same when considered on the basis of its physical and neurological modalities. The primitive Christian religiosity expressed the ultimate meaning for spiritual existence. It had lost much of its dynamic and existential understanding when the symbolic interpretation became the historical objectified faith in the later message of salvation (with the canonical Gospels) within orthodox Christianity.

The persona found in the myth, with its cultural and historical expressions, is well known to most students of the history of religions as well as the study of the philosophy of religion. Thus, the modern secular world and those of various religious persuasions have a basic spiritual commonality -- their common physical existence as humanity. The transformation of meaning concerning existence, by early Christianity (purely within the context of mythology), suggests that it is the reality of human existence that is of primary value and importance. It is not the religious mythological expressions that have been formulated in order to interpret a socio-religious reality. The various spiritual expressions religiously oriented that are mythological in nature and philosophically based, can all be reduced to a common non-metaphysical basis (the physical reality of human existence), which is according to a our modern scientific and rational world-view.

Modern Christian mythology has been and continues to be the significant factor that keeps modern humanity from fully understanding the nature, essence, and basis of our common global, mutual human existence. The symbolic interpretation of the deity's *presence* (as a divine anointing) was understood by the initiates and the members of the christological members and developed without any conceptual confinement to actual physical reality. Symbolism was used to express their religiosity and their spiritual understanding in dynamic metaphorical imagery. Paul was able to adapt various metaphors to his revelatory experience of the cosmic Christ. He could also rely on a long tradition within Judaism that supported ideas of separation from the legalities of the Mosaic tradition.

In view of some diaspora feelings concerning the Temple priesthood, Paul could have entertained ideas within the genre of Jewish, literature as did some members of the Essene community of the Dead Sea Scrolls. VanderKam relates what this connection to ancient Jewish, literature might be:

> The traditions associated with Enoch preserve for us a glimpse at a different option within ancient Judaism – that is, a perspective that put almost no emphasis on the Mosaic Law. It focused its attention, rather, on special revelations granted to Enoch before the flood. These revelations dealt not only with the past but also the future and its meaning for the present. It was a tradition that was hardly to survive but which for a time exercised a noticeable influence among some Jewish people and certainly among some early Christians.[56]

I am not saying that Paul considered himself an Enoch for his own times; but, his revelatory experience and his kerygmatic concerns, having moral and social dynamics, demonstrate that some mythothematic connections are a possibility. His dynamic spirituality, which formed the basis for the Jewish christological communities' religiosity, was the historic and natural symbolic expression of the cult's experiences and relationship with its deity's presence. Paul was their missionary apostle via a revelatory experience; he was 'chosen,' 'approved,' and 'commissioned' by his anointed Savior (Christ Jesus). These religious and christological concepts emerged out of the spiritual meanings derived from the older biblical tradition of the Jewish faith. Theology, plain and simple, is God-talk and for some of the early Jewish gatherings in the diaspora, theology would become Jesus-talk. In *Yeshua*, Jesus, the cult lived and had its spiritual existence (a real experience in mysticism).

Their religious drama had continued to be expressed in eschatological terms by a mythological and christological understanding (evidenced by Paul's middle Platonic categories). This

---

56. VanderKam, *Enoch*, i. See H. S. Kvanvig, *Roots of: The Mesopotamian Background of the Enoch Figure and of the Son of Man*, WMANT 61 (Neukirchen-Vluyn: Neukirchener Verlag, 1988).

drama (*mythos*) found its literary expression as midrashim in the theology of the later, expanded covenantal literary corpora (the N.T.) and marked the historic origin for the emergence of the historical orthodox, Christian faith. It has been assumed that all this evidence to validate the historicity of the earthly Jesus has been lost in antiquity.[57] Thus, the historical Jesus has been the object of historical studies, critical research, and Christological controversy in modern times. It is impossible to penetrate behind the historical sources in critical research in order to uncover any real historical evidence of the historical Jesus. This is the conclusion of modern research.

Consequently, some have concluded that the historical Jesus is not relevant for faith. What is relevant for faith, especially today, is the historic Christ who had been the central figure of the primitive kerygma and explicates the understanding of the Jewish community's origin and religious formation. The real test and ultimate religious value of the early christological community's theologizing, based on the original covenant literary corpora, was to express the fellowship's social location, religious experiences, and christological understanding that they lived in a social and religiously troubled, cultural environment under the oppressive power of Rome. This methodology was taught to the initiates in the early Jewish gatherings via the symbolic hermeneutic and was also retained in its historicized form[58] in the emerging biblical tradition of orthodox Christianity. Thus, it is not surprising to understand that the early gatherings' religious experiences and

---

57. Westcott, *Introduction to the Study of the Gospels*, Chap. III, "The Origin of the Gospels" for an excellent general survey, 174-216. An example of midrashim that was later adapted to a Christian context (cf., 1 Thess. 2:15 and 16b which most biblical scholars agree is an interpolation) concerns a standard motif in early Jewish literature: 'the killing of the prophets.' Setzer notes that "H. J. Schoeps shows the motif of the murder of the prophets to be a traditional one in Jewish circles that surfaces [also] in literature" and "originally, of course, the theme was an in-house critique." See Setzer, *Jewish Responses*, 21. Bracket is mine. See also B. H. Amaru, "The Killing of the Prophets: Unraveling a midrash," *HUCA* 54 (1983), 153-80.

58. See 1 Tim. 6:12, 13, 20; and cf. II Tim. 1:12, 14.

communal celebrations had such a familiar resemblance to the Greek mystery religions' rituals and theosophical expressions, since they were part of the same socio-cultural context.

The diverse religiosity throughout the Greco-Roman world, mythologically based, was perceived philosophically as a united cultural and spiritual expression of one basic and essential religiosity, even with religious diversity. We can see that the variety of religious divination was due to the conceptual limitations of the cultural, historical, and linguistic parameters. Thus, the primitive symbolic tradition of the early, christological gatherings (i.e., the propaganda of the Jesus cult) was easily transmitted "into a universal and easily understandable language"[59] in the Hellenistic world. And thus, it served socially as a religiously-based christological, Jewish, revitalization movement. Some of the eschatological concerns, by the earliest communal gatherings, sometimes are difficult to translate into modern secular terms because of the language and pattern of literalist conceptualization by most conservatives. Wright cautions us that we commit a routine failure to understand that

> When the Jews and early Christians used 'end-of-the-world' *language* to describe this phenomenon [eschatology] they didn't mean it literally. They did not suppose that the world and history were actually going to come to an end. They used 'end-of-the-world' language to invest major and cataclysmic events *within* history with their (as we might say) 'earth shattering' significance. 'Eschatology' thus refers to the belief that history was going to reach, or perhaps that it had just reached, its great climax, its great turning-point. Both the language they used to say this, and the belief itself, are also sometimes referred to as 'apocalyptic,' though this has become so slippery a technical term that some scholars have given up using it altogether.[60]

---

59. Smith, *Ecce Deus*, 222. Note Stark's sociological appraisal in the *Rise of Christianity*: he suggested that the early fellowships cultural presence "revitalized life in Greco-Roman cities by providing new norms ... to cope with many urgent urban problems," 161.

60. Wright, *Saint Paul*, 34.

We should also note especially the language and social direction in the Gospels along with this familiar charge: "to the Jews first then to the Gentiles." Although these Gentiles did become converts to the new faith, their addition to the christological communities was primarily because the primitive tradition was reformulated into Hellenistic terms of religiosity. This type of religiosity (metaphorical and symbolic) was common to the Greek religious world and was perceived with the christological language (in mythological categories) that expressed the mystic realization that they lived in the age of the Spirit and the rule of Christ, communally as the anointed body, in God's Kingdom.[61] All such so-called mythological realities and the systemic, supernatural phenomena in general, which maintained an existence in some other (non-physical) realm above, beyond, or wherever, must be totally rejected as descriptive of a non-scientifically based reality. When this occurs, humanity will have to rely on its own human moral integrity, which would be sustained by a mutual, social rationality that focuses on realistic human resolutions to global and local human issues. In our twenty-first century, the death of innocence, which is life without a mythological understanding of existence, has occurred for many, so that many live in the reality of the present age of modernity with satisfaction, joy, comfort, happiness, and moral integrity.

---

61. See John Noe, *The Apocalypse Conspiracy* (Brentwood, Tenn.: Wolgemuth & Hyatt, Pub., Inc., 1991). Besides being refreshing and original as a student of the Bible, as an evangelical Christian, his non-traditional approach to biblical exegesis identifies the symbolic essence that is necessary for Christian spirituality in his exposition of the biblical themes found in the book of Revelation for modern readers on a popular basis.

BLIOGRAPHY

This bibliography indicates the wide range of scholarship that is available to deal with the complex theological subject at hand. The major scholarship used in this study, whose conceptual foundations have been germane to an understanding of Apocalypticism and eschatological concerns within the early Jewish, christological tradition, as it further relates to the concept of Jewish christological development and the historical Jesus during the Second Temple Period, appears in the body of the text. Additional works have been selected that have had a transformative influence on current theological ideas. Also, included are the recommended works that were helpful in the general formation of this material but were not mentioned in the main body of the study. In no form or fashion is this bibliography considered to be exhaustive; but, it is merely suggestive of the diversified nature and range of the scholarship, which is available to resolve the origins of Christianity without a historical Jesus as an integral factor in its formation.

Aland, Barbara. "Marcion." *TRE* 22 (1992): 89-101.

Alfoldy, G. *The Social History of Rome*. Trans. D. Braund and F. Pollock. London: Croom Helm, 1985.

Allegro, J. M. and Anderson, A. A. Eds. *Discoveries in the Judaean Desert of Jordan*. Vol. 5: Qumran Cave 4 I (4Q1S8-4Q186). Oxford: Clarendon, 1968.

Allen, Charlotte. *The Human Christ: The Search for the Historical Jesus*. New York: Free Press, 1998.

Allison, Dale C. *The End of the Ages Has Come*. Philadelphia: Fortress, 1985.

Altizer, Thomas J. J. *The Contemporary Jesus*. New York: State University of New York, 1997.
_____. *History as Apocalypse*. Albany: State University of New York, 1985.
_____, et. al. Eds. *Truth, Myth, and Symbol*. Englewood cliffs, New Jersey: Prentice-Hall, Spectrum Books, 1962.
_____. *Oriental Mysticism and Biblical Eschatology*. Philadelphia: Westminster, 1961.
_____. "The Religious Foundations of Biblical Eschatology." *The Journal of Religion*. XXXIX (1959).
Andersen, F. "2 Enoch." *OTP*, 1:91-221.
Applebaum, S. "Judea as a Roman Province. The Countryside as a Political and Economic Factor." *ANRW* II, 8 (1980): 355-96.
_____. "The Social and Economic Status of Jews in the Diaspora." *The Jewish People in the First Century*, ed. S. Safrai and M. Stern. Philadelphia: Fortress, 1976.
Argyle, A. W. "The Greek Apocalypse of Baruch." *The Apocryphal Old Testament*. Ed., H. F. D. Sparks. Oxford: Clarendon, 1984.
Armstrong, A. H. *An Introduction to Ancient Philosophy*. 3d ed. London: Methuen, 1957.
Ash, James. "The Dead Sea Scrolls and Jesus." *Midstream: A Monthly Jewish Review* 43/1 (1997): 14-16.
Attridge, H. W. "Historiography." *Jewish Writings of the Second Temple Period*. ed., M. E. Stone. Philadelphia: Fortress, 1984.
_____. "Philo the Epic Poet." *OTP*, 2:781-84.
Atwood, D. J. and Flowers, R. B. "Early Christianity as a Cult Movement." *Encounter* 44 (1983): 45-61.
Axtell, H. L. *The Deification of Abstract Ideas in Roman Literature and Inscriptions*. New Rochelle, N.Y.: Aristilde D. Caralzas, 1987.
Bagnall, R. *Egypt in Late Antiquity*. Princeton: Princeton University, 1993.
Baigent, Michael and Leigh, Richard. *The Dead Sea Scrolls Deception*. New York: Touchstone, 1991.
Baillie, John. *The Idea of Revelation in Recent Thought*. New York: Columbia University, 1956.
Bammel, E. "Christian Origins in Jewish Tradition." *NTS* 13 (1967): 317-35.

Banks, Robert. *Paul's Idea of Community: The Early House Churches in their Historical Setting.* Grand Rapids, MI: Eerdmans, 1980.

Baring, Anne and Cashford, Jules. *The Myth of the Goddess: Evolution of an Image.* London: Penguin, 1993.

Barker, A. *The Lost Prophet: The Book of Enoch and Its Influence on Christianity.* London: SPCK, 1988.

Barker, M. "Some Reflections on the Enoch Myth." *JSOT* 15 (1980): 7-29.

Barnstone, Willis, Ed. *The Other Bible: Ancient Esoteric Texts.* San Francisco: Harper and Row, 1984.

Barthelemy, D. and Milik, J. T. Eds. *Discoveries in the Judaean Desert.* Vol. 1: Qumran Cave I. Oxford: Clarendon, 1955.

Bartlett, J. R. *Jews in the Hellenistic World.* Cambridge: Cambridge University Press, 1985.

Barton, Stephen C. "Paul and the Resurrection: A Sociological Approach." *Religion* 14 (1984): 67-75.

_____. "Paul and the Cross: A Sociological Approach." *Theology* 85 (1982): 13-19.

Bassler, Joutte M. "The Galileans: A Neglected Factor in Johannine Research." *CBQ* 43 (1981): 243-257.

Bauer, Arndt, William F. and Gingrich, F. Wilbur. *A Greek-English Lexicon of the New Testament and Other Early Christian Literature.* 2nd ed., Chicago: University of Chicago Press, 1979.

Beard, Mary et al., Eds. *Religions of Rome.* Vol. 2: A Sourcebook. Cambridge: Cambridge University, 1998.

Beardslee, William A. *Literary Criticism of the New Testament: Guides to Biblical Scholarship.* Philadelphia: Fortress, 1970.

Beckwith, Roger T. *The Old Testament Canon of the New Testament Church and its Background in Early Judaism.* London: SPCK, 1985.

Bellah, Robert N. "Religious Evolution." *American Sociological Review.* (1964): 29:358-374.

Belo, Fernando. *A Materialist Reading of the Gospel of Mark.* Trans. Matthew M. J. O'Connell. Maryknoll, N.Y.: Orbis Books, 1981.

Ben-Dov, M. *In the Shadow of the Temple: The Discovery of Ancient Jerusalem.* Jerusalem: Keter, 1985.

Benko, Stephen. *Pagan Rome and the Early Christians.* Bloomington, Ind.: Indiana University, 1985.

_____. and O'Rourke, J. J. Eds. *The Catacombs and the Coliseum: The Roman Empire as the Setting of Primitive Christianity.* Valley Forge, Pa.: Judson, 1971.

Berger, P. L. and Luckmann, T. *The Social Construction of Reality: A Treatise in the Sociology of Knowledge.* New York: Anchor Books, 1967.

Bernardakis, Ed. *Plutarch on the Delay of the Divine Justice.* Trans. Andrew P. Peabody. Boston: Little Brown, 1885.

Betz, Otto. "Was John the Baptist an Essene?" reprinted in Hershel Shanks' *Understanding the Dead Sea Scrolls.* New York: Random House, 1992.

Bevan, Anthony Ashley. Trans. *The Hymn of the Soul: Contained in the Syriac Acts of St. Thomas.* Cambridge: Cambridge University, 1897.

Bickermann, Elias. *The Jews in the Greek Age.* Cambridge: Harvard University, 1988.

_____. "The God of the Maccabees: Studies on the Meaning and Origin of the Maccabean Revolt." *SJLA* 32, Leiden: Brill, 1979.

_____. *From Ezra to the Last of the Maccabees.* New York: Schocken, 1962.

Black, M. Ed. *The Scrolls and Christianity: Historical and Theological Significance.* London: SPCK, 1969.

_____. *The Scrolls and Christian Origins: Studies in the Jewish background of the New Testament.* New York: Scribner's, 1961.

Black, Matthew. *Models and Metaphors.* Ithaca, N.Y.: Cornell University, 1962.

_____. *The Scrolls and Christian Origins.* Atlanta: Scholars Press, 1961.

Blenkinsopp, J. "Interpretation and Sectarian Tendencies: An Aspect of Second Temple History." *Jewish and Christian Self-Definition.* Eds. Sanders et al. (1968): 2:1-26.

Bloch, J. *On the Apocalyptic in Judaism.* Philadelphia: Dropsie College, 1952.

Bloom, Harold. *Omens of Millennium: The Gnōsis of Angels, Dreams, and Resurrection.* New York: Riverhead, 1996.

_____. "Apocalypse Then." *New York Review of Books* 30/21-22 (January, 1984): 25-26, 31-33.

Boak, Arthur E. R. *A History of Rome to 565 A.D.* 3d Ed. New York: Macmillan, 1947.

Boccaccini, G. *Portraits of Middle Judaism in Scholarship and Arts: A Multimedia Catalog from Flavius Josephus to 1991.* Turin: Zamorani, 1992.

Boff, L. *Jesus Christ Liberator: A Critical Christology for Our Times.* New York: Orbis Press, 1978.

Bokser, B. M. "Wonder-Working and the Rabbinic Tradition: The Case of Hanina Ben Dosa." *JSJ* 16 (1985): 42-92.

Boman, Thorleif. *Hebrew Thought Compared with Greek.* SCM Press, London, 1960.

Bonsirven, J. *Palestinian Judaism in the Time of Jesus Christ.* Trans. William Wolf. New York: MacGraw-Hill, 1965.

Boobyer, G. "Galilee and Galileans in St. Mark's Gospel." *BJRL* 35 (1953): 334-48.

Booth, W. *The Rhetoric of Fiction.* Chicago: University Press, 1961.

Borg, Marcus. *Jesus in Contemporary Scholarship.* Valley Forge, PA: Trinity, 1994.

_____. *Jesus: A New Vision: Spirit, Culture, and the Life of Discipleship.* San Francisco: Harper, 1987.

Borne, Etienne. *Atheism.* New York: Hawthorne, 1961.

Bornkamm, Gunther. *Paul.* Trans. D. G. M. Stalker. New York: Harper & Row, 1971.

_____. *Jesus of Nazareth.* London: SCM. 1960.

Bossman, David M. "Images of God in the Letters of Paul." *BTB* 18 (1988): 18.

Bostock, D. "Jesus as the New Elisha." *ET* 92 (1986): 39-41.

Bourquin, D. R. *First-Century Palestinian Judaism: A Bibliography of Works in English.* San Bernardino: Borgo, 1990.

Bousset, Wilhelm. *Kyrios Christos: A History of the Belief in Christ from the Beginnings of Christianity to Irenaeus.* Nashville: Abingdon, 1970.

Bowersock, G. W. *Greek Sophists in the Roman Empire.* Oxford: Clarendon, 1969.

Braaten, Carl E. *Christ and Counter-Christ: Apocalyptic Themes in Theology and Culture.* Philadelphia: Fortress, 1972.

_____. "The Significance of Apocalypticism for Systematic Theology." *Interpretation*   25/4 (1971): 480-99.

Brandon, S. G. F. *History, Time and Deity.* Manchester University Press, 1965.

Branham, J. "Vicarious Sacrality: Temple Space in Ancient Synagogues." *Ancient Synagogues: Historical Analysis and Archaeological Discovery*. 2 Ed. D. Urman and P. Flesher. Leiden: Brill, 1995.

Braun, Herbert et al. "God and Christ: Existence and Providence." Ed. Robert W. Funk, Vol. V, *Journal for Theology and the Church*. New York: Harper & Row, Harper Torchbooks, 1968.

Breasted, James Henry. *Development of Religion and Thought in Ancient Egypt*. Intro. John A. Wilson. New York: Harper & Row, Harper Torchbooks, 1959.

Brenton, L. Trans. *The Septuagint with Apocrypha (Greek & English)*. Grand Rapids, Mich.: Zondervan, 1851.

Bronner, L. *Sects and Separatism during the Second Jewish Commonwealth*. New York: Bloch, 1967.

Brooke, G. J. Ed. "New Qumran Texts and Studies." *STDJ* 15. Leiden: Brill, 1994.

Brown, Peter. *The Body and Society: Men, Women and Sexual Renunciation in Early Christianity*. New York: Columbia University, 1988.

Brown, Raymond E. *The Death of the Messiah*. 2 vols., I, 1994, New York: Doubleday, II, 1998.

_____. *An Introduction to the New Testament*. New York: Doubleday, 1997.

_____. *The Community of the Beloved Disciple*. New York: Paulist Press, 1979.

_____. "The Eucharist and Baptism in John." *New Testament Essays*. New York: Paulist Press, 1965.

_____. *New Testament Essays*. New York: Paulist Press, 1965.

Bruce, F. F. *Second Thoughts on the Dead Sea Scrolls*. Grand Rapids: Eerdmans, 1977.

Brumfield, A.C. *The Attic Festivals of Demeter and their Relation to the Agricultural Year*. New York: Arno Press, 1981.

Buber, Martin. *Two Types of Faith*. Trans. Norman Goldhawk. New York: Harper & Row, Harper Torchbooks, 1961.

_____. *I and Thou*. New York: Scribner's, 1958.

_____. "Prophecy, Apocalyptic, and the Historical Hour." *Union Seminary Quarterly Review* 11-12 (1957): 9-21.

_____. *The Prophetic Faith*. New York: Harper & Row, Harper Torchbooks, Cloister Library, 1949.

Budge, E. A. Wallis. *Osiris and the Egyptian Resurrection.* Vol. 1. New York: Dover, 1973.

Bull, Malcolm, Ed. *Apocalypse Theory and the Ends of the World.* Oxford: Basil Blackwell, 1995.

Bultmann, Rudolf. "The Idea of God and Modem Man." *Translating Theology into the Modern Age.* New York: Torchbooks, 1965.

_____. *Jesus and the Word.* New York: Scribner, 1934.

Burkert, W. *Orphism and Bacchic Mysteries: New Evidence and Old Problems of Interpretation.* Berkeley: Center for Hermeneutical Studies, 1977.

Burkitt, F. C. *The Gospel History and its Transmission.* Edinburgh: T. & T. Clark, 1925.

Burnett, F. *The Testament of Jesus-Sophia: A Redaction Critical Study of the Eschatological Discourse in Matthew.* Washington, D.C.: University Press of America, 1981.

Burrows, Millar. *The Dead Sea Scrolls.* New York: Viking, 1955.

Camp, C. "Woman Wisdom as Root Metaphor: A Theological in Consideration." *The Listening Heart: Essays in 'Wisdom and the Psalms in Honor of Roland E. Murphy, O Carm.* Ed. K. Hogland et. al. 45-76. Sheffield, England: JSOT Press, 1987.

Campbell, Joseph. :From Darkness to Light: The Mystery Religions of Ancient Greece," in *Transformations of Myth through Time.* Public Media Video, William Free Productions. Vol. 1, No. 5.

_____. *The Masks of God: Occidental Mythology.* Penguin, New York, 1964.

_____. Ed. "The Mysteries." *The Eranos Yearbooks. Bollingen Series* 30, vol. 2. New York: Pantheon, 1955.

Cansdale, L. "Qumran and the Essenes: A Re-Evaluation of the Evidence." *TSAJ* 60. Tubingen: Mohr-Siebeck, 1997.

Carmignac, J. *Christ and the Teacher of Righteousness: The Evidence of the Dead Sea Scrolls.* Trans. K. G. Pedley. Baltimore: Helicon, 1962.

Case, Shirley Jackson. *The Social Triumph of the Ancient Church.* New York: Harper & Brothers, 1933.

_____. "The Acceptance of Christianity by the Roman Emperors." *Papers of the American Society of Church History.* 45-64. New York: Putnam's, 1928.

_____. *The Social Origins of Christianity*. Chicago: University of Chicago, 1923.

Cassirer, Ernst. "The Philosophy of Symbolic Forms." Vol. II. *Mythical Thinking*. Trans. Ralph Manheim. New Haven: Yale University, 1955.

_____. *Language and Myth*. Trans. Susanne Langer. New York: Harper and Brothers, 1946.

Catchpole, David R. *The Trial of Jesus: A Study in the Gospels and Historiography from 1770 to the Present Day*. SPB 18. Leiden: E. J., 1971.

Charles, James H. *Jesus' Jewishness: Exploring the Place of Jesus within Early Judaism*. New York: Crossroad, 1991.

Charles, R. H. Ed. Trans. *The Apocrypha and Pseudepigrapha of the Old Testament*. 2 vols. Oxford: Clarendon, 1913.

_____. Ed. *The Testaments of the Twelve Patriarchs*. London: Adam & Charles Black, 1908.

_____ and Morfill, W. R. *The Book of the Secrets of Enoch*. Oxford: Clarendon, 1896.

Charlesworth, James H. *The Pesharim and Qumran History: Chaos or Consensus?* Grand Rapids, Mich.: Eerdmans, 2002.

_____. *Jesus and the Dead Sea Scrolls*. New York: Anchor-Doubleday, 1995.

_____. "The Origin and Subsequent History of the Authors of the Dead Sea Scrolls: Four Transitional Phases among the Qumran Essenes." *RQ* 10 (1980).

_____. *Jesus Within Judaism*. New York: Anchor-Doubleday, 1988.

_____. Ed. *The Old Testament Pseudepigrapha*. 2 Vols. *Apocalyptic Literature and Testaments*. Garden City, NY: Doubleday, 1983, 1985.

_____. *The Old Testament Pseudepigrapha and the New Testament: Prolegomena for the Study of Christian Origins*. New York: Cambridge University, 1985.

Chase, Richard Volney. *Quest for Myth*. Baton Rouge: Louisiana State University, 1949.

Chenu, M. D. and Heer, Friedrich. "Is the Modern World Atheist?" *Cross Currents* (Winter, 1961).

Chernus, I. *Mysticism in Rabbinic Judaism*. Berlin: de Gruyter, 1982.

Chilton, Bruce and Evans, Craig A. "Studying the Historical Jesus: Evaluations of the State of Current Research." *NTTS* 19. Leiden: Brill, 1994.

Clabeaux, John J. *A Lost Edition of the Letters of Paul: A Reassessment of the Text of the Pauline Corpus Attested by Marcion.* The Catholic Biblical Quarterly Monograph Series No. 21. Washington, D. C.: The Catholic Biblical Association of America, 1989.

Clark, Gillian. *Women in Late Antiquity: Pagan and Christian Life Styles.* Oxford: Clarendon, 1993.

Clauss, Manfred. *The Roman Cult of Mithras: The God and his Mysteries.* Routledge, New York: 2001.

Clement, of Alexandria, Saint. *Stromateis.* Washington, DC: Catholic University of America Press, 1991.

Cochrane, Charles Norris. *Christianity and Classical Culture.* London: Oxford, 1957.

Coggins, R.J. *Samaritans and Jews: The Origins of Samaritanism Reconsidered.* Oxford: Blackwell, 1975.

Cohen, S. J. D. "The Significance of Yavneh: Pharisees, Rabbis, and the End of Jewish Sectarianism." *HUCA* 55 (1984): 27-53.

_____. "Josephus in Galilee and Rome: His Vita and His Development as an Historian." *Columbia Studies in the Classical Traditions.* 8. Leiden: Brill, 1979.

Collins, A. Yarbro. *Cosmology and Eschatology in Jewish and Christian Apocalypticism.* Leiden: Brill, 1996.

_____. Ed. "Early Christian Apocalypticism: Genre and Social Setting." *Semeia* 36. Missoula, MT: Scholars Press, 1986.

Collins, John J. *The Apocalyptic Imagination: An Introduction to Jewish Apocalyptic Literature.* 2d Ed. Grand Rapids: Eerdmans, 1998.

_____. *Apocalypticism in the Dead Sea Scrolls.* New York: Routledge, 1997.

_____. "Apotheosis and Resurrection." Borgen, Peder and Soren Giversen, Eds. *The New Testament and Hellenistic Judaism.* 88-100. Peabody, MA: Hendrickson, 1995.

_____. "The Son of Man in First-Century Judaism." *NTS* 38 (1992): 448-66.

_____ and Charlesworth, J. H. Eds. "Mysteries and Revelations: Apocalyptic Studies since the Uppsala Colloquium." *JSP* Sup 9. Sheffield: JSOT Press, 1991.

_____. *The Apocalyptic Imagination: An Introduction to the Jewish Matrix of Christianity.* New York: Crossroad, 1984.

_____. "The Genre Apocalypse in Hellenistic Judaism." *Apocalypticism in the Mediterranean World and the Near East.* Ed., D. Hellholm, Tubingen: Mohr Siebeck, 1983.

_____. "The Apocalyptic Technique: Setting and Function in the Book of Watchers." *CBQ* 44 (1982): 91-111.

_____. "Symposium: Apocalyptic Symbolism and Social Reality." *Biblical Research* 26 (1981): 4-45.

_____. Ed. "Apocalypse: The Morphology of a Genre." *Semeia* 14. Atlanta: Scholars Press, 1979.

_____. "Cosmos and Salvation: Jewish Wisdom and Apocalyptic in the Hellenistic Age." *History of Religions* 17/2 (1977): 121-42.

_____. "Jewish Apocalyptic Against Its Hellenistic Near Eastern Environment." *BASOR* 220 (1975): 27-36.

Conzelmann, Hans. *History of Primitive Christianity.* Nashville: Abingdon. 1973.

_____. "The Mother of Wisdom." *The Future of Our Religious Past.* Ed. J. M. Robinson, Trans. C. E. Carlston and R. P. Scharlemann, 230-43. London: SCM, 1971.

Cook, L. *Prophecy and Apocalypticism: The Postexilic Social Setting.* Minneapolis: Fortress, 1995.

Cook, M. *Mark's Treatment of the Jewish Leaders.* Leiden: Brill, 1978.

Cooper, D. Jason. *Mithras.* Samuel Weiser, Maine, 1996.

Copenhaver, Brian P. Trans. *Hermetica: The Greek Corpus Hermeticum and the Latin Asclepius.* Cambridge: Cambridge University, 1992.

Cory, Isaac Preston. *Ancient Fragments of the Phoenician, Chaldaean, Egyptian, Tyrian, Carthaginian, Indian, Persian, and other Writers.* 2nd Ed. London: William Picketing, 1832.

Coser, Lewis A. *The Function of Social Conflict.* New York: Free Press, 1964.

Cotton, H. M. and Geiger, J. Masada. 2: The Yigael Yadin Excavations 1963-1965, *Final Reports: The Latin and Greek Documents.* Jerusalem: Israel Exploration Society and Hebrew University, 1989.

Coughenour, R. R. "The Wisdom Stance of Enoch's Redactor." *JSJ* 13 (1982): 47-55.

Countryman, Louis W. *The Rich Christian in the Church of the Early Empire: Contradictions and Accommodations.* New York: Edward Mellen Press, 1980.

Craffert, P. F. "The Origins of Resurrection Faith: The Challenge of a Social-Scientific Approach." *Neotestamentica* 23 (1989).

Cross, F. M. *The Ancient Library of Qumran.* 3rd Ed. Sheffield: Sheffield Academic Press, 1995.

_____. *Canaanite Myth and Hebrew Epic.* Cambridge, Mass: Harvard University Press, 1973.

Crossan, John Dominic. "Why Christians Must Search for the Historical Jesus." *Bible Review* 12 (April, 1996): 42-45.

_____ and Watts, Richard G. *Who Is Jesus? Answers to Your Questions About the Historical Jesus.* San Francisco: Harper, 1996.

_____. *Who Killed Jesus? Exposing the Roots of Anti-Semitism in the Gospel Story of the Death of Jesus.* San Francisco: HarperCollins, 1995.

_____. *The Essential Jesus: Original Sayings and Earliest Images.* San Francisco: Harper, 1994.

_____. *A Revolutionary Biography.* San Francisco: Harper, 1993.

_____. *The Historical Jesus: The Life of a Mediterranean Peasant.* San Francisco: Harper, 1991.

Crouch, James E. "How Early Christians Viewed the Birth of Jesus." *Bible Review* 7/8 (1991): 34-38.

Cullmann, Oscar. *The Johannine Circle.* London: SCM Press, 1976.

_____. *Jesus and the Revolutionaries.* Trans. Gareth Putnam. New York: Harper & Row, 1970.

_____. *Salvation in History.* London: SCM Press, 1967.

_____. *The State in the New Testament.* New York: Scribner's, 1956.

Culpepper, R. Alan. *Anatomy of the Fourth Gospel: A Study in Literary Design.* Philadelphia: Fortress, 1983.

Cumont, Franz. *Oriental Religions in Roman Paganism.* New York: Dover, 1956.

Dahl, Nils Alstrup. "The Origin of the Earliest Prologues to the Pauline Letters." *Semeia* 12 (1978): Pt. 1, 233-77.

_____. *The Crucified Messiah and Other Essays*. Minneapolis: Fortress, 1974.

Dan, J. "Jewish Gnosticism." *JSQ* 2 (1995).

Danby, H. Ed. and Trans. *The Mishnah*. Oxford: Clarendon, 1933.

Danielou, Jean and Marrou, Henri. "The First Six Hundred Years." Vol. 1. *The Christian Centuries*. New York: Paulist Press, 1964.

Daube, D. *The New Testament and Rabbinic Judaism*. London: University of London, Athlone Press, 1956.

Davenport, G. L. *The Eschatology of the Book of Jubilees.* SPB 20. Leiden: Brill, 1971.

Davies, J. G. *The Early Christian Church*. New York: Doubleday, Anchor Books, 1965.

Davies, P. "The Ideology of the Temple in the Damascus Document." *JJS* 33 (1982): 287-301.

Davies, R. "Behind the Essenes: History and Ideology in the Dead Sea Scrolls*."* *BJS* 94. Atlanta: Scholars Press, 1987.

Davies, Stevan L. *Jesus the Healer: Possession, Trance, and the Origins of Christianity*. New York: Continuum, 1995.

_____. *The Gospel of Thomas and Christian Wisdom*. New York: Seabury, 1983.

Davies, W.D. *The Gospel and the Land: Early Christianity and Jewish Territorial Doctrine*. Berkley: University of California Press, 1974.

_____. *Paul and Rabbinic Judaism: Some Rabbinic Elements in Pauline Theology*. Rev. ed. New York: Harper & Row, Harper Torchbooks, 1965.

Deissmann, Adolf. *Light from the Ancient East*. Grand Rapids, MI: Eerdmans, 1978.

_____. *Paul: A Study in Social and Religious History*. Trans. William E. Wilson. New York: Harper & Row, Harper Torchbooks, The Cloister Library, 1957.

_____. *The Religion of Jesus and the Faith of Paul*. Trans. William E. Wilson. London: Hodder & Stoughton, 1923.

Derrett, J. Duncan M. "St. John's Jesus and the Buddha." *JHC* 6/2 (Fall, 1999): 161-174.

Detering, Hermann. "The Dutch Radical Approach to the Pauline Epistles." *JHC* 3/2 (Fall, 1996): 163-193.

_____. "The Synoptic Apocalypse (Mark 13/par): A Document from the Time of Bar Kochba." *JHC* 7/2 (Fall, 2000): 161-210.

Deutsch, C. "Wisdom in Matthew: Transformation of a Symbol." *Nov T* 32 (1990): 13-47.

Dewey, Arthur J. "Four Visions and a Funeral: Resurrection in the Gospel of Peter." *JHC* 2/2 (Fall, 1995): 33-51.

Di Leila, A. A. "Conservative and Progressive Theology: Sirach and Wisdom." *CBQ* 38 (1966): 139-54.

Didache, The. [Ca. 100.] *The Apostolic Fathers*, Ed. J. B. Lightfoot and J. R. Harmer, 229-235. Grand Rapids, MI: Baker, 1984.

Dimant, D. and Schiffman, L. H. Eds. "Time To Prepare the Way in the Wilderness: Papers on the Qumran Scrolls by Fellows of the Institute for Advanced Studies of the Hebrew University, Jerusalem." 1989-90. *STDJ* 16, Leiden: Brill, 1995.

————. *Bibliography of Works on Jewish History in the Persian, Hellenistic, and Roman Periods*. 1981-85. Jerusalem: Historical Society of Israel, 1987.

Dio Cassius. [Ca. 200.] *The Roman History: The Reign of Augustus*. London: Penguin Classics, 1987.

Dix, Gregory. *Jew and Greek*. New York: Harper & Bros., 1953.

Dobschutz, Ernst von. *Christian Life in the Primitive Church*. Trans. Geo. Bremner and Ed. W. D. Morrison. London: Williams & Norgate, 1914.

Dodd, Charles Harold. *The Founder of Christianity*. New York: Macmillan, 1970.

Dodds, E. R. *Pagan and Christian in an Age of Anxiety*. York: Norton, 1970.

Doherty, Earl. "The Puzzling Figure of Jesus in John Dominic Crossan's Birth of Christianity: A Critical Discussion." *JHC* 6/2 (Fall, 1999): 216-258.

————. *The Jesus Puzzle*. Ottawa, Canada: Canadian Humanist Publications, 1999.

Douglas, M. *Natural Symbols: Explorations in Cosmology*. 2nd Ed. London: Barrie and Jenkins, 1973.

Downing, F. Gerald. *Cynics, Paul and the Pauline Churches: Cynics and Christian Origins II*. New York: Routledge, 1998.

Drane, John. *Jesus and the Four Gospels*. San Francisco: Harper & Row, 1979.

Drower, E. G. *The Secret Adam: A Study of Nasoraean Gnōsis*. Oxford: Clarendon, 1960.

Duke, Paul D. *Irony in the Fourth Gospel*. Atlanta: John Knox, 1985.

Duling, Dennis C. *Jesus Christ Through History*. New York: Harcourt Brace Jovanovich, 1979.

_____. "The Therapeutic Son of David: An Element in Matthew's Christological Apologetic." *NTS* 24 (1978): 392-410.

Dungan, David L. *The Sayings of Jesus in the Churches of Paul*. Fortress, 1971.

Dunn, James D. G. *The Evidence for Jesus*. Philadelphia: Westminster, 1985.

_____. "John vi - A Eucharistic Discourse?" *NTS* 17, (1970): 328-338.

Dupont-Sommer, A. *The Jewish Sect of Qumran and the Essenes: New Studies on the Dead Sea Scrolls*. Trans. R. D. Barnett. New York: Macmillan, 1956.

Durkheim, Emile. *The Rules of Sociological Method*. 8th Ed. New York: Free Press, 1966.

_____. *The Elementary Forms of Religious Life*. George Alien & Unwin, 1915.

Earle, William. "Man Is the Impossibility of God" and "The Paradox and the Death of God," *Christianity and Existentialism*. Evanston: Northwestern University, 1963.

Edie, James M. "The Absence of God." *Christianity and Existentialism*. Evanston: Northwestern University, 1963.

Edmonson, George. *The Church in Rome in the First Century*. New York: Gordon Press, 1976.

Efron, J. *Studies on the Hasmonean Period*. Leiden: Brill, 1987.

Ehrman, Bart D. *The Orthodox Corruption of Scripture*. Oxford: Oxford University Press, 1993.

Eisenman, Robert. "Paul as Herodian," *JHC* 3/1 (Spring, 1996): 110-122.

_____. *James the Just and the Habakkuk Pesher*. Leiden: Brill, 1986.

_____. *Maccabees, Zaddokites, Christians and Qumran*. Leiden: Brill, 1983.

Eliade, Mircea. *A History of Religious Ideas: From the Stone Age to the Eleusinian Mysteries*. Chicago: University of Chicago, 1978.

_____. *The Myth of the Eternal Return*. Princeton, N.J.: Princeton University, 1971.

_____ and Joseph M. Kitagawa, Eds. *The History of Religions: Essays in Mythology*. Chicago: The University of Chicago, 1959.

_____. *The Sacred and the Profane: The Nature of Religion*. Trans. Willard R. Trask. New York: Harper & Row, Harper Torchbooks, The Cloister Library, 1959.

_____. *Patterns in Comparative Religion*. Trans. Rosemary Sheed. New York: Sheed and Ward, 1958.

_____. *Rites and Symbols of Initiation: The Mysteries of Birth and Rebirth*. Trans. Willard R. Trask. New York: Harper & Row, Harper Torchbooks, The Academy Library, 1958.

Elliot, James K. *The Apocryphal Jesus. Legends of the Early Church*. Oxford: Oxford University, 1996.

_____. *Home for the Homeless: A Sociological Exegesis of I Peter. Its Situation and Strategy*. Philadelphia: Fortress Press, 1981.

Elliott, John H. "Social-Scientific Criticism of the New Testament: More on Methods and Models." *Semeia* (1986): 35:1-33.

_____. "The Historical Jesus, The Kerygmatic Christ, and The Eschatological Community." *Concordia Theological Monthly* 37/8 (1966): 470-491.

Engels, Friedrich. "On the History of Early Christianity." *Karl Marx and Friedrich Engels: Basic Writings on Politics and Philosophy*. Ed. L. S. Feuer, 168-94. New York: Doubleday, 1959.

Engelsman, J. C. *The Feminine Dimension of the Divine*. Philadelphia: Westminster, 1979.

Enslin, Morton Scott. *Christian Beginnings*. Part I and II. New York: Harper & Row, Harper Torchbooks, The Cloister Library, 1938.

Epstein, I. Gen. Ed. *The Babylonian Talmud*. 35 vols. London: Soncino, 1935-48.

Esler, Philip F. "Political Opposition in Jewish Apocalyptic Literature: A Social-Scientific Approach." *Listening: Journal of Religion and Culture*. (1993): 28.

Eusebius. [Ca. 325.] *The History of the Church*. Trans. G. A. Williamson. Harmondsworth, Middlesex: Penguin, 1965.

Evans, C. F. and Porter, Stanley E. Eds. "The Historical Jesus." A Sheffield Reader. *Biblical Seminar* 33. Sheffield: Sheffield Academic, 1995.

411

Evans, Craig A. "Life of Jesus Research: An Annotated Bibliography." *New Testament Tools and Studies*. 12. Rev. Ed. Leiden: Brill, 1996.

———. "Early Rabbinic Sources and Jesus Research." Seminar Papers *SBL* (1995).

——— and Chilton, Bruce D. *Studying the Historical Jesus: Evaluations of the State of Current Research*. Leiden: Brill, 1994.

———. "The Kerygma." *Journal of Theological Studies*. Vol. VIII, Pt. 1 (April, 1956).

Farmer, W. R. *Maccabees, Zealots, and Josephus*. New York: Columbia University, 1956.

Faure, Paul. "Crete and Mycenae: Problems of Mythology and Religious History," *Mythologies*. Comp. Yves Bonnefoy and Wendy Doniger. Trans. Gerald Honigsblum et. al. 4 vols. vol. I: *Greek and Egyptian Mythologies*. 30-40. Chicago: University of Chicago, 1992.

Fawcett, T. *The Symbolic Language of Religion: An Introduction*. London: SCM, 1970.

Feeley-Harnik, Gillian. *The Lord's Table: Eucharist and Passover in Early Christianity*. Philadelphia: University of Pennsylvania, 1981.

Feldman, Louis H. and Meyer, Reinhold. Eds. *Jewish Life and Thought Among Greeks and Romans*. Minneapolis: Fortress, 1996.

———. *Jew and Gentile in the Ancient World: Attitudes and Interactions from Alexander to Justinian*. Princeton: Princeton University, 1993.

Ferguson, Everette. *Backgrounds of Early Christianity*. 2nd Ed. Grand Rapids: Eerdmans, 1993.

———. "Mithraism." *The Encyclopedia of Early Christianity*. Ed. Everette Ferguson, New York: Garland, 1990, 609.

Festinger, Leon. *A Theory of Cognitive Dissonance*. White Plains, N.Y.: Row, Peterson & Co., 1957.

———. Riecken, H. W. and Schachter, S. *When Prophecy Fails*. New York: Harper, 1956.

Finkel, Asher. *The Pharisees and the Teacher of Nazareth: A Study of their Background, their Halachic, Midrashic Teachings, the Similarities and Differences*. Leiden: Brill, 1974.

Finley, M. I. *The Ancient Greeks*. New York: Penguin, 1991.

_____. *Economy and Society in Ancient Greece.* New York: Viking, 1982.

_____. *Atlas of Classical Archaeology.* New York: McGraw-Hill, 1977.

Fiorenza, Schussler Elisabeth. "The Phenomenon of Early Christian Apocalyptics: Some Reflections on Method." *Apocalypticism in the Mediterranean World and the Near East.* Ed. D. Hellholm, 295-316. Tubingen: J. C. B. Mohr (Paul Siebeck), 1983.

_____. *The History of the Jewish People in the Age of Jesus Christ (175 B.C.-A.D. 135).* Rev. Ed. 3 Vols. Edinburgh: T. & T. Clark, 1973-87.

_____. "Apocalyptic and Gnosis in Revelation and in Paul." *JBL* 92 (1973): 565-81.

Fishbane, M. "Use, Authority and Interpretation of Mikra at Qumran." *Mikra.* Ed. M. J. Mulder. Assen: Van Gorcum, 1988.

Fitmyer, Joseph A. *The Dead Sea Scrolls: Major Publications and Tools for Study.* Atlanta: Scholars Press, 1990.

Fittschen, K. and Foerster, G. Eds. *Judaea and the Greco-Roman World in the Time of Herod in the Light of Archaeological Evidence.* Gottingen: Vandenhoeck and Ruprecht, 1996.

Flusser, D. *The Spiritual History of the Dead Sea Sect.* Trans. C. Glucker. Tel Aviv: Israel, 1989.

_____. *Judaism and the Origins of Christianity.* Jerusalem: Hebrew University Press, 1988.

_____ and Safrai, S. "The Essene Doctrine of Hypostasis and Rabbi Meir." *Immanuel* 14 (1982): 47-57.

Fornberg, Tornd and David Hellholm. Eds. *Texts and Contexts. Biblical Texts in Their Textual and Situational Contexts.* FS Lars Hartman, Oslo and Copenhagen: Scandinavian University, 1995.

Fortna, Robert T. "The Gospel of Signs: A Reconstruction of the Narrative Source Underlying the Fourth Gospel." *SNTSMS* 11. Cambridge: Cambridge University, 1970.

Foss, Martin. *Symbol and Metaphor in Human Experience.* Princeton: Princeton University, 1949.

Fowler, R. "Who is the Reader in Reader-Response Criticism?" *Semeia* 31 (1985): 5-26.

Fox, Robin Lane. *Pagans and Christians.* New York: Knopf, 1987.

Frank, Harry Thomas. *Discovering the Biblical World.* Rev. Ed. Maplewood, NJ: Hammond, 1988.

Frend, W.H.C. *Martyrdom and Persecution in the Early Church.* Oxford: Basil Blackwell, 1965.

Freud, Sigmund. "Obsessive Actions and Religious Practices." *Origins of Religion.* Penguin Freud Library 13, Harmondsworth: Penguin, 1985.

_____. *The Future of an Illusion.* New York: Anchor, 1965.

Freyne, Sean. "Bandits in Galilee: A Contribution to the Study of Social Conditions in First-Century Palestine." Neusner et al. Ed. *The Social World of Formative Christianity and Judaism: Essays in Tribute of Howard Clark Kee.* Philadelphia: Fortress Press, 1988.

_____, Nickelsburg, *G.W.E.* and Collins, J. J. Eds. "The Charismatic." *Ideal Figures in Ancient Judaism. S.B.L.* Septuagint and Cognate Studies 12, Chico: Scholars Press 1980, 223-58.

_____. "The Galileans in the Light of Josephus' Vita." *NTS* 26 (1980): 397-413.

_____. *Galilee from Alexander the Great to Hadrian, 323 B.C.E. to 135 C.E.: A Study of Second Temple Judaism.* Wilmington, Del.: Michael Glazier, 1980.

Fritz, Stern. *The Dogma of Christ: and Other Essays on Religion, Psychology, and Culture.* New York: Holt, Rinehart and Winston, 1963.

_____. *The Varieties of History.* New York: Meridian, 1956.

Fromm, Erich. *Marx's Concept of Man.* New York: Ungar, 1961.

Frymer-Kensky, T. *In the Wake of the Goddesses: Women, Culture, and the Biblical Transformation of Pagan Myth.* New York: Free Press, 1992.

Fuchs, E. *Studies of the Historical Jesus.* London: SCM Press, 1964.

Fuks, A. "Aspects of the Jewish Revolt in A. D. 115-117." *JRS* 51 (1961): 98-104.

Fuks, G. "The Jews of Hellenistic and Roman Scythopolis." *JJS* 33 (1982): 407-16.

Fuller, Reginald H. *The Foundations of New Testament Christology.* New York: Scribner, 1965.

Funk, Robert W. *The Acts of Jesus: The Search for the Authentic Deeds of Jesus.* San Francisco: HarperSanFrancisco, 1998.

_____. Hoover, Roy W. and the Jesus Seminar. Eds. *The Five Gospels: The Search for the Authentic Words of Jesus.*

414

New Translation and Commentary. San Francisco: Harper, 1996.

_____. *Honest to Jesus: Jesus for a New Millennium*. San Francisco: Harper-Collins, 1996.

_____. Ed. "Apocalypticism." *JTC* 6. New York: Herder and Herder, 1969.

Gabba, E. "The Growth of Anti-Judaism or the Greek Attitude towards Jews." *The Cambridge History of Judaism*. Volume 2: *The Hellenistic Age*. Ed. W. D. Davies and L. Finkelstein. Cambridge: Cambridge University Press, 1989.

Gager, J. G. "Social Description and Social Explanation in the Study of Early Christianity: A Review Essay." *The Bible and Liberation: Political and Social Hermeneutics*. Ed. Norman K. Gottwald. 428-440. Maryknoll, N.Y.: Orbis Books, 1983.

_____. *Kingdom and Community: The Social World of Early Christianity*. Englewood Cliffs, N.J.: Prentice Hall, 1975.

Gallagher, Eugene V. "Divine Man or Magician? Celsus and Origen on Jesus." *SBL* Diss. Series. 64. Chico, CA: Scholars Press, 1982.

Galloway, Allen. *The Cosmic Christ*. New York: Harper & Row, 1951.

Gardiner, Patrick. *The Nature of Historical Explanation*. London: Oxford University, 1952.

Gardner, E. Clinton. *Biblical Faith and Social Ethics*. New York: Harper & Row, 1960.

Garnsey, P. "Peasants in Ancient Roman Society." *JPS* 2 (1975): 222-35.

Gaster, Theodore H. *The Dead Sea Scriptures*. New York: Bantam Books, 1976.

Geertz, Clifford. *The Interpretation of Cultures*. New York: Basic Books, 1973.

_____. "Religion as a Cultural System." *The Interpretation of Cultures*. New York: Basic Books (1973): 87-125.

Gibbon, Edward. [1776-1788] *The Decline and Fall of the Roman Empire*. Abridged Ed. D. M. Low. New York: Harcourt, Brace and Company, 1960.

Gilkes, L. N. *The Impact of the Dead Sea Scrolls*. London: Macmillan, 1962.

Gilkey, Langdon B. "Secularism's Impact on Contemporary Theology." *Christianity and Crisis* (April 5, 1965).

_____. "The God is Dead Theology and the Possibility of God-Language." *The Voice*. Crozier Theological Seminary (January), 1965.

Gill, Robin. *The Social Context of Theology: A Methodological Enquiry*. London and Oxford: Alden & Mowbray, 1975.

Ginsburg, C. D. *The Essenes*. Grand Rapids, Mich.: Eerdmans, 1956.

Ginzberg, L. *The Legends of the Jews*. 7 vols. Philadelphia: Jewish Public Society, 1937-66.

Glock Charles Y. *Christian Beliefs and Anti-Semitism*. New York: Harper and Row. Goldstein, Jonathan. 1981.

_____. "Jewish Acceptance and Rejection of Hellenism." *Jewish and Christian Self-Definition*, Ed. E. P. Sanders, A. I. Baumgarten, and Alan Mendelson, 64-87. Philadelphia: Fortress, 1966.

_____. and Stark, Rodney. "The Role of Deprivation in the Origin and Evolution of Religious Groups." *Religion and Social Conflict*, Ed. Robert Lee and Martin E. Marty. New York: Oxford University. 1964, 24-36.

Gnilka, Joachim. *Jesus of Nazareth: Message and History*. Peabody, MA: Hendrickson, 1997.

Golb, Norman J. *Who Wrote the Dead Sea Scrolls? The Search for the Secret of Qumran*. New York: Scribner, 1995.

Goldin, J. *Studies in Midrash and Related Literature*. Philadelphia: Jewish Publication Society, 1988.

Goldstein, J. "Jewish Acceptance and Rejection of Hellenism." *Jewish and Christian Self-Definition* 2: *Aspects of Judaism in the Graeco-Roman Period*. Ed. E. P. Sanders et al. Philadelphia: Fortress, 1981.

_____. *1 Maccabees*. Anchor Bible 41. New York: Doubleday, 1976.

Gollwitzer, Helmut. *The Existence of God*. Philadelphia: Westminster, 1965.

Goodenough, E. R. *An Introduction to Philo Judaeus*. 2nd Ed. Blackwell, Oxford: OUP, 1962.

_____. "Literal Mystery in Hellenistic Judaism." *Quantulacumqu Studies Presented to Kirsopp Lake*. Ed. R. P. Casey, S. Lake, and A. Lake. London: Christophers, 1937.

_____. *By Light, Light: The Mystic Gospel of Hellenistic Judaism*. New Haven: Yale University Press, 1935.

_____. *The Church in the Roman Empire: The Berkshire Studies in European History*. New York: Henry Holt, 1931.

Goodman, M. "Jewish Attitudes to Greek Culture in the Period of the Second Temple." *Jewish Education and Learning*. Ed. G. Abramson and T. Parfitt. Chur, Switzerland: Harwood Academic Publishers, 1994.

_____. *The Ruling Class of Judaea: The Origins of the Jewish Revolt against Rome A.D. 66-70*. Cambridge: Cambridge University, 1987.

_____. *State and Society in Roman Galilee A.D. 132—212*. Totowa N.J.: Rowman and Allenheld, 1983.

Gotesky, R. "The Nature of Myth and Society." *The American Anthropologist*. LIV (1952).

Gottwald, Norman K. Ed. *The Hebrew Bible: A Socio-Literary Introduction*. Fortress Press, Philadelphia, 1985.

_____. *The Bible and Liberation: Political and Social Hermeneutics*. Maryknoll, N.Y.: Orbis Books, 1983.

Gould, Stephen Jay. *Questioning the Millennium: A Rationalist's Guide to a Precisely Arbitrary Countdown*. New York: Harmony Books/Crown, 1997.

Grabbe, Lester L. *Judaism from Cyrus to Hadrian*. 2 vols. Minneapolis: Fortress, 1992.

_____. "The Social Setting of Early Jewish Apocalypticism." *Journal for the Study of the Pseudepigrapha* 4 (1989): 27-47.

Graetz, Heinrich. *History of the Jews*. Philadelphia: Jewish Publication of Society, 1944.

Grant, F. E. "Jesus Christ." *IDB* 2 (1962): 869-96.

Grant, Frederick C. *Hellenistic Religions: The Age of Syncretism*. New York: Liberal Arts Press, 1953.

Grant, Robert Michael. *From Alexander to Cleopatra: The Hellenistic World*. New York: Scribner, 1982.

_____. *Jesus After the Gospels: The Christ of the Second Century*. Louisville: Westminster, 1990.

_____. *The History of Rome*. London: Faber and Faber. 1978.

_____. *Early Christianity and Society*. New York: Harper & Row. 1977.

_____. *Augustus to Constantine: The Rise and Triumph of Christianity in the Roman World*. New York: Harper and Row. 1970.

_____. *Theophilus of Antioch*. Oxford: Clarendon Press, 1970.

_____. Ed. *The Apostolic Fathers* (6 vols.) T. Nelson. New York, 1964-1968.

Grayson, A. Gruenwald, Ithamar. "Jewish Apocalypticism to the Rabbinic Period." *Encyclopedia of Religion* 1 (1987): 336-42.

Greeley, Andrew W. *The Christ Myth*. Garden City, NY: Doubleday, 1971.

Green, Henry A. "The Socio-Economic Background of Christianity in Egypt." *The Roots of Egyptian Christianity*. Ed. Birger A. Pearson and James E. Goehring. 100-113. Philadelphia: Fortress, 1986.

_____. *The Economic and Social Origins of Gnosticism*. Atlanta: Scholars Press, 1985.

Green, Joel B. and Turner, Max. Eds. *Jesus of Nazareth, Lord and Christ: Essays on the Historical Jesus and New Testament Christology*. Grand Rapids: Eerdmans, 1994.

Green, W. Scott. Ed. *Approaches to Ancient Judaism*. Vol. 5. *Studies in Judaism in its Greco-Roman Context*. Brown Judaic Studies 32, Atlanta: Scholars Press, 1985.

Greenfield, J. C. and Stone, M. E. "The Books of Enoch and the Traditions of Enoch." *Numen* 26 (1979): 89-103.

Grenfell, B. P. and Hunt, A. S. Eds. and Trans. *Oxyrhynchus Papyri*. Vol. 11. London: Oxford University Press, 1915.

Griffiths, J. G. "Egypt and the Rise of the Synagogue." *JTS* 38 (1987).

_____. "Apocalyptic in the Hellenistic Era." *Apocalypticism in the Mediterranean World and the Near East*. Ed. D. Hellholm. Tubingen: Mohr Siebeck, 1983.

Grimal, Pierre. *The Penguin Dictionary of classical Mythology*. London: Penguin, 1991.

Grintz, J. M. "Hebrew as the Spoken and Written Language in the Last Days of the Second Temple." *JBL* 79 (1960).

Grobel, K. *The Gospel of Truth: A Valentinian Meditation on the Gospel*. New York: Abingdon, 1960.

Gruen, E. *Heritage and Hellenism: The Reinvention of Jewish Tradition*. Berkeley: University of California Press, 1998.

Gruenwald, I. *From Apocalypticism to Gnosticism*. Frankfurt: Peter Lang, 1988.

_____. *Apocalyptic and Merkavah Mysticism*. Leiden: Brill, 1980.

Gryson, Roger. *The Ministry of Women in the Early Church*. Collegeville, MN: Liturgical Press, 1976.

Guignebert, Charles. *Jesus*. New York: University Books, 1956.

Gundry, R. H. *The Use of the Old Testament in St. Matthew's Gospel, with Special Reference to the Messianic Hope*. (Nov) T Sup 18. Leiden: Brill, 1967.

Guthrie, W. K. C. *Orpheus and Greek Religion: A Study of the Orphic Movement*. 2d Ed. London: Methuen, 1952.

Habel, N. C. "The Symbolism of Wisdom in Proverbs 1-9." *Int.* 26 (1972): 131-57.

Habermas, Gary and Flew, Anthony. *Did Jesus Rise from the Dead? The Resurrection Debate*. San Francisco: Harper & Row, 1987.

Hadas, M. and Smith, M. *Heroes and Gods*. New York: Harper and Row, 1965.

Hagner, D. A. *The Jewish Reclamation of Jesus: An Analysis and Critique of the Modem Jewish Study of Jesus*. Grand Rapids: Zondervan, 1984.

Hahn, F. *The Titles of Jesus in Christology*. New York: World, 1969.

Halow, D. C. "The Greek Apocalypse of Baruch (3 Baruch) in Hellenistic Judaism and Early Christianity." *SVTP* 12. Leiden: Brill, 1996.

Hamerton-Kelly, R. G. *Pre-Existence, Wisdom and the Son of Man: A Study of the Idea of Pre-Existence in the New Testament*. Cambridge, University Press, 1973.

Hanson, Paul D. "Apocalypses and Apocalypticism." *Anchor Bible Dictionary* 1 (1992): 279-92.

_____. *Old Testament Apocalyptic*. Nashville: Abingdon, 1987.

_____. Ed. "Visionaries and Their Apocalypses." *Issues in Religion and Theology* 4. Philadelphia: Fortress, 1983.

_____. "Apocalypticism." *Interpreter's Dictionary of the Bible*. Supplement Vol. Nashville: Abingdon, (1976): 27-34.

_____. "Jewish Apocalyptic against Its Near Eastern Environment." *Revue Biblique* 78 (1963): 31-58.

Happold, F. C. *Mysticism: A Study and an Anthology*. Baltimore: Penguin, 1963.

Hardy, E. R. *Christology of the Later Fathers*. Philadelphia: Westminster, 1954.

Harnack, Adolf von. *History of Dogma*. English Ed. London: Williams and Norgate. 1894.

Harrelson, W. "Wisdom Hidden and Revealed According to Baruch (Baruch 3.9-4.4)." *Priests, Prophets and Scribes: Essays on the Formation and Heritage of Second Temple Judaism in Honor of Joseph Blenkinsopp.* Ed. E. Ulrich et. al. 158-71. *JSOTSS* 149. Sheffield, England: JSOT Press, 1992.

Harrington, Daniel J. "The Jewishness of Jesus: Facing Some Problems." *Jesus' Jewishness: Exploring the Place of Jesus in Early Judaism.* Ed. James Charlesworth. New York: Herder, 1996, 123-152.

_____. "Sociological Concepts and the Early Church: A Decade of Research." *TS* 41 (1980): 181-90.

Harris, O. G. "The Social World of Early Christianity." *Lexington Theological Quarterly* 19 (1984): 102-14.

Harrison, P. N. *Polycarp's Two Epistles.* Cambridge: Cambridge University, 1936.

Hartlich, Christian. "Historical-Critical Method in its Application to Statements Concerning Events in the Holy Scriptures." *JHC* 2/2 (Fall, 1995): 122-139.

Harvey, Andrew. *Teachings of the Christian Mystics.* Shalmbala, 1998.

_____. *Jesus and the Constraints of History.* Philadelphia: Westminster, 1982.

Hayes, John H. *Son of God to Superstar: Twentieth Century Interpretations of Jesus.* Nashville: Abingdon, 1976.

Hayim Goren. *Jesus the Jew: A Jewish Perspective.* Collegeville, MN: Liturgica Press, 1994.

Hechter, Michael. *Principles of Group Solidarity.* Berkeley: University of California. 1987.

Hedrick, Charles. *The Historical Jesus and the Rejected Gospels.* Semeia 44. Scholars Press, 1988.

_____. *The Apocalypse of Adam.* Chico, California: Scholars Press, 1980.

Hegedus, Tim. "Social Scientific Approaches to the Urban Expansion of the Cult of Isis in the Greco-Roman World: An Analysis Based on Forty-four Cities." Un-pub. paper. Centre for Religious Studies, University of Toronto. 1994.

Hegel, G. W. F. *Phenomenology of Mind.* New York: Humanities, n. d.

_____. *Science of Logic.* Trans. W. H. Johnson and L. G. Struthers. New York: Humanities, n. d.

Hegermann, H. "The Diaspora in the Hellenistic Age." *The Cambridge History of Judaism.* Volume 2: *The Hellenistic Age.* Ed. W. D. Davies and L. Finkelstein. Cambridge: Cambridge University Press, 1989.

Hellholm, David, Ed. *Apocalypticism in the Mediterranean World and the Near East.* Tubingen: J. C. B. Mohr (Paul Siebeck), 1983.

Hengel, Martin and Schwemer, Anna M. *Paul Between Damascus and Antioch: The Unknown Years.* London: SCM Press, 1997.

_____. *The Pre-Christian Paul.* London: SCM Press, 1991.

_____. *The Johannine Question.* London: SCM Press, 1989.

_____. *Between Jesus and Paul.* London: SCM Press, 1983.

_____. *The Atonement: A Study of the Origins of the Doctrine in the New Testament.* London: SCM Press, 1981.

_____. *The Charismatic Leader and his Followers.* Edinburgh: T. and T. Clark, 1981.

_____. *Acts and the History of Earliest Christianity.* London: SCM Press, 1979.

_____. *Crucifixion.* London: SCM Press, 1977.

_____. *The Son of God: The Origin of Christology and the History of Jewish-Hellenistic Religion.* Philadelphia: Fortress, 1976.

_____. *Judaism and Hellenism: Studies in Their Encounter in Palestine during the Early Hellenistic Period.* 2 vols. Philadelphia: Fortress, 1974.

_____. *Was Jesus a revolutionist?* Philadelphia: Fortress Press, Facet Books, 1971.

Hennecke, E. and Schneemelcher, W. Eds. *New Testament Apocrypha* (2 vols.) ET: Philadelphia: Westminster, 1963.

Herford, R. Travers. *Christianity in Talmud and Midrash.* Reference Book Publishers, Clifton, N.J.: 1966.

Heschel, Abraham Joshua. *God in Search of Man: A Philosophy of Judaism.* New York: Meridian Books, 1955.

Hilgenfeld, Adolf. *Review of the Hymn of the Soul, by A. A. Bevan.* Berliner Philologische Wochensckrift 13 [or 15] (1898): 389-95.

Hill, C. C. *Hellenists and Hebrews: Reappraising Division within the Earliest Church.* Minneapolis: Fortress, 1992.

Himmelfarb, Martha. *Ascent to Heaven in Jewish and Christian Apocalypses.* York: Oxford University Press, 1993.

_____. "Apocalyptic Ascent and the Heavenly Temple." *SBL* (1987): 210-17, Seminar Papers. Ed. Kent H Richards. Atlanta: Scholars Press, 1987.

_____. *Tours of Hell: An Apocalyptic Form in Jewish and Christian Literature.* Philadelphia: Fortress, 1983.

Hippolytus, *Philosophoumena; or, The Refutation of all Heresies.* Trans. Francis Legge. London: Society for Promoting Christian Knowledge, 1921.

Hobsbawn, E. "Peasants and Polities." *JPS* 1 (1974): 3-23.

Hock, Ronald F. *The Social Context of Paul's Ministry: Tentmaking and Apostleship.* Philadelphia: Fortress Press, 1980.

Hoenig, S. *The Great Sanhedrin.* Philadelphia: Dropsie College, 1953.

Hoffmann, R. Joseph. *On the Restitution of Christianity: An Essay on the Development of Radical Paulinist Theology in the Second Century.* AAR Academy Series 46; Chico, Calif.: Scholars Press, 1984.

Holladay, C. R. "Jewish Responses to Hellenistic Culture in Early Ptolemaic Egypt." *Hellenistic Egypt.* Ed. P. Bilde et al. Aarhus: Aarhus University Press, 1992.

Hollander, H. W. and de Jonge, M. "The Testaments of the Twelve Patriarchs: A Commentary.*" SVTP* 8. Leiden: Brill, 1985.

Hollenbach, Paul W. "Recent Historical Jesus Studies and the Social Sciences." *SBL* 1983 Seminar Papers. Ed. Kent H. Richards. Chico, California: Scholars Press, 1983, 61-78.

_____. "The Historical Jesus Question in North America Today." *Biblical Theology Bulletin* 19 (1989): 11-22.

Honigman, S. "The Birth of a Diaspora: The Emergence of a Jewish Self-Definition in Ptolemaic Egypt in the Light of Onomastics." *Diasporas in Antiquity.* Ed. S. J. D. Cohen and E. Frerichs. Atlanta: Scholars Press, 1993.

Hooker, Morna D. "Christology and Methodology." *NTS* 7 (1971): 480-88.

_____.. *The Signs of a Prophet. The Prophetic Actions of Jesus.* London: SCM Press and Harrisburg, Penn.: Trinity, 1997.

Hoppe, L. *The Synagogues and Churches of Ancient Palestine.* Collegeville, Minn.: Michael Glazier- Liturgical Press, 1994.

422

Hopper, Stanley R. "On the Naming of the Gods in Holderlin and Rilke." *Christianity and the Existentialists.* Ed. Carl Michalson. New York: Scribner, 1956.

Horbury, William. *Jewish Messianism and the Cult of Christ.* London: SCM, 1998.

_____. and Noy, D. *Jewish Inscriptions of Graeco-Roman Egypt.* Cambridge: Cambridge University Press, 1992.

_____. "The Messianic Associations of 'The Son of Man.'" *JTS* 36 (1985): 34-55.

Horner, George William. Trans. *Pistis Sophia.* Intro. George Francis Legge. London: Society for Promoting Christian Knowledge, 1924.

Horsley, Richard. *Archaeology, History, and Society in Galilee: The Social Context of Jesus and the Rabbis.* Valley Forge, PA: Trinity, 1996.

_____. "High Priests and Politics in Roman Palestine." *JSJ* 17 (1986): 23-55.

_____. "The Zealots: Their Origin, Relationship and Importance in the Jewish Revolt." *NT* 18 (1986): 159-92.

_____. "Popular Messianic Movements around the Time of Jesus." *CBQ* 46 (1984): 475-95.

_____. "Ancient Jewish Banditry and the Revolt against Rome." *CBQ* 43 (1981): 409-32.

_____. *Sociology and the Jesus Movement.* New York: Crossroad, 1989.

_____. *Jesus and the Spiral of Violence: Popular Jewish Resistance in Roman Palestine.* San Francisco: Harper, 1987.

_____. "'Like One of the Prophets of Old:' Two Types of Popular Prophets at the Time of Jesus." *CBQ* 47 (1985): 435-63.

_____. "Spiritual Marriage with Sophia." *VC* 33 (1979): 30-54.

_____. "The Law of Nature in Philo and Cicero." *HTR* 71 (1978): 35-39.

Howard, G. "The Letter of Aristeas and Diaspora Judaism." *JTS* 22 (1971): 337-48.

Howlett, D. *The Essenes and Christianity.* New York: Harper & Row, 1957.

Hughes, Graham. *Hebrews and Hermeneutics.* Cambridge University, 1979.

Hunt, Morton. *The Universe Within: A New Science Explores the Human Mind*. New York: Simon and Schuster, A Touchstone Book, 1982.

Huxley, Julian. *Religion Without Revelation*. New York: Mentor, 1958.

Hyatt, J. Philip. Ed. *The Bible in Modern Scholarship*. Nashville: Abingdon Press, 1965.

Hynes, W. J. *Shirley Jackson Case and the Chicago School: The Socio-Historical Method*. Chico, Calif.: Scholars Press, 1981.

Irenaeus. *Adversus haereses. St. Irenaeus of Lyons against the Heresies*. Trans. Dominic J. Unger and John J. Dillon. New York: Paulist Press, 1992.

Isenberg, Sheldon R. "Some Uses and Limitations of Social Scientific Methodology in the Study of Early Christianity." *SBL* 1980 Seminar Papers. 29-49. Ed. Paul J. Achtemeier. Chico, California: Scholars Press, 1980.

_____. "Power Through Temple and Torah in Greco-Roman Palestine." *Christianity, Judaism and Other Graeco-Roman Cults*. Pt. 2. *Early Christianity*. Ed. J. Neusner, 24-52. Leiden: Brill, 1975.

_____. "Millenarism in Greco-Roman Palestine." *Religion* 4 (1974): 26-46.

Jacobson, Arland. *The First Gospel: An Introduction to Q*. Polebridge Press, Calif., 1992.

_____. "The History of the Composition of the Sayings Source Q." *SBL* Seminar Papers, 1987.

_____. "The Literary Unity of Q." *JBL* 101 (1982): 365-89.

Jagersma, H. *A History of Israel from Alexander the Great to Bar Kochba*. Trans. J. Bowden. Philadelphia: Fortress, 1986.

James, Montague Rhodes. *Apocrypha Anecdota*. 2nd series. Cambridge: Cambridge University Press, 1897.

Jasper, Karl. *Nietzsche and Christianity*. Chicago: Gateway, 1961.

_____. *The Origin and Goal of History*. Trans. Michael Bullock. London: Routledge and Kegan Paul Ltd., 1953.

Jenks, G. C. "The Origin and Early Development of the Antichrist Myth." *BZNW* 59. Berlin: de Gruyter, 1991.

Jenson, Robert W. *Alpha and Omega*. New York: Nelson, 1963.

Jeppesen, K. et al. Eds. *In the Last Days: On Jewish and Christian Apocalyptic and Its Period*. Aartius: Aarhus University Press, 1994.

Jeremias, Joachim. *Jerusalem in the Time of Jesus: An Investigation into Economic and Social Conditions during the New Testament Period*. Trans. F. H. Cave and C. H. Cave. London: SCM, 1969.

――――. *The Eucharistic Words of Jesus*. New York: Scribner, 1966.

――――. *The Problem of the Historical Jesus*. Philadelphia: Fortress, 1964.

Johns, Lindley Ross. *The Historic Origin of the Jesus Myth*. Th.D. Diss. Florida Theological University, *Research Abstracts*. University Microfilms International, 1991.

Johnson, F. Ernest, Ed. *Religious Symbolism*. New York: Institute for Religions and Social Studies, 1955.

Johnson, Luke T. "The Search for (the Wrong) Jesus." *Bible Review* 11 (1995): 20-25, 44.

――――. *The Real Jesus: The Misguided Quest for the Historical Jesus and the Truth of the Traditional Gospels*. San Francisco: Harper, 1995.

Johnson, M. D. "Reflections on a Wisdom Approach to Matthew's Christology." CBQ 36 (1974): 44-64.

Johnson, Thomas F. "Sectarianism and the Johannine Community." *JBL*. Originally read at the Society of Biblical Literature annual meeting, Atlanta, Georgia, November 23, 1986.

Jonas, Hans. *The Gnostic Religion: The Message of the Alien God and the Beginnings of Christianity*. 2nd Ed. Rev. Boston: Beacon, 1963.

Jonge, Marinus de. *Jesus, the Servant Messiah*. New Haven: Yale University, 1991.

――――. *Jesus: Stranger from Heaven and Son of God. SBLSBS* 11. Missoula, Mont.: Scholars Press, 1977.

Josephus, Flavius. [Ca. 100.] *Complete Works*. Trans. W. Whiston Kregel. Grand Rapids, 1973.

Judge, Edwin A. "The Social Identity of the First Christians: A Question of Method in Religious History." *JRH* 11 (1980): 201-17.

――――. "The Early Christians as a Scholastic Community." *JRH* 1 (1960-61): 4-15, 125-37.

――――. *The Social Pattern of Christian Groups in the First Century*. London: Tyndale. 1960.

Julian (the "Apostate"). Orations 4 and 5 in *The Works of the Emperor Julian*. Loeb Classical Library (Greek & English) Cambridge, Mass.: Harvard University, 1980.

Jung, C. G. *Knowing the Truth: A Sociological Approach to New Testament Interpretation.* Minneapolis: Fortress, 1989.

_____. *Aion: Researches into the Phenomenology of the Self* (Collected Works, vol. ix, part 2). New York: Pantheon, 1959.

Kalthoff, Albert. *The Rise of Christianity.* London: Watts & Co., 1907.

Kanter, Rosabeth Moss. *Commitment and Community.* Cambridge: Harvard University, 1972.

Karlsaune, Erik. Ed. *Religion as a Social Phenomenon: Theologians and Sociologists Sharing Research Interests.* Trondheim: Tapir, 1988.

Kasemann, Ernst. "The Problem of the Historical Jesus." *Essays on New Testament Themes.* Philadelphia: Fortress, 1982.

_____. "On New Testament Apocalyptic." *In New Testament Questions of Today.* London: SCM, 1959. 108-138.

Katz, Steven T. "Issues in the Separation of Judaism and Christianity after 70 C.E.: A Reconsideration." *Journal of Biblical Literature* (1984): 103:43-76.

Kautsky, Karl. *Foundations of Christianity.* Trans. Henry F. Mins. New York: Russell & Russell, 1953.

Keck, Leander E. "On the Ethos of Early Christians." *JAAR* 42 (1974): 435-52.

Kee, Howard Clark. *Miracle in the Early Christian World: A Study in Sociohistorical Method.* New Haven: Yale University, 1983.

_____. *Christian Origins in Sociological Perspective: Methods and Resources.* Philadelphia: Westminster, 1980.

_____. *Jesus in History: An Approach to the Study of the Gospels.* 2d Ed. New York: Harcourt, Brace, Jovanovich, 1977.

_____. *Community of the New Age: Studies in Mark's Gospel.* Philadelphia: Westminster, 1977.

Kelber, W. H. *The Oral and the Written Gospel.* Philadelphia: Fortress Press, 1983.

Kelly, J. N. D. *Early Christian Doctrines.* San Francisco: Harper, 1960.

Kennedy, H. A. A. *St. Paul and the Mystery Religions*. London: Hodder and Stoughton, 1913.

Kirk. G. S. *The Nature of Greek Myths*. Baltimore: Penguin, 1974.

Kisemann, Ernst. *The Testament of Jesus*. London: SCM Press, 1968.

Kittel, G. and G. Friedrich. Eds. *The Theological Dictionary of the New Testament*. 10 vols. Grand Rapids, Mich.: Eerdmans, 1964-1976.

Klausner, Joseph. *The Messianic Idea in Israel from the Beginning to the Completion of the Mishnah*. New York: Macmillan, 1955.

_____. *Jesus of Nazareth*. London: George Alien & Unwin, 1947.

_____. *From Jesus to Paul*. Trans. William F. Stinespring. Boston: Beacon, 1943.

Kloppenborg, John S. "The Sayings Gospel Q and the Quest of the Historical Jesus." *Harvard Theological Review* 89/4 (1996): 307-344.

_____. "The Transformation of Moral Exhortation in Didache 1-5." *The Didache in Context*. Ed., Clayton Jefford, 88-109. Leiden: E. j. Brill, 1995.

_____. "Isis and Sophia in the Book of Wisdom." *HTR* 75 (1982): 57-84.

_____. *Q Parallels: Synopsis, Critical Notes, and Concordance*. Sonoma, Calif.: Polebridge, 1988.

_____. "Wisdom Christology in Q." *LTP* 34 (1978): 129-47.

Knibb, M. A. *Jubilees and the Origins of the Qumran Community: An Inaugural Lecture in the Dept. of Biblical Studies, King's College*. London: King's College, 1989.

_____. "Apocalyptic and Wisdom in Fourth Ezra." *JSJ* 13 (1982): 56-79.

Knight, Christopher and Robert Lomas. *The Second Messiah*. Boston: Element, 1997.

Knox, John. *Marcion and the New Testament: An Essay in the Early History of the Canon*. Chicago: University of Chicago, 1942.

Knox. W. E. "The Divine Wisdom." *JTS* 38 (1937): 230-37.

Koch, Klaus. "The Rediscovery of Apocalyptic." *SBT*. 2d. series. 22. 1970.

Koester, Helmut. "The Disappearance of the 'God-Fearers.'" *Diaspora Jews and Judaism: Essays in Honor of, and in Dia-*

logue with, A. Thomas Kraabel. Ed. J. A. Overman and R.
S. MacLennan. Atlanta: Scholars Press, 1992.
_____. *Ancient Christian Gospels: Their History and Develop-
ment*. Philadelphia: Trinity, 1990.
_____. "Monastic Jewish Women in Greco-Roman Egypt: Philo
of Alexandria on the Therapeutrides." *Signs* 14 (1989):
345-80.
_____. *History, Culture and Religion of the Hellenistic Age*. New
York: Walter de Gruyter, 1987.
_____. "History and Development of Mark's Gospel." *Colloquy
on New Testament Studies: A Time for Reappraisal and
Fresh Approaches*, 35-57. Bruce Corley, Ed., 1983.
_____. *Introduction to the New Testament* (Vol. 1: *History, Cul-
ture and Religion of the Hellenistic Age*. Vol.2: *History
and Literature of Early Christianity*). Philadelphia: For-
tress, 1982.
_____. "Apocryphal and Canonical Gospels." *HTR* 73 (1980):
105-130.
_____. "Nomos Physeos: The Concept of Natural Law in Greek
Thought." *Religions in Antiquity: Essays in Memory of E.
R. Goodenough*. Ed. J. Neusner. Leiden: Brill, 1968.
Kohler, Kaufmann. "Wisdom." *The Jewish Encyclopedia*. Ed. I.
Singer. 12:537-8. New York: Funk & Wagnalls, 1901-6.
Kortner, Ulrich H. J. *The End of the World: A Theological
Interpretation*. Louisville: John Knox, 1995.
Kraeling, C. H. "The Jewish Community at Antioch." *JBL* 51
(1932): 130-60.
_____. *The Excavations at Dura-Europas: The Synagogue*. New
Haven: Yale University, 1956.
Kraft, Robert. *Barnabas and the Didache*. Vol. 3. In *The Apostolic
Fathers*. Ed., Robert Grant, 20. New York: Thomas
Nelson, 1965.
Kreuziger, Frederick A. *Apocalypse and Science Fiction: A
Dialectic of Religious and Secular Soteriologies*. Chicago:
Scholars Press, 1982.
Kuhrt, A., and S. Sherwin-White Eds. *Hellenism in the East*.
London: Duckworth, 1987.
Kvanvig, Helge S. "The Relevance of the Biblical Visions of the
End Time: Hermeneutical Guidelines to the Apocalyptic
Literature." *Horizons of Biblical Theology* 11 (1989): 35-
58.

_____. "Roots of Apocalyptic: The Mesopotamian Background of the Enoch Figure and of the Son of Man." *WMANT* 61. Neukirchen-Vluyn: Neukirchener, 1988.

Kyrtatas, Dimitris J. *The Social Structure of the Early Christian Communities*. London: Methuen & Co, 1987.

Lacroix, Jean Paul. *The Meaning of Modern Atheism*. New York: Macmillan, 1965.

Ladd, George Eldon. "The Place of Apocalyptic in Biblical Religion." *Evangelical Quarterly* 30 (1958): 75-85.

Lake, Kirsopp, Trans. *The Apostolic Fathers* (2 vols.) *Loeb Classical Library* (Greek & English). 1912-13.

Lancellotti, Maria Grazia. *Attis: Between Myth and History*. Brill, Leiden, 2002.

Lang, B. *Wisdom and the Book of Proverbs: A Hebrew Goddess Redefined*. New York: Pilgrim, 1986.

Lapide, Pinch. *Encountering Jesus - Encountering Judaism*. New York: Crossroad, 1987.

Layton, Bentley. *The Gnostic Scriptures*. New York: Doubleday, 1987.

Lease, Gary. "Mithraism and Christianity." *ANRW* 11.23.2 (1987): 1306-1332.

Leach, E. *Culture and Communication: The Logic by Which Symbols Are Connected*. Cambridge: Cambridge University, 1976.

Lebram, J. C. H. "The Piety of the Jewish Apocalyptists." In *Apocalypticism in the Mediterranean World and the Near East*. Ed. D. Hellholm, 171-210. 2nd Ed. Tubingen: J. C. B. Mohr (Paul Siebeck), 1989.

Leclant, Jean. "The Cults of Isis among the Greeks and the Roman Empire," *Greek and Egyptian Mythologies*. Comp. Yves Bonnefoy and Wendy Doniger. Trans. Gerald Honigsblum et. al. 4 vols. Vol. 5, 245-51. Chicago: University of Chicago, 1992.

Legge, Francis. *Forerunners and Rivals of Christianity*. New York: University Books, 1964.

Leipoldt, Johannes "The Resurrection Stories, A Religious-Historical Perspective." *JHC* 4/1 (Spring, 1997): 138-149.

Leon, H. J. *The Jews of Ancient Rome*. Philadelphia: Jewish Publication Society, 1960.

Levine, L. I. *The Rabbinic Class of Roman Palestine in Late An-tiquity.* New York: Jewish Theological Seminary of America, 1989.

_____. "Ancient Synagogues: A Historical Introduction." *Ancient Synagogues Revealed.* Ed. L. I. Levine. Jerusalem: Israel Exploration Society, 1981.

_____. Ed. *Ancient Synagogues Revealed.* Jerusalem: Israel Exploration Society, 1981.

_____. "Rabbi Abbahu of Caesarea." *Christianity, Judaism and Other Greco-Roman Cults: Studies for Morton Smith at Sixty.* 4. Ed. J. Neusner. Leiden: Brill, 1975.

Lewis, John Wren. "Does Science Destroy Belief?" *Faith, Fact and Fantasy.* London: Fontana, 1964.

Lietzmann, Hans. *A History of the Early Church.* 4 Vols. Trans. Bertram Lee Woolf. New York: World, Meridian Books, I and II, 1953.

Lightstone, J. N. "The Commerce of the Sacred: Mediation of the Divine among Jews in the Graeco-Roman Diaspora." *BJS* 59. Chico, Calif.: Scholars Press, 1984.

Lightley, J. W. *Jewish Sects and Parties in the Time of Jesus.* London: Epworth, 1925.

Lohse, E. *The New Testament Environment.* Trans. J. E. Steely. Nashville: Abingdon, 1976.

Long, A. A. and Sedley, D. N. *The Hellenistic Philosophers.* Cambridge: Cambridge University Press, 1987.

_____. *Hellenistic Philosophy.* Duckworth, London, 1977.

Ludemann, Gerd. *What Really Happened to Jesus? A Historical Approach to the Resurrection.* Louisville: John Knox, 1996.

_____. "Concerning the History of Earliest Christianity in Rome: I. Valentinus and Marcion; II. Ptolemaeus and Justin." *JHC* 2/1 (Spring, 1995): 112-141.

_____. *The Resurrection of Jesus: History, Experience, Theology.* London: SCM Press, 1995.

_____. "The Acts of the Apostles and the Beginnings of Simonian Gnosis." *NTS* 33 (1987): 279-359.

Maccoby, Hyam. *Judaism in the First Century.* London: Sheldon, 1989.

_____. *Paul and Hellenism.* Philadelphia: Trinity, 1991.

Macdonald, Alexander B. *Christian Worship in the Primitive Church.* Edinburgh: T. & T. Clark, 1934.

Mach, M. "From Apocalypticism to Early Jewish Mysticism." *The Encyclopedia of Apocalypticism*. Volume 1: *The Origins of Apocalypticism in Judaism and Christianity*. Ed. J. J. Collins. New York: Continuum, 1998.

Mack, Burton L. *Studies in Hellenistic Judaism*. Atlanta: Scholars Press, 1991.

_____. "Wisdom and Apocalyptic in Philo." *Studia Philonica Annual*. Ed. David T. Runia (1991): 3:21-39.

_____. *A Myth of Innocence: Mark and Christian Origins*. Philadelphia: Fortress, 1988.

_____. "Wisdom, Myth, and Mythology." *Int* 24 (1970): 46-60.

Mackey, James P. *Jesus, the Man and the Myth: A Contemporary Christology*. New York: Paulist Press, 1979.

MacMullen, Ramsay and Lane, Eugene N. Eds. *Paganism and Christianity 100-425 CE: A Sourcebook*. Minneapolis: Fortress, 1992.

_____. *Paganism in the Roman Empire*. New Haven: Yale University, 1981.

_____. *Roman Social Relations: 50 B.C. to A.D. 284*. New Haven: Yale University, 1974.

Macquarrie, John. *The Scope of Demythologizing: Bultmann and his Critics*. New York: Harper & Row, Harper Torchbooks, The Cloister Library, 1960.

MacRae, George W. "Sleep and Awakening in Gnostic Texts." *Le origini dello Gnosticismo*. Ed. U. Bianchi. (1970): 496-507.

_____. "The Jewish Background of the Gnostic Sophia Myth." *Novunt Testamentum*. XII (1970): 86-101.

Malherbe, Abraham J. "Moral Exhortation: A Greco-Roman Sourcebook." *Library of Early Christianity* 4. Philadelphia: Westminster, 1989.

_____. *Paul and the Popular Philosophers*. Minneapolis: Fortress, 1989.

_____. *Social Aspects of Early Christianity*. 2d Enlarged Ed. Philadelphia: Fortress, 1983.

_____. Ed. and Trans. "The Cynic Epistles." *Sources for Biblical Study* 12. Missoula, Mont.: Scholars Press, 1977.

Malina, Bruce J. "Jesus as Astral Prophet." *Biblical Theology Bulletin* 27/3 (1997): 83-99.

_____. *Windows on the World of Jesus: Time Travel to Ancient Judea*. Louisville: Westminster, 1993.

431

_____. and Richard L. Rohrbaugh. *Social-Science Commentary on the Synoptic Gospels*. Minneapolis: Fortress, 1992.

_____. *Calling Jesus Names: The Social Value of Labels in Matthew*. Sonona: Polebridge, 1988.

_____. *Christian Origins and Cultural Anthropology*. Atlanta: John Knox. 1986.

_____. "Normative Dissonance and Christian Origins." *Social-Scientific Criticism of the New Testament*. Ed. John H. Elliott, 1986, 35-59.

_____. *The Gospel of John in Sociolinguistic Perspective*. 48 Berkeley, Calif.: the Center for Hermeneutical Studies in Hellenistic and Modern Culture, 1985.

_____. "The Social Sciences and Biblical Interpretation." *The Bible and Liberation: Political and Social Hermeneutics*. Ed. N. K. Gottwald. Maryknoll, N.Y.: Orbis, 1983, 11-25.

_____. *The New Testament World: Insights from Cultural Anthropology*. Atlanta: John Knox, 1981.

Malina-Jacobs, Diane. "Gender, Power, and Jesus' Identity in the Gospels." *Biblical Theology Bulletin* (1994): 158-66.

Malinowski, Bronislaw. *Myth in Primitive Psychology*. Westport, Conn.: University Press, 1971.

Manson, T. W. *Ancient Egypt: Light of the World.* 2 vols. London: Stuart &Watkins, 1970.

_____. "The Quest of the Historical Jesus -- Continued." *STUDIES IN THE GOSPEL AND EPISTLES*. Ed. M. Black. Manchester: MUP (1962): 3-12.

_____. "The Life of Jesus: A Study of the Available Materials." *BJRL* 27 (1943): 323-38.

_____. *The Historical Jesus and the Mythical Christ*. Springfield: Star Publishing, 1886.

Manson, William. *The Servant-Messiah: A Study of the Public Ministry of Jesus*. Cambridge: Cambridge University, 1953.

Mantel, Hugo. "The Causes of the Bar Kokba Revolt." *JQR* 58 (1968): 224-242, 274-296.

Marsh, C. "Quests of the Historical Jesus in New Historicist Perspective." *Biblical Interpretation* 5 (1997): 403-437.

Martini, Cardinal Carlo Maria. "Christianity and Judaism: A Historical and Theological Overview." James H. Charlesworth. Ed. *Jews and Christians: Exploring the Past, Present, and Future,* 19-34. New York: Crossroad, 1990.

Martyn, J. Louis. *History and Theology in the Fourth Gospel.* 2nd Ed. Rev. and Enlrg. Nashville: Abingdon, 1979.

Marxsen, Willi. *The Resurrection of Jesus of Nazareth.* Fortress, 1970.

Mason, S. *Flavius Josephus on the Pharisees: A Composition-Critical Study.* Leiden: Brill, 1990.

Matthews, Shailer. *New Testament Times in Palestine.* Rev. Ed. New York: Macmillan, 1933.

May, Gerhard. "Marcion in Contemporary Views: Results and Open Questions." *The Second Century* (1987-1988): 6:129-151.

McCormack, Thomas Joseph. Trans. *The Mysteries of Mithra.* Franz Cumont. Chicago: Open Court, 1903.

McFague, Sally. *Metaphorical Theology: Models of God in Religious Language.* Philadelphia: Fortress, 1982.

_____. *Speaking in Parables: A Study in Metaphor and Theology.* Philadelphia: Fortress, 1975.

McGinn, Bernard. "Early Apocalypticism: The Ongoing Debate." *The Apocalypse in English Renaissance Thought and Literature.* Ed. C. A. Patrides and Joseph Wittreich. 2-39. Ithaca, NY: Cornell University, 1984.

_____. "Apocalypticism in the Western Tradition. And Apocalyptic Spirituality." *Classics of Western Spirituality.* New York: Paulist Press, 1979.

McKnight, Edgar V. *What Is Form Criticism? (Guides to Biblical Scholarship).* Philadelphia: Fortress, 1969.

McKnight, S. *A Light among the Gentiles: Jewish Missionary Activity in the Second Temple Period.* Minneapolis: Fortress, 1991.

Mead, George Robert Stow. *The Gnostic John the Baptizer: Selections from the Mandaean John-Book, Together with Studies on John and Christian origins, the Slavonic Josephus' Account of John and Jesus, and John and the Fourth Gospel Proem.* London: Watkins, 1924.

_____. *The Gnosis of the Mind. Echoes from the Gnosis 1.* London: Theosophical Publishing Society, 1906.

_____. *Thrice-Greatest Hermes: Studies in Hellenistic Theosophy and Gnosis, Being a Translation of the Extant Sermons and Fragments of the Trismegistic Literature.* 3 vols. London: Theosophical Publishing Society, 1906.

_____. *Fragments of a Faith Forgotten: Some Short Sketches among the Gnostics, Mainly of the First Two Centuries*. London: Theosophical Publishing Society, 1900. 2nd. Ed., 1906.

_____. "Notes on the Eleusinian Mysteries," *Theosophical Review* 22 (April 1898): 145-57.

_____. *Pistis Sophia: A Gnostic Gospel (with Extracts from the Books of the Savior Appended) Originally Translated from Greek into Coptic and Now for the First Time Englished from Schwartze's Latin Version of the Only Known Coptic MS. and Checked by Amelineau's French Version*. London: Theosophical Publishing Society, 1896.

_____. *Plotinus*. London: Theosophical Publishing Society, 1895.

_____. *Simon Magus: An Essay*. London: Theosophical Publishing Society, 1892.

Meecham, H. G. *The Epistle to Diognetus*. Manchester: Manchester University, 1949.

_____. *The Letter of Aristeas*. Manchester: Manchester University Press, 1935.

Meeks, Wayne A. *The Origins of Christian Morality. The First Two Centuries*. New Haven: Yale University, 1993.

_____. "Social Functions of Apocalyptic Language in Pauline Christianity." *Hellholm* (1983): 687-705.

_____. "The Social Context of Pauline Theology." *Interpretation* 36 (1982): 267-77.

_____. and R. A. Wilken. *Jews and Christians in Antioch in the First Four Centuries of the Common Era*. Missoula, Mont.: Scholars Press, 1978.

_____. "'Am I a Jew?' -- Johannine Christianity and Judaism." *Christianity, Judaism and Other Greco-Roman Cults: Studies for Morton Smith at Sixty*. Ed. Jacob Neusner, 1:163-186. 4 vols. *SJLA* 1 Leiden: E. J. Brill, 1975.

_____.. "The Image of the Androgyne: Some Uses of a Symbol in Earliest Christianity." *HR* 13 (1974): 165-208.

_____. "The Man from Heaven in Johannine Sectarianism." *JBL* 91 (1972): 44-72.

_____. "The Prophet-King: Moses Traditions and the Johannine Christology." (Nov.) *T Sup* 14. Leiden: E. J. Brill, 1967.

Meier, John P. *A Marginal Jew: Rethinking the Historical Jesus*. Vol. 1. Garden City, New York: Doubleday, 1991.

_____. "Evidence for Jesus Outside the Bible." *Bible Review* 6/1 (1991): 20-25.

Mendelson, A. *Secular Education in Philo of Alexandria.* Cincinnati: Hebrew Union College, 1982.

Merkur, Daniel. *Gnosis: An Esoteric Tradition of Mystical Visions and Unions.* Albany, NY: State University of New York, 1993.

Merleau-Ponty, Maurice. *The Primacy of Perception.* Ed. and Intro. James M. Edie. New York: Northwest University, 1964.

Metzger, Bruce. *A Textual Commentary on the Greek New Testament.* New York: United Bible Societies, 1977.

_____. *The Canon of the New Testament: Its Origin, Development and Significance.* Oxford: Oxford University Press, 1987.

Meyer, Marvin W. *The Gospel of Thomas: The Hidden Sayings of Jesus.* San Francisco: Harper, 1993.

Meyerhoff, Hans. *The Philosophy of History in Our Times.* New York: Doubleday, 1959.

Meyers, Eric M. "Early Judaism and Christianity in the Light of Archaeology." *Biblical Archaeologist* (1988): 51:69-79.

_____. "Galilean Regionalism as a Factor in Historical Reconstruction." *BASOR* 221 (1976): 95-101.

Milik, J. T. with Black, M. *The Books of Enoch: Aramaic Fragments of Qumran Cave 4.* Oxford: Clarendon, 1976.

_____. *Ten Years of Discovery in the Wilderness of Judea.* London: SCM, 1959.

Miller, Alan S., and John P. Hoffman. "Risk and Religion: An Explanation of Gender Differences in Religiosity." *Journal for the Scientific Study of Religion* (1995): 34:63-75.

Miller, David. "The Symbolizing of the Symbol," *Brethren Life and Thought.* (Summer, 1963).

Miller, Joseph Hillis. *The Disappearance of God: Five Nineteenth Century Writers.* Cambridge: Harvard University, 1963.

Miller, Robert J. Ed. *The Complete Gospels.* San Francisco: Harper, 1994.

Minear, Paul S. *New Testament Apocalyptic: Interpreting Biblical Texts.* Nashville: Abingdon, 1981.

Mink, Hans Aage. "The Use of Scripture in the Temple Scroll and the Status of the Scroll as Law," *SJOT* 1 (1987): 20-50.

Momigliano, A. *On Pagans, Jews, and Christians.* Middletown, CT: Wesleyan University, 1987.

_____. *Alien Wisdom: The Limits of Hellenization.* Cambridge: Cambridge University, 1975.

Montefiore, C. G. *Lectures on the Origin and Growth of Religion.* 2nd Ed. London: Williams and Norgate, 1893.

Moore, G. F. *Judaism in the First Centuries of the Christian Era: The Age of the Tannaim.* New York: Shocken, 1971.

Moore, Hamilton. "The Problem of Apocalyptic as Evidence in Recent Discussion." *Irish Biblical Studies* 8 (1986): 76-91.

Morenz, S. *Egyptian Religion.* Trans. Ann E. Keep. London: Methuen, 1973.

Morgan, Robert, Ed. "The Nature of New Testament Theology." *SET* 25, London: SCM, 1973.

Morris, L. *Apocalyptic.* Grand Rapids: Eerdmans, 1972.

Moule, C. F. D. *The Birth of the New Testament.* New York: Harper & Row, 1962.

Mowry, L. *The Dead Sea Scrolls and the Early Church.* Chicago: University of Chicago Press, 1962.

Mulder, Jan M., Ed. *Mikra, Text, Translation and Interpretation of the Hebrew Bible in Ancient Judaism and Early Christianity.* Philadelphia: Fortress, 1988.

Munby, D. L. *The Idea of a Secular society and Its Significance for Christians.* Oxford: Oxford University, 1963.

Murphy, Frederick. J. *The Religious World of Jesus: An Introduction to Second Temple Palestinian Judaism.* Nashville: Abingdon, 1991.

_____. "Sapiential Elements in the Syriac Apocalypse of Baruch." *JQR* 48 (1986): 311-27.

_____. "The Structure and Meaning of Second Baruch." *SBLDS* 78. Atlanta: Scholars Press, 1985.

_____. "2 Baruch and the Romans." *JBL* 104 (1985): 663-669.

Murphy-O'Connor, J. and Charlesworth, J. H. Eds. *Paul and the Dead Sea Scrolls.* New York: Crossroad, 1990.

_____. "The Essenes and Their History." *RB* 81 (1974).

_____. "Demetrius I and the Teacher of Righteousness." *RB* 83 (1976).

Murray, R. "Jews, Hebrews, Christians: Some needed Distinctions." *NT* 24 (1982): 194-208.

Mussies, G. "Greek in Palestine and the Diaspora," *The Jewish People in the First Century*. 2 Ed. S. Safrai and M. Stern. Philadelphia: Fortress, 1976.

Mylonas, George E. *Eleusis and the Eleusinian Mysteries*. Princeton: Princeton University, 1961.

Neusner, Jacob. "History, Time, and Paradigm in Scripture and in Judaism." *JHC* 7/1 (Spring, 2000): 54-84.

_____. *Judaism in the Matrix of Christianity*. Atlanta: Scholars, 1991.

_____. *The City of God in Judaism and Other Comparative and Methodological Studies*. Atlanta: Scholars, 1991.

_____. *Judaism and Its Social Metaphors: Israel in the History of Jewish Thought*. Cambridge: Cambridge University, 1989.

_____, Borgen, P., Frerichs, E., and Horsley, R. Eds. *The Social World of Formative Judaism: Essays in Tribute of Howard Clark Kee*. Philadelphia: Fortress Press, 1988.

_____. *Torah: From Scroll to Symbol in Formative Judaism*. Philadelphia: Fortress Press 1985.

_____. *Judaism in the Beginning of Christianity*. London: SPCK, 1985.

_____ and Frerichs, E. S. Eds. "To See Ourselves as Others See Us." *Christians, Jews, "Others" in Late Antiquity*. Chico, California: Scholars Press, 1985.

_____. "Galilee in the Time of Hillel: A Review in Formative Judaism. Religious, Literary and Historical Studies." *Brown Judaic Studies* 37, Chico: Scholars Press, 1982.

_____. Ed. *Christianity, Judaism, and Other Greco-Roman Cults: Studies for Morton Smith at Sixty*, Four Parts, Leiden: Brill, 1975.

_____. *First-Century Judaism in Crisis: Johanan ben Zakkai and the Renaissance of Torah*. Nashville: Abingdon, 1975.

_____. *From Politics to Piety: The Emergence of Pharisaic Judaism*. Englewood Cliffs, N.J.: Prentice-Hall, 1973.

_____. *Development of a Legend: Studies in the Traditions concerning Yohanan ben Zakkai*. Leiden: Brill, 1970.

Newman, B. "The Pilgrimage of Christ-Sophia." *Vox Eenedictina* 9 (1992): 9-37.

Newsome, J. D. *Greek, Romans, Jews: Currents of Culture and Belief in the New Testament World*. Philadelphia: Trinity Press International, 1992.

Neyrey, Jerome H. *The Resurrection Stories*. Collegeville: M. Glazier, 1992.

_____. Ed. *The Social World of Luke-Acts: Models for Interpretation*. Peabody, MA: Hendrickson, 1991.

_____. *Christ is Community: The Christologies of the New Testament*. Collegeville: M. Glazier, 1991.

_____. *Ideology of Revolt: John's Christology in Social-Science Perspective*. Philadelphia: Fortress, 1988.

Nickelsburg, George W. E. "I Enoch and Qumran Origins." K. Richards. Ed. *SBL* Seminar Papers. Atlanta: Scholars Press, 1986.

_____. "Social Aspects of Palestinian Jewish Apocalypticism." *Apocalypticism in the Mediterranean World*. Ed. David Hellholm. 641-54. 1983.

_____. "The Epistle of Enoch and the Qumran Literature." *JBS* 33 (1982): 333-48.

_____. *Jewish Literature between the Bible and the Mishnah: A Historical and Literary Introduction*. Philadelphia: Fortress, 1981.

_____. "Enoch, Levi, and Peter: Recipients of Revelation in Upper Galilee." *JBL* 100 (1981): 575-600.

_____. "The Apocalyptic Message of 1 Enoch 92-105." *CBQ* 39 (1977): 309-28.

_____. *Resurrection, Immortality and Eternal Life in Intertestamental Judaism*. Harvard University Press, 1972.

Niebuhr, B. G. *The History of Rome*. London: Walton and Maberly, 1855.

Niebuhr, H. Richard. *Christ and Culture*. New York: Harper & Row, Harper Torchbooks, Cloister Library, 1963.

_____. *Radical Monotheism and Western Culture*. New York: Harper & Row, 1960.

Nietzsche, Friedrich. *Thus Spoke Zarathustra*. Trans. R. J. Hollingdale. Baltimore: Penguin, 1961.

Nilsson, Martin P. *The Dionysiac Mysteries of the Hellenistic and Roman Age*. New York: Arno Press, 1975.

Nock, Arthur Darby. "The Question of Jewish Mysteries." *Essays on Religion and the Ancient* World. Ed. Z. Stewart, 2 vols. Oxford: Clarendon, 1972.

_____. *Conversion: The Old and the New in Religion from Alexander the Great to Augustine of Hippo*. Oxford: Clarendon. 1933.

438

_____. Ed. and Trans. *Concerning Gods and the Universe (Sallustius, Neoplatonist)*. Cambridge University, 1926.

Novak, D. *The Image of the Non-Jew in Judaism: An Historical and Constructive Study of the Noahide Laws*. Lewiston: Mellen Press, 1983.

Novak, Michael. *Belief and Unbelief*. New York: Macmillan, 1965.

Oakesmith, John. *The Religion of Plutarch: A Pagan Creed of Apostolic Times*. London: Longmans, Green, 1902.

O'Dea, Thomas F. "The Sociology of Religion." *Foundations of Modern Sociology Series*. Englewood Cliffs, New Jersey: Prentice-Hall, 1966.

Ogden, S. *The Point of Christology*. London: SCM, 1982.

Olivier, J. P. "Schools and Wisdom Literature." *JNSL* 4 (1975): 49-60.

O' Neill, J. C. The "Jesus in Hebrews." *JHC* 6/1 (Spring, 1999): 64-82.

_____. *Theology of Acts in its Historical Setting*. London: SPCK, 1970.

_____. *The Puzzle of I John*. London: SPCK, 1966.

Oppenheimer, A. *The Am Ha-Aretz: A Study of the Social History of the Jewish People in the Hellenistic-Roman Period*. Leiden: Brill, 1977.

Orage, A. R. "Review of the Gnosis of the Mind." *Theosophical Review*. 39 (January 1907): 466.

Orlinsky, H. M. "The So-Called Servant of the Lord in Second Isaiah." *Studies in the Second Part of the Book of Isaiah*. Leiden: Brill, 1967.

Orton, D. E. "The Understanding Scribe: Matthew and the Apocalyptic Ideal." *JSNTSS* 25. Sheffield, England: Sheffield Academic Press, 1989.

Ostow, Mortimer. "The Fundamentalist Phenomenon: A Psychological Perspective." *The Fundamentalist Phenomenon*. Ed. Norman J. Cohen, 99-125. Grand Rapids, MI: Eerdmans. 1990.

Otto, Rudolph. *The Kingdom of God and the Son of Man*. Trans. Floyd V. Filson and Bertram Lee Woolf. London: Lutterworth, 1938.

Otto, Walter F. *Dionysus: Myth and Cult*. Bloomington, Indiana University Press, 1965.

Otzen, B. *Judaism in Antiquity: Political Development and Religious Currents from Alexander to Hadrian.* Trans. F. M. Cryer. Sheffield: JSOT Press, 1990.

Overman, J. A. *Matthew's Gospel and Formative Judaism.* Philadelphia: Fortress, 1970.

Pagels, Elaine H. *Beyond Belief: The Secret Gospel of Thomas.* New York: Random House, 2003.

_____. *The Gnostic Gospels.* New York: Vintage, 1989.

_____. "The Mystery of the Resurrection: A Gnostic Reading of I Corinthians 15." *JBL* 93.2 (1974): 276-288.

_____. "The Johannine Gospel in Gnostic Exegesis: Heracleon's Commentary on John." *SBLMS* 17. Nashville: Abingdon, 1973.

_____. "A Valentinian Interpretation of Baptism and Eucharist and Its Critique of 'Orthodox' Sacramental Theology and Practice." *HTR* 65.2 (1972):153-169.

Pamment, M. "The Son of Man in the First Gospel." *NTS* 29 (1983): 116-29.

Parrinder, Goerffrey. *Jesus in the Qur'an.* New York: Oxford University, 1977.

Parry, D. W. and Ricks, S. D. Eds. "Current Research and Technological Developments on the Dead Sea Scrolls: Conference on the Texts from the Judean Desert." Jerusalem, 30 April, *1995. STDJ* 20. Leiden: Brill, 1996.

Patterson, Stephen J. *The Gospel of Thomas and Jesus.* Sonoma, Calif.: Polebridge, 1993.

Pearson, Birger A. *The Future of Early Christianity: Essays in Honor of Helmut Koester.* Minneapolis, Minn.: Fortress, 1991.

_____. "Earliest Christianity in Egypt: Some Observations." *Roots of Egyptian Christianity.* Ed. Berger A. Pearson and James E. Goehring, 132-156. Philadelphia: Fortress, 1986.

_____. Ed. "Friedlander Revisited: Alexandrian Judaism and Gnostic Origins." *Studio Philonica* (1973): 2:23-39.

Peel, Malcolm L. "Gnostic Eschatology and the New Testament." *Novum Testamentum.* XII (1970):141-165.

_____. "The Epistle to Rheginos: A Valentinian Letter on the Resurrection: Introduction, Translation, Analysis and Exposition." *New Testament Library.* London: SCM, 1969.

Pelikan, Jaroslav. *Jesus through the Centuries: His Place in the History of Culture.* New York: Harper & Row, 1987.

Perdue, L. G. "Liminality as a Social Setting for Wisdom Instructions." *ZAW* 93 (1981): 114-26.

Perkins, A. *The Art of Dura-Europos*. Oxford: Clarendon, 1973. Israel Exploration Society, 1994.

Perkins, Pheme. "The Resurrection of Jesus of Nazareth." *Studying the Historical Jesus: Evaluations of the State of Current Research*. Ed. Bruce Chilton and Craig A. Evans, 423-42. Leiden: Brill, 1994.

Perrin, Norman. *Jesus and the Language of the Kingdom: Symbol and Metaphor in New Testament Interpretation*. Philadelphia: Fortress Press, 1976.

_____. and Duling, Dennis C. *Jesus and the Language of the Kingdom*. Philadelphia: Fortress, 1976.

_____. "Apocalyptic Christianity." *The New Testament: An Introduction*. New York: Fortress, 1974.

_____. "What Is Redaction Criticism?" *Guides to Biblical Scholarship*. Philadelphia: Fortress, 1969.

Petersen, Norman R. *Literary Criticism for New Testament Critics. Guides to Biblical Scholarship*. Philadelphia: Fortress Press, 1978.

Philo, of Alexandria. *About the Contemplative Life*. Oxford: Clarendon, 1895.

Plato. *Republic*. New York: Modern Library. 1941.

_____. *Timaeus and Critias*. New York: Penguin Classics, 1965.

Pomeroy, Sarah B. *Goddesses, Whores, Wives, Slaves: Women in Classical Antiquity*. New York: Schocken Books, 1975.

Popper, Karl R. *The Logic of Scientific Discovery*. New York: Harper and Row, 1959.

_____. *The Poverty of Historicism*. London: Routledge & Kegan Paul Ltd., 1957.

Powell, Evan. *The Unfinished Gospel: Notes on the Quest for the Historical Jesus*. Westlake Village, CA: Symposium Books, 1994.

Price, George R. "Science and the Supernatural." *Science*. CXXIL (August, 26), 1955.

Price, Robert M. *Deconstructing Jesus*. Prometheus Books, 2000.

Pulikottil, Paulson. *Transmission of Biblical Texts at Qumran*. Sheffield, UK: Sheffield Academic, 2000.

Quispel, G.; Guillaumont, A.; Puech, H. Ch.; Till, W.C.; 'Abd al Masih, Y. *The Gospel According to Thomas: Coptic Text Established and Translated*. New York: Harper, 1959.

Rabin, C. *Qumran Studies.* New York: Schocken, 1975.

Rahner, Karl. "The Hermeneutics of Eschatological Assertions." *Theological Investigations.* Vol. IV. Baltimore: Helicon, 1966.

Raisanen, Heikki. *Beyond New Testament Theology: A Story and a Programme.* London: SCM, 1990.

_____. "The Torah and Christ: Essays in German and English on the Problem of the Law in Early Christianity." SESJ 45, Helsinki: Kirjappaino Raamattutalo, 1986.

Rajak, T. "Jews and Christians as Groups in a Pagan World." *To See Ourselves as Others See Us: Christians, Jews, 'Others' in Late Antiquity.* Ed., J. Neusner and E. S. Frerichs. Chico, Calif.: Scholars Press, 1985.

_____. "The Hasmoneans and the Uses of Hellenism." *A Tribute to Geza Vermes.* Ed., P. R. Davies and R. T. White. Sheffield: JSOT Press, 1990.

_____. "Was There a Roman Charter for the Jews?" *JRS* 74 (1984): 107-203.

Ramsey, W. M. *The Church in the Roman Empire: Before A.D. 170.* New York: Putnam, 1911.

Randall, J. H. *Hellenistic Ways of Deliverance and the Making of the Christian Synthesis.* New York: Columbia University, 1970.

Rappaport, U. "The Hellenization of the Hasmoneans." *Jewish Assimilation, Acculturation, and Accommodation: Past Traditions, Current Issues, and Future Prospects.* Ed. M. Mor. Lanham, Md.: University Press of America, 1992.

Reed, S. A. Rev. and Ed. Lundberg, M. J. with Phelps, M. B. "The Dead Sea Scrolls Catalogue: Documents, Photographs and Museum Inventory Numbers." *SBLRBS* 32. Atlanta: Scholars Press, 1994.

Reese, J. M. "Hellenistic Influence on the Book of Wisdom and Its Consequences." *AnBib* 41. Rome: Biblical Institute, 1970.

Reicke, Bo. "A Synopsis of Early Christian Preaching." *The Roots of the Vine: Essays in Biblical Theology.* Ed. A. Fridrichsen and others. New York: Philosophical Library, 1953.

Reider, J. *The Book of Wisdom.* Dropsie College Series. New York: Harper, 1957.

Remus, Harold E. "Sociology of Knowledge and the Study of Early Christianity." *Sciences Religieuses* 11 (1982): 45-56.

_____. "Pagan-Christian Conflict over Miracle in the Second Century." *Patristic Monograph Series*, No. 10. Cambridge, Mass.: Philadelphia Patristic Foundation, 1983.

Renan, Ernest. *The Life of Jesus*. New York: Prometheus, 1991.

Rensberger, David K. *As the Apostle Teaches: The Development of the Use of Paul's Letters in Second-Century Christianity*. Ph.D. diss. Yale University, 1981.

Reumann, John. *Jesus in the Church's Gospels: Modem Scholarship and the Earliest Sources*. Philadelphia: Fortress, 1968.

Rhoads, D. *Israel in Revolution, 6-74 CE: A Political History based on the Writings of Josephus*. Philadelphia: Fortress, 1976.

Riches, John. *The World of Jesus: First-Century Judaism in Crisis*. Cambridge: University Press, 1990.

_____. *Jesus and the Transformation of Judaism*. London: Darton, Longman & Todd, 1980.

Ricoeur, P. *Hermeneutics and the Human Sciences*. Cambridge: University Press, 1981.

Riddle, Donald W. *The Martyrs: A Study in Social Control*. Chicago: University of Chicago Press, 1931.

Rigby, Cynthia L. Ed. *Power, Powerlessness, and the Divine*: *New Inquiries in Bible and Theology*. Atlanta: Scholars Press, 1997.

Riley, Gregory J. *One Jesus, Many Christs*: *How Jesus Inspired Not One Christianity, but Many*. San Francisco: Harper San Francisco, 1998.

Rives, J. B. *Religion and Authority in Roman Carthage from Augustus to Constantine*. New York: Oxford University, 1995.

Robbins, Thomas. *Cults, Converts and Charisma: The Sociology of New Religious Movements*. Beverly Hills, CA.: Sage, 1988.

Robbins, Vernon K. *Jesus the Teacher: A Socio-Rhetorical Interpretation of Mark*. 2nd Ed. Philadelphia: Fortress, 1992.

Roberts, Colin H. *Manuscript, Society, and Belief in Early Christian Egypt*. London: Oxford, 1979.

Robertson, John M. *Pagan Christs*. New York: University Book, 1967.

_____. *The Problem of History in Mark*. London: SCM, 1957.

_____. "Dr. Conybeare and the Jesus Problem -- A reply to 'The Historical Christ. '" *The Literary Guide* (June, July, and August), 1914.

_____. *Christianity and Mythology.* London: Watts, 1910.

Robinson, James M and Koester, Helmut. *The Nag Hammadi Library in English.* HarperSanFrancisco, 1990.

_____. Ed. *The Nag Hammadi Library.* 3rd Ed. Rev. San Francisco: Harper & Row, 1988.

_____. Ed. *Trajectories Through Early Christianity.* Philadelphia: Fortress, 1968.

Robinson, John A. T. "Very Goddess and Very Man: Jesus' Better Self." *Images of the Feminine in Gnosticism.* Studies in Antiquity and Christianity. Ed. K. King, 113-27. Philadelphia: Fortress, 1988.

_____. "Jesus as Sophos and Sophia." *Aspects of Wisdom in Judaism and Early Christianity.* Ed. R. L. Wilken, 1-16. *CSJCA* 1. Notre Dame, Ind.: University of Notre Dame, 1975.

_____. *Redating the New Testament.* Philadelphia: Westminster, 1976.

_____. *The New Reformation.* Philadelphia: Westminster, 1965.

_____. *Honest to God.* Philadelphia: Westminster, 1963.

_____. "Jesus: Myth or History?" *Thinker's Library* No. 110. London: Watts, 1949.

_____. *A Grammar of the Greek New Testament in the Light of Historical Research.* Nashville: Broadman, 1934.

Robinson, John Mansley. *An Introduction to Early Greek Philosophy.* Boston: Houghton Mifflin, 1968.

Roetzel, Calvin J. *The World That Shaped the New Testament.* Atlanta: John Knox, 1985.

Rollins, Wayne. "The New Testament and Apocalyptic." *New Testament Studies.* 17 (1971): 454-76.

Rordorf, Willy. "An Aspect of the Judeo-Christian Ethic: The Two ways." *The Didache in Modern Research.* Ed., Jonathan Draper, 148-64. Leiden: E. J. Brill, 1996.

Rose, H. J. *A Handbook of Greek Mythology.* New York: Dutton, 1959.

Rowland, Christopher. *The Open Heaven: A Study of Apocalyptic in Judaism and Early Christianity.* New York: Crossroad, 1982.

Rowley, H. H. *The Relevance of Apocalyptic: A Study of Jewish and Christian Apocalypses from Daniel to the Revelation.* Rev. Ed. Greenwood, S.C.: Attic, 1980.

Rubenstein, J. L. *The History of Sukkot in the Second Temple and Rabbinic Periods.* Atlanta: Scholars, 1995.

Rubenstein, Richard. "Person and Myth in the Judaeo-Christian Encounter." *Christian Scholar* (Winter, 1963).

_____. "The Symbols of Judaism and Religious Existentialism." *The Reconstructionist* (May, 1959).

Russell, D. S. *Divine Disclosure: An Introduction to Jewish Apocalyptic.* Minneapolis: Fortress, 1992.

Russell, Jeffrey Burton. *The Devil: Perceptions of Evil from Antiquity to Primitive Christianity.* Ithaca, NY: Cornell University, 1977.

Rutgers, L. V. *The Jews in Late Ancient Rome: Evidence of Cultural Interaction in the Roman Diaspora.* Leiden: Brill, 1995.

Rylands, L. G. *Did Jesus Ever Live?* London: Watts, 1935.

S, Acharya. *Suns of God.* Adventures Unlimited Press, Kempton Illinois, 2004.

_____. *The Christ Conspiracy.* Adventures Unlimited Press, Kempton Illinois, 1999.

Safrai, S. and Stern, M. Eds. *The Jewish People in the First Century: Historic Geography, Political History, Social, Cultural and Religious Life and Institutions.* CRINT 1/1. Philadelphia: Fortress, 1977.

Saldarini, Anthony J. *Matthew's Christian-Jewish Community.* Chicago: University of Chicago, 1994.

_____. *Pharisees, Scribes, and Sadducees in Palestinian Society: A Sociological Approach.* Wilmington, Del.: Glazier, 1988.

_____. "Apocalypses and 'Apocalyptic' in Rabbinic Literature and Mysticism." *Semeia* 14 (1979): 187-205.

_____. "The Uses of Apocalyptic in the Mishna and Tosephta." *Catholic Biblical Quarterly* 39/3 (1977): 396-409.

Sandelin, Karl-Gustav. "Wisdom as Nourisher: A Study of an Old Testament Theme, its Development within Early Judaism and its Impact on Early Christianity." *AAAbo* 64, 3, Aabo Akademi, 1986.

Sanders, E. P. *Schismatics, Sectarians, Dissidents, Deviants.* Valley Forge, PA: Trinity International. 1993.

_____. *The Historical Figure of Jesus*. New York: Penguin, 1993.

_____. *Judaism: Practice and Belief, 63 BCE-66 CE*. Philadelphia: Trinity Press International, 1992.

_____. *Jewish Law from Jesus to the Mishnah: Five Studies*. Philadelphia: Trinity International, 1990.

_____. Baumgarten, A. I., and Mendelson, Alan. Eds. *Jewish and Christian Self-Definition*. Philadelphia: Fortress, 1981.

_____. *Paul and Palestinian Judaism: A Comparison of Patterns of Religion*. London: SCM Press, 1977.

Sanders, Jack T. *Ben Sira and Demotic Wisdom*. Chico: Scholars, 1983.

_____. *The New Testament Christological Hymns*. London: Cambridge University, 1971.

Sandmel, Samuel. *Philo of Alexandria: An Introduction*. Oxford: Oxford University, 1979.

_____. *Judaism and Christian Beginnings*. New York: Oxford University Press, 1978.

Santayana, George. *Reason in Religion*. New York: Scribner, 1906.

Sapir, J. D. "The Anatomy of Metaphor." *The Social Use of Metaphor: Essays on the Anthropology of Rhetoric*. Ed. J. D. Sapir and J. C. Crocker, 3-32. Philadelphia: University of Pennsylvania, 1977.

Sartre, Jean-Paul. "Existentialism Is a Humanism." *Existentialism from Dostoevsky to Sartre*. Ed. Walter Kaufmann. Cleveland: Meridian, 1957.

Schauss, Hayyim. *The Jewish Festivals: From their Beginnings to Our Own Day*. Cincinnati: Union of American Hebrew Congregations, 1938.

Schiffman, L. H. *Reclaiming the Dead Sea Scrolls: The History of Judaism, the Background of Christianity, the Lost Library of Qumran*. Philadelphia and Jerusalem: Jewish Publication Society, 1994.

_____. Ed., *Archaeology and History in the Dead Sea Scrolls: The New York University Conference in Memory of Yigael Yadin*. Sheffield: Sheffield Academic Press, 1990.

_____. *The Halakah of Qumran*. Leiden: Brill, 1975.

_____. and Scholem, G. *Jewish Gnosticism, Merkavah Mysticism, and Talmudic Tradition*. New York: Jewish Theological Seminary, 1960.

Schillebeeckx, E. *The Christ: The Experience of Jesus Christ as Lord*. New York: Seabury, 1982.

Scleiermacher, Friedrich. *On Religion*. New York: Harper, 1958.

Schmithals, W. *The Apocalyptic Movement: Introduction and Interpretation*. Trans. J. E. Steely. Nashville: Abingdon, 1975.

_____. *Paul and the Gnostics*. Trans. J. Steely. Nashville: Abingdon, 1972.

_____. *Gnosticism in Corinth*. Trans. J. Steely. Nashville: Abingdon, 1971.

Schoedel, William R. "Ignatius and the Reception of the Gospel of Matthew in Antioch." *Social History of the Matthean Community: Cross Disciplinary Approaches*. Ed. David L. Balch. 129-177. Minneapolis: Fortress, 1991.

Schoeps, Hans-Joachim. *Jewish Christianity*. Philadelphia: Fortress, 1964.

_____. *Paul: The Theology of the Apostle in the Light of Jewish Religious History*. London: Lutterworth, 1959.

Scholem, G. *Sabbatai Sevi: The Mystical Messiah*. New Jersey: Princeton, 1973.

_____. *Jewish Gnosticism, Merkabah Mysticism, and Talmudic Tradition*. New York: Jewish Theological Seminary, 1965.

_____. *Major Trends in Jewish Mysticism*. New York: Scholem, 1960.

Scholes, R. and Kellogg, R. *The Nature of Narrative*. New York: Oxford University Press, 1966.

Schurer, E. *The History of the Jewish People in the Age of Jesus Christ*. Rev. G. Vermes, et al. 3 vols. Edinburgh: T. & T. Clark, 1973-87.

Schutz, Alfred. *The Phenomenology of the Social World*. Trans. George Walsch and Fredrick Lehnert. Intro. George Walsh. New York: Northwestern University, 1967.

Schweid, E. *Judaism and Mysticism According to Gershom Scholem: A Critical Analysis and Programmatic Discussion*. Atlanta: Scholars, 1985.

Schweitzer, Albert. *The Kingdom of God and Primitive Christianity*. Ed. Intro. Ulrich Neuenschwander. Trans. L. A. Garrard. New York: Seabury, 1967.

Schweizer, Edward. *The Church as the Body of Christ*. Richmond, Virginia: John Knox, 1964.

Scott, Bernard Brandon. "From Reimarus to Crossan: Stages in a Quest." *Currents in Research: Biblical Studies* 2 (1994): 253-80.

_____. *Jesus, Symbol-Maker for the Kingdom*. Philadelphia: Fortress, 1981.

Scott, R. B. Y. "Solomon and the Beginnings of Wisdom." *Studies in Ancient Israelite Wisdom*. Ed. J. L. Crenshaw, 262-79. New York: KTAV, 1976.

Scroggs, Robin. "Eschatological Existence in Matthew and Paul: Coincidentia Oppositorum." *The Text and the Times: New Testament Essays for Today*. Ed. Scroggs, 234-56. Minneapolis: Fortress, 1993.

_____. *Rebecca's Children: Judaism and Christianity in the Roman World*. Cambridge: Harvard University, 1986.

_____. "The Sociological Interpretation of the New Testament." *The Bible and Liberation: Political and Social Hermeneutics*. Ed. Norman K. Gottwald, 337-356. Maryknoll, N.Y.: Orbis, 1983. Originally in NTS 26 (1980): 164-179.

_____. "The Political Dimensions of Anti-Judaism in the New Testament." Unpublished paper. Segal, A. F.

_____. "Heavenly Ascent in Hellenistic Judaism, Early Christianity and Their Environment." *ANRW* 11.2 (1980): 1333-94.

_____. "The Earliest Christian Communities as Sectarian Movement." *Christianity, Judaism, and other Graeco-Roman Cults II*. Ed. J. Neusner. Leiden: Brill, 1975.

Seager, A. and Kraabel, A. T. "The Synagogue and the Jewish Community," *Sardis from Prehistoric to Roman Times*. Ed. G. M. A. Hanfmann. Cambridge: Harvard University, 1983.

Seeley, David. "The Background of the Philippians' Hymn (2:6-11)." *JHC* 1 (Fall, 1994): 49-72.

_____. "Jesus' Death in Q." *NTS* 38 (1992): 222-234.

Segal, Alan F. "Matthew's Jewish Voice." *Social History of the Matthean Community: Cross Disciplinary Approaches*. Ed. David L. Balch, 3-37. Minneapolis: Fortress, 1991.

_____. *Rebecca's Children: Judaism and Christianity in the Roman World*. Cambridge: Harvard University, 1986.

_____. "Heavenly Ascent in Hellenistic Judaism: Early Christianity and their Environment." *Semeia* 14 (1979): 1334-1394.

Segelberg, Eric. "The Coptic-Gnostic Gospel According to Philip and Its Sacramental System." *Numen* 7 (1960): 189- 200.

Sevenster, J. N. *Do You Know Greek? How Much Greek Could the First Jewish Christians Have Known?* Leiden: Brill, 1968.

Shafer, Robert. *Christianity and Naturalism.* New Haven: Yale University, 1928.

Shanin, T. "The Nature and Logic of Peasant Economies." *JPS* 1 (1974): 186-204.

Shanks, Hershel. *The Mystery and Meaning of the Dead Sea Scrolls.* New York: Random, 1998.

_____. Ed. *The Search for Jesus: Modem Scholarship Looks at the Gospels.* Washington, D.C: Biblical Archaeological Society, 1994.

Sheehan, Thomas. *The First Coming: How the Kingdom of God Became Christianity.* New York: Random House, 1986.

Sheler, Jeffrey L., with Tharp, Mike and Seider, Jill Jordan. "In Search of Jesus." *U.S. News & World Repo*rt 120/14 (April 8, 1996): 47-53.

Sherwin-White, A.N. *Roman Society and Roman Law in the New Testament.* Oxford: University Press, 1963.

Shiner, Larry. "Toward a Theology of the Secular." *Journal of Religion* (October), 1965.

Silberman, Neil Asher. "Searching for Jesus." *Archeology* 47/6 (1994): 31-40.

Silver, Abba Hillel. *A History of Messianic Speculation in Israel: From the First Through the Seventeenth Centuries.* Boston: Beacon, 1959.

Silverman, S. "Patronage as Myth." *Patrons and Clients in Mediterranean Societies.* Ed. Gellner and Waterbury, 7-19.

Simon, Erika. *Festivals of Attica: An Archaeological Commentary.* Madison, WI: University of Wisconsin, 1983.

Simon, Marcel. *St. Stephen and the Hellenists in the Primitive Church.* New York: Longmans, 1958.

Singer, Isidore, Ed. *The Jewish Encyclopedia: A Descriptive Record of the History, Religion, Literature, and Customs of the Jewish People from the Earliest Times to the Present Day.* 12 vols. New York: Funk & Wagnalls, 1901-6.

Slater, Thomas B. "On the Social Setting of the Revelation to John." *New Testament Studies* 44 (1998): 232-256.

Smallwood, E. Mary. "The Jews under Roman Rule." *SJLA* 20. Leiden: Brill, 1976.

_____. "High Priests and Politics in Roman Palestine." *JTS* 13 (1962).

Smith, D. M. *Johannine Christianity*. Columbia, SC.: University of South Carolina, 1984.

_____. *The Use of the Old Testament in the New and Other Essays*. Durham, N.C.: Duke University, 1972.

Smith, George Adam. *The Historical Geography of the Holy Land*. Intro. H. H. Rowley. New York: Harper & Row, Torchbooks, Cloister Library, 1966.

Smith, Jonathan Z. *Drudgery Divine: On the Comparison of Early Christianities and the Religions of Late Antiquity*. Chicago Studies in the History of Judaism. Chicago: University of Chicago, 1990.

_____. "Wisdom and Apocalyptic." *Visionaries and Their Apocalypses*. Ed. P. D. Hanson, 101-20. Philadelphia: Fortress, 1983.

_____. "The Social Description of Early Christianity." *RSR* 1 (1975): 19-25.

Smith, Morton. "On the History of Apokalyptk and Apokalypsis." *Hellholm*, David, Ed. *Apocalypticism in the Mediterranean World and the Near East*. Tubingen: Mohr (Siebeck), 1983.

_____. "Ascent to the Heavens and the Beginnings of Christianity." *Eranosjahrbuch* 50 (1981): 403-24.

_____. *Jesus the Magician*. San Francisco: Harper & Row, 1978.

_____. "On the Differences Between the Culture of Israel and the Major Cultures of the Ancient Near East." *JANESCU* 5 (1973): 389-95.

_____. "Tannaitic Parallels to the Gospels." *SBLDS* 6. Philadelphia: SBL, 1968.

_____. "The Description of the Essenes in Josephus and the Philosophoumena." *Hebrew Union College Annual* 29 (1958): 273-323.

_____. *Clement of Alexandria and a Secret Gospel of Mark*. Cambridge: Harvard University, 1958.

_____. "Palestinian Judaism in the First Century." *Israel: Its Role in Civilization.* Ed. M. Davis, 67-81. New York: Jewish Theological Seminary of America, 1956.

Smith, Ronald Gregor. "A Theological Perspective of the Secular." *Christian Scholar* (March, 1960).

Smith, William. Ed. *Dictionary of Greek and Roman Geography*. London: Walton and Maberly, 1857.

Snyder, Graydon F. *Ante Pacem: Archaeological Evidence of Church Life before Constantine*. Macon, GA: Mercer University, 1985.

Sobrino, Jon. *Jesus the Liberator: A Historical-Theological Reading of Jesus of Nazareth*. Maryknoll, NY: Orbis, 1995.

Sordi, Marta. *The Christians and the Roman Empire*. Norman: University of Oklahoma, 1986.

Spong, John. *Born of a Woman: A Bishop Rethinks the Birth of Jesus*. San Francisco: Harper, 1992.

Staniforth, Maxwell, Trans. *Early Christian Writings*. Penguin Classics, 1968.

Stanley, John E. "The Apocalypse and Contemporary Sect Analysis." *SBL* 1986. Seminar Papers, Ed. Kent H. Richards, 412-21. Atlanta: Scholars Press, 1986.

Stanton, Vincent Henry. *The Jewish and the Christian Messiah: A Study in the Earliest History of Christianity*. Edinburgh: T. & T. Clark, 1886.

Stark, Rodney and Iannaccone, Laurence R. "Sociology of Religion." *Encyclopedia of Sociology*. Edgar F. Borgata. Editor-in-chief. New York: Macmillan, 1991.

_____. *A Theory of Religion*. New York: Peter Lang, 1987.

_____. "Networks of Faith: Interpersonal Bonds and Recruitment to Cults and Sects." *American Journal of Sociology* (1980): 85:1376-1395.

_____ and Bainbridge, William Sims. "Of Churches, Sects, and Cults: Preliminary Concepts for a Theory of Religious Movements." *Journal for the Scientific Study of Religion* (1979): 18:117-131.

_____. "Class, Radicalism, and Religious Involvement." *American Sociological Review* (1964): 29:698-706.

Stauffer, E. *Jesus and the Wilderness Community at Qumran*. Trans. Hans Spalteholz. Biblical Series, No. 10. Philadelphia: Fortress, Facet Books, 1964.

Stein, Robert H. *The Synoptic Problem: An Introduction*. Grand Rapids: Baker Book House, 1984.

Steinberg, Stephen. "Reform Judaism: The Origin and Evolution of a 'Church Movement.'" *Journal for the Scientific Study of Religion* (1965) 5:117-129.

Stemberger, G. *Jewish Contemporaries of Jesus: Pharisees, Sadducees, Essenes.* Trans. A. W. Mahnke. Minneapolis: Fortress, 1995.

Stendahl, Krister. *Paul among Jews and Gentiles and Other Essays.* Philadelphia: Fortress, 1976.

_____. Ed. *Immortality and Resurrection.* New York: Macmillan, 1965.

_____. "The Apostle Paul and the Introspective Conscience of the West." *HThR* 56 (1963): 199-215.

Stendhal, C. Ed. *The Scrolls and the New Testament.* New York: Harper, 1957.

Stern, Menahem. "The Jewish Diaspora." *The Jewish People in the First Century* 1, Ed. S. Safrai and M. Stern. Philadelphia: Fortress, 1974.

_____. *Greek and Latin Authors on Jews and Judaism.* Jerusalem: Israel Academy, 1976.

Stevenson, E. "Some Insights from the Sociology of Religion into the Origin and Development of the Early Christian Church." *Expository Times* 90 (1989): 300-305.

Stone, A. E. *Scriptures, Sects and Visions: A Profile of Judaism from Ezra to the Jewish Revolts.* Philadelphia: Fortress, 1980.

Stone, Michael. E. Ed. "Jewish Writings of the Second Temple Period: Apocrypha, Pseudepigrapha, Qumran Sectarian Writings, Philo, Josephus." *CRINT* 2/2. Philadelphia: Fortress, 1984.

_____. "Apocalyptic Literature." *Jewish Writings of the Second Temple Period.* Ed. Michael E. Stone. *CRINT* 2.2; 383-441. Philadelphia: Fortress, 1984.

_____. "Reactions to Destructions of the Second Temple." *JSJ* 12 (1981): 195-204.

_____. *Scriptures, Sects and Vision: A Profile of Judaism from Ezra to the Jewish Revolts.* Philadelphia: Fortress, 1980.

_____. "The Book of Enoch and Judaism in the Third Century B.C.E." *CBQ* 40 (1978): 479-92.

_____. "Lists of Revealed Things in the Apocalyptic Literature." *Magnalia Dei: The Mighty Acts of God: G. Ernest Wright in Memoriam.* Ed. F. M. Cross, et al. 414-52. Garden City, N.Y.: Doubleday, 1976.

452

Stowers, Stanley Kent. "The Social Sciences and the Study of Early Christianity." *Approaches to Ancient Judaism*, Ed. Gerd W. Theissen. Philadelphia: Fortress Press, 1982.

Strange, James Riley "Defining Judaism in its Classical Age: What is at Stake in the Academic Study of Religion" *JHC* 6/2 (Fall, 1999): 175-185.

Strauss, David F. *The Life of Jesus Critically Examined*. Ed. Intro. Peter C. Hodgson and Trans. George Eliot. Philadelphia: Fortress, 1972.

Strecker, Georg. "On the Problem of Jewish Christianity." Appendix 1. *Walter Bauer, Orthodoxy and Heresy in Earliest Christianity*. Philadelphia: Fortress, 1971.

Suetonius. *Lives of the Caesars*. Loeb Classical Library (2 vols.), 1924.

Suggs, M. J. *Wisdom Christology and Law in Matthew's Gospel*. Cambridge: Harvard University, 1970.

Sugirtharajah, R. S. Ed. *Asian Faces of Jesus*. Maryknoll, NY: Orbis, 1999.

Sullivan, Clayton. *Rescuing Jesus from the Christians*. Harrisburg: Trinity, 2002.

Super, Charles William. *Between Heathenism and Christianity: Being a Translation of Seneca's De Providentia, and Plutarch's De Sera Numinis Vindicta*. Chicago: Revell, 1889.

Swanson, Guy E. *The Birth of the Gods*. Ann Arbor: University of Michigan, 1960.

Swidler, Leonard and Mojzes, Paul, Eds. *The Uniqueness of Jesus: A Dialogue with Paul Knitter*. Maryknoll. New York: Orbis, 1999.

Tacitus. *Annals and History*. Loeb Classical Library (2 vols.), 1932.

_____. Talbert, C. H. "The Myth of a Descending-Ascending Redeemer in Antiquity." *NTS* 22 (1976): 418-440.

Talmon, I. *The Dead Sea Scrolls or the Community of the Renewed Covenant*. Tucson: University of Arizona Press, 1993.

Tasker, R.V.G. *The Old Testament in the New Testament*. 2nd rev. Ed. London: SCM, 1954.

Taubes, Susan A. "The Absent God," *Journal of Religion* (Jan., 1955).

Teixidor, J. *The Pagan God: Popular Religion in the Greco-Roman Near East*. New Jersey: Princeton University Press, 1977.

Telford, W. T. "Major Trends and Interpretive Issues in the Study of Jesus." *Studying the Historical Jesus: Evaluations of the State of Current Research.* Ed. B. Chilton and C.A. Evans. *NTTS* 19. Leiden: Brill, 1994.

Temple, Richard. *Icons and the Mystical Origins of Christianity.* Rockport: Element, 1992.

Theissen, Gerd and Merz, Annette. *The Historical Jesus.* London: SCM, 1998.

_____. *The Gospels in Context: Social and Political History in the Synoptic Tradition.* Edinburgh: T. & T. Clark, 1992.

_____. "The Wandering Radicals. Light Shed by the Sociology of Literature on the Early Transmission of Jesus Sayings, Social Reality and the Early Christians," *Theology, Ethics and the World of the New Testament,* 33-59. Minneapolis: Fortress, 1992.

_____. *In the Shadow of the Galilean.* Philadelphia: Fortress, 1987.

_____. *Psychological Aspects of Pauline Theology.* Trans. J. P. Gavin. Philadelphia: Fortress, 1987.

_____. *Biblical Faith: An Evolutionary Approach.* Philadelphia: Fortress, 1985.

_____.. "The Sociological Interpretation of Religious Traditions: Its Methodological Problems as Exemplified in Early Christianity." *The Bible and Liberation: Political and Social Hermeneutics.* Ed. N. K. Gottwald, 38-48. Maryknoll, New York: Orbis, 1983.

_____. *The Miracle Stories of the Early Christian Tradition.* Trans. F. McDonagh from the German 1974. Ed. J. K. Riches. Philadelphia: Fortress, 1983.

_____. "Social Stratification in the Corinthian Community: A Contribution to the Sociology of Early Hellenistic Christianity." *Theissen, Social Setting* (1982): 69-119.

_____. *The Social Setting of Pauline Christianity.* Ed., Trans., and Intro. J. H. Schutz. Philadelphia: Fortress, 1982.

Thiering, Barbara. "From Qumran to Nag Hammadi, Noah, Melchisedek, and Calendar" *JHC* 7/1 (Spring, 2000): 93-108.

_____. "Christian History and the Dead Sea Scrolls: More About Method," *JHC* 5/1 (Spring, 1998): 88-112.

_____. *Jesus and the Riddle of the Dead Sea Scrolls.* San Francisco: HarperSanFrancisco, 1992.

_____. *Jesus the Man: A New Interpretation from the Dead Sea Scrolls*. San Francisco: Harpers, 1992.

Thompson, Leonard. "A Sociological Analysis of Tribulation in the Apocalypse of John." *Semeia* 36 (1986): 147-74.

Thompson, William Irwin. *The Time Falling Bodies Take to Light: Mythology, Sexuality, and the Origins of Culture*. New York: St. Martin, 1981.

Thurston, Bonnie Bowman. *The Widows: A Women's Ministry in the Early Church*. Minneapolis: Fortress, 1989.

Tiller, A. *Commentary on the Animal Apocalypse of 1 Enoch*. Atlanta: Scholars Press, 1993.

Tillich, Paul. *Systematic Theology*. 3 vols. Chicago: University of Chicago, 1963.

_____. "Being and Love," Will Herberg. Ed. *Four Existentialist Theologians*. New York: Doubleday-Anchor, 1958.

_____. "Theology and Symbolism." *Religious Symbolism*. Ed. F. Ernest Johnson. New York: Institute for Religious and Social Studies, 1955.

_____. *The Courage to Be*. New York: Scribner, 1952.

_____. *The Interpretation of History*. New York: Scribner, 1936.

Tobin, T. H. "4Q 185 and Jewish Wisdom Literature." *Of Scribes and Scrolls: Studies on the Hebrew Bible, Intertestamental Judaism and Christian Origins*. Ed. H. W. Attridge, J. J. Collins, and T. H. Tobin, 145-52. *College Theology Society Resources in Religion* 5. Lanham, Md.: University of America, 1990.

Tolstoy, Leo. *The Kingdom of God Is Within You*. New York: Noonday, 1905.

Tracy, D. *The Analogical Imagination: Christian Theology and the Culture of Pluralism*. London: SCM, 1981.

Trebilco, P. *Jewish Communities in Asia Minor*. Cambridge: Cambridge University Press, 1991.

Tresmontant, Claude. *A Study of Hebrew Thought*. New York: Desclee, 1960.

Trevor, J. C., Cross, F. M., Freedman, D. N. and Sanders, J. A. *Scrolls from Qumran Cave I*. Jerusalem: The Albright Institute, 1972.

Trotter, F. Thomas. "Variations on the Death of God Theme in Recent Theology." *Journal of Bible and Religion* (January, 1965).

Tsafrir, Y. "The Byzantine Setting and Its Influence on Ancient Synagogues," *The Synagogue in Late Antiquity.* Ed. L. I. Levine. Philadelphia: American Schools of Oriental Research, 1987.

Tucker, Robert. *Philosophy and Myth in Karl Marx.* London: Cambridge, 1964.

Tuckett, Christopher. *Q and the History of Early Christianity.* Edinburgh: T. & T. Clark, 1996.

_____. Ed. *The Messianic Secret.* London: SPCK, 1984

Turner, Victor. *The Sages: Their Concepts and Beliefs.* 2 vols. Trans. I. Abrahams. Jerusalem: Magnes (Hebrew University), 1975.

_____. "Metaphors of Anti-Structure in Religious Culture." *Changing Perspectives in the Scientific Study of Religion.* Ed. A. W. Eister, 63-84. New York: John Wiley and Sons, 1974.

_____. *The Ritual Process: Structure and Anti-Structure.* Chicago: Aldine Press, 1969.

Ulrich, I. C. and VanderKam, J. C. Eds. *The Community of the Renewed Covenant: The Notre Dame Symposium on the Dead Sea Scrolls.* Notre Dame: University of Notre Dame Press, 1994.

Underwood, Richard. "Hermes and Hermeneutics: A Viewing from the Perspectives of the Death of God and Depth Psychology." *The Hartford Quarterly* (Fall, 1965).

Uro, Risto. Ed. "Symbols and Strata: Essays on the Saying Gospel Q." *SESJ* 65. Gottingen: Vandenhoeck & Ruprecht, 1996.

Vahanian, Gabriel. *Wait Without Idols.* New York: Braziller, 1964.

_____. "The Future of Christianity in a Post-Christian Era." *The Centennial Review* (Spring, 1964).

_____. "Beyond the Death of God." *Dialog* (Autumn, 1962).

_____. *The Death of God.* New York: Braziller, 1961.

Van Buren, Paul. "The Dissolution of the Absolute." *Religion in Life* (Summer, 1965).

_____. "Theology in the Context of Culture." *Christian Century* (April 7, 1965).

Vanderkam, C. and Adler, W. Eds. *The Jewish Apocalyptic Heritage in Early Christianity.* CRINT 3/4. Minneapolis: Fortress, 1996.

456

_____. "Enoch and the Growth of an Apocalyptic Tradition." *CBQMS* 16. Washington: Catholic Biblical Association of America, 1984.

Van der Leeuw, Gerhardus. *Religion in Essence and Manifestation*. Trans. J. E. Turner. London: Allen and Unwin, 1938.

Van der Ploeg, J. *The Excavations at Qumran: A Survey of the Judean Brotherwood and Its Ideas*. Trans. K. Smyth. New York: Longmans, Green, 1958.

Van Henten, J. W. *The Maccabean Martyrs as Saviors of the Jewish People: A Study of 2 and 4 Maccabees*. Leiden: Brill, 1997.

Van Staden, Piet. "Compassion --The Essence of Life: A Social-Scientific Study of the Religious Symbolic Universe Reflected in the Ideology/Theology of Luke." *Hervormde Teologiese Studies*. Supplement 4. Pretoria: University of Pretoria, 1991.

Van Unnik, C. "The Newly Discovered Gnostic 'Epistle to Rheginos' on the Resurrection." *JEH* 15 (1964):141-52; 153-67.

Vawter, Bruce. *This Man Jesus: An Essay Toward a New Testament Christology*. New York: Doubleday, 1973.

_____. "Apocalyptic -- Its Relation to Prophecy." *Catholic Biblical Quarterly* 22 (1960): 33-46.

Veitch, James. "The Jesus Seminar: What it Is and What it Isn't and Why it Matters." *JHC* 6/2 (Fall, 1999): 186-209.

Vermaseren, Maarten. *Cybele and Attis: Myth and Cult*. London: Thames & Hudson, 1977.

_____. *Mithras the Secret God*. New York: Barnes & Noble, 1963.

Vermes, Geza. *The Changing Faces of Jesus*. New York: Penguin, 2002.

_____. *The Complete Dead Sea Scrolls in English*. New York: Penguin, 1997.

_____. *The Religion of Jesus the Jew*. Minneapolis: Fortress, 1992.

_____. *Jesus and the World of Judaism*. London: SCM, 1983.

_____. *Jesus the Jew: A Historian's Reading of the Gospels*. Philadelphia: Fortress, 1981.

_____. *Scripture and Tradition in Judaism*. Leiden: Brill, 1973.

_____. "The Etymology of Essenes." *Revue de Qumran* 7, no. 2 (June, 1960): 427-43.

Vermes, J. *The Dead Sea Scrolls: Qumran in Perspective.* 3rd Ed. London: SCM, 1994.

Verseput, D. *The Rejection of the Humble Messianic King.* Frankfurt: Peter Lang, 1986.

Vielhauer, Philipp. "Paul and the Cephas Party in Corinth." *JHC* 1 (Fall, 1994): 129-142.

———. *The Dawn of Qumran: The Sectarian Torah and the Teacher of Righteousness.* Cincinnati: Hebrew Union College, 1983.

———. *Eupolemus: A Study of Judaeo-Greek Literature.* Cincinnati: Hebrew Union College, Jewish Institute of Religion, 1974.

———. "Apocalypses and Related Subjects." *New Testament Apocrypha.* Ed. E. Hennecke and W. Schneemelcher. Vol. 2. 581-607. Philadelphia: Westminster, 1965.

Vogel, C. J. De. *Greek Philosophy III: The Hellenistic-Roman Period.* Leiden: Brill, 1959.

Von Balthasar, Hans Urs. *Science, Religion, and Christianity.* London: Burns and Gates, 1958.

Von Rad, G. *Wisdom in Israel.* Trans. J. D. Martin. Nashville: Abingdon, 1981.

Wagner, Gunter. *Pauline Baptism and the Pagan Mysteries.* Edinburgh: Loiver & Boyd, 1967.

Walker, William. "The Burden of Proof in Identifying Interpolations in the Pauline Letters." *NTS* 33 (1987): 610-618.

———. "The Son of Man: Some Recent Developments." *Catholic Biblical Quarterly* 45 (1983): 584-607.

Wallace, Anthony F. C. *Religion: An Anthropological View.* New York: Random House, 1966.

Wallis, Roy. *Millennialism and Charisma.* Belfast: Queen's University, 1982

———. Ed. *Sectarianism.* New York: Wiley, 1975.

Walzer, Michael. *Interpretation and Social Criticism.* Cambridge, Mass.: Harvard University, 1987.

Watson, Francis. "Paul, Judaism and the Gentiles: A Sociological Approach." *SNTSMS* 56. New York: Cambridge University, 1986.

Weber, Max. *The Sociology of Religion.* Trans. Ephraim Fischoff. Intro. Talcott Parsons. Boston: Beacon, 1963.

_____. "Religion and Social Status." *Theories of Society*. Ed. Talcott Parsons, Edward Shills, Kaspar D. Naegele, and Jesse R. Pitts. 1138-1161. New York: Free Press, 1961.

_____. "The Sociology of Charismatic Authority." *From Max Weber: Essays in Sociology*. Ed. H. H. Gerth and C. Wright Mills. 245-252. New York: Oxford University, 1946.

Webster, T. B. L. "Personification as a Mode of Greek Thought." *Journal of the Warburg and Courtauld Institutes* 17 (1954): 10-21.

Wedderburn, A. J. M. "Philo's 'Heavenly Man'." *Test* (Nov., 1973).

Weidmann, Frederick . "The Good Teacher: Social Identity and Community Purpose in the Pastoral Epistles." *JHC* 2/2 (Fall, 1995): 100-114.

Weinert, F. D. "A Note on 4Q159 and a New Theory of Essene Origins." *RQ9* (1977).

Weingrod, A. "Patronage and Power." *Patrons and Clients in Mediterranean Societies*. Ed. Gellner and Waterbury, 41-51.

Weiss Halivni, D. *Midrash, Mishnah, and Gemara: The Jewish Predilection for Justified Law*. Cambridge: Harvard University, 1986.

Weiss, Johannes. *Jesus' Proclamation of the Kingdom of God*. Eng. Trans. 1971.

_____. *Earliest Christianity: A History of the Period A. D. 30-150*. Vol. II. Trans. Frederick C. Grant. New York: Harper & Row, Torchbooks, 1937.

Weiss, Z. and Netzer, E. *Promise and Redemption: A Synagogue Mosaic from Sepphoris*. Jerusalem: Israel Museum, 1996.

Wells, George Albert. *The Jesus Legend*. Chicago: Open Court, 1996.

_____. *Who Was Jesus? A Critique of the New Testament Record*. La Salle: Open Court, 1989.

_____. *Did Jesus Exist?* London: Pemberton, 1986.

_____. *The Historical Evidence for Jesus*. Buffalo: Prometheus, 1982.

_____. *The Jesus of the Early Christians*. London: Pemberton, 1971.

Wenham, D. *Metaphor and Reality*. Bloomington: Indiana University, 1964.

Werner, Martin. *The Formation of Christian Dogma*. Trans. S. G. F. Brandon. London: Adam and Charles Black, 1957.

Wessels, Anton. *Images of Jesus: How Jesus is Perceived and Portrayed in Non-European Cultures.* Grand Rapids: Eerdmans, 1986.

White, L. Michael. Ed. "Social Networks in the Early Christian Environment: Issues and Methods for Social History." *Semeia* 56. Atlanta: Scholars Press, 1992.

_____. *Building God's House in the Roman World: Architectural Adaptations among Pagans, Jews, and Christians.* Baltimore: Johns Hopkins University, 1990.

_____. "Shifting Sectarian Boundaries in Early Christianity." *BJRL* 70 (1988): 7-24.

_____. "Adolf Harnack and Early Christian 'Expansion:' A Reappraisal of Social History." *Second Century* (1986): 5:97-127.

_____. "Sociological Analysis of Early Christian Groups: A Social Historian's Response." *Sociological Analysis* 47 (1986): 249-66.

Whitehead, Alfred North. *Symbolism, Its Meaning, and Effect.* New York: Macmillan, 1927.

Whittaker, M. *Jews and Christians: Greco-Roman Views.* Cambridge: Cambridge University Press, 1984.

Wilde, James Alan. *A Social Description of the Community Reflected in the Gospel of Mark.* Ph.D. diss. Drew University, 1974.

Wilde, Robert. *The Treatment of the Jews in the Greek Christian Writers of the First Three Centuries.* Washington, D.C.: Catholic University of America, 1949.

Wiles, Maurice F. *The Spiritual Gospel: The Interpretation of the Fourth Gospel in the Early Church.* Cambridge: Cambridge University, 1960.

Wilken, Robert L. *The Christians as the Romans Saw Them.* New Haven: Yale University, 1984.

_____. *Judaism and the Early Christian Mind.* New Haven: Yale University, 1971.

Williams, Michael. "The Immovable Race: A Gnostic Designation and the Theme of Stability in Late Antiquity." *Nag Hammadi Studies.* vol. 29. Leiden: Brill, 1985.

Williams, Sam K. *Jesus' Death as Saving Event.* Scholars Press, 1975.

Williamson, Ronald. *Jews in the Hellenistic World: Philo.* Cambridge: Cambridge University, 1989.

Wills, L. "The Form of the Sermon in Hellenistic Judaism and Early Christianity." *HTR* 77 (1984).

Wilson, A. N. *Jesus: A Life*. New York: Norton, 1992.

Wilson, Bryan R. *Magic and the Millennium: A Sociological Study of Religious Movements of Protest Among Tribal and Third-World Peoples*. New York: Harper & Row, 1973.

_____. *Sects and Society*. Berkeley and Los Angeles: University of California, 1970.

_____. *Religious Sects*. New York: McGraw-Hill, 1961.

Wilson, Ian. *Jesus: The Evidence*. San Francisco: Harper & Row, 1984.

Winston, David. *Logos and Mystical Philosophy in Philo of Alexandria*. Cincinnati: Hebrew Union College, 1985.

_____. Ed. *Philo of Alexandria: The Contemplative Life, the Giants, and Selections*. Classics of Western Spirituality. New York: Paulist, 1981.

_____. "The Sage as Mystic in the Wisdom of Solomon." *The Sage*. Ed. Gammie and Perdue (1980): 383-97.

_____. *The Wisdom of Solomon*. Doubleday, Garden City, N.Y.: 1979.

Winter, Paul. *On the Trial of Jesus*. Berlin: de Gruyter, 1974.

Wire, Antoinette Clark. "Gender Roles in a Scribal Community." *Social History of the Matthean Community*. Ed. David L. Balch. 87-121. Minneapolis: Fortress, 1991.

Wise, M. and Tabor, J. "The Messiah at Qumran." *Biblical Archaeology Review* 18. no. 6 (November/ December 1992): 60-65.

Witherington III, Ben. *Jesus the Sage: The Pilgrimage of Wisdom*. Minneapolis: Fortress, 1994.

_____. *Jesus, Paul & the End of the World*. Minneapolis: Fortress, 1990.

_____. *The Christology of Jesus*. Minneapolis: Fortress, 1990.

Witt, R. E. *Isis in the Graeco-Roman World*. Ithaca, N.Y.: Cornell University, 1971.

Wolfson, E. "Female Imaging of the Torah: From Literary Metaphor to Religious Symbol." *From Ancient Israel to Modern Judaism: Intellect in Quest of Understanding: Essays in Honor of Marvin Fox*. Ed. J. Neusner, E. S. Frerichs, and N. M. Sarna, 2:271-307. *BJS* 173. Atlanta: Scholars Press, 1989.

Wright, G. Ernest. *The Bible and the Ancient Near East*. London: Routledge, 1961.

Wright, N. T. *The Original Jesus: The Life and Vision of a Revolutionary*. Grand Rapids: Eerdmans, 1997.

_____. *Jesus and the Victory of God*. London: SPCK, 1993.

_____. *Who Was Jesus?* Grand Rapids: Eerdmans, 1993.

_____. "Jesus, Quest for the Historical." *Anchor Bible Dictionary* 3 (1992): 796-802.

Wyatt, N. "Understanding Polytheism: Structure and Dynamic in a West Semitic Pantheon." *JHC* 5/1 (Spring, 1998): 23-62.

Wylen, M. *The Jews in the Time of Jesus: An Introduction*. New York: Paulist, 1996.

Yadin, Yigael. *The Temple Scroll*. New York: Random, 1985.

Yates, Frances Amelia. *Giordano Bruno and the Hermetic Tradition*. Chicago: University of Chicago, 1964.

Young, Frances M. *Sacrifice and the Death of Christ*. London: SPCK, 1975.

Zuurdeeg, William F. *An Analytical Philosophy of Religion*. New York: Abingdon, 1958.

58238085R00263

Made in the USA
Charleston, SC
06 July 2016